SOCIAL MOBILITY IN TRADITIONAL CHINA

SOCIAL MOBILITY
IN
TRADITIONAL CHINA

BY

WOLFRAM EBERHARD

LEIDEN
E. J. BRILL
1962

Copyright 1962 by E. J. Brill, Leiden, Netherlands.

All rights reserved. No part of this book may be reproduced or translated in any form, by print, photoprint, microfilm or any other means without written permission from the publisher.

PRINTED IN THE NETHERLANDS

CONTENTS

INTRODUCTION 1

PART 1: THE PROBLEM 5
    1. Chinese theories on social class and mobility . . 5
    2. Legal position of social classes in Chinese history 10
    3. Social mobility and migrations in medieval China 22
    4. Families and their genealogies 33

PART 2: SOCIAL MOBILITY OF THE WU CLAN OF SOUTH CHINA 51
    1. The material for the study of the clan 51
    2. Origin and earliest traditions 58
    3. The period of dispersal and migrations 60
    4. The Ch'iu-kuan house 70
    5. The Han-yüan house from P'u-t'ien 75
    6. The Sha-pei house from P'u-t'ien 82
    7. The An-hai house from P'u-t'ien 82
    8. The Lü-wei (Chu-kuo) house 85
    9. The Jung-kui house 102
  10. The T'ien-hsiung (Ch'ing-lung) house 105
  11. The Lung-yen house 111
  12. General conclusions: Migrations and mobility of
      the Wu clan 114

PART 3: CHANGES IN THE STRUCTURE OF THE POPULATION . . 121
    1. Systems of intermarriage 121
    2. Plural marriages 129
    3. Age difference between husband and wives . . . 132
    4. Divorce and re-marriage 135
    5. Marriage age 140
    6. Duration of a generation 146
    7. Life expectancy 147
    8. The number of children 153
    9. Adoptions 159
  10. Birth rate 164
  11. Emigration into Overseas countries 167
  12. Summary of results 168

PART 4: SOCIAL MOBILITY OF THE JUNG CLAN OF SOUTH CHINA   174
    1. Early history of the Jung   174
    2. Divisions and the early history of the eight houses   178
    3. Social mobility of the Jung clan   182
    4. General conclusions: Migrations and mobility of the Jung clan   194

PART 5: GENERAL REMARKS ON SOCIAL MOBILITY   197
    1. Introduction   197
    2. The Gentry   204
    3. The Farmer   219
    4. Artisans and Craftsmen   236
    5. Merchants: 238
        a. shopkeepers   240
        b. itinerant merchants   242
        c. big merchants   245
        d. merchant ethics   247
        e. financial organization   254
        f. was there a bourgeois culture in China?   259

PART 6: CONCLUDING OBSERVATIONS   264
    1. General observations on mobility   264
    2. Village and city   266
    3. Population change   269
    4. Migrations   277

APPENDIX: The Names of the members of the Wu clan   280
BIBLIOGRAPHY   287
INDEX   296

INTRODUCTION

The study of social mobility, always a topic of great interest to sociologists, has recently turned to its inter-cultural aspects, and the question has been raised whether social mobility was much greater in the United States than in Europe. It had been tacitly assumed that social mobility is greatest in the United States and more or less limited in other societies. To this was added the assumption that a strong turnover, especially within the leading elite or elites, is desirable because it will bring able new persons into the leading positions, and less capable men who stay in the elite purely for reasons of their social origins, will be removed.

The subject of social mobility in China has until recently never been thoroughly studied [1], although a number of hypotheses have been brought forth. For more than two centuries now, a group of Western as well as Chinese scholars have been convinced that China was basically "democratic", in spite of its monarchic form of state: a country in which scholars ruled and in which scholars were selected purely on the basis of their competence. Concurrently, another group holds that such conditions are found only in the early period of a ruling dynasty. Later on, they reason, a decadence sets in, unworthy persons come into the elite, and finally, the dynasty breaks down in general decay. The following dynasty restores the good principles of selection of the best and a new period of glory follows. Finally, there is a third group of scholars who believe that social mobility in China was always very limited, if not impossible. This, they think, is one of the aspects of a despotic regime which is basically static and against change. None of these hypotheses has been sufficiently tested, we believe. To some degree, they contain preconceived ideas, and to some degree they try to explain certain facts without really delving into the sources.

We do not expect to solve this problem completely. The following chapters should rather be regarded as another step towards its solution. Our main difficulty, as will be seen, has been to find a body of data which can supply reasonably reliable information.

---

[1] A discussion of relevant recent studies will be given later in this study.

We will try to find out to what degree family genealogies can be used to clarify the social and geographical mobility of Chinese families in South China. We selected South China, because many South Chinese moved into foreign countries and, therefore, many members of the families under investigation are now living in the United States and can be studied there today.

The bulk of our material consists of all data supplied by the genealogies of two South Chinese clans, the Wu and the Jung clan, both from almost the same place in the Southwestern part of Kuangtung province. Each of these clans represents one of the two main types of clan structure. Neither clan is of top-level or the elite, but represent more a middle level. It would certainly be desirable to analyze a much greater number of genealogies; yet even our limited material deals with over 12,000 persons. We doubt, also, whether the addition of many more genealogies would essentially change our final conclusions. However, it is necessary to state that our conclusions are valid only for South China, or more clearly, only for the provinces of Kuangtung and Fukien. We do not think that our conclusions can—without modifications and further research—be applied to conditions in Central or in North China. Our data from the two clans and their genealogies are supplemented by other data from other genealogies of Kuangtung and Taiwanese families. This material is not of a character which yields to statistical analysis. It is used mainly to underline certain conclusions which have been derived from the main data. The Taiwanese families which we studied are all of Fukienese origin; none of them is Hakka or otherwise of Kuangtung origin. We can easily call the Fukienese who came to Taiwan "colonists", who settled in an area which was populated by non-Chinese, often quite hostile tribes. But our Kuangtung families, too, were colonists—only they were a few hundred years earlier. And at least one of our main two families had its origin in Fukien, although it did not come from the same stock and place as did the later Taiwan colonists.

As will be seen later, our discussion of social mobility involves problems of population. Thus, some demographic data will also be discussed. In order to clarify some demographic problems, modern data, collected in Taiwan (as collection in Mainland China was impossible), will occasionally be used.

We cannot claim that we explain in our study social mobility in China before the eleventh century, nor that we found a suitable method for its study. For all periods before this time, we still have to rely upon insufficient data and we can, therefore, reach only tentative conclusions [1]. But even a period as long as 800 or 900 years is a very long period in which—we should expect—many changes may have occurred. However, China during these centuries was a very large and populous country and conditions may have differed from province to province. What we shall have to say about social mobility in China will be limited to South China only; we think that in many, but by no means in all points, the situation may have been similar in other parts of China, although probably mobility was more restricted than in South China. We also believe that with more extensive studies than ours, sub-periods shall emerge much clearer than they did in our study, so that our results will be modified and become more precise by further research. This work, therefore, should be regarded as a kind of pilot project, and not as the definitive study.

Social mobility can be studied from two points of view, and we have tried to use both: a) What was the attitude of society toward social mobility? This attitude can be found in the writings of thinkers and legislators who set up or codified the values of their society. We made a brief survey of the main Chinese theories and legal formulations concerning social mobility. Here, too, there is much more material available and a detailed study is desirable which then would probably bring out changes in attitudes over time much more clearly than we could do in this survey.

b) What actually were the facts of social mobility in China? At the present time, of course, field work in Mainland China is impossible. And in any case, even were it possible, such field work would give us information on only about one or two generations, and would cover a period of great internal change. It is, in the opinion of this writer, a weakness of many sociological studies that they are short-term and do not consider long-term developments. In any study of China with its extensive documentation in almost all fields, a study which does not try to get historical depth can certainly not be regarded as satisfactory. In our case, the type of data which we have at our disposal allows us to get a historical depth of over 800 years, and conclusions drawn from a study over such a time span should have a greater general weight than short-term studies. For persons who

---

[1] cf. my *Das Toba-Reich Nordchinas*, Leiden, E. J. Brill, 1949.

are only interested in present-day China, a long-term historical study will give the necessary background against which they can measure present conditions. The present regime in China has certainly removed the old elite from its position; but where does the new elite come from: is there now greater mobility than before? Is the process now basically different from what it was? This study closes with the period before World War II; most of the documents which we used end at about 1932. It could be continued, if new material from China were available, and perhaps this will some day become possible.

PART ONE

THE PROBLEM

1. Chinese Theories on Social Class and Social Mobility

With the beginning of written documents, China emerges as a stratified society in which at least three classes are clearly evident: the nobility, the commoner, and the slave classes. Yet, some Chinese and Western writers have consistently argued that from the end of the Chou dynasty on (according to others, from the end of the feudal period, i.e., ca. the third century B.C.), China has not had social classes and always has shown great social mobility. It was said that already Confucius had stated, "With education, there is no class" [1], and that the Chinese civil examination system prevented the formation of classes [2].

It is true that the so-called "classics" (*ching*) do not contain clear references to ideas about social classes; Confucius, too, did not study or discuss social classes. The literature until about the fourth century B.C. deals almost exclusively with the actions of the nobility and their followers. If any person of a lower class, such as a slave, a farmer, a merchant, is mentioned, it is only in order to give the background for some report on the upper class. We may say that down to the fourth century B.C. the existence of social classes was so much taken for granted that no thinker ever seriously discussed this problem.

From then on, however, we find discussions about this topic in the literature. We are not going to give here a complete analysis of Chinese thought on social classes and mobility through all ages, but we will try to show the main lines of thinking and the most important changes in attitudes.

From about the fourth century on, texts either speak of the "four (classes of) people" (szŭ-min) or mention the four classes. We are from now on using the term "class" in the Chinese sense, and not in the sense in which sociologists at present use it, especially, as there is no generally accepted definition in existence.

These four classes (szu-min) are: *shih, nung, kung, shang. Shih* means

---

[1] Hu Shih, in H. MacNair, *China*, Berkeley 1946, p. 226.
[2] Hu Shih, *ibid.*, p. 226.

the educated person in government service or a candidate for service. A *shih*-family is at the same time usually a landlord family, as possession of land means wealth and prestige. We can, therefore, call the *shih*-class the "gentry", using a term which is now widely adopted [1]. *Nung* means farmer; independent landowners, as well as tenants, but not landless laborers. *Kung* means craftsman, artisan; *shang* is a merchant who travels from place to place. Sometimes a distinction is made between the *shang* and the *ku* within this group: a *ku* is a resident merchant or shopkeeper, and his social status is always below that of a *shang*.

The accepted stratification was: gentry, farmer, craftsman, merchant [2], and the rationalization behind this sequence was that the gentry as officials are leaders of society and direct the moral education of the people. The farmers have to be led, but they produce. The craftsmen produce, but unnecessary things, thus inducing the farmers to indulge in luxuries instead of saving. The merchants are persons who transport unnecessary things from place to place, making money without producing anything. Moreover, they induce even more people to luxury than the craftsmen.

Actually, a number of texts offer a different sequence. The *Ku-liang-chuan* [3] gives the second place to the merchants and then says that farmers and craftsmen "serve their superiors" which may imply that these two classes were not really "free" [4]. Yet other texts put the merchants into the third class, above the craftsmen [5], but this may have been done for stylistic reasons only. In any case, it is clear from many texts that craftsmen and merchants are one group, and a lower group, while gentry and farmers are another, and higher. On the other hand, some texts put the farmers into the first place [6]: these authors, often writers on agriculture, proceed "historically":

---

[1] See my "Conquerors and Rulers", passim; *Bull. School Orient. & Afric. Studies*, vol. 17, 1955, p. 373 and the literature quoted there. The modern words which mean "class", such as *chieh-chi* (階級) and *teng* (等) and its composita, do not occur in this sense in the classical literature; *teng* in early texts often means "rank".

[2] *Huai-nan tzu* 11, 1b; *Kuo-yü*, Ch'i-yü; *Kuan-tzu* 48/Maverik p. 94; *Kuan-tzu* 5/Maverik p. 51; *Han-shu* 91, 1b; *Han-shu* 24a, 3a; *Shuo-yüan* 7, 24b; *Han Yü, Yüan-tao*, etc.

[3] Ch'eng 1,4.

[4] see p. 12.

[5] *Kuan-tzu* 5 and *Kuan-tzu* 48.

[6] *Kuan-tzu*, l.c. and others.

in the beginning of human life there were producers, before what we would now call a "leisure class" could emerge. Agriculture, for them, is the most basic necessity [1]. Some add that in earliest times all leaders of society (*shih*) were also farmers [2].

Texts which refer to these four classes in the early period, exhibit two main ideas:

a) The lower classes—especially the farmers—have to serve the upper class (*shih*). Typically, the Tso-chuan says: "The *hsiao-jen* (little people) do farmwork, in order to serve the upper (class)" [3].

The term "hsiao-jen" means, according to Ch'en Meng-chia [4], a free farmer; in the school of Confucius, the term got a derogatory connotation: it became the opposite of the "*chün-tzu*", the "gentleman", and designated a person of no high moral qualities, poor behavior—in general, a person oriented toward material values.

b) In an orderly society, people will remain in the class in which they are born. It is a bad sign for a society, if farmers turn to crafts or business. A static society, it was held, is the ideal society; mobility is not desirable.

Implicit in these arguments is the belief that the class structure expresses a moral structure: the upper class has the "good" persons, the lower classes the "bad" persons. In this area of belief, we find significant change over time. The early philosophers of the fourth and third centuries B.C. did not believe that all men are equal: Confucius had already stated "By nature people are near to one another, but through practice they have become apart" [5]. His follower Meng-tzu added "It is the nature of things that they are not equal" [6]. But they believed that people, if they wished, could improve and become good. When the medieval gentry society was firmly established, we find the theory of the "three grades" (*san -p'in*), first pronounced by Hsün Yüeh (148-209 A.D.), later refined by Han Yü (768-824), according to which theory there are three grades of men: the highest who are good, the lowest who are bad, and the medium people who can become either good or bad [7].

---

[1] so still in Ch'en Fu's *Nung-shu*, Introduction.
[2] Wang Chen, *Nung-shu*, p. 8.
[3] *Tso-chuan*, Hsiang 13.
[4] *Yin-hsü pu-tz'u tsung-shu*, 1956, p. 616-7.
[5] *Lun-yü* 17,2.
[6] *Meng-tzu* 3A, 4.
[7] see Wing-tsit Chan, "The Neo-Confucian Solution of the Problem of Evil" in *Bull. Institute History & Philology, Academia Sinica*, vol. 28, Taipei 1957, p. 778.

In Sung time the theory is broadened: there is a "material force" (*ch'i*), called by others "ether", which can be clear or muddy: "As regards (the ether) with which human beings are endowed, there are differences in it according to its opaqueness or clarity, purity or turbidity" [1]. These theories represent a transition in thought: from a belief in an inequality of individuals due to the fact that some work harder than others to become perfect, through the assumption that only medium people can change by developing or rather controlling their feelings, to the final assumption that people are different in their basic endowments and have to remain different.

The classical statement, as far as our topic is concerned, is found in a treatise on agriculture from the Sung time:

> After stating that basically all men are equal, Wang Chen continues:
> "Only in the allowance of *ch'i* (material force), there are differences in that there is clear and muddy *ch'i*. Those persons with clear *ch'i* are the shih (gentry), and those with muddy *ch'i* are the farmers, the craftsmen, and the merchants. The gentry elaborate the rules of human relations (*jen* and *i*); the farmers produce clothing and food; the craftsmen make implements, and the merchants distribute the goods. These four classes are instituted by Heaven, so that they supplement one another, and the holy men have set up laws and rules, and regulated the ranks and differentiations. They cultivate (the people) by their instruction, so that everybody in the world has his clothing and his food, treats his relatives as relatives, and his elders as elders. But as instructors, none are better than the gentry; as feeders, none are better than the farmers. The real (qualification) of the gentry is their scholarship, and the real (qualification) of the farmers is their ploughing. Therefore, the gentry are on top (of the social scale) and the farmers are below them; craftsmen and merchants are at the bottom. Thus, what is root and what is branch, what is unimportant and what is important, can clearly be seen" [2].

Wang Chen then proves that in antiquity, the man of the gentry also worked on the fields and describes the simple life of the farmer, who lives in a straw hut, dresses himself in simple materials, eats simple food, cares for his cows and pigs, goes out when the stars are still visible and returns when the moon is shining:

> "In his public (relations), he pays his taxes and does his corvée service; at home, he feeds his parents, and rears wife and children. In addition, he concludes marriage relationships and has social contacts with his

---

[1] Chu Hsi (1130-1200), as quoted by D. Bodde, in *Harvard Journal of Asiatic Studies*, vol. 7, 1942, p. 31.

[2] *Nung-shu*, chapter 1, p. 7-8.

neighbors. In the field of simple customs, nobody is better than the farmer. Craftsmen, on the other side, rely upon their skills, and merchants manipulate surplusses. They move around and are without a definite place (to live). They cannot be perfect in the (fulfillment of their) duties in caring (for their parents) and their feelings of friendship [1]."

He then concludes that if everybody does his duty, then

"each family has its living, each person has enough. Upper and lower (classes) observe their hierarchy, and close and distant relatives observe their ceremonies. People who do the secondary things (i.e., craftsmen and merchants) then will be rare [2]."

This text expresses clearly not only the ideal that in a good society there will be no social mobility, but also explains why craftsmen and merchants are lower than the farmers: they are "the branches", the "unimportant", and they are also morally inferior because they cannot care for their parents as the gentry or the farmers can, because they have to move around.

This ideology basically remained unchanged until the modern age. There are few voices which sound differently.

The philosopher-essayist Yüan Mei (1716-1797) takes quite a radical position in a famous essay, "Analysis of the *shih*" (*Yüan-shih*):

"If there are few *shih*, then the world is in order. Why is this so? In the world, farmers, craftsmen and merchants came first, and only then appeared the *shih*. The farmers produce grain, the craftsmen make implements; the merchants circulate products. All these 3 classes feed the *shih*, but the so-called *shih* cannot feed the three other classes; they cannot even feed themselves. Then, why are the *shih* in high esteem? It is said: 'These three classes cannot be governed without counts, ministers and high officials, and counts, ministers and high officials cannot do anything without the *shih*...' " [3]

Yüan Mei wrote this introduction in order to criticize the *shih* (officials-scholars) of his time whose training was too simple: everybody who can read can become a *shih*, so that farmers, craftsmen and merchants whose abilities are just enough for their jobs, all try to become *shih* and to get into high positions. He does not want to change the social system; he, too, in the last analysis, favors social stability; but he proposes a stricter selection of officials and a reduction in their number.

---

[1] *Nung-shu*, chapter 1, p. 8.
[2] *Nung-shu*, chapter 1, p. 8-9.
[3] *Hsiao-ts'ang-shan-fang wen-chi*, chapter 1, p. 7.

The only real protest against the social system came from the small group of anarchists; in the book of Lieh-tzu, a text of unknown age and composition, but written not later than the third century A.D. and perhaps much earlier, a Confucian is described who defended the social order: the *shih* are the ruling class and by their activities they make the life of the lower classes possible as animal breeders keep their cows alive. Therefore, the ruling class can use the lower classes as a farmer can use (and kill) his animals. The opponent, an anarchist, tries to show that the function of the *shih* is really to coordinate, and the producing classes appoint the *shih* as their servant for the purpose of coordination only [1]. This opinion, however, never gained acceptance in China.

2. Legal Position of Social Classes in Chinese History

The attitudes of the philosophers reflect, at least in part, the actual situation.

In the Chou period, before 400 B.C., ten different ranks (*teng*) were recognized [2], each rank regarding the next lower rank as its subject and servant. The first four ranks, down to the *shih* [3], are the well-known ranks of the nobility; the following six ranks start with *ts'ao* (曹), office servants. Later commentators refer to these ts'ao as "*ch'ien-jen*", "cheap people" or "commoners". This differentiation into *kui-jen*, "valuable people" or "noblemen", and commoners was quite widely accepted in the fourth century B.C. or earlier [4]), and the commoner had to serve the nobleman as the young person had to serve the old man [5]. Philosophers of the Confucian school gave to both terms moral connotations: a commoner was at the same time also morally inferior. It is not clear whether at this early time, the term "commoner" already implied that the person was not a free man, although it may well have had that specific meaning.

The other pair of concepts, *chün-tzu*, "gentleman", and *hsiao-jen*, "little people", "ordinary people", definitely applied only to noblemen and free "burghers" respectively. Rarely, instead of *hsiao-jen*, the

---

[1] *Lieh-tzu*, transl. R. Wilhelm, p. 45.
[2] *Tso-chuan*, Chao 7.
[3] At this time, the term meant roughly a "knight". It later got the meaning "official" or a "scribe" and from circa 100 B.C. on the term can roughly be translated as "gentry".
[4] *Tso-chuan*, Ai 17 and *Li-chi*, Fang-chi 5.
[5] *Li-chi*, Nei-tz'ê 11.

term *pi-jen*, "low-class people" is used, as in the proverb which a scholar quoted when he heard that an emperor (in the first century B.C.) planned to marry a woman of ordinary origin: "A rotten wood cannot be used as a pillar; a low-class person cannot be used as ruler" [1].

A third pair of concepts is *po-hsing*, "the hundred family names", and "*chao-min*" the miriads of people" or "*li-min*", "numerous people". The *po-hsing* are the aristocracy which alone used family names at that time, and the others are the ordinary people [2].

In the period of gentry society, i.e., from the third century B.C. on, the aristocracy disappeared as a special class, and the old terms changed their meaning. *Chün-tzu* and *hsiao-jen* became purely moral connotations; *chao-min* and *li-min* became antiquated words; and *po-hsing* now meant farmers [3], or rather "tax-paying burgher" [4] because by that time every free citizen already had a family name [5]. The term *kui-jen* disappeared, and the term *ch'ien-jen* soon got a specific meaning: non-free commoners. None of these classifications mentions slaves (*nu*), because slaves were not members of a human society, they were pieces of property [6]. Only later, the slaves were included with the commoners [7].

We have, then, in medieval China, four classes of free burghers: the *shih* or gentry as leading class; the *nung* or farmers as second class. This second class was, at least legally, completely free, and it was

---

[1] *Han-shu* 77, 3b.

[2] The term is mentioned for example in *Ku-liang-chuan*, Huan 1; *Kung-yang-chuan*, Yin 4. Explanations of the meaning in O. Franke, *Geschichte*, vol. 3, p. 47; Hsü T'ung-hsin in *Historical Annual*, vol. 2, No. 2, p. 161-164a; Ch'en Meng-chia, *Yin-hsü pu-tz'u tsung-shu* p. 626.

[3] Hsü T'ung-hsin, *l.c.*, p. 164.

[4] *T'ang hui-yao* 20, as quoted by Shigeru Kato, *Studies in Chinese Econ. History*, vol. 2, 1953, p. 339.

[5] W. Eichhorn (in *Deutsche Akademie d. Wissenschaften, Inst. f. Orientforschung*, vol. 3, No. 2, 1953, p. 294 note) believes that in Han time the term still referred to the gentry only.

[6] *T'ang-lü su-i* 6.

[7] Ch'en Meng-chia, *Yin-hsü*, p. 616, believes that the term "*ch'ou*" (ugly) and the expression "*chung-jen*" (mass people) which occur in Shang texts before the eleventh century B.C., meant slaves. E. G. Pulleyblank in *Journal Econ. & Social History of the Orient*, vol. 1, No. 2, 1958, p. 219 believes that "the institution of slavery as it was known in imperial China originated in the state of Ch'in in the fourth and third centuries B.C.", and that the word "*nu*" which down to the present time meant "slave" had the meaning of "child" in earlier time (p. 193). The terminology and legal definitions indeed changed, but there is no doubt that there was slavery in the strict sense of the word in Shang and Chou times in addition to serfdom.

assumed that able farmers who passed the civil service examinations could move up into the gentry.

With the next two classes, the situation was different: they were legally free, but under severe restrictions. We can classify artisans into 3 groups: a) farmers who in their spare time or in the off-season worked as craftsmen for their own households or for friends. Such persons were legally farmers. b) landless farmers who worked in villages for other farmers. They were also legally farmers. If landless farmers moved around and worked in different villages, they were legally farmers if they were still on the taxation lists of their home districts. If they had permanently left their home districts, they were "*liu-min*" (vagabonds), and as such were criminals. c) real craftsmen who worked in cities [1]. Only these were legally "craftsmen" (*kung*). We have very little information about this class, and no special study has yet been made. We know that in ancient China, the craftsmen lived in blocks close to the palace of the ruler, and we know that they were tied to the ruling aristocracy and had to work for them. Apparently, their position was quite similar to the Indian system: to each family of the aristocracy a number of craftsmen families were attached. They did all the work the lord's family wanted to have done, and got a fixed payment in yearly or half-yearly installments in kind. The conditions in earliest Japan, too, seem to have been quite similar. The craftsmen, thus, might be called bondsmen.

When the feudal order of ancient China broke down, the position of the craftsmen changed. We even read of craftsmen who were unemployed, participating in a revolt [2]. In the medieval gentry society, craftsmen lived in special quarters of the cities and towns, each craft in one lane, or around the markets. They could sell their products to other citizens. But their freedom was restricted. They were under obligation to work for the government a certain number of days every year. Such work could be in the capital, and the craftsmen then had to travel to the capital; or it could be in any provincial town, where they then would have to work for the local official. All craftsmen were registered in lists. Before 1400, for instance, there were 232,089 registered carpenters in China, and each of them had to work 10 days per month in his home district for the government. If he was to be used in the capital, the periods of work were longer,

---

[1] R. Tawney, *Agrarian China*, p. 224.
[2] *Tso-chuan*, Chao 22.

but mobilization occurred only once a year or even once every 5 years [1]. The government could also send the craftsmen to any other place, where they were needed: in 839, for instance, thirty-six master carpenters, together with carpenters, ship builders and founders were sent to Central China, in order to repair some Korean ships [2]. In 952 the emperor ordered the craftsmen to come to the capital in order to create state workshops there. At the same time, he closed provincial workshops which the governors had opened in order to produce "gifts" for their superiors [3]. In 957, the emperor ordered numerous craftsmen into the capital in order to have ships built; in a year, a hundred ships were constructed [4]. State-owned workshops and factories which produced lacquer ware or porcellain for the imperial household, or arms for the imperial armies probably had a very long history; we know them very well from the Han dynasty on (206B.C.-220 A.D.). Most of the trained workers in these factories were certainly craftsmen; others were slaves or criminals who had been temporarily enslaved; still others were commoners.

The craftsmen were under still other restrictions. According to a law of 719 [5], the state had models of bows, arrows, swords and other implements made and kept lists of craftsmen who were allowed to make these implements. Only the standard models could be sold and only by licensed craftsmen. Similar rules applied even to items of fashion. As late as 1118 A.D. the state had 30 standard models of court shoes made and distributed to shoemakers in the then capital K'ai-feng [6]. We tend to assume today, that the governmental lists of craftsmen and the standardization of implements led to the creation of guilds in a later period.

Over many periods of medieval China, land was allotted to each family according to a fixed system. The law of 737 states that families of craftsmen and merchants should get half of the land which farmers' families would get, and if there was not enough land, they should not get any [7]. Thus, craftsmen were under special restrictions in a number of ways. Most important of all, they could not have a per-

---

[1] *Sung-chuang meng-yü* 4, as quoted in *Li-shih yen-chiu* 1955, no. 3, p. 107.
[2] *Ennin's Diary*, transl. Reischauer, p. 76.
[3] *Chiu-Wu-tai shih* 112: p. 4343c.
[4] *Chiu-Wu-tai shih* 117: p. 4351a.
[5] N. Niida, *T'ang Law*, p. 720.
[6] *Neng-kai chai man-lu* 13, 5b.
[7] N. Niida, *T'ang Law*, p. 632

manent home, as they could at any time be shifted around by the government. Therefore, the above-mentioned philosopher who said that artisans and merchants could not really fulfill their obligations towards their parents, was correct.

This situation remained until 1485. From summer 1485 on, the service obligations of craftsmen could be cancelled, if the craftsman paid 6 cash per month as special tax. This way out was soon taken by many craftsmen, so that by 1562 the number of registered carpenters was only 142,486 [1]. From the 15th century on, then, we find a "liberation" of the craftsmen; the state from then on paid for the services it needed from the craftsmen's tax payments.

The situation of merchants and shopkeepers was still more restricted. We are not going to enumerate the numerous taxes and customs which they had to pay when transporting goods or selling on the market and the strict control to which they were subjected in every transaction and often even in their pricing policies. From the second century B.C. on they were not allowed to own land; later [2], their allotments were kept low. They were also not allowed to enter the civil service examination to become officials [3]. They had to wear dress of special material and color, indicating their low status [4]; they were not allowed to ride on horseback [5].

Down to the Ming dynasty (1368-1644), the material of their dress had to be inferior to that of farmer's dress and if even one man in a farmer's family became a merchant, the whole family had to wear the merchant's garb [6].

These restrictions began to be loosened from the eleventh century on. From that time, the proposition was made that merchants and craftsmen should be allowed to take the examination, but in actuality, access remained illegal: by bribery, by initiating forbidden marriages with gentry families, by other connections [7]. From the late tenth century on, merchants and craftsmen were allowed to ride on horseback, but had to use special colors for the saddle and ride in a special way [8].

---

[1] *Li-shih yen-chiu* 1955, no. 3, p. 107 and *Memoirs Inst. Orient. Culture*, 10, 1936, p. 412 with references.
[2] W. Eberhard, *Landwirtschaft*, p. 81 and M. Wilbur, *Slavery*, p. 199.
[3] A. Hulsewé, *Remnants of Han Law*, vol. 1, p. 152.
[4] M. Wilbur, *Slavery*, p. 207 and Ch'ü T'ung-tsu, p. 109.
[5] Ch'ü T'ung-tsu, p. 117.
[6] Ch'ü T'ung-tsu, p. 110.
[7] Sung Hsi in *Ta-lu tsa-chih*, vol. 4, no. 11, 1952, p. 11 and 26.
[8] *Shih-lin yen-yü* 3, 1b.

Finally, they were legally allowed to take the examinations, but on a special quota which in the early 19th century was 81 persons per examination, later becoming 110 persons [1].

Of course, we know of powerful merchants, mainly in the transition period between feudal and gentry China; but even later we read of many wealthy merchants. Yet, their status remained low, they were legally discriminated against, and always at the mercy of the officials.

These brief remarks which only give those details which are of utmost importance to our topic, allow the following conclusions: medieval Chinese society consisted of 4 classes of free burghers [2]. Each class had special rights and restrictions, which were fixed by law. Merchants certainly were most discriminated against, but the situation of craftsmen was not much better. Both classes gained some freedom only after the eleventh or even the 15th centuries.

As members of both classes were, until quite recently, not allowed to compete for the civil service, there was legally no possibility for members of these classes to move up into the gentry. The farmers, on the other hand, could try their luck in the examinations. Of course, farmers also were not completely free : they had to be registered and their land was registered. In long periods land was allotted to them according to special rules, and they could not legally sell such land. As they were obliged to pay taxes, and as the tax was in relation to the land they had (often paid in kind), they had to cultivate the land and could not move away. To leave the land and to live unregistered in another place was a crime and severely punished. Moreover, the remaining farmers had to pay the taxes of those who had fled. Finally, in most periods of medieval history, the Chinese farmer had to do corvée labor.

To the gentry, the upper class of the period after 1000 A.D., belonged persons who had passed the civil service examination (they were then often called "Ju-hu", "Confucian families"), as did their families. They had special privileges, such as a permission to have larger rooms and houses, special decorations on the houses, special dress, etc. These privileges remained in the gentry family even if at a given time, no member of the family actually was in the civil service [3].

---

[1] Ch. L. Chang, *China's Gentry*, p. 62; the total quota per examination in the 19th century, according to Chang was 25,089.
[2] *Ch'ing-shih kao*, Shih-huo-chih is the first text which states this clearly.
[3] Ch'ü T'ung-tsu, p. 125.

And with such privileges remained social status [1]. To belong to the gentry, therefore, was not an achievement of an individual, as Chang tried to show. Class consciousness was always strong. As an example, let us mention a social club of the 18th century that admitted only gentry members, expressly excluding farmers, craftsmen, merchants, shopkeepers, office clerks and commoners [2].

Thus, classes of free burghers were clearly divided by law and behavior; and many rules and regulations were made in order to allow a person to know immediately to which class another person whom he met, belonged. Clearly, the ideal was a stable, static society. Only then, the economy could function: only then could the state know exactly how many carpenters there were so that it could have the labor supply for a building program; only then could the state know exactly how many farmers cultivated how many acres, could calculate the average production and make its plans for wars, etc. Any shift naturally involved a great deal of legal paper work and inconvenience to the gentry officials who had to do this work. Thus, they were certainly against such shifts. Shifts on a larger scale would mean imbalances and, therefore, social unrest—another reason to be against changes in status.

Downward mobility was not desirable either; and in most cases, the families would try to keep downward mobility secret; if, for instance, a gentry member engaged in business, he would try to have the actual business done by a merchant and would only be manager or investor. Or, if he were actively engaged in business, he would avoid registration as a merchant, thus protecting the status of his family.

In medieval China, the members of these four free classes were called "*liang-jen*" (good people). Below them, we have the classes of the "*ch'ien-jen*", "cheap people" or commoners. The lowest of the classes of the commoners are the slaves (*nu*), and as such, were not really members of society, but merchandise which could be bought and sold. Many of these slaves were foreigners who had been kidnapped or bought from specialized traders. Others were prisoners of war. Still others were the relatives of criminals who had been executed. Some persons sold themselves as slaves. Slaves could be state slaves, temple slaves or private slaves. Their children were slaves. They

---

[1] *Li-shih yen-chiu* 1955, no. 4, p. 122 and M. Freedmann, *Lineage*, p. 55 with a discussion of the term.
[2] *Ming-chai hsiao-shih* 3, 8b.

were subject to special laws and had hardly any legal rights. They could gain their freedom by buying themselves off, if they had money [1], or the owner could free them by a special legal document which had to be signed as well by sons of the owner [2]. A freed slave remained a commoner. In the Sung period (960-1287) a case is reported in which a slave owner gave court rank to all his slaves when he became chancellor [3], but such action was immediately prohibited by law [4].

State slaves (*kuan-nu* or *kuan-hu*) were sent to state factories if they knew a craft. Others were handed over to the Ministry of Agriculture. The men had to care for the storehouses, collect firewood, care for the chickens, ducks, pigs, and the vegetable gardens at court; the women had to sew, to embroider and to serve as nurses at court. If they were over 14 when enslaved, they were sent to South China to serve in the city offices there. The Ministry of Agriculture distributed food and clothing to them, gave them 3 days vacation per year, and one month leave in case of childbirth, death of parents or for weddings. They were only allowed to marry other state slaves—nobody else [5]. Female (state) slaves who were over 60 years of age,[6] or were sold to private persons were freed to become burghers when they reached an age of 70 more [7]. Otherwise, they had to wait until the state proclaimed an amnesty. An amnesty made them *fan-hu*, commoners of the second class [8].

Fan-hu were state servants; as such they were comparable to the *pu-ch'ü* of private persons in early medieval China [9]. They were not registered as citizens, but were under the control of the Ministry of Agriculture and were normally descendents of state slaves. They were under obligation to serve the state 3 months per year and got some

---

[1] *T'ang-lü su-i* 17.
[2] N. Niida, *Legal documents*, p. 187.
[3] *Tung-hsien pi-lu* 2, 2b-3a.
[4] *Neng-kai chai man-lu* 12, 8b.
[5] *Studies in Chinese Economic History*, p. 150-154.
[6] *San-kuo Wei-chih* 4, 1a.
[7] *San-kuo Wei-chih* 4, 2b and *T'ang-hui-yao*, as quoted by N. Niida, *Legal Documents*, p. 739.
[8] *T'ang-liu-tien*, as quoted by Niida, *Legal Documents*, p. 739.
[9] We cannot discuss the meaning of pu-ch'ü here, nor their legal status. See *Studies in Chinese Economic History*, p 110f.; p. 180-183; Wang Yi-t'ung in *Harvard Journal of As. Studies*, vol. 16, 1953, p. 352-3; Yang Chung-i in *Shih-huo*, vol. 1, 1935, no. 3, p. 97-107; H. Maspero, *Les Institutions de la Chine*, Paris 1952, p. 76; N. Niida, *Legal Documents*, p. 739-740; N. Niida, *T'ang Law*, p. 261. They are mentioned since ca. 180 A.D. (W. Eichhorn in *Deutsche Akademie d. Wiss., Inst. f. Orientforschung*, vol. 3, no. 2, 1955, p. 319 note 93).

18 THE PROBLEM

pay during this period of work. In case of land allotments, they were given 50% of the amount of land given a burgher. Like the slaves they, too, were not allowed to marry a person of any other class [1]. In the event of an amnesty, the *fan-hu* became *tsa-hu*. This class has existed legally since the 5th century A.D. The *tsa-hu* were registered in their home districts, but were under the rule of the local officials. They were hereditarily bound to perform specific services, and were, accordingly, variously called "tomb families" (who cared for the imperial tombs), "shepherd families" (for the imperial herds), "musician families", (for the imperial orchestra), "postal families", "kiln families", "medical families", "soothsayer families", etc [2]. They, too, could marry only within their own groups [3]. In the event of an amnesty, these *tsa-hu* could become free burghers.

The survey of the commoners reveals that such persons are similar to serfs or true slaves. Their behavior and their actions are regulated by law; they are legally inferior persons. Upward mobility is possible for them only by a special act of clemency by the state or by their owners.

To the *tsa-hu* belong also some small, local groups which—so far as we can see—were originally non-Chinese tribes which in the course of the expansion of the Chinese lost their livelihood and specialized in certain professions which then became hereditary. We can call such groups castes, and actually, the process of their formation is similar to that of many, though by no means all, Indian castes. A good example of such caste groups in China are the To-min of Chekiang [4]. The To-min made lamp shades, while their wives were go-betweens and hairdressers for ladies, and were mentioned in the law books as commoners until the early 18th century [5], by which time they were already completely sinified. Special rules applied to non-Chinese tribal groups who still lived in China; after the 17th century they were given a special quota in the state examinations [6]. Thus, the Chinese class system included even tribes of non-Chinese.

If we review the period under consideration, i.e., from the fourth century B.C. to the early 20th century A.D., it becomes quite clear

---

[1] *Studies in Chinese Economic History*, p. 157-9.
[2] Wang Yi-t'ung in *Harvard Journal of Asian Studies*, vol. 16, 1953, p. 344 ff.; E. Balazs, *Le Traité économique du "Souei Chou"*, p. 209; *Studies in Chinese Economic History*, p. 196-8.
[3] *Studies in Chinese Economic History*, p. 161.
[4] W. Eberhard, *Kultur und Siedlung der Randvölker Chinas*, p. 206-7.
[5] Ch'ü T'ung-tsu, p. 173, note 4.
[6] Ch. L. Chang, *China's Gentry*, p. 79-80.

that certain patterns emerge: Whereas social relationships were more or less in a state of flux in the first centuries of our study, with few if any laws regulating the relations of social classes, there develops a growing tendency to stabilize society from the Han period (206 B.C.) on. Paralleling this, we find the early philosophers thinking that every person could change, whereas the later philosophers tended to assume that certain persons had fixed personality traits which predestined them to certain positions in society. From the eleventh century on, however, we find in actuality a loosening of these attitudes: at first, the possibility and desirability of admitting lower class people to the elite group is discussed; then one restriction after another is revoked and a slow "liberation" of the lower classes can be found.

Our brief review mentioned the attitude of pre-modern Chinese thinkers toward migration and the legal problems involved in migration. The thinkers regarded migration as undesirable, because it meant that the migrant would have to leave his parents and thus could not fully care for them; at the very least, he would have to leave his dead ancestors (even if he took the ancestral tablets with him), and could no longer take care of the tombs. He could take the ancestral tablets only if the whole family under its head were to emigrate.

Legally, migration was not permitted: farmers who left their land and went away, committed a crime. Craftsmen who migrated would fail to fulfill their labor obligations, and migrating merchants would fail to pay their taxes. The whole system of control would break down.

Of course, the government could send people to settle anywhere at its convenience. History is full of such examples in all periods of time. When an emperor decided to move into a new capital, the citizens of the old capital as well as people from other places would be ordered to move into the new place in order to fill it up and to create the basis for an economically sound capital. When floods occurred, the goverment might decide to resettle formers. Most important however, were settlements by soldiers and/or criminals.

Soldiers, not yet mentioned in our survey of the class system, fell into two main types: the militia and the professional soldiers. The militia soldiers were ordinary farmers who did military service as a part of the labor obligations of every farmer. In the Han period, every free farmer was registered upon reaching 20 years of age. At 23 he became an ordinary, regular soldier. He was supposed to serve the first year in the guards; in the second year he would serve in special services, as crossbow man, horseman, light vehicle man or boatman. From then on, he remained in the reserves until age 65. Actual service was only a month per year. Wealthy people could pay instead of serving; the sum was 2000 "cash" per month. In addition to these service obligations there were also frontier guards who theoretically were to serve 3 days per year, but were always called for a much longer period. This obligation, too, could be discharged with a cash payment (300) [1]. Similar regulations existed in other periods. There were, in addition, in certain periods, local militia armies [2] for which extra recruitments were ordered, such as that every seven families had to supply one soldier [3]. Normally, such soldiers returned after some time, except those who were paid by rich people to serve in their employ. Professional soldiers, on the other hand, were a kind of caste, belonging to the commoners. We find them from the Han time on [4]; they were registered in special lists [5] and if the man who was in the service, died or became unfit for service, the family had to replace him either by a brother [6] or by a son. The emperor could, if he liked, also use the children of such families; in one case, he had 500 boys collected to serve as imperial rooster breeders [7].

While the militia soldiers were free burghers (*liang-jen*) [8], and also soldiers in the imperial guards were free burghers [9], the others had low status. They were joined by criminals or relatives of executed criminals. Such soldiers could then be settled anywhere by the government. In the early period, military/agricultural settlements which produced their own food supply in time of peace, were called "*t'un*"; and the *t'un* system has been in existence since the 2nd century B.C. [10] Normally, such *t'un* were created along the borders, mainly along the Inner-Asian borders. But in some periods, in addition to

---

[1] H. Maspero, in *Bull. Inst. Phil. & Hist.*, Academia Sinica, vol. 28, part 1, 1956, p. 200; slightly different is N. L. Swann, *Food and Money*, p. 50-51. The following notes are not a "history of Chinese military institutions" but intend only to bring forth some data which are of sociological importance. Details in the regulations changed over time, of course; but we are interested in the main lines of the institutions only.

[2] On their low quality in T'ang time see Kikuchi Hideo in *Tōyō shigaku,*, vol. 13, 1955, p. 61-96. For the 10th century see *Chiu-Wu-tai shih* 103: p. 4332d

[3] *Chiu-Wu-tai shih* 107: p. 4335b.

[4] H. Maspero, l.c. p. 200; *Tōhō gakuhō*, vol. 11, part 1, p. 293-304.

[5] *Ying-shih* 5, 4a, for the early 13th century.

[6] *Chin-shu* 36; p. 1185a.

[7] *T'ai-p'ing kuang-chi* 485; vol. 39, 13b for T'ang time.

[8] Lo Chen-yü, *Liu-sha tui-chien*, vol. 2, p. 22a.

[9] Lo Chen-yü, *l.c.*, p. 22b.

[10] Ōshima Toshikazu in *Tōyōshi kenkyu*, vol. 14, 1955, p. 1ff.

military settlements under the management of the governors and/or the Ministry of Finance, civil t'un settlements were also started. Between 200 and 265 the Ministry of Agriculture opened civil settlements near the capital Lo-yang. The settlers were landless farmers who instead of paying rent to landlords, delivered 50 to 60% of their production to the government and were in addition freed from the obligations of military service [1]. This system, though, did not function well because of corruption.

In the 5th century, professional soldiers were called *"ying-hu"* 營戶, "camp families" [2] and settlements were afterwards often called *"ying"*, "camp". Especially in the early Ming time (14th-15th centuries) many *ying* were created in SW China among non-Chinese tribes [3].

In addition to hereditary soldiers and convicts, the government also could settle prisoners of war: the Mongols settled farmers from Central China in villages around Peking, in order to raise more rice near Peking [4]; they also settled people from the Near East near Peking, in order to use their technical skills in different crafts. Similar cases are known throughout Chinese history [5]. Such foreign settlers, in the course of generations eventually became Chinese.

Legal migration, then, was limited to such government actions and to lowclass people. An official could be transferred to any place, but he would retain his registration in his home province. He could, if he liked to remain in some place (especially if he had property there and if he already had lived there for a long time or even over generations), change his registration and become a citizen of the new place. This would mean that he also separated from the main family and that he established a recognized branch house. In several periods of Chinese history, such separations were legally restricted because of possible losses of income for the state by the creation of small, split families.

Illegal migration, in the other hand, was always practiced. Farmers, if put under too strong pressure by landlords or officials, would disappear. They could try to move into cities as workers for industrialists or craftsmen. Or they could become tenants of some landowner

---

[1] Sadao Nishijima in *Memoirs Inst. Orient. Culture*, vol. 10, 1956, p. 1-84.
[2] Wang Yi-t'ung in *Harvard Journal Asian Studies*, vol. 16, 1953, p. 346.
[3] *Yü-kung*, vol. 7, 1937, No. 1, p. 232ff.
[4] *ibid.*, p. 231.
[5] Plans to settle Hsiung-nu tribesmen in the northern provinces as hunters and shepherds were discussed (*Han-shu* 49, 6a).

in a new area. In both cases, they were at the mercy of their employers, because they were not registered.

They could also move into uninhabited areas inside China, especially into the hill areas. Hill land was often either not taxed (because regarded as village commons or as state land) or under different tax laws. In the hills, they could live as charcoal producers, wood-cutters, or as hillside farmers. Chinese control over the farmers required settlement in closed villages, and villages of different settlement forms are found everywhere in China; but there are a few areas in which open settlement in isolated farmsteads does occur. If we find open settlement in border areas, we can be quite sure that these had their origin in unauthorized settlements [1].

Farmers could also move into an area outside the borders of China and become subjects of a foreign power. This was a pattern very common in Mongolia and Manchuria [2], but we also find Chinese who settled in territory belonging to some tribal chieftain south of the border. In due time, the whole area usually became so thoroughly Chinese that it was incorporated into China proper.

Merchants, too, could move into foreign countries or among foreign tribes. We find many examples of this [3]. They were, in the new environment, completely free of all restrictions which the Chinese government had set up for them; and usually the other country was either loosely organized as a tribal state, or had no special restrictions for the merchant class, or no legislation affecting foreigners, so that they could easily amass wealth and property. For many centuries under Ming and Manchu regimes, such emigration was forbidden, but it still occurred.

3. Social Mobility and Migrations in Medieval and Pre-Modern China

After the discussions in the preceding chapter, we should not expect much social mobility in medieval China and little more in modern China. Nor should we expect to find much documentation for social mobility or migrations, since both were so often in violation of the laws. Yet, Chinese and Western authors have consistently argued that the civil service examination system as it was practiced

---

[1] H. Scholz in *Sinologica*, vol. 3, 1953, p. 43-44 describes these areas.
[2] examples in O. Lattimore, *The Mongols of Manchuria*, New York 1934.
[3] see the fine study by H. Wada, "The Chinese Colonies in the South-East Asia in the Sung Period" in *Tōyō gakuhō*, vol. 42, no. 1, 1959, p. 76-106.

from Han time on (to 1904)[1] was a democratic institution which made upward mobility possible for every person who was capable. As no nobility existed in medieval China, there was a permanent rotation of the elite, and this, it was believed, was one of the reasons why Chinese civilization continually flourished without showing signs of decay.

It can be shown that these authors did not realize that large sectors of the population (including, of course, all women) were deprived of the right to participate in the examinations, or they did not try to find out how large the underprivileged groups were. They also did not study how the examination system functioned in large periods of medieval China.

A satisfactory study of the examination system in Chinese history has not yet been written, but several facts which are of importance for our topic, are well known and will be mentioned here:

a) Only burghers of the first two classes (gentry, farmers) were admitted; admission of merchants was allowed only in very late times and under a tiny quota (0.3% of the total quota), as already mentioned. Sons of criminals, even if they were of the first two classes, were excluded; monks were also excluded, in spite of their class origin [2]. Participation of non-Chinese was already forbidden in Han time [3] and only rarely permitted later, in special cases.

b) Down to the 7th century, no free competition was possible. Candidates had to be recommended by the local authorities according to a quota system. In the Earlier Han period, there were 3 categories; candidates for the second category could be recommended at the rate of one per 200,000 registered inhabitants per year (most commoners, as was mentioned, were not registered).

Candidates for the first category could be recommended at the rate of one per *chou*, i.e., about 1 : 7,000,000 [4]. The provincial governor (of the *chün*), or the head of the *chou* who made these recommendations, was personally responsible for their candidates; if the candidates

---

[1] H. O. H. Stange in *Orientalistische Literaturzeitung* 1961, no. 3, p. 199-200 believes that "die Auffassung, das Prüfungssystem Chinas sei in der Han-Zeit geschaffen, ..., vollkommen falsch ist" but H. G. Creel has shown that the earliest written examinations can be shown to have been held in 165 B.C. and "tests for officials" already in the 3rd century B.C. (*Bull. Ac. Sinica, Phil-hist.*, extra vol. 4a, 1961, *Studies Presented to Tung Tso-pin*, p.633).

[2] P. Buriks, *Fan Chung-yen's Versuch einer Reform des chineseschen Beamtenstaats*, Ph. D. thesis, manuscript, Göttingen, 1954, p. 40.

[3] *Hou Han-shu* 67, 7a.

[4] L. S. Yang in *Ch'ing-hua Journal*, vol. 11, 1936, pp. 1031-1032.

succeeded at court, the officials were praised, if the candidates were failures, they could be punished. If we consider the chance which the man who made the recommendations had to take and the pressures to which he certainly was subject, it can be assumed that he would not easily recommend a farmer's boy whom he did not know well, nor reject candidates who were recommended to him by powerful local families or candidates from his own clan whom he did know well. Even if the farmer's boy was qualified, it was always possible that the powerful local families would denounce him or the selecting official and bring both into trouble for snubbing them.

It is not easy to analyze the actual results of this system, especially because data on family background in the Han time are often insufficient to establish safely the class origin of a person. An attempt with a very limited set of data (n = 78 for the Early Han; 117 for the later Han period) indicated [1]: in the special examinations of the earlier period, 21.8% of the candidates belonged to the nobility (i.e., were relatives of the imperial family), 57.7% were from officials families, 10.1% were unknown, 6.4% from poor families, and more than 1% from military families. In the special examinations of the later period, 49.6% came from the nobility, 25.6% came from families of officials, 12.8% were unknown. The data do not permit much interpretation [2].

c) Social pressure upon all persons involved in the examinations was so strong, that corruption was unavoidable. Corruption, naturally, worked in favor of the class in power, i.e. the gentry. In the tenth century, which was one of the worst periods, people were granted the degree not because of merit, but only because of belonging to a prominent family [3]. A proverb of the time said, "One does not have to study books in order to pass the examinations; and who does have to work, in order to be an official?" The text which gives us this proverb states that there were fixed prices for which one could buy degrees [4].

An order of 955 stated that the practice of passing candidates without any examination, or of giving them a degree because the

---

[1] *Bulletin of Chinese Studies*, vol. 2, 1941, p. 100; vol. 3, 1942, p. 35; percentages calculated by myself.
[2] L. S. Yang in *Ch'ing-hua Journal* 11, 1936, p. 1038 about the misuses of the system.
[3] For instance the case of Ts'ui I-sun in *Chiu-Wu-tai shih* 69: p. 4287d.
[4] *Hou-ching-lu* 4, 2a.

candidate tried hard for a long period and never passed, or because he belonged to a prominent family should be abolished [1].

d) Some of the higher officials came under the *yin* privilege. Already in Han time, high officials had the right after 3 years of service to propose a son or nephew for court office, i.e., for the beginning of a career as an official [2]. Later, this privilege was extended, so that, according to Fan Chung-yen (1043 A.D.), an official could secure twenty appointments of relatives to positions at court in 20 years of service [3]. Although the government later tried to curb the *yin* privilege, it remained an important institution which clearly favored the gentry, especially, as there was always a fixed quota for candidates.

e) There were three ways to acquire the education which was required in the examinations, and in all of them the gentry was favored. There were state schools. According to the rules of 466, a province of medium size had two professors, two assistant professors and 80 students. Students were selected according to their abilities, but with the remark that first all able boys of the "high gates", i.e., the important gentry families should be taken and only after them, if there were still openings, boys from "middle families" [4]. In the T'ang time, there were six types of higher schools: the Kuo-tzu school ("School for the sons of the state") was open only for 300 sons and grandsons of civil or military officials of at least the third rank; the graduates immediately got high ceremonial jobs in the capital [5]. The T'ai-hsüeh ("Great school") accepted 500 sons and grandsons of officials of rank five or higher [6]. When in 1010 it was proposed to change the rules for internship in this type of school the political opposition openly declared that this would help the rich, but not the poor [7]. The third school was the Szu-men school, ("Four Gates school") which accepted 1300 students. Five hundred were descendants of officials from rank three or, exceptionally from rank four on, and 800 would come from able *shu-jen* families [8].

---

[1] *Chiu-Wu-tai shih* 115: p. 4347c.
[2] L. S. Yang, *loc. cit.*, p. 1033.
[3] P. Buriks, *loc. cit.*, p. 19, The author concludes: „Es scheint mir, dass — wenigstens für die Sungzeit — diese Zahlen nicht viel übriglassen von der traditionellen Annahme, in China hätte man nur durch die staatlichen Prüfungen Beamter werden können" (p. 46).
[4] *Wei-shu* 48: p. 2009a, and 6: p. 1915c.
[5] *Wen-hsien t'ung-k'ao* 41: p. 391c.
[6] *Wen-hsien t'ung-k'ao* 41: p. 391a.
[7] *Neng-kai-chai man-lu* 13, 3b.
[8] *Wen-hsien t'ung-k'ao* 41: p. 391c.

Shu-jen in this period are persons without government position or honorary rank [1] or "persons holding the lowest four of the twenty grades" [2]. In addition to these three main schools, there were special schools, such as a law school which also accepted only sons of officials or *shu-jen* who already had training. Students in such schools had to pay a certain amount of silk, wine, and meat every day [3]. These schools, clearly, did not give access to boys who did not come from the gentry.

There were private schools, from the eleventh century on, often financed by a foundation. The grant was only in rare cases made by the state [4]; more commonly, wealthy members of a family made a family or clan school for their own boys [5]. If the clan was wealthy and had a school and if this school functioned, even boys from poorer branches of the clan could get an education. The importance of this institution as an avenue to upward mobility for farmers who belonged to a wealthy clan, cannot be calculated; although the total amount of land set aside for schools was small [6]. The third possibility of acquiring an education was to hire a private tutor; this required even more money, and good teachers were not easily available.

In conclusion, from these data we can say that the examination system cannot be expected to have contributed much to upward social mobility. This problem can be studied from still another aspect. We have lists of successful candidates for the later periods. These lists can be studied as to the social origin of the candidates. For the Sung period, such a study has been made [7] but for our purposes,

---

[1] *Historical Annual* 2, no. 2, 283a, and N. L. Swann, *Food and Money*, p. 19.

[2] N. L. Swann, *Food and Money*, p. 31.

[3] Law of 719, quoted by N. Niida, *T'ang Law*, p. 271.

[4] Grant of 1138, see N. Niida, *Legal Documents*, p. 400 and P. Buriks, *l.c.*, p. 39, note 1.

[5] Hu Hsien-chin, *The Common Descent Group in China*, p. 71; detailed analysis by J. Nakamura in *Tōhō gakuhō* 11, 1955, pp. 100-109 and in *Shien* 64, 1955, pp. 43-63.

T. Grimm's valuable study *Erziehung und Politik im konfuzianischen China der Ming-Zeit*, Hamburg 1960, stresses the importance of private academies (*shu-yüan*) for the education in the Ming period and states that in general education became more widely available in the latter part of the Ming period, a conclusion with which we agree but which does not, in general, change our conclusion that education was not easily available for the lower classes in that time.

[6] In modern Kuang-tung the percentage changed from 0.1% to 5% of the cultivated land (Ch'en Han-seng, *Landlord and Peasant*, p. 25). We must bear in mind that these schools ordinarily provided only elementary education.

[7] E. A. Kracke, *Civil Service in Early Sung China*, 960-1057, Cambridge, 1953; and E. A. Kracke, "Region, Family, and Individual in the Chinese Examination System", in J. K. Fairbank (edit.), *Chinese Thought and Institutions*, Chicago, 1957, pp. 251-268.

the value of this study is very limited: the author has only attempted to find out whether a father, grandfather or other close relative on the male side of a successful candidate had also passed the examinations. He did not attempt to find out whether the candidate came from a gentry family or a farmer's family. In addition, we know that just passing the examinations did not automatically mean success in entering the civil service [1]. We know a good number of names of candidates about whom nothing else is known: perhaps some of them did not want an appointment; but others seem not to have gotten an appointment of any consequence. It seems safe to conclude that a correlation between social origin and success not only in the examinations but also in the careers after the examinations might exist.

If we take the successful gentry, defined as persons who were regarded as important enough to be included in the dynastic histories, and study the social origin of these persons, we find out [2] that in those periods which have already been analyzed almost nobody rose from low social origins. Exceptions are periods of civil war in which bandits and soldiers could make a career and could enter the circle of the gentry. One such case is the period of the Five Dynasties (906-960): the wars of this period removed many old gentry families from their high positions and brought a number of new families into the gentry.

On the other hand, we find many families which belong to the gentry over periods of many centuries [3].

With the Ming period (1368-1644) our historical data become so abundant, that new methods can be used to study social mobility. Two recent studies which cover the period from the Ming dynasty to the near-present have to be mentioned in this connection, partly because of the method which they used, partly because of the conclusions drawn.

The study by Robert M. Marsh [4] uses a sample of 572 persons to cover the period from 1590 to 1900. His sample comes from a standard biographical dictionary (A. Hummel) in which the politically and culturally leading persons of the time are mentioned. Marsh is

---

[1] S. van der Sprenkel, *Legal Institutions in Manchu China*, London 1962, p. 53.
[2] W. Eberhard, *Das Toba-Reich Nord-Chinas*, Leiden, 1949, pp. 364-387; *Conquerors and Rulers*, Leiden, 1952, pp. 103-121; *BOSS*, 1955, vol. 17, pp. 373-374.
[3] Cf. note 2 and "Research on the Chinese Family" in *Sociologus*, vol. 9, 1959, pp. 1-11.
[4] *Mandarin and Executive*, Ph. D. thesis, University of Michigan, 1959, manuscript.

conscious of the possibility that such a dictionary, which was published under the direction of Americans, not Chinese, may have certain biases; he also knows that his sample really takes only a small fraction of the very top level of Chinese society. Yet, we would agree with him, that with limitations valid conclusions can be drawn from such a sample. More serious is another limitation of his study. He measures the degree of social mobility by comparing the status of the person mentioned in the dictionary with the status of the ancestors in the main male line of this person in the last three generations. Status again is defined as membership in the official bureaucracy, i.e. rank and or title. Thus, he finds that in 51% of all cases, only ego and one of his next direct ancestors was an official; in 32% of all cases, two of the four generations (ego included) were officials, in 13% three and only in 4% all four generations were officials. The consequences of his limitation are:

a) He does not take into account that a family may have legal "gentry" status, as indicated by the social privileges enjoyed by such families (see above, pages 15-16) and has, therefore, also the social prestige of the gentry class; yet it may not have produced a member of the bureaucracy for a number of generations. If a son of such a family becomes an official, the status of the family does not actually rise, just as a European noble family remained a toplevel family even if for several generations no member was a ruler; if a member became a ruler, this did not mean upward mobility.

b) Secondly, if social mobility is measured by membership in the bureaucracy, another important group is left out. Normally, none of the official biographies mention the lowest ranks of the bureaucracy or the low provincial posts of a person. Only more "significant" posts are mentioned. Also, if a person just passed through the lower examinations and thus, for the Chinese, reached gentry status, the normal biographies do not mention this fact unless the man went on and reached a higher position. Such a person, naturally, did not belong to the political leaders of Chinese society, but in his home district, he belonged to the gentry and could, even if he never accepted any office or never tried to get a position, make his voice heard in matters of local importance [1], just as a European country gentleman of the nobility could, by just talking matters over with the officials, straighten out situations in a way other persons could not.

---

[1] Ch'ü T'ung-tsu, *Local Government in China under the Ch'ing*, Cambridge, Mass. 1962, p. 175.

With these reservations in mind, some of Marsh's results can be summarized as follows: In Manchu time (1644-1911) members of the imperial family, nobility, hereditary officials and tribal chieftains, i.e., members of the Manchu conquerors, had better chances to reach the top level of society than others [1]. Chinese from official families (i.e. families in which a member of the last three generation had been an official) rose higher, though not necessarily more quickly than sons of commoners, even if the sons of officials did not take the "proper path", i.e. the examinations. Sons of commoners were about as successful as sons of officials in reaching high-rank posts, once they got into office, but they were not as successful in holding these high-rank posts over a long period of time [2].

The tiny fraction of the population who were officials or holders of degrees were tremendously over-represented, and the mass of the population greatly under-represented. What really mattered was to get into the bureaucracy. Once a person was "in", his chances were not much worse than those of the sons of official families [3]. One good way for commoners to move up by the "miscellaneous path" was to start a military career; this career had lower prestige and, therefore, it was easier to get into by simply buying oneself a low rank. But it promised quick and high promotion in case of military success, as in periods of war [4].

Marsh, in conclusion, finds that social mobility in China was about as high as in America [5], and varied in different periods: it was relatively high in the first period (1590-1684: 36% of the persons came from families below elite status), was low in the period of greatest strength of the dynasty (1685-1780: 19%), and rose again in the period of civil and foreign wars (1781-1900: 29%) [6].

The study of Ho Ping-ti [7] is, in my opinion, the best study thus far produced in which degree-holders and or officials are used and their ancestry is analyzed. Ho takes into consideration that there was a belief in human inequality in the period he studied (1370-1904) and there was legal stratification. Yet, he thinks that from 1550 on

---

[1] *Loc. cit.*, p. 246.
[2] *Loc. cit.*, p. 248.
[3] *Loc. cit.*, p. 249.
[4] *Loc. cit.*, p. 250.
[5] Some studies rate upward mobility in the U.S. as around 60%.
[6] R. M. Marsh, *loc. cit.*, p. 236.
[7] "Aspects of Social Mobility in China, 1368-1911", in *Comparative Studies in Society and History*, vol. 1, no. 4, 1959, pp. 330-359.

the laws regulating status broke down [1]; that degrees could be bought (from 1450 on) and thus wealthy commoners could move into the elite; and that after 1720 the "declassed" group was less than 1% of the population and even the descendants of such people got chances for social mobility because after three or four generations they could compete for the examinations [2].

The strength of his research lies in his definition of "ruling class" as "consisting of officials, people holding official ranks and titles, sub-officials, and degree-holders above *sheng-yüan* for the Ming period, with the same definition for the Ch'ing period except for the exclusion of *chien-sheng* [3]. *Sheng-yüan* are persons who passed only the first examination (*hsiu-ts'ai*, in popular terminology): *chien-sheng* were *hsiu-ts'ai* who were sent to the Academy and got higher jobs; but this rank could be bought. Ho calls this group "transitional status group", because these persons still had semi-privileges recognized by law and were not allowed to take up jobs as clerks, brokers, runners, or bookkeepers of merchants [4]. It seems to me that Ho is right in making a difference between these two groups; yet both together belong to the leading sector of Chinese society. If we take the percentages of persons whose ancestors belonged to the ruling class, as defined by Ho, and to the transitional group together, we find that from 1652-1703, 76.4% of the ruling class members came from these groups; between 1822-1868, 85.1% and between 1871-1904, 83.3% [5] Because of his different method, his results cannot be directly compared with those of R. Marsh, yet certain similarities are recognizable, and both studies reveal a higher degree of social mobility between 1370 and the present than we had formerly suspected. It is significant, also, that both studies come to the conclusion that periods of war are periods of greater social mobility.

Although direct comparisons of the situation in the medieval and the recent period are impossible because we cannot use the same research methods for both periods, we get the impression that until around 1000 A.D. social mobility was quite restricted in China; that the civil wars of the 10th century and the economic developments of the 11th century were periods of greater mobility; and that in more recent periods, mobility has become more common and easier.

---

[1] *Loc. cit.*, p. 336.
[2] *Loc. cit.*, p. 336.
[3] *Loc. cit.*, p. 342.
[4] *Loc. cit.*, p. 344.
[5] Calculated on the basis of *loc. cit.*, p. 347, table.

Instead of taking persons in the social elite and investigating their ancestry—as all previous studies have done, we attempted another approach—that of studying, among certain clans, all the male members (as far as possible) over a long period of time (generally 300 years). Since status was ascribed by law not to individuals but to families, it seems to be important to study what happens to a whole clan or family over a long period of time and not to limit the study to an analysis of the fate of individuals only. Naturally, if one or more individuals succeed in rising to a high status, or if one man because of a crime is deprived of his class status, this has strong reactions upon his family and, often, upon his clan. Social mobility of families and clans is not independent of social mobility of the individuals which make up the family or the clan; but social mobility of individuals is also strongly influenced by their families or clans. We will later on go more into details and will also clarify the interrelations between families and the clans to which they belong.

Our study was also designed to attack another problem. Some of the critics of my concept of "gentry" and "gentry society" have said: "If you study the genealogy of any family, you will come up with some officials. Then, logically, all Chinese families are gentry families". The first statement is true: Chinese population has increased greatly: The total number of clans today, however, is not too much greater than 1000 years ago, and thus, at some place in the genealogy we will indeed invariably find some high official. Yet, today, the family in question may have no gentry status at all. Clans split into branches, houses, and families; some of these families lost their status by the fact of splitting off the main house. Other families became extinct and thus, gentry status came to an end. These processes will be discussed later in more detail.

This problem can be formulated differently. As certainly not all Chinese families are gentry families, a process of downward mobility must have been involved. In fact, many authors have, on the basis of Chinese proverbial sayings, spoken of a kind of cyclical social mobility. A family needs, they contend, 2 or 3 generations of hard work to reach high social status, and in the following 2 or 3 generations, the same family is again down at the bottom.

Now, we know from practically all available studies made on samples of modern Chinese populations that the wealthier the family, the more children they have on the average; the poorer, the fewer [1].

---

[1] Data on family size will be given below.

We have reason to assume that the wealthier families are at the top level of society, in fact, the gentry families are also, on the average, the wealthier families. If, then, gentry families increase at a greater rate than commoners' families, it must in the long run become near to impossible to place all sons in top-level positions, even if they have all other moral and intellectual abilities for leadership, simply because the number of jobs will at best increase in proportion to the increase in the population, and therefore more slowly than the increase in the number of gentry sons. Studies in European societies have shown that the elite produced fewer children than the commoners, so that, in order to fill the top level positions, sons of commoners had to be accepted because there were more job openings than sons of the elite. Thus, if we follow this deduction, there must always have been a fairly high degree of upward social mobility in Europe while upward social mobility in China should have been limited. It seems to me to be a poor, a priori argument to assume that the "normal" son of an elite family was so decadent that he could not preserve the status of his family or father, in spite of the advantages which family status must have given him. Yet, for logical reasons we must assume downward social mobility to be in existence, if the upper class increased more quickly than the lower class. We believe that with our method, we can reach some understanding of this process.

We know from other studies that upward social mobility is often connected with geographical, horizontal mobility: it is easier to change social status or class in a place where one's background and origins are not well known. We decided, therefore, to include a study of migration in our discussion.

The addition of a study of migration poses several problems. We know that China's political and ethnic boundaries have expanded over the centuries and, therefore, we know that large-scale migrations have taken place. The sources report directly about forced migrations of low-class people (as discussed above), and of migrations of gentry families in connection with political catastrophies, such as a conquest of North China by non-Chinese invaders. But we feel that these two kinds of migrations cannot be all. Several attempts to study migrations more closely have, indeed, been made [1]. Li Chi studied the spread of city-building over the last 3,000 years and could thus map out the

---

[1] We leave aside here the modern labor migrations. For these see Ta Chen, *Emigrant Communities in South China*, New York, 1940; K. J. Pelzer, *Die Arbeiterwanderungen in Südostasien*, Hamburg, 1935, and his *Pioneer Settlement in the Asiatic*

main lines and the main periods of migrations [1]. H. Bielenstein analyzed census reports and could by this method map out lines and periods of migrations [2]. In a more recent study [3], he adopted a method which is close to that of Li Chi and reached results which explain quite well the pattern of settlement of the present-day province of Fukien. But none of these methods determines who migrated, where to, and why.

One good source for the study of both mobility and migration, are actual census sheets and office files. The excavations in Tun-huang have brought forth some such documents and valuable information can be drawn from them [4]; but the body of data is too small to be of great use. We expect that with our method, which uses data contained in genealogies, we can get close to an understanding of social and geographical mobility.

4. Families and Their Genealogies

A history of the development of the Chinese family has yet to be written, in spite of the existence of many books on the Chinese family. We can here not discuss this, but we will try to outline a few facts which are of importance to our main topic [5]. The form of the family, of the group which regarded themselves as Chinese, has always been patrilinear and patriarchal; other forms of the family occurred among non-Chinese populations within the area of present-day China and outside of it.

In Chou time (from the eleventh century B.C. on) we find large clans characteristic of the elite, the nobility. The clans, with the geographical dispersal of their members over a large area, began to dissolve soon after the Chou came into power. Their place was taken by aristocratic lineages.

Tropics, New York, 1945; G. W. Skinner, *Chinese Society in Thailand*, Cornell University Press, 1957, and many other special studies.

[1] Chi Li, *The Formation of the Chinese People*, Cambridge, 1928.

[2] H. Bielenstein, "The Census of China During the Period 2 — 742 A.D.", in *Bull. Museum Far Eastern Antiquities*, vol. 19, 1947.

[3] H. Bielenstein, "The Chinese Colonization of Fukien until the End of T'ang", in *Studia Serica, Bernhard Karlgren Dedicata*, Copenhagen, 1960, pp. 98-122.

[4] W. Eberhard, "The Origin of the Commoners in Ancient Tun-huang", in *Sinologica*, vol. 4, 1955, pp. 141-155, and "The Leading Families of Ancient Tun-huang", in *Sinologica*, vol. 4, 1956, pp. 209-232.

[5] For a broader approach see "Research on the Chinese Family" in *Sociologus*, vol. 9, 1959, pp. 1-11.

In the period of transition to the gentry society of medieval times, lineages broke up into families, who then often lost their aristocratic status, and this was especially true if they had descended from concubines. Primogeniture which had existed [1], at least in parts of Chou China and in relation to the transmission of fiefs, disappeared. Families of commoners and even of non-Chinese had become so much assimilated that they, too, accepted family names as the nobility had done; they also now owned land, which formerly had not been possible [2]. In the early gentry period, then, we find a class society of the type which has already been briefly described; in this society we find patrilinear, patrilocal, and patriarchal families of the form of extended families. Although philosophers and moralists at all times praised the large family in which "5 generations live under one roof", such cases were always rare and were often especially reported in the dynastic histories. The size of an average family was more often around 5 persons; only gentry families showed larger numbers. Legislation had a strong influence upon the size of the family. Shang Yang, for instance, statesman and philosopher of the early fourth century (died 338 B.C.), taxed families in which several sons lived in the house [3]. Such a regulation brought about a sudden dispersal of large families. The Han dynasty (206 B.C. - 220 A.D.) abolished this rule [4] and thus favored the formation of extended families.

The size of the household also depended upon the wealth of the family; large landowners always had larger families than small farmers [5]. Gentry families had larger than average families because many children insured success of their "dynastic marriages".

Each family was controlled by a family head, usually the oldest male in the main line. If no man was alive, a woman could be legal chief of the household [6]. Although, as was mentioned, primogeniture did not exist in the medieval period, the successor head of a family

---

[1] The Shang practiced minorate (Fu Szŭ-nien in *An-yang fa-chüeh pao-kao*, vol. 2, p. 367) but once the brothers were all dead, the elder sons were preferred. Ultimogeniture can be proved in traces, especially among China's northern neighbors.

[2] These processes are described in more detail in my *A History of China*, second edition, London, 1960, p. 72 ff.

[3] J. J. L. Duyvendak, *The Book of Lord Shang*, p. 15.

[4] A. Hulsewé, *Remnants of Han Law*, vol. 1, p. 50.

[5] *Yenching Journal of Social Studies*, vol. 3, p. 13; Fr. L. K. Hsu, *Under the Ancestors Shadows*, p. 214; O. Lang, *Family and Society in China*, p. 147; G. W. Skinner, "A Study in Miniature of Chinese Population" in *Population Studies*, vol. 5, 1951, p. 101.

[6] N. Niida, *Legal Documents*, pp. 625-626 and p. 745.

should always be the first son of the main wife, even though there was an older son from a concubine. In the event of his death, the next son of the main wife would become his successor. Only if there were no sons of the main wife, could a son of a concubine become head of the family [1]. The family chief administered the family property, as well as the property belonging to his brothers, although he probably did not legally own this property. Members of nuclear families until the Sung period (ca. 11th century) could not sell family land without the permission of the family head, nor could the chief sell land or give freedom to slaves without the counter-signature of his own sons and of the heads of the other nuclear families in the extended family [2]. Individuals could have their own property, and their salaries were always under their own control [3]. From Sung time on, as the individual family got more independence, the family head began to be regarded as owner, and could then often sell land even without the counter-signatures of his sons.

Tensions within the extended family always led to the break-up of the family. Such tensions were, as N. Niida stated [4], mostly tensions between daughters-in-law, but tensions with the in-laws in general, tensions between brothers, and even tensions between father and sons were not rare. The family could break up after the death of the father or the parents, or when the father (the head of the family) was old or permitted a separation. In some periods, separation was illegal as long as parents and grandparents were alive [5]. If the family chief initiated a separation during his own life-time, he could set up special conditions [6]. He could also make a will with special conditions [7]: he could, for instance, give land to relatives other than his sons [8]; he could set up foundations and even make gifts [9].

---

[1] *An-ping Kao-shih tsu-p'u chih lüeh*, p. 92a. Similarly, sons of concubines and servant girls received only half a share in inheritance, and sons of other families who had been adopted into the family only one quarter share in pre-modern Taiwan among Taiwanese Chinese (Mrs. Yang Ch'ing-yü, "T'ai-wan-ti min-su", in *Hsin-shê-hui*, vol. 12, no. 4, April, 1960, p. 16).

[2] *T'ang-lü su-i* 20, as quoted in *Studies in Chinese Economic History* p. 178. For the modern period see E. Kroker, "The Concept of Property in Chinese Customary Law", in *Transact. Asiatic Society of Japan*, 3rd series, vol. 7, 1959, p. 141.

[3] N. Niida, *Legal Documents*, pp. 566-567.
[4] N. Niida, *Village Family*, pp. 104-105.
[5] N. Niida, *Legal Documents*, p. 559.
[6] N. Niida, *Legal Documents*, pp. 592-593.
[7] N. Niida, *Legal Documents*, p. 593.
[8] Hu Hsien-chin, *Common Descent Group*, p. 106.
[9] N. Niida, *Legal Documents*, pp. 624-628.

However, some kinds of property could not be given to non-relatives, and the percentage of money which could be given as gifts was limited [1]. Such wills were legal documents and had to be sealed by an official [2]. If there was no will, all sons shared equally, although unmarried sons got an extra share in order to be able to marry, and unmarried female descendants also got some extra share [3]. Sons of concubines got the same share as real sons and got even a share of the property which the main wife had brought into the marriage [4], except during the Mongol period, when sons got 4 shares, sons of concubines 3 shares, and sons from low-class wives only one share [5]. It seems that from this period on, fathers indicated by the specific form of the name who among their sons was not a son of the main wife [6], but we cannot yet prove this point.

These are some of the general characteristics of the Chinese family from medieval times on which did not change much; the two changes which we observed and which occurred after 1000 A.D. accentuated even more the patriarchal, patrilinear character of the family.

Marriage within the same family, and, in most periods of Chinese history, even marriages with maternal cousins who, according to Chinese custom, had a different family name, were not allowed. By definition "same family" meant "same family name", even if the relationship could no longer be proved [7], and if, in case of a concubine of low class origin, her family name was unknown (or if she had none), the oracle had to be consulted[8]. This was a tightening of an earlier, feudal period rule according to which a marriage was allowed if no common ancestors within the last 5 generations could be found[9]; after five generations, relationship ended[10], and a new independent family came into being [11]. From Han time on, a family could indeed become independent if they had split from the main house five generations earlier; but inter-marriage remained forbidden.

---

[1] N. Niida, *Legal Documents*, p. 628.
[2] N. Niida, *Legal Documents*, p. 633.
[3] N. Niida, *Legal Documents*, p. 583.
[4] N. Niida, *Legal Documents*, p. 586.
[5] N. Niida, *Legal Documents*, p. 586.
[6] Actually, a Chinese could have only one legal wife; all others were legally concubines.
[7] *Li-chi, Ch'ü-li* 1: Couvreur, vol. 1, p. 31.
[8] *Ibid.*, and *Tso-chuan*, Chao 1.
[9] Sing Ging Su, *Chinese Family System*, p. 24.
[10] *Li-chi, Ta-chuan* 7; translated by Couvreur, vol. 1, p. 781.
[11] Sing Ging Su, *Chinese Family System*, p. 32.

All these regulations concerning marriage, inheritance, property rights, make it understandable that wealthier families had to have genealogies in order to keep track of family members and to prevent imposters [1].

In the early gentry period, feudal traditions were still alive, and gentry families tried to prove their "good" origin, and in some cases also their right to become an imperial house [2], by tracing their genealogy back to a feudal or early ruling house. In some cases, this may have been historical fact, in others, very probably not.

The existence of the above-mentioned social classes was another reason why genealogies were necessary. If a family wanted to conclude a marriage relation with another family, it had to prove that it belonged to the gentry class and that it was a "good", "old", and "high" family. We know how important genealogies in this respect were even among the non-Chinese populations at the borders of China: [3] Lolo could recite long genealogies of interrelated families [4]. They usually sang them, but their leaders and their shamans also had written genealogies [5]. In one case, 110 generations were claimed [6], but in many other cases, genealogies seemed to go back to and to be reliable from the 13th and 14th centuries on [7]. They were used to establish the relative status of the families who wanted to intermarry.

As the class to which a family belonged also indicated the rights and obligations of that family, the government was as much interested in genealogies as were the families themselves. The first systematic way of checking was probably the census lists which mentioned the status of each family as early as Han time. Later, the so-called *t'u-tuan* were created [8], lists which apparently established the geographical

---

[1] In a story, a man looks up in the family genealogy to check upon a stranger who said that he was a relative (*Nan-Ch'u hsin-wen*, as quoted in *T'ai-p'ing kuang-chi* 238; vol. 19, p. 20a).

[2] The Liu family of the Han imperial house proved that they were descendants of emperor Yao; Wang Mang, who dethroned them in order to create his own dynasty, proved that his family descended from emperor Shun and, therefore, were rightful successors to the Liu, because Shun followed Yao (text in *Han-shu*, 99b, 3a).

[3] H. H. Vreeland, *Mongol Community and Kinship Structure*, New Haven, 1952, pp. 11 and 15.

[4] *Frontier Affairs*, vol. 4, no. 9/12, pp. 1-20.

[5] *Frontier Studies*, 1942/4, p. 52.

[6] *Frontier Affairs*, vol. 4, no. 5/6, p. 13.

[7] *Frontier Affairs*, vol. 4, 5/6, p. 20 and *Frontier Affairs*, vol. 4, no. 7/8, pp. 20-24.

[8] H. Maspero, *Les Institutions de la Chine*, Paris, 1952, p. 79.

origin and home of important families. These lists were of greatest importance in the fourth and fifth centuries, when innumerable families fled to the South as a result of the conquest of North China by nomadic tribes. Disruption of families and migration made it easy for impostors to be accepted.

About a century later, we find the first "p'u" (list) of gentry families, the "Chinese Gotha" [1]. These lists were arranged according to districts and enumerated all gentry families of each district. There are many later lists, from 634, 638, 681, 749, etc [2]. The list of 634 had 398 family names; the list of 638 had 293 family names with 1651 individual families, divided into 9 classes. According to other texts [3] the 638 list had only 193 families and was used to check upon candidates for offices as well as for marriages. They were made on the basis of local lists and historical data, and families mentioned in these lists, when proved not related, could intermarry.

In addition to these lists, it was the privilege of officials above a certain rank to be mentioned in the dynastic histories by a biography or at least by a reference [4]; and if the state historians needed information, they asked members of prominent families to provide facts on their families [5]. Thus, important families could always prove their status by referring to the dynastic histories, wherein their ancestors and relatives were mentioned.

In this period, i.e. roughly between 200 B.C. and 900 A.D., gentry families seem not to have remained together for more than the traditional five generations. After five generations, a branch would become an independent house, and, if it happened to live in a district other than the home district of the old house, it would register locally. This would mean—to give an example—that a branch of the famous Ts'ui house of Tung-wu in Ch'ing-ho which registered in An-p'ing in Po-ling would now be called the "Po-ling Ts'ui" and no longer the "Ch'ing-ho Ts'ui" [6], and as such would automatically relinquish its original gentry status.

---

[1] Composed in 508, cf. Mou Jun-sun in *T'ai-wan Ta-hsüeh, Wen-shih chê-hsüeh pao*, vol. 3, 1951, p. 70.

[2] Mou Jun-sun, *loc. cit.*, p. 61 f.; and On Kidea in *Tōyō Gakuhō*, vol. 4, no. 1, 1958, p. 64.

[3] *Lin-shih tsung-ch'in-lu* 1937, p. 13, guiding text from 1113 A.D.

[4] *Ch'ü-yu chiu-wen*, 10, p. 2b, for Sung time.

[5] *Chiu-Wu-tai shih* 10: p. 4212b-c for the year 920.

[6] The exact relation of both branches is, incidentally, not yet clear. It may be the other way around. Both houses were gentry families and are mentioned in the lists.

The main house, then, in its own private genealogy (which was checked by the state) would carry only the names of the main house and no longer mention the branch houses [1]. The branch house, on the other hand, would mention the earlier generations, but only in a summary, and give complete data from time of separation on [2].

The upheavals of the period of the Five Dynasties (906-960) brought a change in the system of genealogies. Low-class families which had entered the elite by way of a career as bandits and successful soldiers were ashamed to discuss their ancestors [3]. The state no longer exercised control over the correctness of genealogies which then became the private concern of families [4].

Later, however, new factors in Sung time favored the tradition of keeping genealogies: from the eleventh century on, a new element of capitalistic activity was introduced into the family economy. Not only do we find individual property, but there is also family property controlled by the head of the extended family. Now, in addition, we find clan property, commonly owned by as many as several hundred persons. Clan property took the form of land which was set aside for the welfare of the clan: [5] to pay for a school; to make regular rice rations available to all members of the clan and thus guarantee a minimum living standard; to pay for the expenses of travel to the capital for examinations; to give premiums to successful candidates and thus to induce young men to compete for high education; or to pay the expenses of ancestral sacrifices [6] or weddings or funerals. The clan, in this way, tried to establish a system of social security for its members at a time when upheavals in politics made state assistance tenuous. As may be seen, often quite large investments had to be administrated. The clan appointed special administrators (who were paid) and auditors who had to see that the property was

---

[1] See the case of Tu Cheng-lun who was not allowed to include relatives from a branch house in the South of the city, because the relationship was too far (preface of 1413 of the *Ling-nan Wu-shih tsung-p'u*, 2, p. 24b).

[2] Such was Ou-yang Hsiu's (1007-1072) opinion, see T. Makino, p. 55.

[3] Makino, p. 43.

[4] Makino, *loc. cit.*, p. 40.

[5] See D. Twitchett, "The Fan Clan's Charitable Estate", in D. Nivison, *Confucianism in Action*, Stanford, 1959, pp. 97-133, but also J. Fischer, *Fan Chung-yen*, Ph. D. thesis, Göttingen 1954, 78, manuscript, and Makino *loc. cit.*, p. 131. Fan is regarded as the initiator of this type of foundations and is, therefore, highly praised by most Chinese authors. However, serious accusations concerning his character were made by other authors (*Jung-ch'uang hsiao-p'in* 18, 8b; a Ming source); this would make a special biographical study desirable.

[6] On the cost of the cult see Makino, *loc. cit.*, p. 29.

used in the best way: land had to be rented out to tenants, but care had to be taken when clan members wanted to be the tenants, because they might prove to be poor rent payers. Cash income could be invested in shops or other business concerns. There might also be land with buildings which could be rented and thus need control and repair. Naturally, whoever controlled the clan land was in a key position. In practice, this meant that the main house of the clan was strengthened, and that the branch houses tended to keep in contact with the main house in order to profit from the clan property. From Sung time on, therefore, we find the formation of large clans of many hundred individuals with much land and great power. These clans played a special role in Central and South China, because economic conditions there were more favorable: a) there was still land available, either virgin land or land in the hands of native tribes. b) Investment could make poor land fertile, as, for instance, by installation of irrigation. c) Even rice land could be made much more fertile by agricultural techniques such as deep fields, combined use of fields for rice and pisciculture, etc. d) Business opportunities were great for enterprises among the native tribes or with coastal shipping.

The genealogies changed their form from approx. the eleventh century on. The main purpose remained: to establish who was related and to what degree. The degree of relationship determined not only mourning obligations [1], but also the inheritance upon death. A genealogy should "investigate branches and twigs, enumerate high and low (family members), should not flatter the rich and influential, and not omit the low and distant (relatives)" [2]. They now included introductory chapters which contained what was called the "chia-fa" (house rules): a moral code, often also a set of legally binding rules for the members of the clan regulating inheritance, use of clan property, appointment of clan officials, and the like [3]. These clan rules have recently been studied [4] as to their Confucian content. They also provide a rich source for the study of internal changes in the clans and in the economic attitudes of the clans. A clan rule of 890 A.D., of which only a few fragments are reported—it seems to be one of the oldest rules known—stated, for instance, that the clan

---

[1] Sung P'ei, in his preface of 1169 in the *Ling-nan Wu-shih tsung-p'u* 2, p. 19a; Tseng Ti in his 1343 preface, *loc. cit.*, p. 21b.

[2] Li Chen in his 1370 preface in the *Ling-nan Wu-shih tsung-p'u*, 2, p. 22a.

[3] Ch'ü T'ung-tsu, *loc. cit.*, p. 18.

[4] Wang-Liu, Hui-shen, "An Analysis of Chinese Clan Rules" in D. Nivison, *Confucianism in Action*, Stanford, 1959, pp. 63-96.

should not keep slaves; that nobody should be allowed "to play with falcons and dogs" (i.e., go hunting), and "the sciences of the maps, the field of astronomy, the ideas of alliances and shifts of power (i.e., political and military science), the words of Buddha and the monks, the profit-ways of merchants and businessmen must not be practised"[1]. Similarly, another genealogy stated that *shih* (officials) are the best people, followed by farmers, craftsmen, merchants, shop-keepers; after these come the medical doctos and soothsayers. But to be a soldier is to be in a dishonorable profession[2]. Both rules show that the clans definitely discriminated against members engaging in business. We will later see that soothsayer, geomancer ("the science of maps") and local doctors (i.e., those who have not passed special government examinations by which they qualified as officials) are low-status professions which often were selected by men who wanted to climb socially. Clan rules often warn of Buddhist and other monks, because monks do not marry, do not therefore, propagate the family, and cost the family much money and wealth, because the family often has to care for their upkeep in order to maintain the family prestige.

Because of the importance of the clan rules to the whole problem of social mobility and migration—especially as they bear on the relationship between the main and other branches of the clan—I am summarizing, as a typical example, the 32 rules which the Ch'en clan[3] set up for its members:

1) Provision is made for a manager and two assistants who are responsible for all clan affairs. They pay the expenses, at the proper time, for the marriages of sons and daughters, and the "tea money" for food and drink the three times of the year at festivals, and on new moon days.

2) These men should not be appointed according to age, but on the basis of their knowledge of economics; they should be men of ideas, who are decent and can restrain themselves, men who are forgiving and understanding.

3) Two treasurers keep the accounts of the whole clan and set up the standards for the group. They handle rewards and punishments, take care of public and private affairs, admonish superiors and inferiors.

---
[1] *T'ai-wan Ch'en Ta-tsung tz'u Tê-hsing-t'ang chung-hsiu chi-nien t'ê-k'an*, Taipei, 1958, p. 96.
[2] Makino, *loc. cit.*, p. 77.
[3] *T'ai-wan Ch'en Ta-tsung*, pp. 91-93.

manage manors and houses, handle the taxes for each house as well as all contracts and papers concerning manors. They are obliged, every year, to collect and deliver the Emperor's taxes and the money needed by the public. They also give clothing to men and women; they control the accounts of all manors. In the case of these treasurers, again, age should not be taken into account, but active and courageous men should be appointed who can conscientiously control the affairs of the manors.

4) For each manor there should be two men appointed from among relatives (brothers and cousins), one to act as head man, one as vice-chief. They work together in the management of the manor—measuring fields, giving permission to those under them to carry on business away from the manor, even punishing or rewarding for disobedience or good behavior—and the rules even stated that no father and son should work together in this activity, to avoid suspicion.

5) Eleven brothers and cousins should be selected, each to be given specific duties: two are responsible for the wine, vinegar, and making of flour; two control the mortars and distribute to each manor the necessary amounts, including portions for guests. The amount of rice which is hulled every day must be entered in a book, controlled by the general manager. Two take care of the gardens, vegetable fields, cows, horses, pigs, sheep, etc., and hire regularly the manor "guests" (laborers), so that there is the necessary daily supply. One man controls the gates—opening them in the morning and closing them at night—and keeps track of the comings and goings of the brothers and cousins. Four men control the basic supplies in the fields: the rice and mulberry harvests, and the firewood collections in order that daily needs are always on hand. Here, again, good work is to be rewarded, bad behavior punished.

6) The clan has one representative who is responsible for the marriages of sons and daughters; who keeps track of the rank and order of men and women. He keeps a "Long-Life List" (birth and death register), into which he writes every year the months and days. He enters into his book the birth of each child of all the houses, assigning each a number according to birth dates, up to 99, and then beginning anew. Degrees of relationship are not herein considered—only birth sequence. Boys are entered in one column, girls into the other. When the sons reach 18, this representative makes arrangements for a bride and prepares the ceremonies. The boys in this clan were to have only one wife, no "servant-girls". The girls must wait until there is a request from another family.

7) Every married man should remain under the control of the manager. Every day, he should do agricultural or other work, as the manager has ordered him. If he should not obey, he should be reported to the head of the family for further action.

8) Sons and nephews should not only do what they have been told to do. But they should, when they go out or return, in the morning and the evening, wear a sash and full dress. If they are negligent in this respect, an investigation would follow.

9) There is a study in the East-family Farm. All sons and nephews who are bright, should study there. The best students should be sent for the examination. Educated persons should be allowed to take books in and out, without consideration of the degree of relationship, and any visitors who want to stay there and study, should be made welcome by the East-family Farm.

10) There is a school west of the East-family Farm, for the education in elementary things. From a lucky day in the first month on, to a lucky day in the 12th month, boys of the age of seven should go to this school, until they are 15 and then to the university. In the Library of the East-family Farm, there should be two teachers during the whole year, one regular and one assistant. The needs for paper, brushes, and ink should be supplied by the Treasurer.

11) There is also a Taoist place, and a Taoist should be there. He should take care of the burning of incense in the morning and the evening. He should pray to the powers above for long life, and to the powers below for peace. All necessary sacrifices should be arranged by him.

12) There is a house for the old shamanistic practices. The necessary actions for exorcism, in the case of house-building, of selecting a tomb, of oracles or of imprecations should be taken there.

13) There should be one doctor for the treatment of the ills of old and young. One should select a man who knows the drugs and the prescriptions.

14) In the kitchen, eight young women should work. Their job is the preparation of food. Two prepare the vegetables, four cook the rice, two keep a supply of hot water. For all services in the interior of the house, throughout the year, the young brides should be used, one after the other.

15) For the meals of the day, the men should sit down twice a day in the hall of the outer verandah. Those between 40 and 50 should be served first, because they have duties. From 50 up and including

the head of the family, they should be served later because they have nothing to do. There should be two waitresses to supply hot water, other water, tea, etc. The women eat in the rear hall and eat also in 2 sessions, the old and the young. Salt, soja, vegetables, and fresh fruit are supplied by the vice-manager.

17) On ordinary days—non-festive days—men who go out and work, should each receive every 5 nights one porcelain bottle of wine as a reward for their services. The old men are free to drink as much as they want. A person who understands something of wine should test whether it has the right temperature.

20) Concerning home visits of wives: in the first three years, they should be sent home twice a year, in the Spring and Fall, and the time should be limited to 15 days. After these three years, they should be sent at the festivals, and the time limit is 20 days.

21-27) Detailed rules as to what sons and daughters should be given when they marry, and how many dresses, quilts, shoes, etc., should be given annually to each man and woman.

28) Sons and nephews who violate the rules of the house should be punished at the "Place for punishment and beating".

29) Persons who commit wrongs either by mistake or because of drunkenness should be forgiven, if their crime is small. But if they do not react upon admonishment and commit serious crimes, they should be given 50 strokes.

30) Persons who do not obey the family laws, who do not follow the orders of their superiors, who do wrong, persons who gamble and fight, should all be given 20 strokes. Their (ceremonial) dresses should be taken away from them, and they should be put to work for a year. If they then change, they should be reinstated.

31) Persons who misuse farm funds, who go to the bazaar and indulge there in wine and women, should receive 30 strokes, their (ceremonial) dress should be taken away, and they should be sent to work for 3 years. If they then change, they should be reinstated.

To the modern reader, these seem like the rules for a commune or a business enterprise [1]. In fact, the business-like attitude and the strong control which leaves the individual almost no freedom, is astonishing, even if we accept that much of these rules may have been mostly

---

[1] For a general content analysis of clan rules see now Wang-Liu, Hui-chen, *The Traditional Chinese Clan Rules*, Monogr. of the Assoc. for As. Studies, no. 7, New York 1959.

on paper. Max Weber would have been surprised if such texts had become known to him; here is no respect for status and seniority in the family. Efficiency and qualification are what matters. The main house, in which the family head lives, controls all those branch houses in nearby places which have not yet officially and legally separated from the main house. Their activities, especially their financial activities, are strictly controlled by the main house. This is, as stated above, one of the reasons why the main house remains financially strong and maintains its position of leadership. Employees in the manors, i.e. in places other than the seat of the family, may be sent to town to buy, or sell, but each step they take is controlled. The main house controls the age of marriage and the form of marriage; as well as the dowry. Members of the family should wear formal dress in public; their goings and comings when they leave the house are controlled and they must do whatever work the manager assigns to them.

Intelligent boys from all branches of the family receive education. The special provision that everybody, "without consideration of the degree of relationship", can get books to read, indicates that there was a tendency to restrict access to books in the library of the main house to members of the main house.

The clan provides not only its teachers, but also its doctors, priests and magicians. As these persons are employees of the clan and members of other families, their status is not much above that of servants; therefore, members of the family should not enter such professions.

Even the rules governing the taking of meals indicate that economic factors take precedence over seniority; those who work should get their meals as quickly as possible; but wine should be available for the old man rather than for those of working age.

"House rules" such as these are quite similar to Japanese clan rules, though the structure of Japanese clans and families differs in many significant aspects from Chinese clans.

The genealogies were distributed among family members and their distribution was strictly controlled. At the time of the great ancestral sacrifices each year in Spring they were checked and brought up to date if this had not yet been done [1]. People who defaced them, were

---

[1] According to typical clan rules (such as the text quoted by Huang Tien-ch'üan in *T'ai-wan wen-chien*, vol. 5, no. 2, 1956, p. 23 from a Formosan Chinese family) when a baby is over a month old, it should be presented ceremoniously to the parents of the father. At that occasion, the baby's name and date of birth

punished by the clan authorities [1]. Yet, I have seen a genealogy in which a correct entry was later falsified. The sentence "Xth of the Xth month of 1952, he was shot by the Kuo-min-tang" was replaced by the sentence "he died in 1952". The reason for this change was that the family had reasons to fear government action if an official found that the family had reported this illegal slaying of a Formosan [2].

Examples such as this bring up the question as to the reliability of genealogies. Clan genealogies are not complete. They frequently do not contain the names of all daughters, nor their birth and death dates. There are other omissions in genealogies, which vary from clan to clan. In the following, I give excerpts from a genealogy which states some typical rules governing the writing of genealogies:

1) Five generations are on one Table. If one Table is finished, then one begins again with the fifth generation and starts again another table, so that, in fact, there are four (different) generations (per table) only.

2) The main (wife's) son (of the main house) is the leading son; sons of branch families and other sons (i.e. second, etc., sons) come after him. Whether they are close or distant (relatives) the name of each one is given. Thus, the oldest sons go down as on a string, and all other sons follow on the left side, one after the other. In each case, there are two lines of notes under the name. The right (line) has his *tzu* (manhood name) and his rank number (as son), his office, work, death name and *hao* (honorific name). It reads: such and such an office, such and such a *hao*, such and such a death name. If he had none, nothing is written. If he moved away, it is written: moved to such and such a place. If he was given away in adoption, it is written: given in adoption to such and such a relative. The left line has: married Miss X, had so and so many sons. If this is not known, a "missing" is noted. If a man died early and his wife remained chaste, it is written "Married Miss X who became a widow at early age, after she had children or not". If she remarried, this is not written; if he married such a woman, it is only written "he died early" after

---

should be entered into the "manuscript genealogy", i.e. the text which later would be printed. Similarly, 3 days after the wedding the bride is ceremoniously presented to the house deities, and at that occasion, family name and birth date of the bride should be entered into the "manuscript genealogy". This means, that ideally, all babies who survived the first month should be found in the genealogies. This is, however, not always the case.

[1] Makino, *loc. cit.*, pp. 37-39.

[2] From a manuscript in a Formosan family. I was asked not to reveal the name and place nor the day and the month. Full data in my hands.

having had children or ("he died early" and) had no children. If he had married but remained without children, a "successor" is set up to serve as his descendant, and it is written "Such and such a relative's son X was his descendant". If there is a (person) who never married, his death is not reported (as of date of death), and if no descendant was set up for him, it is written "Stopped". If he had descendants but there is no information about them, or if he went to some other place as a "live-in son-in-law", and nothing is known about him, it is written "no report". If a man becomes the descendant of another person, it is written "Went out as descendant of X, such and such a relative", and his *tzu*, wife and place of burial are all reported under the name of his adopted father. If a man became a Buddhist or Taoist monk, he is treated as a son who died in infancy. Only on the Table and in the life histories a note is entered under such a name as "Eldest (or "Middle" or "Youngest"), died early".

3) If a man gives up his clan name and (illegally) accepts another person's register and birth place; or if he attaches his genealogy to the genealogy of a man with the same clan name and thus creates confusion in his clan, or if he has illegitimate children and thus darkens his sib; or if he takes a child born by some other woman and pretends that it is fathered by himself; all such types of behavior are against the rules of the holy men for the conservation of the family. If this is written (in the book) (the entries under his name) come to an end with his person. His sons or grandsons are no longer noted. This is done out of respect for the clan.

4) When one takes a wife, one does not take one with the same clan name. The rules stress exogamy. A remarrying wife or a beloved concubine are not mentioned. This is written only in the life histories because, according to the rites, there is no second marriage. Monogamy is stressed.

5) If children or grandchildren behave against reason and if they make trouble and personally receive punishments, nothing is written. This is so in order to punish them. If a man acts against his superiors and violates the elders, he is punished severely according to the laws; but nothing is noted. This is the way to blame unloving sons or unbrotherly sons. If a son's wife behaves badly and heaps shame upon herself, if she loses her chastity and destroys her name, she also is not mentioned, in order to criticize her" [1].

---

[1] *An-p'ing Kao-shih tsu-p'u chih-lüeh*, 1955, p. 13a-13b.

From this example we see that genealogies cannot be used for a study of criminality, and that a genealogy may have certain gaps in cases where family members were involved in crimes. We also see that not all wives are mentioned, though some genealogies which I have used give all the wives and concubines. Adoptions are fully mentioned, except for cases in which a child was given away to strangers or an illigitimate child or a stranger's child was taken in. Yet some genealogies report faithfully on such cases. An entry "Died early" indicates not always early death, but also death without having children. Other omissions are the result of lack of information. On the basis of our actual work with genealogies we tend to regard them on the whole as highly reliable. I have read texts in which persons who had been expelled from the clan because of crimes they committed were mentioned with a note "Expelled"; in such cases their descendants are not mentioned.

Finally, it should be mentioned that genealogies were expected to be printed, if money was available, and the printing should be financed by individual contributions as well as by income from clan land [1].

This new organization of clans, from the eleventh century on, has had great influence upon the ecology of Central and South China. Studies in this special field are still rare and more studies necessary, but from an investigation made by T. Makino in Yen-yüan hsiang (Feng-hua hsien in Chêkiang), some facts are already clear. He found in his investigation of 169 villages and 22 hamlets belonging to these villages (9,492 families; average 4.5 persons [2], average size of villages 497 persons), that 47.3% of the villages consisted of only one single clan [3], and even if a village had more than one clan, the largest clan included usually more than 50% of the population [4].

The villages had from one to 27 clans and from one to 659 families [5]. One-clan villages had an average of 14 families per village [6], and this can be taken as an indicator of the age of a village. We can assume that the mother house originally acquired the land on which it later settled a branch house. If the settlement now has an average of 14 individual families, the settlement cannot be very old, if we assume

---

[1] Makino, pp. 45-46.
[2] Makino, pp. 185-191; calculations by myself.
[3] Makino, pp. 208-209.
[4] Makino, p. 213.
[5] Makino, p. 210.
[6] Makino, p. 210, calculated by myself.

that the village has not sent out a daughter settlement of its own. T. Makino studied the settlement question separately and found that in the course of time, 27 clans with now 3.285 families immigrated into the area (i.e. 118 families per clan), and while ten clans which immigrated after 1644 had an average of 20 families now, eight clans which immigrated between 1368 and 1644 now had an average of 143 families [1]. The majority of the immigrants came, as T. Makino showed [2], from nearby districts of Chêkiang, with a general direction from SW to NO. Further study of materials of the type used by Makino would probably enable us to map out the migrations of individual clans with a fairly high degree of reliability. He also pointed out another area of source of material; the ancestor temples. According to him, 10% of all clans, comprising 68% of all families (average of 97 families per clan) had an ancestral temple in their own village, 30% of the clans with 18% of the families (average 8.5 families per clan) regarded themselves as branches and had their ancestral temple in another village. Such families, then, had separated only recently from the main house. Twenty-one per cent of all clans, comprising 6% of all families, still have their family records in the old home [3], and are, therefore, also fairly recent branches.

Three further sources of ecological character have not yet been mentioned. One is the inscriptions on temples other than ancestral temples. Such inscriptions contain the names of persons who contributed financially to the erection or repair of the temple and are normally dated. From a study of the names which occur on such inscriptions and, to some degree, from the place where a certain name occurs on the inscription, some conclusions as to the spread and importance of clans can be drawn. A second possible source is to be found in cemeteries and tomb inscriptions. These inscriptions sometimes indicate the clan home, and usually the family home, often the name and original family of the wife and always the title of the dead person, if he had any. Temple inscriptions even of emigrant Chinese communities can also be revealing; they not only prove how many and which members of a given clan or family lived in the foreign place at a known time, but as such temples are usually erected by emigrants from the same home country, conclusions upon their home district can be drawn. We have used below information from

---

[1] Makino, p. 284.
[2] Makino, p. 287.
[3] Makino, pp. 224-225.

1868 and 1871 inscriptions on one Chinese temple in Rangoon; other temples in Rangoon did not provide a single name of members of the clan under investigation, because they were erected by persons from an area in which the clan under investigation did not live.

Chinese cemeteries in foreign countries are arranged according to their home districts and not according to clans. Thus, one of the four Chinese cemeteries in Colima (south of San Francisco, California) contained 57 persons of the clan under investigation; the others, among them one very large cemetry, only 6, 3 and 3 persons each, because they represented districts in which our clan was only poorly represented. The third possible source of information is land registers. This source has never yet been tapped. A superficial look at land registers from Tun-huang and the period before 1000 A.D. showed clearly that members of the same clan often had adjacent plots and that by a study of the distribution of the plots, the history of clan settlement could be worked out.

PART TWO

SOCIAL MOBILITY OF THE WU CLAN OF SOUTH CHINA

1. The Material for the Study of the Wu Clan

The source for the following discussions is the "General genealogy of the Wu Clan of Ling-nan" (Ling-nan Wu-shih tsung-p'u) [1], as compiled by Wu Yao-kuang, a member of the 76th generation of the clan. His preface is dated 1933 and his material in most cases is up to date. This genealogy is not the first and only genealogy of the clan which has been written.

The earliest genealogy which was known to the Chinese author had an introduction by Sung P'ei (宋裴) dated 1169 [2]. It dealt with the Wu clan of Tou-tung in Ling-nan. Tou-tung (斗洞) is the home settlement of the Lü-wei house of the Wu clan in Hsin-ning hsien in SW Kuangtung.

The next known genealogy was prefaced by Tseng Ti (曾迪), dated 1343 [3]. It mentioned mainly the Fukien branch of the clan, but indicated that the clan was widely spread all over South-Central China. It mentioned that two brothers, both with a *chin-shih* degree, created houses, one in SW Kuangtung (the Lü-wei house), and the other in Fukien near P'u-t'ien (the An-hai and Sha-pei houses).

Our source mentions a number of other genealogies: a general Wu clan genealogy with a preface dated 1370 by Li Chen (黎貞) [4]. Li Chen was a writer who lived in the home-district of the Han-yüan house of the Wu clan, Hsin-hui. He was the educational officer there until he became involved in an affair and was exiled to Liao-tung, where he remained for 18 years [5]. It is said that many persons followed him into exile, and we know that at least one member of the Han-yüan

---

[1] 嶺南伍氏總譜. Size of the text 7: 12.5".
[2] Tsung-p'u 2a, 19a (from now on, all references in which no Chinese source is mentioned, refer to the *Ling-nan Wu-shih tsung-p'u*).
[3] 2a, 21a.
[4] 2a, 22a.
[5] *Ming-shih* 285: K'ai-ming edition, p. 7792 c-d.

house was exiled to Liao-tung at the same time. Three members of the Han-yüan house (generation 55 and two cousins in gen. 60) and one member of the Lü-wei house (gen. 58) married into the Li clan. Thus, the connections of Li Chen with our clan were quite close.

The next reported genealogy, again a general genealogy, had a preface by Wu K'an (吳侃), dated 1411 [1].

Two prefaces, both dated 1413, and written by Ch'en Kang (陳綱) and Ch'en K'ai (陳塏) dealt with the whole clan [2]. Finally, Wu Yen-shou of the Lü-wei house, wrote a genealogy of his own house in 1425 [3]. Although he belongs to our clan, he is not otherwise mentioned; perhaps his name Yen-shou is only a "style" (*tzu*) and he might be mentioned somewhere under his unknown real name (*ming*).

There was yet another genealogy, of 1427, with a preface by Wu Sheng, also a member of the clan and otherwise unknown [4], but this genealogy dealt with a branch of the clan which is not studied in our genealogy, the socalled Chiang-shan house in Chekiang. The relation of this house to the others seems to have been unclear even at Wu Sheng's time. Wu thought that the house came from Ning-hua in Fukien and settled in Chiang-shan after 1299 [5].

On the basis of these sources of information, other early genealogies, and inquiries made by the author, the present genealogy of 1933 was compiled.

It can be regarded as a scholarly work. The author Wu Yao-kuang has tried to bring as much evidence as he could find to co-ordinate the different houses and to establish their inter-relationship. On the basis of the earlier material, the author believed that all Wu originally came from one single family which can trace its origin far back into the first millenium B.C. He intended to write the genealogy of only the Ling-nan houses, i.e. those Wu houses which are found in Kuangtung and Kuanghsi. Here, he found eight great houses. The best information he had was about his own house, the Lü-wei house. He succeeded quite well, clearly on the basis of earlier studies, in establishing a connection between the Lü-wei house and the Han-yüan house, which always was geographically near the Lü-wei house. The Lü-wei

---

[1] 2a, 23a.
[2] 2a, 24a and 25b.
[3] 2a, 27a.
[4] 2a, 27a.
[5] 2a, 28a.

house certainly had the longest written history: it had a genealogy dated 1169 and another one dated 1425. The genealogy of 1343 already established a link between the Lü-wei house and those branch houses which claimed an origin from Fukien, i.e. the An-hai, the Sha-pei and the Han-yüan houses. The genealogy of 1370 was even then a "general genealogy" which brought several houses together, in this case the Han-yüan and the Lü-wei houses.

A study of Table 1 gives further insight into his sources. We see in this table that certain branches show an increase of members from generation to generation; after a peak, however, there follows a complete break and only very few members are mentioned. This indicates clearly that our author had at his disposal genealogies for such branches, which came to an end at the peak generation. After the peak, he tried to arrange other available material to complete the genealogy. Usually the information is very clear up to the peak, and becomes quite unclear after the peak [1]. We, too, often experienced difficulties in establishing the generation for persons of the houses who lived after the peak period but centuries before our author. From the "peaks" we can see that a genealogist who lived at the time of generations 58/59, i.e. between 1400 and 1450, (and, therefore, probably the genealogist who wrote around 1413,) co-ordinated the four main houses: Lü-wei, Han-yüan, Ch'iu-kuan and An-hai. The Sha-pei house was already, as we had seen, closely connected with the other houses in the 14th century.

The 15th century then emerges as the period in which the family showed great interest in their genealogy, and the period during which the main work, namely to tie together different houses, was done.

A study of Table 1 shows further, that at the time of gen. 65-66, i.e. around 1650, other genealogists had been at work; the genealogies of the Sha-pei, T'ien-hsiung and Lung-yen houses must have been compiled at this time. It would seem that our author, on the basis of these genealogies from ca. 1650, succeeded in connecting the T'ien-hsiung and the Lung-yen houses with the other houses. We will see later that these links are quite tenuous.

The greatest difficulty, obviously, was created by the Jung-kui house. The genealogist of 1413 seems to have relied upon verbal information and established a weak link between the Jung-kui and the Han-yüan houses. But he openly admitted that he did not have a

---

[1] *Italics* on Tab. 1 indicates such a "break".

TABLE 1. SIZE OF THE BRANCHES OF THE WU CLAN
(male clan members reported in genealogy)

genr.	Ch'iukuan	Hanyüan	Lüwei	Shapei	Anhai	T'ienhsiung	Yungkui	Lungyen	Total
1-39	—	—	—	—	—	—	—	—	47
40-49	—	—	—	—	—	—	—	—	40
50	5	3	3						11
51	7	5	3						15
52	8	3	6	1	1				19
53	14	10	12	4	4	5	3		52
54	19	18	24	5	1	—	7		74
55	23	32	46	1	1	6	3		112
56	30	32	106	2	1	1	9		181
57	51	31	147	2	1	4	5	1	242
58	*66*	64	*206*	5	*4*	5	*6*	1	357
59	10	*106*	26	8	—	4	2	1	157
60	9	8	20	11	—	6	1	3	58
61	19	6	28	14	—	17	—	8	92
62	14	4	23	19	—	29	1	7	197
63	7	6	36	39	—	58	2	11	159
64	7	5	27	63	—	85	3	16	206
65	5	8	54	*94*	1	*129*	1	22	314
66	6	8	33	—	1	4	4	*41*	97
67	14	7	41	—	2	5	4	9	82
68	6	8	75	—	4	5	6	7	111
69	12	13	63	1	8	4	8	19	128
70	15	10	109	—	9	12	3	*45*	203
71	16	16	67	1	28	14	—	8	150
72	3	22	139	—	*68*	9	14	11	266
73	10	31	153	—	5	7	5	22	233
74	—	14	208	—	—	3	7	26	258
75	—	4	202	—	—	2	1	8	217
76	—	3	57	—	—	—	4	2	66
77	1	—	25	—	—	—	5	—	31
78	2	1	8	—	—	—	11	—	22
79	—	—	—	—	—	—	11	—	11
80	—	—	—	—	—	—	5	—	5
81	—	—	—	—	—	—	4	—	4
82	—	—	—	—	—	—	13	—	13
83	—	—	—	—	—	—	10	—	10
84	—	—	—	—	—	—	5	—	5
85	—	—	—	—	—	—	4	—	4
	379	478	1947	270	139	414	167	268	4149
un-known	7	31	128	6		10			182
	386	509	2075	276	139	424	167	268	4331

complete record of the Jung-kui house. The house never seems to have had a genealogy and information down to the present time remained very scanty. In fact, we can establish the fact that this house is a Hakka family, while the others are not Hakkas; thus, we have serious doubts as to whether the Jung-kui house really ever was connected with the other houses.

When our author had brought together all the data he could get from written sources and from informants, data about a total of over 4,000 persons, he had to admit that his work was still far from being complete. He mentions [1] that there are five settlements in Kuanghsi and one in Kuangtung in which Wu from unknown branch houses live. He believes that these settlements were created by Wu from Fukien and Hunan, who settled as soldiers or as merchants.

He admits furthermore that the Ch'iu-kuan house, for which he obviously had no printed genealogy after gen. 58, has at present six settlements, four of which are close to Canton and the others (in Nan-hai and Tseng-ch'eng) also not far from Canton, and that he knows that the San-shan settlement in Nan-hai possesses a genealogy down to gen. 66 (i.e. 1650). But he does not seem to have been able to use this genealogy. And he has no information of the other settlements, either. In his opinion, only the San-shan (三 山) settlement has a relatively high social status, while the others have a low social status [2].

He certainly knew that the clan had more than the few hundred living members which he mentions at the time of his writing; his general information seems to indicate that by 1933 far more than a million people in Kuangtung and Kuanghsi had the clan-name Wu and claimed to belong to the clan he studied. Most of these people were simple farmers, as the names of the places in which they live indicate. Here, the author has limited himself to find all villages in which Wu live and to establish the name of the first settler. In most cases, then, he succeeded in identifying the founder with one of the main branches and with a definite generation. Our genealogy, therefore, does not claim to enumerate all living Wu, but to trace the history of all settlements of Wu members and to connect the founders with the main houses; thus, the history of the houses emerges. He mentions, in addition, famous family members.

---
[1] 2a, 2a.
[2] 1b, 23a.

And he tries to give a complete list of all family members only when he had an early complete genealogy at his disposal. This situation limits the value of the genealogy for our purposes: it has a definite bias in favor of famous persons.

The individual houses counted their generations, always starting with the founder of the house; for the older houses, the counting begins with the settlement in Kuangtung or Kuanghsi. The author tried to synchronize the different counting systems and to identify the generation number of the branch houses with the generation number from the time of the founding of the Wu clan in the Chou period. We have summarized his results in Table 2, and have added rough estimates as to the time at which each individual generation "flourished". These data should be taken as approximations only. In the case of the Jung-kui house, for instance, gen. 25 did not flourish in 1870, but much earlier, because generations 84-85 are now living. In our later analysis of the individual houses and the important events in the development of the houses, we often have need to refer to this Table 2 for the purpose of establishing an approximate date for an event, if the genealogy does not supply the exact date.

The genealogy has obvious weaknesses, apart from the limitations which have already been noted. It is incomplete insofar as not all branches and settlements have been included. It does not make any attempt to include all living members of the clan. Thus, to give only one example, an inscription on a temple in Rangoon, dated 1868, mentions seventy-three members of the Wu clan. Only one of these can (perhaps) be identified with a person mentioned in our genealogy. But from the structure of the names which occur on the inscription, we can show that many of the persons belonged to our generations 72-74 and to the Lü-wei branch house. They were probably not important enough to be mentioned in our genealogy, or our author was unable to get information about them.

Our genealogy does not mention daughters, only rarely mentions wives. Even in those parts in which we feel certain that the genealogy attempts to be complete, i.e. for the parts before gen. 58 for the three main houses, we gain the impression that some family members have been left out. Finally, the work mentions only honorable deeds; if a man was exiled for having committed some crime, this is normally described only as an "appointment" without indication of the character of that appointment.

Considering all these weaknesses, we cannot expect to get results

TABLE 2. SYNCHRONISTIC TABLE OF THE HOUSES OF THE WU CLAN

Time	General Clan	CHK	LW	Branch generations Ths ChHs	JK	HY	An	Sha	LY	PL
1050	47	1	0—————————0							
1080	48	2	0			0				
1120	49	3	1———————1			0				
1160	50	4	2		2	1				
1190	51	5	3		3	2				
1120	52	6	4		4	3				
1250	53	7	5——1		5	4———1———0				
1280	54	8	6	2	6	5	2	0		
1310	55	9	7	3	7	6	3	0		
1340	56	10	8	4/1	8	7	4	1		
1370	57	11	9	5/2	9	8	5	2	1	
1400	58	*12*	*10*	6/3	*10*	9	*6*	3	2	
1430	59	13	11	7/4	11	*10*	7	4	3	
1460	60	14	12	8/5	12	11	8	5	4	
1490	61	15	13	(9/6)	13	12	9	6	5———1	
1530	62	16	(14)	10/7	14/1	13	10	7	6	2
1560	63	17	15	11/8	15/2	(14)	11	8	7	3
1590	64	18	16	12/9	16/3	15	12	9	8	4
1630	65	19	17	*13/10*	17/4	16	13/1	*10*	9	5
1670	66	20	18	14/11	18/5	17	14/2	11	10	6
1710	67	21	19	15/12	19/6	18	3	12	11	7
1740	68	22	20	16/13	20/7	19	4	13	12	8
1770	69	23	21	17/14	21/8	20	5	14	13	9
1795	70	24	22	18/15	22/9	21	6	15	14	10
1815	71	25	23	19/16	23/10	22	7	16	15	11
1845	72	26	24	20/17	24/11	23	8	17	16	12
1870	73	27	25	21/18	25/12	24	9	18	17	13
1895	74	28	26	22/19	26/13	25	10	19	18	14

Key to Table 2

ChK   Ch'iu-kuan house.
Ths   T'ien-hsiung house.
ChHs   Ch'ing-hsiang branch of the T'ien-hsiung house.
LW   Lü-wei or Chu-kuo house.
HY   Han-yüan house.
An   An-hai house, which had common origin with the Han-yüan house; In generation 13 a new count starts.
Sha   Sha-pei or Hsiang-lung house, which had common origin with the Han-yüan.
JK   Jung-kui house, which claims common origin with the Han-yüan.
LY   Lung-yen house.
PL   Pei-liu branch of the Lung-yen house.

Italics: Here a genealogy came to an end.
In parenthesis: Here, a name code was accepted by the house.

which are of the highest degree of reliability. Yet, I believe that the following discussions will show that a genealogy of this type does yield significant results. And this is another reason for undertaking this study: to show that, and to what degree, a family genealogy can yield results if it is regarded as a sociological source.

In the following chapters, we will analyze the clan from several points of view: first its general traditional history until the split into branch houses, i.e. until generation 47. We shall not discuss the mechanism of the establishment of branch houses, nor the further splits into still smaller units, because these points have already been discussed in detail and with great clarity by M. Freedman [1].

We will then study the development of the main branches, in each case from two viewpoints: a) social, and b) geographical mobility of the house. These discussions will then be tied together by a general history of the relevant migrations and the comparison of the changes in social status in the individual branches. Later chapters deal with details such as the marriages and the children of the family and family policies in both cases. A chapter on the names used by the clan and the importance of a study of names for a study of the clan will follow.

2. Origin and Earliest Traditions

According to family tradition of the 14th century, the Wu clan came from the ancient, mythical emperor Chuan-hsü and first entered history in the 7th century B.C. as a clan in the town of Chiao in the feudal state of Ch'u, a clan which belonged to the lower aristocracy (ta-fu 大夫), intermarrying with the royal Ch'u clan. The town of Chiao, unfortunately, cannot be identified, but a number of indications point toward an area in western or northwestern Anhui. In any case, the Wu clan is always clearly identified as a Ch'u clan, and no trace of any northern origin can be found.

Family tradition holds that by the time of the 4th generation, the clan had moved to T'ang-i, today's Liu-ho in Kiangsu near Nanking, and that Wu Tzu-hsü (ca. 500 B.C.), a minister in Wu [2], a feudal state in Kiangsu-Kiangsi, belonged to this clan [3]. After Wu Tzu-hsü's

---

[1] *Lineage Organization in Southeastern China* (London, 1958).
[2] *Han-shu* 45: 3b regards the clan as a Ch'u clan in the beginning of the Han dynasty (ca. 200 B.C.).
[3] *Han-shu* 37: 1a calls the clan a Wu clan in Chou time. A man in the generation 24 who served in Ju-nan (*Hou Han-shu* 102: p. 859d of the K'ai-ming ed.) belonged, according to the commentary, to the Wu house.

violent death, some of his nephews fled to Wu-ling in SW-Hunan and settled there. We hear of this Wu-ling branch only some 750 years later, when a member of the clan, living in the Han-shou district in Wu-ling (close to the present Chang-tê in Hunan) was recommended to a court office.

From then on to the tenth century (generation 40) we have no details in the genealogies of the Wu clan. If we analyze the average length of a generation, we find that between, roughly speaking, 500 B.C. and 120 B.C. (generation 4-14) it was 38 years, between 120 B.C. and 180 A.D. (gen. 14-24) 30 years; between 180 and 270 (gen. 24-28) 22 years, and between 270 and 950 (gen. 28-40) it was 56 years. A duration of 38 or 56 years for an average generation is unrealistic and indicates that the genealogy is not trustworthy.

As Wu Tzu-hsü is regarded as an ancestor of the Wu clan, temples erected in his honor can be used as means of achieving a rough estimate of the distribution of the clan. In Han time, Tzu-hsü already had temples in Kiangsu, Chekiang and the whole lower Yangtse region [1]. In Sung time (later than generation 40) an important family temple was in Lu-chou, near the present Ho-fei in Anhui, and close to the hypothetical home of the clan [2]. Other temples were in Chien-ch'ang (Kiangsi) [3] and on the upper Yangtse, above the present Han-k'ou [4]. These data, again, point to an original home close to the Yangtse, perhaps in western Anhui.

The fact that the genealogy does not mention high officials down to the tenth century, except the ancestor Wu Tzu-hsü, might indicate that the clan did not belong to the leading, central gentry of China. From what will be shown below, it seems rather probable that the Wu's did not really belong to high Chinese society before the tenth century.

According to the genealogy, a change occurred in the 40th generation: an ancestor held a court office in the partial Southern T'ang Dynasty. The partial dynasties of the 10th century were avenues along which local families moved into power positions, and families not yet quite assimilated into Chinese culture were able to make the next

---

[1] According to *Lun-heng* 4, part 1 (Forke transl. vol. 2, p. 247-8), quoted in *T'ai-p'ing yü-lan* 60: 6b and *San-kuo chih*, *Wu-chih* 19: 9b.
[2] *Yü-chih-t'ang* 23: 13a and *T'ai-p'ing kuang-chi* 291: vol. 25: 45a, both quoting from different sources.
[3] *I-chien-chih* 13: 4a.
[4] *Ju-Shu-chi* 6: 2b. The *Hua-man-chi* 7: 3b again mentions a temple in Yang-chou (Kiangsu), the *Ying-shih* 10: 2a a temple in Wu-shan, probably also in Kiangsu.

step towards sinification. The dignitaries of the Southern dynasties and their families were in part integrated into the Sung dynasty in the second part of the tenth and the eleventh centuries. Thus, in the 43rd generation, a family member moved into the capital of the Sung dynasty and got a provincial appointment as assistant to the governor of Fukien, while a nephew of his lived in the capital as a scholar. The Fukien appointment, in connection with what we know about the family might indicate that the family already had a home in Fukien. We are now given the impression that the whole Wu clan lived in the Sung capital of K'ai-feng down to the 48-49th generations. Many members, it is claimed, attained the highest degrees and the family became a central gentry family: a member of gen. 45 attained the *chin-shih* degree in 968 and the post of district magistrate. His two sons attained the same degree in 1013 and one of them again became a magistrate. One of their sons (gen. 47) won the same degree in 1028 and again became a magistrate, and his son passed the *chin-shih* in 1091 and received a high court appointment. A cousin of his won the degree in 1097 and was appointed to a high post in the Department of Justice.

3. The Period of Dispersal and Migration

The genealogy derives the main branches of the Wu clan from these men of the generations 47 and 48. And they link the dispersal of the family all over South China to a political event in North China: in 1126 the capital of the Sung fell and when the ruling house fled to Chêkiang, families in the capital which were highly identified with this regime fled too. This flight from the North is regarded as responsible for the basic splits in the clan.

It all starts with the man in gen. 45 who had a degree. His two sons also held degrees. One of the chin-shih of gen. 46 had two sons. Of these, Wu Yüan (gen. 47) had a son, Wu Hsi-wen, who won a *chin-shih* degree and an office in the Justice Department (Ch'iu-kuan). Wu Hsi-wen moved down to the Canton region and started the house which, after his title, was called the Ch'iu-kuan house. Wu Yüan's brother Wu Lü had no title. Wü Lü's son also migrated to the Canton area and a descendant of this son became the founder of a Hupei branch which is otherwise unknown. This Ch'iu-kuan house and a second branch of it near Canton have existed down to the present.

It is significant to note here that the genealogy indicates that Wu Yüan was born in Nan-hsiung, a place in NE Kuangtung province. Nan-hsiung was an important place at that time for three reasons: a) it was a place to which political exiles were sent, b) it was an important military center, guarding the passage from coastal Kuangtung province through the mountains into Kiangsi and North China, and c) it was the main thoroughfare of trade from all southern coastal ports to the interior of China. Boats could come up north to Nan-hsiung; merchandise would be unloaded and transported by land to the upper reaches of the Chang River, where it was again shipped by river boats to the north. It is possible that Wu Yüan's father was an official in Nan-hsiung; we do not know. It seems more probable that here we must take into consideration another fact. Several other prominent Kuangtung families also trace their genealogy back to Nan-hsiung. The Chang's, who claim to be descendants of the famous scholar Chang Chiu-ling of T'ang time, and who state that they had settled around 630 in Shao-chou, a coastal port in NE-Kuangtung, later moved to Nan-hsiung. Here they lived in the same village as the Wu: Chu-chi-hsiang, the "Pearl street" or (written slightly differently) the "Pearl county" or "Pearl block village" (Chu-chi li ts'un) in "Cow field quarter" (Niu-t'ien fang). In the early 10th century, the Chang's moved to the South and bought property in the direct vicinity of the place where later the Wu settled [1], namely Ku-kang-chou 古岡州. The Wei clan, also near neighbors of the Wu, left the same village in Nan-hsiung in 1273, when the Mongol conquerors arrived, went South and married there into a local family [2]. T. Makino [3] has pointed out that "Pearl village" is mentioned as the home of a great number of families all of whom we now call "Cantonese" by language. As there are other cases in which many families claim an origin from a small, unknown place, Makino has doubts of the truth of such a statement. The genealogy claims [4] that rumors of a mobilization started to circulate in Nan-hsiung, whereupon 98 persons (with their families?) under the leadership of a Su Ju-hsing 蘇汝興 left for the South. In another

---

[1] *Ch'ing-ho tsu-p'u* 清河族譜 1: 16a.
[2] *Wei-shih tsu-p'u* 韋氏族譜 1: 85a.
[3] In *Japanese Journ. of Ethnology*, vol. 14, 1950, no. 3, p. 212.
[4] 2b: 23b.

place [1] the date of emigration is put in the middle of the 12th century and it is said that it started with government permission. If these traditions are correct, these Pearl Village families might have been farmers in Nan-hsiung and ventured into the South as a more or less organized emigrant group. This seems, seen from other information, not to be impossible. In fact, the Ch'iu-kuan branch of our Wu clan remained a farming family for centuries and made no claim to high offices.

The genealogy of another clan, the T'an clan, gives an explanation. The first part of this explanation seems to be a story, but the rest can be fairly well documented. Let me, therefore, report the story in detail:

> In the year 1265 the Imperial consort Hu committed a mistake when playing music while the emperor visited her harem. She was, therefore, ordered into the "cold" harem. But because the harem gate was not well guarded, the consort ran away. She disguised herself as a vagrant woman and secretly left the capital. She strolled around everywhere always finding someone to stay with. At that time, there was a rich man, Huang Chu-wan, who lived in Nan-hsiung-fu, in the district Shih-hsing, in the Oxfield ward (Niu-t'ien fang). Upon imperial order he moved grain to the capital (i.e. he was a merchant). Upon his return, he moored at Kuan-k'ou-shih (possibly in Honan, T'ai-k'ang district), where he sacrificed to the deities and did good works. There he saw a woman singing and dancing on a nearby boat. Chu-wan began to flirt with her and she came from the boat and talked to him. She was accommodated by him and wanted to spend her life with him. Chu-wan, thereupon, hid her in his boat and brought her home.
>
> Later, the emperor gave amnesty to the consort without knowing that she had run away. When she could not be found for a long time, he gave orders to Chang Ying-kui, head of the Department of War, asking him to send orders to all provinces and districts to have them search for her. Over the years, she could not be found, and finally, the Head (of the War Department) reported this and was permitted to give up the search. Nobody knew that the girl whom Huang Chu-wan had met was consort Hu. She had changed her name to Chang, and had become his favored concubine and nobody noticed anything amiss.
>
> But, later, Liu Chuang, a servant in Huang Chu-wan's house, revolted against his master and ran away. Then the secret began to leak through, and the rumor reached the capital. At this time, the Head of the War Department, Chang Ying-kui, knew that mischief and disaster could arise and was, therefore, afraid the emperor could investigate the matter again and he could then lose his life. Thus,

---

[1] 2b: 24a and 24b.

he brought all officials of all Departments together and they discussed the situation and made a secret plan to mow down the population in order to eliminate all traces. Therefore, he falsely claimed that the population of Nan-hsiung-fu, Shih-hsien district, Oxfield ward, had become bandits and had revolted and had committed harm to good citizens. He reported this to the court and got permission to build in Oxfield Ward forts and bring in soldiers and guards in order to protect the good and to pacify the bandits, so that there was well-being in the country and peace among the people. At that time, there was a Mr. Liang Ch'iao-hui, husband of aunt Lo, in Pearl street, who was in the capital on official business. He heard these rumors and sent a man home with the news. Everybody was frightened. Less than ten days later, the Ministry's letter came to the Province (*fu*) and district, with strict orders to evacuate. All people in the 58 villages of Oxfield Ward in Shih-hsing district were sad and afraid.

But 97 families in Pearl street, among them Lo Kui, Mai Hsiu, Li Fu-jung and others, made a plan: 'From our ancestors we have heard that in the malaria-infested South there is much land and little population. Let us all go and open a new home there. There is certainly food available and we can see one another in the morning and in the evening, just as we now do here at home'. Thus, they agreed, informed the district magistrate, and got permission and an introductory letter. They again went to Nan-hsiung-fu for report (with the letter of introduction), and got permission, gave themselves a (group) name and organized a *chia* (mutual assistance group). Then they formed a military unit (*t'ui*) and each with his letter and his family slowly went south.

When they came to Lai-shih Mountain, there was no ferry boat and they tied bamboo together as a raft. Thus, they came to Lien-chiang-k'ou and moored. During the night, a big storm came and most of their rafts were destroyed by the waves and many were drowned. All survivors dispersed in fear. Only the raft of the 97 families of Pearl street had somehow been able to find shelter in time, and their losses were not very great.

After the storm, they reformed their group and continued south. After over 20 days, they came to Kang-chou. At the time, there were few people in Kang-chou and much land. So they settled there and, relying upon a native, went to the district official and reported themselves and had themselves registered. Each then looked for some land and settled. They cleaned the jungle, worked hard on their fields and later their descendants became numerous and dispersed into all adjacent districts. Among them were probably also many who were not on the raft of the 97 families which migrated together to the south. But because histories and genealogies are not complete, the details cannot be established [1].

---

[1] *T'an-shih shih*, vol. 2, pp. 266b-267b.

The text of the genealogy which reports this story also reproduces the "permits" of the district and the province. These state that the men were farmers who always paid their taxes, but who could no longer live in this area. The permit shows that they were allowed to pass through all control points and contains an order to the local magistrate to have them registered locally. All these details concerning the administrative side of the migration fit into what we know of the bureaucracy of the time. Actions of similar character against whole areas are well known, especially in outlying and coastal areas. The intrigues which occur in the story are also possible. Yet, we have not been able to check the story of the concubine and her lover, nor the personality of the Minister of War. This part of the report sounds much like a part of a popular novel. The editor himself, who relied upon family traditions, states that the man who supposedly was a member of the group and supposedly belonged to the fourth generation of the clan, was, according to family history, born 200 years before the event. And already in the second generation of the clan there was a man of the family in South China. Certainly, the tradition about "Pearl Ward" (*Chu-chi*) is very strong among the clans in the neighborhood of the Wu. The ancestors of the important Ch'en clan, into which many Wu married and which is one of the thirty-five clans, also state that they came from Pearl Ward, but that around 1270 one ancestor moved to Hsin-hui (Kuangtung province) and settled there. When Nan-hsiung and the Pearl Ward definitely fell into the hands of the Mongols, he decided to stay in Hsin-hui for good [1], and there is now a ward in Hsin-hui which carries the name Pearl Ward [2]. Such a transfer of a name from one area (usually the home) to another area is well known for China and other parts of the world. Such cases may indicate a migration which at first was temporary and later became final. The T'an genealogy does not, therefore, necessarily contradict itself. The list of the 97 families (of 35 clans) contains two members of the Wu clan. One of them is called Wu Yüan-lou and this man might be identical with our Wu Yüan who lived in Nan-hsiung-fu (gen. 47)—but again over 100 years earlier. The other, Wu Hsien-ts'ai might be identical with or related to Wu Hsien-tsu, who was born in 1176—almost a century before the time of our story. But it is true, that around the time of our story, members of many clans migrated to the South. Whether

---

[1] *Hsin-hui hsien-chih*, edition of 1840, Chapt. 8, p. 45.
[2] *Hsin-hui hsien-chih*, Chapt. 2, p. 54b.

this had to do with our story is hard to say: by the time of the story, most of the Sung empire was already in the hands of the Mongol invaders; and in 1273 Nan-hsiung was occupied by them. It is possible that the Mongols were responsible for the migration to the south.

But what remains of the story is a) a tradition among a great number of South Chinese families that they came from Nan-hsiung at the end of the 13th century and that they had been farmers before their departure, and b) a feeling among these families of belonging together, which is expressed in a high percentage of marriages within the group.

Let us return to the brothers in gen. 46 who were both *chin-shih*. The second of these brothers had a son who again won the degree. He had a son Wu Hsin (gen. 48) who also was a *chin-shih* (in 1091). He attained high positions—among others, employment in the Han-lin academy. He is buried in Ch'ing-chiang p'u [1]. Although not exactly identifiable, this place seems to have been in Southern Kiangsi along the main trade route. Wu Hsin had four sons. Wu Shih won a *chin-shih* degree in 1109 [2], and an office in Hsing-hua (the later P'u-t'ien in Fukien) and settled there in 1125, when the Northern Sung dynasty came to an end [3]. He is the ancestor of the Fukien house. Like Nan-hsiung, P'u-t'ien is the ancestral home of many families which are now regarded as Fukienese families and spread all over South China, mainly as businessmen. The specific home is "Sugarcane village" [4]. Wu Shih (gen. 49) had two sons, each of whom had a son (gen. 51) who started a new branch settlement near Canton: the An-hai and the Sha-pei branches.

The second son of Wu Hsin (gen. 48), Wu Lü (gen. 49) remained at the Imperial court and seems to have had an office. His son, Wu Cheng (gen. 50) was also a member of the Han-lin academy and his branch house is now called the "Han-yüan" house. He moved to Nan-hsiung at the time of the end of the Northern Sung. He then went farther south and settled in Ku-kang-chou, close to the Chang family. His own wife was a Chang, daughter of a Kiangsi high official [5], but I could not find out whether she came from this same Chang clan. Wu Cheng died in 1205, his son Wu Pei (gen. 51) married

---

[1] 1b: 22a-b.
[2] 1a: 25a. According to another tradition, Wu Shih was exiled to Hsing-hua (2, 21a).
[3] 1b: 22b.
[4] s. T. Makino in *Jap. Journ. of Ethnol.*, vol. 17, 1952, no. 3/4, p. 224.
[5] 2a: 28a.

a daughter of an official in Nan-hsiung [1] and settled in the South together with his father. He had no office, nor had his son. But this son (gen. 52) bought much land and became a rich landowner. One of his sons (gen. 53) also married a wife from Nan-hsiung. The connections of the Han-yüan house with Nan-hsiung are thus quite close, while there are no connections with P'u-t'ien. This Han-yüan house did not go into business, but became a landlord family as did the Ch'iu-kuan branch; in addition they kept their gentry status, as will be seen later.

Wu Hsin (gen. 48) had another son, Wu Min (gen. 49), who won his *chin-shih* degree in 1123, and also had high court titles, among others the title Shang Chu-kuo; he was made a general and exiled to Nan-en-chou (later: En-p'ing hsien in Kuangtung) [1] because of his criticisms of the policy of the government. He died in the South and was buried close to the home of his wife, born a Mai, from Hsin-ning hsien, Wen-chang tu, Tou-tung county. This home of his wife became the seat of his family which was later called either the Chu-kuo house or the Tou-tung house. The family name of his wife would seem to indicate that she might have belonged to a local, non-Chinese family.

There seems to be considerable uncertainty among the genealogists whether Wu Min really was the brother of Wu Lü; Wu Min's family has no connections with Nan-hsiung. Neither has it any connections with P'u-t'ien and Wu Min's alleged brother Wu Shih. But Wu Min's Chu-kuo house and Wu Lü's Han-yüan house always lived very closely together and maintained close connections.

Wu Ch'ao-tso (gen. 50), one of Wu Min's many sons, himself had two sons, one of whom passed a special local examination (gen. 51) In the next generation (gen. 52) one son of this successful father and one of his cousins both had fairly high administrative positions. It is from these men that another branch of the Wu clan supposedly took its origin, the Jung-kui branch. We do not hear much about the Jung-kui branch, as the genealogy is unclear and interrupted several times. It is said, however, that a member of generation 58 moved to Mei-hsien in Kuangtung, while earlier members seem to have lived in Fukien. In gen. 60 we hear that a family member (from Fukien?) moved to Ning-hua hsien in Fukien, to the "Stone wall county"

---

[1] 2a: 28b.
[1] 2a: 14a and 2a: 49b-50a.

(Shih-pi-hsiang). We know from Makino [1] and Lo Hsiang-lin [2] that many Hakka families claim to come from this "Stone wall county"; and we know that Mei-hsien is a center of Hakka people. There is little doubt, therefore, that the Jung-kui branch of the Wu is a Hakka family. Our genealogy thus combines the three major population elements of Kuangtung province into one clan. This, together with the gaps in the genealogy, proves that the writers constructed a frame which could accept all Wus now existing, disregarding their ethnic origins. We will later mention still other branches which the genealogists could not integrate into this framework, and where they admit that the degree of relationship remains unclear. But we can, from now on, regard the individual "houses" or branches as independent families, and study each of them individually as examples of South Chinese clans, thus broadening our scope from the study of one clan to the study of a number of clans with the same name.

TABLE 3. THE BRANCHES OF THE WU CLAN

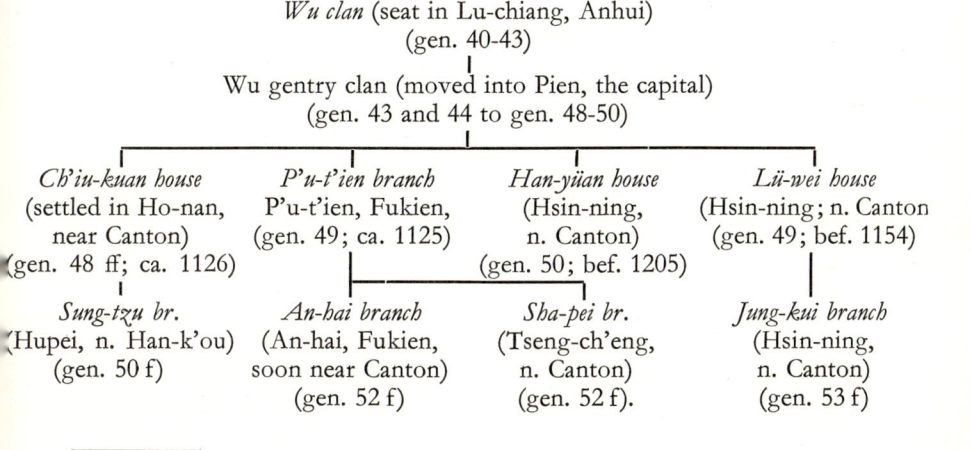

Wu clan (seat in Lu-chiang, Anhui)
(gen. 40-43)
|
Wu gentry clan (moved into Pien, the capital)
(gen. 43 and 44 to gen. 48-50)

Ch'iu-kuan house	*P'u-t'ien branch*	*Han-yüan house*	*Lü-wei house*
(settled in Ho-nan, near Canton)	P'u-t'ien, Fukien,	(Hsin-ning,	(Hsin-ning; n. Canton
(gen. 48 ff; ca. 1126)	(gen. 49; ca. 1125)	n. Canton)	(gen. 49; bef. 1154)
		(gen. 50; bef. 1205)	
Sung-tzu br.	*An-hai branch*	*Sha-pei br.*	*Jung-kui branch*
(Hupei, n. Han-k'ou)	(An-hai, Fukien,	(Tseng-ch'eng,	(Hsin-ning,
(gen. 50 f)	soon near Canton)	n. Canton)	n. Canton)
	(gen. 52 f)	(gen. 52 f).	(gen. 53 f)

---

[1] *Jap. Journ. of Ethnol.* 14, no. 3, p. 212.
[2] Lo Hsiang-lin, *K'o-chia*, pp. 41-42; 43, 47, 48, 51. Many Taiwan clans claim origin from here.

APPENDIX TO PART 2, CHAPTER 3
List of Titles Mentioned

The purpose of this list is to enable the reader to evaluate status or official rank (given in parenthesis; highest rank is 1A, lowest is 9B).

Families in which at least one member had one of the below-mentioned titles or ranks were often called "Ju-hu" 儒戶, scholar families.

A. *Examinations and training*:

1) *chin-shih* 進士 passed highest examinations in capital.

2) *chü-jen* 舉人 passed highest provincial examinations (*sheng* 省).

3) *wu-chü* 武舉 passed highest provincali military examinations.

4) *kung-sheng*, comprising *pa-kung* 貢生, 拔貢, a student who had passed the local examinations. Once every 12 years, the best were brought to the capital, where they could become *chin-shih*. Others could get a low rank in the capital, appointment as magistrate or, the lowest, appointment as teacher.

5) ——, comprising *sui-kung* 歲貢, the best candidate in the local examinations. One person per year was brought to the capital and into the school for government officials.

6) ——, comprising *en-kung* 恩貢, successful candidate in local examinations, selected in a special, irregular selection.

7) ——, comprising *fu-kung* 副貢, second-class, successful candidate in local examinations; sometimes some of these were also selected.

8) *sheng-yüan*, 生員, comprising *lin-sheng* 廩生, *tseng-sheng* 增生, and *fu-sheng* 附生, different grades of students who studied on government expenses for higher degrees.

9) *hsiang-sheng* 庠生, divided into *I-hsiang-sheng* and *fu-hsiang-sheng*, students in district or *fu*-schools; the *fu* being an administrative unit comprising several districts.

10) *I-sheng* 佾生 student specializing in ritual dances for the Confucian cult.

11) *Ju-t'ung* 儒童 elementary students.

B. *Teaching*:

1) *chiao-shou* 教授 educator for a whole *fu* (group of districts) (7A)

2) *hsüeh-cheng* 學正 director of education for a *chou* (smaller group of districts) (8A)

3) *chiao-yü* 教諭 educational officer for a district (8A)

4) *hsün-tao* 訓導 educational instructor for a district (8B)

SOCIAL MOBILITY OF THE WU CLAN OF SOUTH CHINA 69

C. *Ranks*:

Persons in active service or with honorary ranks, for which they often made payments.

Persons with the title of successful candidates which they got by a payment.

1) *Tzu-chêng ta-fu* 資政大夫, a title, usually posthumously given (2A)
2) *Pu-chêng-szu* 布政司, high provincial administrative position (2B)
3) *Wu-kung chiang-chün* 武功將軍, a military title (2B)
4) *Chao-wu tu-wei* 昭武都尉, a military title (4A)
5) *Chung-hsien ta-fu* 中憲大夫, a civil title (4A)
6) *Ch'ao-i ta-fu* 朝義大夫, a civil title (4B)
7) *T'ung-chih* 通治, administrative official in charge of a *fu* area (5A)
8) *Feng-chêng ta-fu* 奉政大夫, a title, usually posthumously given (5A)
9) *Wu-tê ch'i-wei* 武德騎尉, a military title (5A)
10) *T'ung-p'an* 通判, administrative official in a *fu* (6A)
11) *Ch'êng-tê-lang* 承德郎, a title (6A)
12) *Yen-yün ta-shih* 鹽運大使 (Salt transportation high officer), administrative officer in the provincial areas (6B?)
13) *Hsüan-tê-lang* 宣德郎, a civil title (6B)
14) *Ju-lin-lang* 儒林郎, a civil title, often given to persons who reach the age between 59 and 68 years (6B)
15) *Wu-lüeh tso tu-wei* 武略佐都尉, a military title (6B)
16) *Ch'e-wu lang* 奮武郎, a military title (7A)
17) *Chih-hsien* (Magistrate) 治縣, a civil administrative officer, in charge of a district (7A)
18) *Wen-lin-lang* 文林郎, a civil title, preferably given to persons who reach an age above 89 years (7A)
19) *Chêng-shih-lang* 徵使郎, civil title (7B)
20) *An-ch'a-shih chih-shih* 安差使知事, civil administrative officiel in the provinces (8A)
21) *Hsiu-chih-lang* 脩職郎, a civil title, normally given to persons who reach an age between 79 and 88 years (8A)

22) *Hsiu-chih-tso-lang* 脩職佐郎, a civil title often given to a person whose brother(s) already had received a title (8B)
23) *Teng-shih-lang* 登仕郎, a civil title, normally given to persons who reach an age between 69 and 78 or more (9A)
24) *Teng-shih tso-lang* 登仕佐郎, a civil title, often given to persons whose brothers already had received a title (9B)
25) *Hsiang-yin ta-pin* 鄉飲大賓, purely honorific title, given to persons who reach an age between 69 and 78 (below the rank order)
26) "Headdress": permission to wear the insignia of a low rank without giving the actual rank, given to persons who reach an age above 79 years.

4. The Ch'iu-kuan House

a) Social Mobility

As already pointed out, the ancestor of this house, Wu Yüan (gen. 47 = Ch'iu-kuan gen. 1) lived in Nan-hsiung and had two sons, one of whom won the *chin-shih* degree in 1097 (Wu Hsi-wen, gen. 48/2) and had a position in the Justice Department. He fled to the South when the Chin conquered the capital of the Sung dynasty. With him came his brother and his cousin. Two settlements near Canton were started and the family from then on was a Cantonese family.

But from this time on, the family loses its social prominence. Wu Hsi-wen's son (gen. 49/3) could have had a government job because he was the son of a prominent father, but he did not accept the post. In gen. 50/4, a member of the family had an unimportant court job and stayed briefly in the capital. In the next generation Wu Hsiao-wu (1133-1195) had a small military job which he gave up when his father died. His son had some education but no post, because he gave up too early and became a local teacher (gen. 52/6; 1162-1225). His son did not accept any job; it is said that his grandson (gen. 54/8) had some education. In the following generation (55/9) the Mongols conquered South China. A great-grandson of the teacher was wealthy but had no official position; he used his wealth to fight for the dynasty against the Mongols (Wu Yen-ch'u, 1239-1299). His son (56/10; 1266-1326) was also active against the Mongols. He had some education, but no degree. We hear no more about achievements of members of this family during the Ming period.

When the Manchu threatened China, we read of a man (gen. 64/18) who failed in the local examination and later moved to the West, to Ling-shan. In the new place, a family member in the next generation (65/19) had a small office job; later (gen. 66/20) a member had a military job and fought often against bandits and the Manchus, so that the powerful men in the place respected him.

At about this time, the Ling-shan branch begins its upward move: one member of gen. 67/21 had some military successes; another one was a student, and a third passed highest in the local examinations and was offered a post as inspector of instruction (*chiao-yü*) in Nan-hsiung, the old family home. He did not accept this appointment, though. In the next generation, one family member was a student at the national school (*kuo-hsüeh-sheng*), a sign of high education, while another member went into business and thus started a new family tradition. The reason for this move was, says the genealogy, a local revolt which created unsettled conditions.

In generation 69/23 we have 6 members with careers in the bureaucracy: again, one was the best candidate in the local examination (*sui-kung-sheng*), three others were local students. One of them failed in the examination and devoted himself to social work in his community, as did a successful candidate. One member had military interests and was also active in social work; and one member got posthumous honorific titles because of the career of his son. On the other hand, three members of the family were successful in business and became influential local leaders. One of these businessmen bought a title, so that he, at least nominally, was also a member of the gentry.

In generation 70/24, i.e. in the beginning of the 19th century, three members of the Ling-shan branch were prominent: one had military success, one passed the examination with great success (*pa-kung* in 1789), and a third held a low provincial job through his father-in-law. In this generation, however, another branch of the Ch'iu-kuan house, in Pin-yang, began to rise; one member got a military degree, one was best candidate (*sui-kung-sheng*) and got several educational jobs, and one was nominated as successful candidate in a special examination (*en-kung-sheng*). Finally, one family member was a successful businessman and civic leader in Pin-chou.

The Pin-yang branch rose higher in the generation 71/25: there were two students in this generation. One man became an engineer (1892-?), another one became owner of a mine with 8,000 workers after having accumulated the capital through business, while another was in business and had a bookstore. The Ling-shan branch had another military member, who failed in his examinations but was successful in fighting against the T'ai-p'ing rebels. Another man paid for a title; one was a student and a fourth one had high jobs with the central government in Shantung and other places. In generation 72/26 we hear of a school president in the Pin-yang branch, and in the following generation there is one *chü-jen* and a student in the provincial examinations mentioned together with a graduate from a textile school who had a shop in Hong Kong.

Reviewing the longtime development of the Ch'iu-kuan branch, we can say that after the settlement near Canton the family lost its status as a gentry family and seems to have been a wealthy farmer's family with some, but not too much, education. They may have been local leaders of their community, but were not important in provincial or state politics. There was some interest in military jobs which indicates a fairly low status.

A definite change did not occur until the 17th century—a change which came about through a personal contact: the family member had a friend, a Mr. Huang, who took him with him to Ling-shan when he got a job there. Mr. Wu thought that thinly settled places were better than cities if the country were to be conquered by the Manchu, and followed Mr. Huang to Ling-shan. It seems that by this contact, his sons got a chance in the examination. But it took another three generations for the first member of the family to become nationally prominent. In the 18th century the business developed in the city of Ling-shan and by buying titles these new businessmen tried to get back into the ranks of the gentry. The Pin-yang branch had gone into business around 1650, and remained essentially a business family, although some members by the 19th century had titles. It seems that their wealth more than their education got them the titles.

b) *Geographical Mobility*

The family home in the South was established by three family members with two settlements, both close to Canton (in P'an-yü, Yang-wu-tu and in Ho-nan, Hsia-tu), in the 48th generation. In the next generation one member got a job near Han-k'ou and established another branch there, about which nothing more is known.

The next move is in the generation 52/6 in which two new settlements near Canton were started. More mobility occurred in the generation 53/7 with four new settlements, all close to Canton (two in P'an-yü and two in Nan-hai). It is mentioned in one case that the move was due to the fear of Mongol attacks (in 1259). A further move to a neighboring village took place in gen. 55/9. In generation 57/11 a branch moved into Canton city—the first really urbanized branch of the family. We do not know anything further about them, but can assume that they were businessmen.

In the late 13th century, another group came down from the ancestral home in Nan-hsiung: two members of our family together with 2 commanders and 136 soldiers left Nan-hsiung and settled in Huai-chi among the Miao tribes. The genealogy indicates that this migration was in connection with the end of the Mongol dynasty.

TABLE 4. CH'IU-KUAN HOUSE, NEW SETTLEMENTS

	gen. 51-56	gen. 57-60	gen. 61-65	Total
1) P'an-yü (and Ho-nan and Sha-pei)	6	1		7
2) Nan-hai	2			2
3) Huai-chi		4		4
4) Yü-nan			1	1
5) Ling-shan			2	2
6) Kao-chou			1	1
7) Pin-yang			1	1
	8	5	5	18

This cannot be proved, but a settlement of commanders together with their soldiers could easily indicate a military colonization scheme of the government or that exile had been imposed upon them[1]. It can be safely assumed that these men were not of high rank. This seems to be another proof that the family home was really in Nan-hsiung. Gradual migrations are very typical for all farm families. This group created three settlements in Huai-chi and one in Ts'en-ch'i (Kuanghsi).

The next reported migration is a secondary one from a village in Shun-tê to a place in Yü-nan, in generation 63/17. We do not know when the Shun-tê settlement was founded; the text mentions only a settlement of the Lü-wei branch house there (since gen. 56). In gen. 64/18 the movement to Ling-shan (already mentioned) began. When

---

[1] This tradition might reflect the above-mentioned romantic story of Pearl ward.

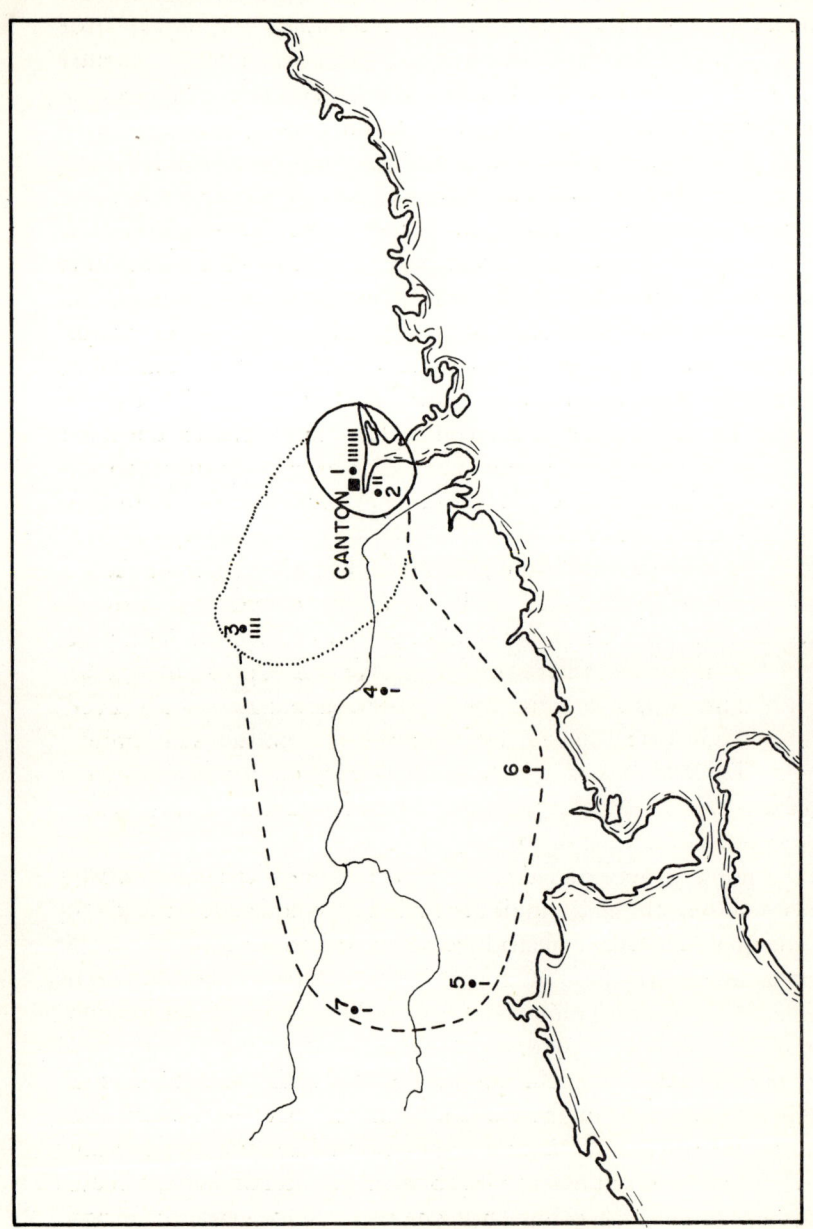

Map 1: The movements of the Ch'iu-kuan branch.
(numbers indicate the sequence of settlements; strokes at the side of the numbers indicate the number of individual settlements at each place)

Mr. Wu joined his friend and went with him to Ling-shan, he became his financial councillor there. This may indicate that there was some earlier connection with business in the family; it almost certainly indicates, however, that Mr. Wu had some capital which he seems to have invested in land near Ling-shan. In the next generation (65/19) the family in Ling-shan moved to a nearby place, because the first settlement was too low and was often inundated. A separate migration in generation 64/18 had created the branch in Kao-chou.

In generation 65/19 the settlement in Pin-yang (Kuanghsi) was created from Shih-hsing; Shih-hsing is in Nan-hsiung. This is the last migration from the original home Nan-hsiung to the South. The settler this time was a farmer; he started an indigo plantation and a dye business and because the natives in Pin-yang did not know the technique he quickly became rich. His family branch remained in business. The story of this branch is a good example of the transition of a family from farming to business in a colonial setting. No further migrations are reported.

Thus we see how, in a period of more than 800 years, the family continuously moved farther south, from the northeastern part of Kuangtung into the Canton area and then into Kuanghsi. There are not many migrations; this seems to indicate that the family was an ordinary farming family without too many connections or too much wealth, so that it was not easy to create new settlements. The family's military tradition points in the same direction. Several branches succeeded in going into business, became wealthy, and in some cases attained positions of influence.

It should be pointed out that the family did not hesitate to accept settlers who for 11, or even 18 generations continued to come from the old home, as legitimate branches of their own house.

5. The P'u-t'ien Han-yüan House

a) *Social Mobility*

As already mentioned, Wu Hsin's son Wu Shih (gen. 49) settled around 1125 in P'u-t'ien in Fukien where he held an official job. He is regarded as the ancestor of all Fukien branches of the main house. His two brothers still remained in the capital. Of the three grandsons (gen. 51) of the founder, one had two sons; the other two became founders of branch houses, one in Sha-pei, district of Tseng-ch'eng and the other in Nan-hai, district of Ho-nan, both places near Canton. The genealogy, however, states that the exact genealogy of the founder of the An-hai branch is uncertain. This is quite important for the later development. The Sha-pei and the An-hai houses will be studied later.

Wu Shih's brothers Lü (gen. 49) and Shang remained in the capital. Shang's family soon died out, but Lü's son Wu Cheng became the founder of the Han-yüan branch (gen. 50/1). Wu Cheng (1122-1205) was a member of the Han-lin academy, moved to Nan-hsiung some time after the fall of the capital and finally settled in Ku-kang chou near Canton. One of his sons, married to the daughter of a judge in Nan-hsiung, settled in the new home and registered as a citizen there (1154-1225), while another son held a court title (Wu Li; gen. 51/2). This pattern remains the same in the next generation. While the one brother (Wu Ch'ao-yung, 1202-1276) had no position, but enlarged the family property so that the family became very wealthy, one of his cousins passed the examination (as *kung-sheng*) (gen. 52/3). Of Wu Ch'ao-yung's sons, one held an honorific title, while the other handed his wealth over to his brother, studied, and passed the examination to hold high titles and an administrative job in Kao-chou, close to the family home. His wife, incidentally, was from Nan-hsiung. This man, Wu Ch'i-lung (gen. 53/4; 1236-1303) created a family manor on the land he acquired in his career, adding to the wealth of his family. One of his second cousins also had a court title, but no job. These men created a new tradition: both served under the Mongols, i.e. the enemies of the dynasty under which their fathers had served. The Han-yüan branch follows their example, as the only branch of the Wu clan to do so; all others remained antagonistic to the Mongols.

Wu Ch'i-lung's son Wu T'ing-feng (gen. 54/5; 1262-1311) had several administrative posts all in South China and continued to acquire large tracts of land, so that the family increased its wealth still further. His brother Wu Wen-feng, also had government posts; and a third brother, Wu I-feng (1292-1329), had the highest posts, lived in the city of Canton and one of his three wives was a Mongol woman. One further member of this generation (54/5) got the *chin-shih* degree as an honorific degree from the Mongols. This shows the degree of affiliation of this family with the Mongol rulers. The star of the family continued to shine: two members passed their examinations, a third made the *chü-jen* examination and later became director of education in Feng-ch'eng in Kiangsi; three others had administrative jobs in South China.

In gen. 56/7 one man got the *chin-shih* degree and, later, educational jobs; another passed the local examination. One got a high post in Canton and the last one was an important officer of the Mongols, who died in a fight against sea rebels in 1357. In the time of gen. 57/8 the Mongol dynasty came to an end.

One member who had a job with the Mongols was exiled in 1387. Another member had scholarly friends and was a writer, besides being very wealthy, but he held no high position; and a third man passed the local examinations.

The high position of the family was short-lived. In gen. 58/9 we find three men who passed the local examinations, one who came to the school in the capital and one who made the *chü-jen* examination (in 1411). Two other members of this generation made large contributions during a famine and got honorific titles from the government (ca. 1440 and 1445). In the next generation we find nine members who passed local examinations, and one who passed the *chü-jen* examination (ca. 1488/1505). This *chü-jen* got a job as magistrate; one of the other successful candidates got a small job in Fukien.

In the following generations the level of the family tended to go down: in gen. 60/11 four men had education: one of them was a magistrate, another a poet. In gen. 61/12 we find another poet, a *chin-shih* and a man with a local Kuangtung job [1]. In gen. 62/13 there was only one man of the clan represented in the local examinations. It seems that by this time the wealth of the family had decreased. In the following two generations it is to be noted that the wealth of the family again increased. There was a *chü-jen* and four other men in gen. 63/14 who had passed local examinations. In gen. 64/15 and 66/17 we find only one man each who had a higher education, while a man in gen. 65/16 seems to have been wealthy but not very well educated. This is the time of the beginning of the Manchu dynasty, a period of many disturbances. There is only one man in gen. 67/18 who passed the local examinations and nobody in gen. 68. The new ascendancy of the clan did not begin until around 1700,

---

[1] In this generation 61, our house is closely allied with the philosopher Ch'en Hsien-chang (陳獻章) or Ch'en Pai-sha (陳白沙), 1428-1500, also a native of T'ai-shan, who got his *chin-shih* degree but retired to his home where he became the head of an important Confucianist school (2b, 9a and 12b, 15a; see also *Jung-ch'uang hsiao-p'in* 16, 6a 湧幢小品 and *Jen-ming ta tz'u-tien*, p. 1106b). This man seems to have developed the name codes which were later adopted by the Han-yüan and the Lü-wei houses for the following 20 generations.

when conditions were more settled; in gen. 69/20 a man passed the military *chü-jen* examination, and two others passed the examinations and were brought to the capital for further study (pa-kung). In the following generation (70/21) a man got the *chü-jen* by imperial grace, and another one passed the local examinations by imperial grace. Two other men were students. One man who started out as a teacher, later went overseas as a businessman, and a sixth man went directly into business.

With generation 71 we are already in the later 19th century. Three men passed examinations, one by imperial grace. In the following generation (72/23) there is a definite trend away from government careers: one man passed the military examination and got military posts; another one became a magistrate. One failed however in the examinations and became a wealthy businessman; another was appalled the corruption in the government, gave up learning and went into business; two went directly to Australia as poor businessmen and returned wealthy. One later owned a building firm and a restaurant in Canton, the other became a leading member of the KMT party; and one man went to New York University for modern Western study. In the present-day generation we find again five persons who passed the old examinations, but one of these took over his father's business in Hong Kong and in San Francisco. Two others owned business firms in the United States, one in Hong Kong and one in China. One became a KMT party boss, two others had jobs in the Kuangtung provincial government and one was a teacher. Only one took an old-fashioned administrative job such as his ancestors often had held.

It is important to note that down to gen. 67/18 all famous men came from the family seat, but that from gen. 69/20 on all famous men came from more recent branch settlements in En-p'ing (settlement began in gen. 57/8), Hsin-hsing (settled since gen. 55/6) and T'ai-shan (since gen. 55/6); thus, it took more than ten generations for members of these new branches to climb to importance. In general the connections of the Han-yüan house with Fukien seem to be quite weak, while the house had stronger connections with Nan-hsiung. The family can, therefore, be called a Cantonese family. The family quickly became wealthy in the Ku-kang home near Canton; the wealth was agricultural and remained so. But some members of the family as early as Sung time had education and government jobs in the fields of education or local adminstration. Because the family collaborated with the Mongol invaders, they rose to high importance in their home province during the 14th century. They retained their importance, partly by their wealth, to the end of the 15th century. But from then on the importance of the Han-yüan house decreased until the late 18th century. The re-emergence seems to have been achieved in part by going into a military career, i.e. the low-prestige career. It was limited to more recent branches; the main Han-yüan house did not regain its position. The new branch houses showed an increasing tendency to go into business and to emigrate in the course of the 19th and 20th centuries, but educational and local administrative positions were still taken, following old family traditions.

b) *Geographical Mobility*

After the establishment of the Han-yüan house in Ku-kang (later: Hsin-hui) near Canton in the late 12th century, four relatives of the founder followed him in gen. 53/4, i.e. during the Mongol period, and established settlements in Yang-chiang, in Tseng-ch'eng, Hsiang-shan and in two military areas which seem to be in eastern Kuanghsi province. The names of these military areas indicate that they were largely settled by non-Chinese and were, therefore, colonial areas. One more settler arrived and settled near Ku-kang in gen. 54/5; but from then on all later movements come from the Ku-kang home: four branches in gen. 54, all in nearby places, two more in gen. 55/6. These new settlements were all created in the period of the greatest wealth and power of the Han-yüan branch.

One migration in gen. 56/7 is interesting: Wu Tsung-i (55/6), himself educated, had married the daughter of a scholar in Ch'üan-chou (Fukien). His son remained in Ch'üan-chou, much against common tradition, learned there geomancy from his maternal relatives, and his profession brought him finally to Hsin-hsing, where he married a local girl and settled, creating an important new branch. There is a second geomancer in this family (gen. 57/8), who settled in Canton. The first urban settlement was started in gen. 56/7 in Canton. The number of new settlements increased in the next generations: four in gen. 57/8, four in gen. 58/9 and seven in gen. 59/10, all from the main house. But one of the Kuanghsi settlements created a new branch back in Kuangtung province (Kuang-ning) (gen. 57/8), and the Hsin-hsing house also created a new branch nearby (gen. 59/10).

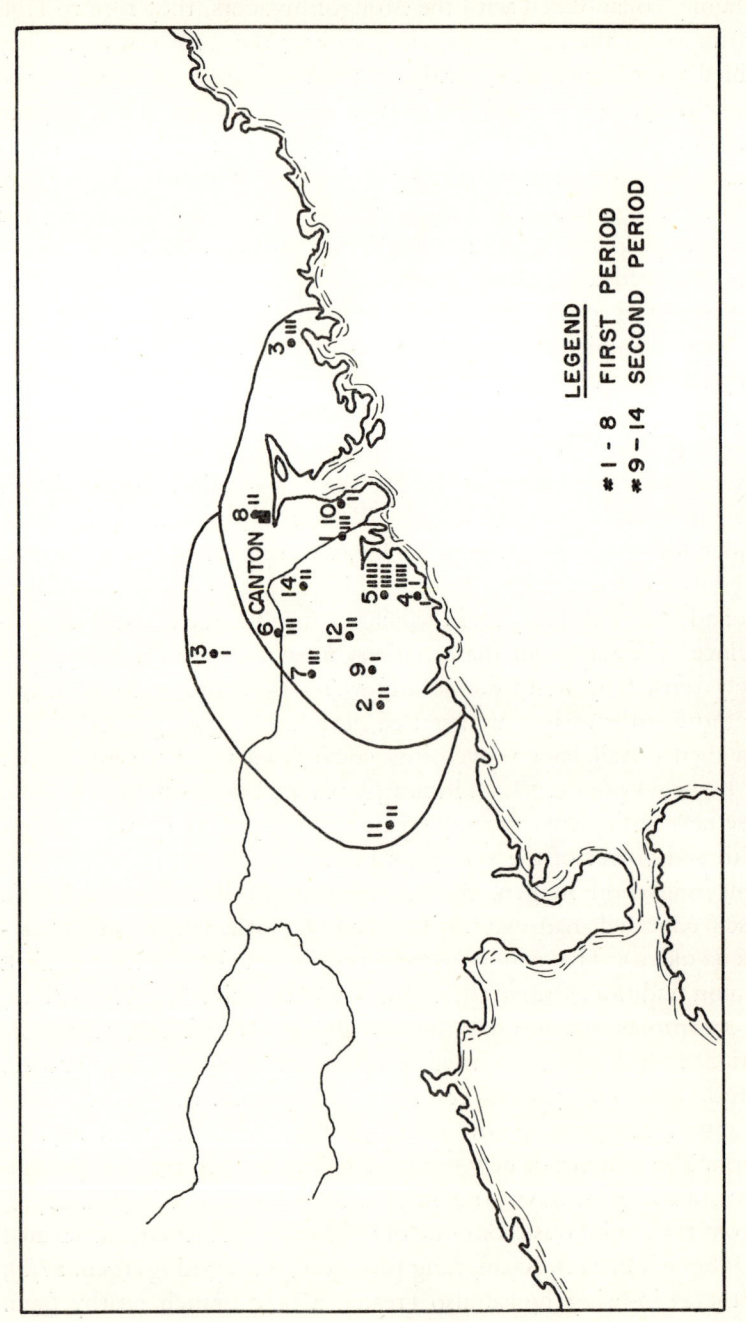

Map 2: The movements of the Han-yüan house.

TABLE 5. HAN-YÜAN HOUSES, NEW SETTLEMENTS

	gen. 51-56	gen. 57-60	gen. 61-65	gen. 66-73	Total
1) Hsin-hui	2	1			3
2) Yang-ch'un	2				2
3) Hsiang-shan	2	1			3
4) Kuang-hai	1				1
5) T'ai-shan	4	5	3	4	16
6) Kao-yao	1	1	1		3
7) Hsin-hsing	1	2			3
8) P'an-yü (Canton)	1	1			2
9) En-p'ing		1			1
10) Chung-shan		1			1
11) Hsin-i		1			1
12) K'ai-p'ing		2			2
13) Kuang-ning		1			1
14) Kao-ming		1		1	2
	14	18	4	5	41

With the general downfall of the family after 1500, new settlements decrease:

gen. 60/11: one
　　 61/12: one
　　 62/13: one
　　 63/14: one
　　 64/15: one
　　 65/16: two
　　 66/17: one (from a branch house in Kao-yao)
　　 67/18: one
　　 68/19: one
　　 69/20: one
　　 70/21: one
after 70: none

Only in the migration in gen. 64/15 do we hear of the reason: robbers threatened the home. One man with his sons planned to emigrate and first went to a place where the water was salty; they then went to another place where a family Liu gave them land. We are not told why this grant was made.

All migrations remained restricted to Kuangtung, with one brief exception. In the last ten generations T'ai-shan became an important migration center.

6. The P'u-t'ien/Sha-pei House

As already stated, this house supposedly broke away from the P'u-t'ien house in gen. 52 and settled in Sha-pei near Canton, in the district of Tseng-ch'eng. No information is given for the next three generations. In gen. 56 one man had an official position in Canton while another moved into the city of Tseng-ch'eng. It is this man, Wu Hsiang-lung, who gave his name to a whole branch, the "Hsiang-lung" branch. But if a move into a city is mentioned in a genealogy without any further detail as to an official or other job, the possibility exists that such persons were businessmen. In any case, although Hsiang-lung was not important, both of his sons (gen. 57) passed the *chin-shih* examinations and held official positions of some small importance, one dealing with economics. The rise of this branch did not continue, however: in gen. 58 only one man had an educational job (*chiao-yü*). Another man created a branch settlement near Sha-pei. From then on, we have many names of members, but with little information. One member each, possibly of gen. 59 and 60, was a *chü-jen*, and so it was in gen. 64 and 65. In gen. 65 a second man passed the local examinations. During these generations a settlement was started in Tung-wan (gen. 62) and two in Pao-an and Tseng-ch'eng (gen. 63), all close to the home house.

With gen. 65, information on this branch stops suddenly. This coincides roughly with the beginning of the Manchu dynasty (1644). We hear only that two brothers in Tseng-ch'eng got a military degree in 1666 (gen. 68), and that a new settlement in Pao-an was started in gen. 71. But down to the present time this is all we find. The branch still exists in several settlements in Sha-pei as well as in Tseng-ch'eng and Pao-an, but it cannot be regarded as a family of the elite. What little we have of information seems to indicate that down to ca. 1600 the family held some social status, but that a downward mobility began with the advent of the Manchu.

7. The P'u-t'ien/An-hai Houses

This house, too, claims to come from P'u-t'ien in gen. 52 and believes that the family settled in An-hai in Fukien for reasons which are not indicated. It is not impossible that business activity was the main occupation of this family at that time. We have some information on this family down to gen. 58, but no details. None of the members had passed an examination or held an official position.

From gen. 58 on, i.e. roughly speaking 1420 on, to gen. 65, around 1600, we have no information at all. With gen. 65 a new branch emerged which moved into Nan-hai near Canton as a merchant family from An-hai. This second An-hai family claimed to descend from the earlier An-hai branch. This is possible, but cannot be proved. In any case, the second An-hai family is a typical Fukienese business family—the only one of the P'u-t'ien houses which clearly shows this trait which, according to Makino, is typical of P'u-t'ien families.

Wu Ch'ao-feng (gen. 66/14/2) was a merchant (1613-1694) who moved from Fukien down to Canton, registered as a citizen in Nan-hai and lived close to Canton's western gate. He seems to have had some success, because he brought his father Wu Tien-pei to the new home; he is now regarded as the first settler of the new An-hai house, corresponding to the 13th generation of the first An-hai house (65/13/1). Not too much is known about the family down to gen. 69/17/5. In this generation, two men are described as being very wealthy; one earned a posthumous title. But the other one, Wu Kuo-jung (1731-1810), was the real founder of a prominent house: in his youth, he traveled to and from Fukien to Canton. He then created an overseas trading house (I-ho yang-hang 怡和洋行) and asked his third son Wu Ping-chien (70/18/6; 1769-1843) to conduct overseas trade, i.e. trade with the Western countries.

Ping-chien became the head of the 13 Hong merchants of Canton and was one of the four biggest of them. When war was impending he gave the provincial government of Canton 260,000 taels in silver and one American warship, worth 18,000 taels [1]. He also made a gift of 100,000 for buildings of military character [2]. It is interesting to see that his three brothers joined the government bureaucracy: one was in the Ministry of the Interior (Hu-pu) and in other jobs; he also was interested in literature and published a collection of poems (Wu Ping-yung, 1764-1824) [3]. His second brother Wu Ping-chün (1777-1799) was in the same Ministry, and later was given the second court rank and posthumous titles [4]. His third brother Wu Ping-chen

---

[1] 4b, 6b.
[2] 4b, 2a.
[3] 2a, 44a; 4a, 63a; 6b, 32a.
[4] 2a, 44a; 4a, 63a.

(1770-1835) got the fifth rank and had a job in the Ministry of Justice [1]. By this time, the family was so powerful that the cousins also profitted from its strength—four of them had government positions. One was in charge of mining in Hei-lung-chiang province near the Siberian border, and later controlled the armaments of ships at the Tiger's Gate near Canton [2].

In gen. 71/19/7 we have no less than 20 famous men: 5 persons with the *chü-jen* degree, although we learn that for three of these five the degree was the result of large financial contributions to the government and not of learning; four had the second rank and three the third rank, again often as a result of contributions. But five of these men of gen. 71 wrote poetry or calligraphy and were well educated. Most of the famous men, in addition to the rank or titles which they bought, had some active government position, too. Only one of them went to the Military Academy in Tokyo and one opened a business firm in Hong Kong. These latter two lived toward the close of the 19th century, while the others lived in the earlier part of the century.

In generation 72/20/8 we find 26 persons of distinction. In most cases, however, the distinction is an honorific title or a posthumous honor; few have had active government duty. Two members of this generation had a post in the Salt Administration, as had a member of the preceding generation. The Salt Administration was one of the most lucrative government jobs. Again, one member of gen. 72 was in business with Western countries.

The generation 73/21/9 is a 20th century generation and many members are still alive and thus not yet at the end of their careers when the genealogy was written. We hear of four persons in actual administrative positions. Another man had a degree in engineering taken in the United States. Two of the officials had law degrees. This family did not migrate: it has remained since its re-emergence around 1700 a merchant family, living in cities and not in villages. It is interesting to observe that the wealth of the family was limited until they got into business with foreigners, at which time their wealth increased tremendously. And as soon as there was wealth enough, the family tried, successfully, to enter government service and to make its fortune in the government.

---

[1] 2a, 44a-b; 4a, 63a; 5, 20a.
[2] 10, 56b.

8. The Lü-wei (Chu-kuo) House
1. *Social Mobility*

This is the largest house of the Wu clan, split into a number of sub-houses. The home in Hsin-ning-hsien, Wen-chang tu, Tou-tung county, was created by Wu Min (gen. 49/1), who died there as an exile living in the house of his wife. Of Wu Min's two sons, one had a low court position, but both seem to have lived close to their father's tomb (gen. 50/2). The son of the official passed a special local examination together with a cousin and got a low local job in Yang-ch'un, near the family home (Wu Chih-ts'ai, died 1229; gen. 51/3).

One of Wu Chih-ts'ai's sons became educational officer in Chao-ch'ing-fu (Kuangtung Province) (*chiao-shou*), while the son of the other successful candidate of the gen. 51 became Censor of Kao-chou (Kao-chou lu *tz'u-shih*), a relatively high post. One of his brothers was adopted by an uncle who had no sons at the time, although he later had one of his own. It is from this adopted son Wu Yü-tsu (other name: Jung-kui; gen. 52/4) that a new house took its origin, the so-called Jung-kui house. The ancestor Wu Yü-tsu, it is reported, had an office in Fukien.

In generation 53/5, the son of the educational officer also became educational officer in Kao-yao (Kuangtung Province) (*chiao-yü*) after he had passed a local examination. He liked Kao-yao very much and recommended to his sons that they settle there. One of his cousins, Wu T'ien-hsing (1199-1286), passed the local examination as the best candidate and got court jobs in the capital of the Sung Dynasty, while his brother Wu T'ien-lin (1201?-1268) passed the *chin-shih* examination and took several appointments, among these the post of a Transportation Officer of Hu-Kuang Province [1]. The family by this time was quite elevated and can be called a local gentry family, because in spite of some jobs outside the province, the majority of the positions in this and other generations were in the home province of Kuangtung.

There is a certain concentration on educational offices which continues in the following period. Generation 54/6 brings us close to the end of the Sung Dynasty. Two of the Wu T'ien-lin's sons also passed the *chin-shih* examinations and both held court positions at the end of the Sung period. Their eldest brother Wu Lung-ch'i fled with the Sung imperial house when the Mongols captured

---

[1] 2b, 3b-4a; 2a, 16a and 1a, 32b.

Hang-chou and fought for the dynasty in Kuangtung province until one of his men murdered him and surrendered to the Mongols. It is reported that he had made large contributions in grain to the dynasty to finance the fight [1]. The family remained basically anti-Mongol and thus differed from the Han-yüan branch which lived nearby and was pro-Mongol. There were six cousins of these three famous brothers who also reached prominence: one was a *chin-shih* (Wu Huan-chang, 54/6; *chin-shih* in 1247) and held high court and administrative positions; two others had educational jobs (*hsüeh-cheng*) and two had court titles or positions.

In gen. 55/7 three persons held educational positions (*hsüeh-cheng, hsüch-shih* and *chiao-yü*), one made his *chin-shih* before the end of the Sung rule. His father had passed the local examinations. Finally, one man, Wu T'ung-lao changed the family attitude towards the Mongols and passed his *chin-shih* under the Mongols in 1333 [2] and got offices in the north.

Four of the sons of T'ung-lao got government posts through the *yin* privilege; but we do not learn what types of jobs they accepted. We have two more educational officers (*hsüeh-cheng*) in gen. 56/8, and two men who passed the examinations. One of them got a job in Kiangsi Province and his sons decided to live there. In gen. 57/9 we find again three educational officers (*chiao-yü*) all active in the home province. Two other men had education but rejected offers for jobs, yet another passed the local examinations and one became a magistrate. The level of the family in this generation which lived in the 14th century, was lower than in the preceding generation.

To this generation belonged Wu Yüan-chung, whose genealogy is well attested, but who is reported to have lived in the 16th century. It is said that he "gave up learning" and became a businessman settling in Ku-shui in Kuang-ning. From the place name we might conclude that he was a small businessman in an unimportant place. His move took place between 1522 and 1566 [3], although one should expect this man to have lived in the 15th century, from the data on his generation.

The members of gen. 58/10 all lived under the Ming dynasty.

---

[1] 1a, 42b; 3, 14a; 6b, 4b; 8, 7b; 8, 26a; 9, 11b.

[3] 2b, 5a; 2a, 18 b; 1a, 48a; 8, 7b; 9, 13a.

[2] 4a, 22b. We have given these page references only as examples to show how often and at how many places information is given. From now on, we do not refer to all these data.

We find among them two *chü-jen*, and two who passed the local examinations. One of the *chü-jen* got a provincial educational post (*hsüeh-shih*) in Kuanghsi, another man was first educational officer (*chiao-shou*) and later magistrate in Kuanghsi, and a third man was tax collector in Kuanghsi and settled there. Two other men got honorific titles. One last man became quite wealthy as a geomancer; but he was educated, for he also composed poems.

For the next few generations, the genealogy is extremely vague and incomplete. In a good number of cases which would interest us, the attribution of a given person to a definite generation and a definite branch of the family is uncertain. All this seems to indicate that the family, at least in its main branch, remained at a fairly low social level. In gen. 59/11 we read of one man of the main house who got his *chin-shih* degree and two years later a job as educational officer (*chiao-yü*) in a place near Yang-ch'un where he settled and later died. He is also reported as having fought against the local Yao tribes. His son, however, is said to have been the first from a poor family who attained wealth, though only a later descendant was able to buy a shop in Yang-ch'un city. This would seem to indicate that the educational officer, in spite of his high degree, did not have a career and remained poor; that one of his sons went into business and made some money, which enabled one of his descendants to become a businessman in a city. These events must have taken place in the early 15th century.

There are five persons belonging to this Lü-wei lineage mentioned with a *chü-jen* degree and probably belonging to generation 59; only one came from the main house. All the others lived in settlements about which we do not read earlier, and no further details are given. There is, in addition to these, also a man who was first in the *chü-jen* examination.

In gen. 60/12 we hear nothing about the main house. One *chü-jen* and one judge (*t'ung-p'an*) are mentioned, but both are from branch houses about which no further information is available.

It remains essentially the same for gen. 61/13: there was one *sui-kung-sheng*, i.e. the best in the local examination, from the main house, and another from a branch house, as well as a *chü-jen* from a branch house. But no information nor other details are given. In gen. 62/14 we hear of a man who passed his *chin-shih* and got a high post in Nan-ch'ang (Kiangsi) around 1510, but we do not know exactly from which branch he came. Three members of a branch in Feng-ch'uan all passed the local examinations and were sent to Peking (as *pa-kung*); one became an educational officer and another a local magistrate. The third one seems to have failed in the final examination. The Feng-ch'uan branch had been created in gen. 60/12, but no details about this step are known. With gen. 63/15 the main family seems to move upward again; we are now in the latter half of the 16th century. The family had two *chü-jen*, two *sui-kung-sheng* and one *pa-kung*. One of its members became a general, fought against Japanese pirates and drowned. And of one other man it is said that he gave up study and became a farmer. The Feng-ch'uan branch produced another *pa-kung* who later got a civil job in Kuanghsi. The Yang-ch'un branch also produced a *chü-jen*; he was probably a descendant of the *chin-shih* of gen. 59. Two more men with degrees, but from unknown side branches, are mentioned.

With gen. 64/16 we come to the end of the Ming dynasty and the beginning of the Manchu regime. There are two *chü-jen* and one *sui-kung* in the main branch, while it is said of two other men that they chose to become farmers. One man apparently failed in his examinations and opened a small medicine shop in Jung-hsien; he later settled there as a relatively poor farmer (ca. 1580), at the same time that other relatives of his settled in near-by villages. There are three other persons from unknown side-branches with degrees.

In gen. 75/17 we find a number of prominent persons from different places: there is one man from a village close to the family home who went to Kiangsi to learn geomancy—a profession which had at an earlier time been taken up by members of his clan. Another man decided to become a farmer—a fact which indicates that other members of his family had higher education. A third man also from T'ai-shan became famous because he gave a loan which he did not reclaim; he gave grain away during a famine and he built a bridge—all showing his concern for his community. In other branches we find more prominent men: in Hsin-hsing Wu Kuang-wen passed the examinations and became educational officer (*chiao-shou*) in Kuanghsi; in Hsin-hui another man passed his examinations (*sui-kung-sheng*) and was later honored by the Manchu conquerors. In Kao-yao a member of the family took military jobs under the Manchu regime. And in Chung-shan Wu Jui-lung placed highest in the *chü-jen* examinations of 1621, became educational officer sometime after 1625 and author of a provincial gazetteer and other books and essays. He served in the capital in different positions at the time of the end of the Ming dynasty.

In the middle of the 17th century the home of our clan was seized by bandits, and some of the members moved into the city of T'ai-shan to fight the bandits until the end of the rebellion, and returned later to the village (in 1667). Another branch family in T'ai-shan was spared by the bandits (in 1677) because the household chief was famous as a model of piety. Two of the T'ai-shan men also became farmers, as in the earlier generations. One man in T'ai-shan got a military degree (1669). In Hsin-hui the son of a candidate passed his *chü-jen* and became magistrate in Kiangsi, and the son of the educational officer from Hsin-hsing also passed his examinations (*sui-kung-sheng*). Finally, we hear of a *chü-jen* in Canton who came from our clan. While all these men selected professions which were traditional in their family, we now find a textile merchant in Wu-chou (Kuanghsi), a man whose father had left Hsin-hui for the city of Wu-chou—and we can safely say that the father was poor when he started life in Wu-chou. This branch remained in business in the town for many generations. His son (gen. 67/19) became wealthy enough to make a gift of land and to build a wharf for ships in Wu-chou. Thus he helped other businessmen in their problems of transportation.

All four sons of the famous man in Hsin-hsing went to school, one later got the *chü-jen* degree and another the *sui-kung-sheng* degree, but none of them seems to have occupied any official posts (gen. 67/19).

In the main house, we hear of a man who passed some examinations, but who apparently did not hold any positions. He was famous for his welfare activities; he built bridges, roads, burned debt-receipts, sold grain at low prices in times of famine; he fed the poor and let rents go by the board. He had a garden where he passed the time with his friends, as a real gentleman should do. A relative of his in a nearby village was the author of a book on omina; he gained more fame, however, by reaching the great age of 101 years (in 1733). And another relative near by was a farmer who succeeded in increasing the landed property considerably. There are four civil and two military *chü-jen* and one *sui-kung-sheng* in different branches in this generation. All this seems to indicate that the Lü-wei house weathered the transition from Ming to Manchu rule quite well, and that most of their branches showed an upward social mobility.

In gen. 68/20, the Hsin-hsing branch of the Lü-wei house is most famous: five men had degrees, one of them was even a *chin-shih* (in 1799) and served 12 years in various positions. His brother served as a magistrate in Kuangsi.

In the vicinity of the main home in T'ai-shan we hear of yet another farmer, of a man who failed in his examinations and passed only when he was 70 years old, and another one who failed and finally got a title because of a large gift of money to the government. A third man liked books but had no degree; he excelled in social welfare by not reclaiming debts and by otherwise helping his clansmen. There were eight other men in this generation in different branches—all with degrees.

In gen. 69/21, the main house in T'ai-shan had six famous members, four of whom were descendants of the same grandfather. One of the six was a writer and calligrapher and became educational officer (*chiao-yü*); his brother attained the age of 101 years and was renowned because he helped the poor during a famine. The Hsin-hsing branch had three members in the bureaucracy; two of them were educational officers. The branch in Wu-chou now also shows upward mobility: a man who lost his father at the age of nine acquired an education and even passed an examination but did not take any positions. He had some knowledge of medicine and wrote some poems and essays. His house was burned in 1857 during the T'ai-p'ing rebellion; he died in 1883.

A settlement of the Lü-wei house in En-p'ing many generations ago (61/14) had brought forth only farmers. In this generation (69/21) the main occupation of the family is still described as farming. But now we find a man who took a tutor and entered the local school. His three older brothers started businesses in addition to farming. Business began on a small scale, but the eldest brother soon became very rich and bought land and farm houses in many neighboring places, so that his descendants could settle there. He rented most of the land out, helped by his two brothers. There are four other members of the Lü-wei house who passed examinations; but no other details on them are known.

The En-p'ing branch house had in gen. 70/22 (1831) one *chü-jen* who later became educational officer (*chiao-yü*), and one other man who passed, while three other brothers, though educated, did not pass the examinations.

The Wu-chou house produced a calligrapher with some education, but no position. The Hsin-hsing house did not produce famous men in this generation, and the main house also remained weak in gen. 70/22: two men went to school and one planned to erect a school. But now, in the early 19th century, new developments became visible everywhere: a man in a village near T'ai-shan emigrated to Mexico and returned as a wealthy man, started a textile factory in Hong Kong and grew even wealthier. From what we know of such emigrants and of the place from which he came, we can safely say that he began as a poor farmer.

In Hsin-hui were several settlements of the Lü-wei house. In the city of Hsin-hui we find a man who passed the *chin-shih* in 1781 and became a magistrate in Fukien and in Hunan. He also was a writer. But in that same family, we also find a man who went to Singapore as a businessman and returned as early as 1846. And outside the city we meet another merchant (born 1819), who started out as an orphan working in town as a laborer, who then became a businessman in town and made much money. He got his brother started in an independent business, assisted all poor farmers of his clan, paid off the debts of a friend in Canton, kept five concubines and married the sister of his wife after her death.

In a settlement of the family in Shun-tê we find two brothers who passed their examinations. One of these, Wu Lan-wei, took a number of official jobs as magistrate, which brought him into Yünnan. He wrote about Yünnan and also published poetry, but he was more important as an entrepreneur in Yünnan and the adjacent Shan States of Burma, where he dealt with the tribes, and as the creator of a large agricultural irrigation project in Yünnan (ca. 1880) which made him rich.

Similarly, a branch family in Jung-hsien produced four famous brothers in the 7th generation of settlement in Jung-hsien. The most interesting of these brothers had no ability for learning, but some military interests. Yet, because the family was poor, he became a farmer and cultivated a large property on a sandy hill which had never yet been under cultivation and this made him wealthy. He used some of the wealth to build bridges, Confucian temples and study halls, and he made a financial contribution to the government for a war in Annam (1788). His brother organized a village militia, when the famous "salt-bandits" threatened their village. Later, he also financed the building of examination halls, and made gifts of land to his clansmen. A third brother became wealthy by administering the family properties. He fought against bandits and later burned all debt certificates. The fourth brother had honorary government posts.

There are more famous men in this generation in various branches of the house: four scholars in Feng-ch'uan, one of whom was a *chü-jen* (after 1810) and represented a philosophical school which was in opposition to the orthodox school. Hsin-hsing had four scholars, one of whom also was a *chü-jen*. And there are seven other scholars with degrees, or men known as writers.

In general, for this generation which lived in the beginning of the 19th century, the new development is represented by the spread into South-east Asia and America where the emigrants quickly got rich and returned home to make further investments there.

Many members of gen. 71/23 are still alive today. The En-p'ing house had five scholars; the branch in Wu-chou produced a writer who was also once in the salt administration in Swatow, and a magistrate. In Hsin-hui we find another successful man in the merchant family branch; but this man made the *chü-jen* (in 1889) and the *chin-shih* (in 1892) and took high positions in the capital. His brother, however, always failed in the examinations and finally bought a rank. The other Hsin-hui branch also produced a *chü-jen*. The Jung-hsien family kept up the military tradition it enjoyed; the leader in this generation (71/23) became in 1847 chief of the local guard; he had several fights with the T'ai-p'ing and saved thousands in a fortress which he constructed and defended. Later he granted land for the settlement of refugees. His cousin, too, gave large gifts for road and bridge construction and for weddings of poor people. He had also some interest in geomancy.

In T'ai-shan, near the main home, we find another geomancer, but with a *chü-jen* degree. In Republican times he opened a school. Another T'ai-shan man failed the examinations and became a teacher; and there is a third man from T'ai-shan who deserves mention as a local delegate in 1921.

A hitherto undistinguished branch in Pao-an produced two brothers who both attained their degrees in 1892. The older one fought against Great Britain, was taken prisoner and was to be executed, if his clan had not intervened. He was later released. He gave money for the contruction of hospitals.

The members of gen. 72/24 in Jung-hsien were all involved in the fight against the T'ai-p'ing and some lost their lives. Nine members in Jung-hsien or near by are mentioned in this connection. One of them was a drugstore owner, as his father and grandfather had been before him.

By now there are more and more members of the Lü-wei house in prominent positions. We will only mention those whose lives exhibit special attainments. There is, for instance, the son of the Hsin-hui merchant who had been in Singapore; he studied in a Christian school in Hong Kong, and later created the first modern newspaper in China. He then went to London to study law and became the first foreign law student with a London degree. He was in Moskow, in 1898, and after 1900 in the United States, both times on diplomatic missions. He made international treaties and created trade laws in China. He died in The Hague in 1924. A relative of this man in Hsin-hui attained his wealth through his business and then bought titles. In the Shun-tê branches we find four men with degrees. One of these passed his *chin-shih* in 1890 and then became director of examinations in Szu-ch'uan, where he interested himself in mining and railway construction as well as in the cultural development of Tibetans.

In the settlements close to the old home we find 13 men who were teachers or who created schools in the 20th century. Two others wrote essays (one on the T'ai-p'ing). Seven others passed the old-time examinations. One man was a druggist in Canton; another one became a medical man who was against Western medicine. He also was active in the field of law. Two men were businessmen in the United States. One worked for years on a steamship and finally bought his own boat and became wealthy both overseas and in Hong Kong. One other man was in business and bought titles for himself. Although a writer at first, he participated in an abortive revolution against the Manchu. He had to leave the country and lived in Malaya, Thailand and Burma until 1921, after a short unsuccessful interlude in China in 1912. He was closely allied with Sun Yat-sen in 1921.

In gen. 73/25 we find 28 teachers or prospective teachers in modern schools, and 12 men have studied and been active in the old way.

In the Jung-hsien house we find four men in military positions. One of these failed in his military examinations and went into business and welfare activities. Eleven members went to the United States (mostly to the East Coast). Many of these later returned and worked in South China. Only one of this group learned some law (in San Francisco) as a translator for a lawyer; he later defended the Chinese in Mexico which gave him the idea of opening a ship line from China to Mexico; this was a failure, but he was refinanced by Harriman and then his Mexico line was a success. In 1920 he was Salt Commissioner in Kuangtung and Kuanghsi; he died in 1927. Another family member worked in the British naval construction yards in Hong Kong, became a shipbuilder and thus very rich. Another man was a merchant in Penang. But most of the others remained in Hong Kong or South China as businessmen (five persons). One man had a rice shop in Hong Kong, another a building firm there. Most interesting is a young man from Hsin-hui (Wu Hung-kuang, born 1848) who failed the examinations and went into business. He settled in a village with many whorehouses and opened a dye shop there when he was not older than twenty. He later opened an oil, sugar, honey and wax shop, made medicines and wrote a booklet on smallpox. He did much for the public welfare in the form of a dyke against floods, resthouses, fords, and a contribution to a hospital.

There are now some more men with Western degrees in our family: a medical doctor, a political scientist who studied in Japan, an engineer from Shanghai, a law student from London and the United States who later became ambassador to the United States (Wu Ch'ao-shu, died 1934) and another student in the United States. Finally, we also find a specialist in geomantic books.

In gen. 74/26 we find 45 persons who were or still are teachers or created schools or planned to create schools. An additional 11 persons studied under the old system and four wrote essays in the old style. There are many businessmen in this generation: the owner of a medicine shop in Hong Kong; of a lumber and rice transportation business in Wu-chou (Kuanghsi) and Hong Kong; of a building shop in Hong Kong; of another drug store in T'ai-shan; of an insurance business in Hong Kong; of a textile factory with over 2000 workers in Hong Kong with a Canton branch; and eight other businessmen about whom no details are given. Fourteen other businessmen got their start in the United States. Most of these later opened their own establishments in China; one opened a medicine shop. Nine persons went to other foreign countries: one of them had a restaurant in Manila and ten other shops there, another started in Manila. The restaurant owner and a relative both first started out in the United States before they went with the Americans to the Philippines. Of two other relatives in the Philippines we have no further details. Two men of this group were in Penang where one of them had a restaurant, although he later went to Bangkok. The other man from Penang studied medicine and was an instructor in Hong Kong from 1912 on. Of the last man in this group we know only that he was in South-East Asia.

In the professions we find many graduates from United States universities: among the 10 students one studied naval construction.

One studied political science at Harvard and he and a distant relative who also had studied in the United States became revolutionaries and followers of Sun Yat-sen. There are two more political scientists from Harvard and Columbia; one law student (Wu Ta-kuang) who later was Chinese representative at the Versailles Conference 1919. No details are given about the fields of four other graduates from United States universities. Three men studied law and three others political science in Chinese colleges; one graduated from a teacher's school and one showed an interest in medicine.

The gen. 75/27 is in part still young and their life histories are not completely reported. Twenty-three men are teachers or have created schools. Four men still had an old-style education and three others wrote old-fashioned essays or poems. One man went to an old-style military school and took military jobs in the imperial time.

Five men were businessmen in the Philippines: two were businessmen in Peru, and two others in undisclosed foreign countries. Four were in business in the United States and a fifth man later went from the United States to the Philippines and then, as so many others, returned to China. Two men had shops only in China.

Three men graduated from Columbia University (engineering, education and possibly political science), one from George Washington University (field unknown). A fifth student also studied engineering in the United States. One student each studied in France (medicine), Germany, and England. Six students studied in China (medicine, law, political science and naval science).

The following three generations do not supply new data: the trend seems to continue, but most members are still too young to be mentioned in detail in the genealogy.

In general: the very large and greatly subdivided Lü-wei house started out as a landowning gentry family, always in civil or educational positions. They created more and more new settlements which they manned with such members of the family as were not interested in or capable of study. The first move into business began in the 16th century. In the 18th century the main house declined, and by the 19th century few men in this house were still in important jobs in the bureaucracy. At the same time, during this period, more and more of them were going into business. A certain inclination is to be seen toward drug stores and medicine in general; the trend toward geomancy disappears in the 19th century. In the early 19th century, with the new possibilities given by the foreign powers, more and more men of the poorer settlements emigrated to South-East Asia, the Philippines and North or South America. Most of these returned to establish their own shops in South China. Towards the end of the 19th century the descendants of these men entered the colleges in China or in the United States. In the 20th century more and more members of the house became teachers or at least helped in establishing schools; they shunned government jobs, although some were closely allied with Sun Yat-sen and the revolutionaries. Many were local leaders in the 1930's, but none of them was a leader in the KMT.

2. *Geographical Mobility*

The main house of this branch in Hsin-hui (later: T'ai-shan), Tou-tung, was started in gen. 49, as already mentioned. The first move came five generations later, to a settlement near by, in Tou-tung (gen. 54).

During the life of gen. 55 the Mongol invasion of South China took place, and as our branch was against the Mongols, this event influenced the fate of the house adversely. Two brothers, whose father was killed in the war against the Mongols fled from home and settled in new places: one in Shun-tê, the other in Sha-pei. Another family member also fled to Shun-tê and settled there because he was afraid of the Mongols. Wu Tzu-li went into the family of his mother (Chang) and was adopted by them; his grandson, however, returned to the Wu family and took the Wu family name again. Although there is no explanation for this unusual move, it is possible that Tzu-li did this in order to escape the threats of further danger from the Mongols. The man who moved to An-chiao in Shun-tê moved into the home of his wife—in a manner similar to Tzu-li's action. Further moves in gen. 55 are to Hui-chou, Kui-shan, to Feng-ch'uan and to P'an-yü, T'ang-pien.

From now on the number of migrations increases so much that it is feasible to present them in abbreviated form, especially so because not many details are known about the reasons for the migrations. We differentiate, however, migrations into primary (from the family home) and secondary settlements (created from a branch or primary settlement).

In gen. 56 we learn about 17 migrations; only three of them secondary in nature. In only one case do we know that it was in connection with troubles of the late Mongol period. All these migrations were into villages. The three secondary migrations took place one generation after the primary migration. Two of these secondary migrations go into areas farther away than the other migrations had taken Wu family members.

In generation 57 twenty-nine migrations are reported. Among them are two very important settlements: one in En-p'ing which later produced many well-known persons, and one in Kuang-ning which became another major center. Only in this latter case do we know the reason for the migration: the founder, Wu Yüan-chung, gave up learning to go into business in Kuang-ning, Ku-shui. His son started to acquire land and to invest in irrigation systems, as soon as new land was opened. He became a farmer and around his settlement soon many other village settlements came into existence. The five secondary migrations do not offer much of interest: they, too, are settlements in near-by villages. One migrant left the province: his father got a position in Kiangsi province and he settled there too. Nothing else is known about this branch. All settlements are rural, none is urban, except a short period during which the founder of the Kuang-ning settlement lived in town.

In generation 58, i.e. in the early Ming period, 39 new settlements are mentioned. Of these 39, seven were created by secondary migration. Three secondary migrations started from Kuang-ning, Ku-shui, into three near-by villages; two came from An-chiao in Shun-tê and went into villages in other districts, some distance away. The family began a strong move into Kuanghsi province in this generation. But most migrations were, as before, into villages close to the family home. Two emigrants were officials, and both moved farther away: one was a *chü-jen*, who moved into Ho-p'u, and we can assume that this was in connection with an office he held there; the other one had an office in Kuanghsi and moved first into Kui-hsien city, but later into a village near Kui-hsien, i.e. he had acquired land while an official.

We know about 11 migrations in generation 59, but we have to consider that the number of persons reported for this generation is less than one quarter of the number of persons mentioned in gen. 58, so that the percentage of migrants may be even higher. On the other hand, we have to keep in mind that the genealogy from this generation on is rather incomplete and that persons who started a new settlement had a much greater chance to be remembered than others. Of the eleven migrations, five were secondary, and of these, three were from Kuang-ning. This settlement seems, therefore, to have been

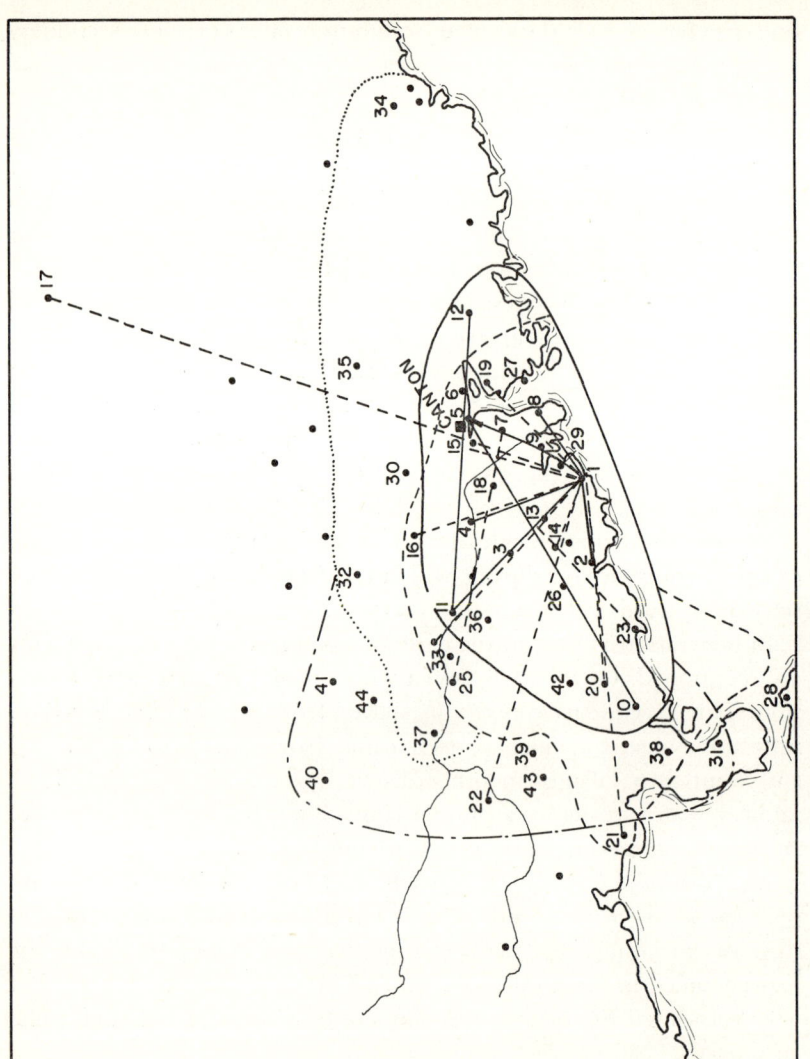

Map 3: The Expansion of the Liü-wei House Settlements: 1-12; 13-29; 30-37; 38-44.

very vigorous. In only one case (of a primary migration) do we hear of a founder who had a *chin-shih* degree and fought against Yao tribesmen in his home province.

In generation 60 we hear of eight migrations and at least three are secondary. All these migrations go into distant places, even to Hai-nan island. In only one case do we have some detail: the settler is a man who had made money by doing business in Yang-ch'un, so he settled

Map 4: Density of Lü-wei Settlements

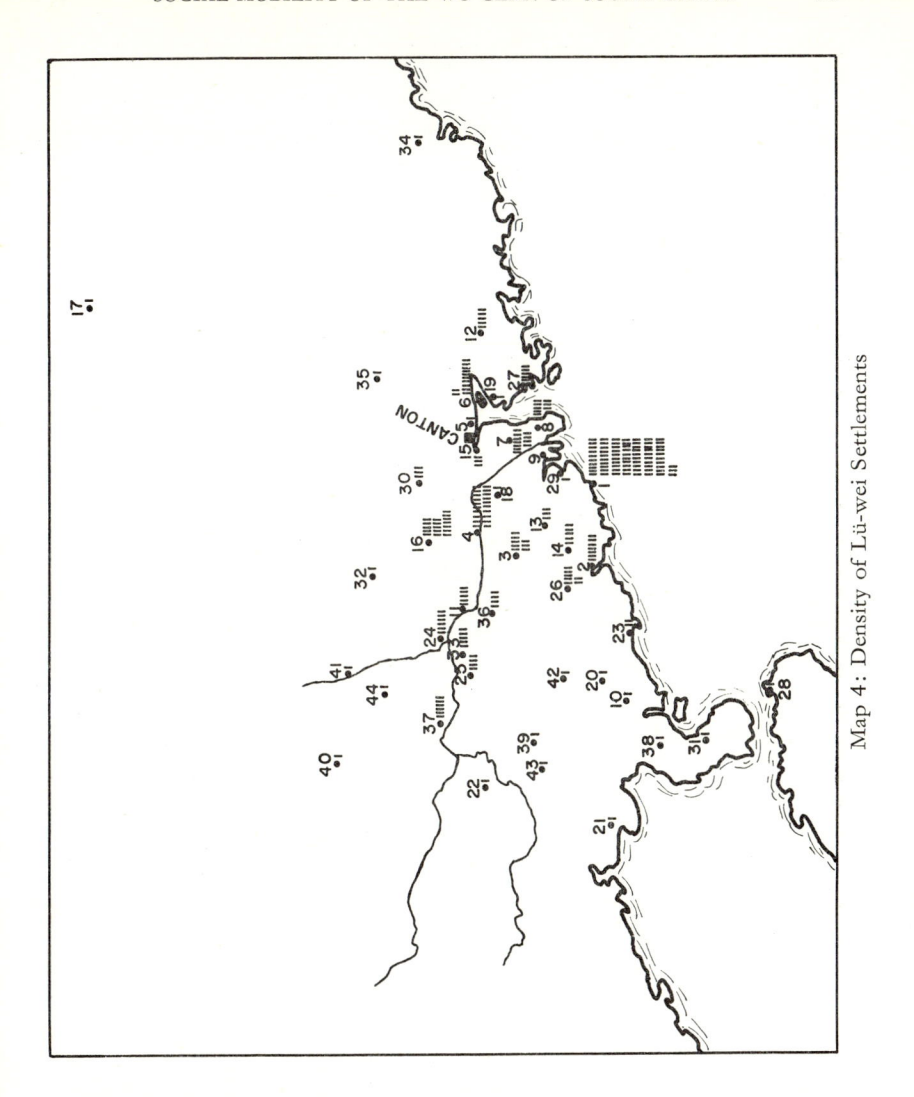

in the town, and his descendant later bought a shop in the town. Perhaps the Hai-nan settler, too, was a businessman, although nothing is said about him.

In generation 61 we know of 12 moves; at least seven were secondary. One migration went into the town of Hui-ch'eng close to the family seat, but no reasons are given.

Eleven migrations are known in generation 62, and only three were primary. Two of these primary migrations were into near-by villages, but one was to En-ping. This migrant left his family home together with his neighbor, a Mr. Lei, and both moved around a bit. They came to En-p'ing, liked it, acquired land there and settled. Later, the Lei's left the place and left all their land to the Wu's, so that the settlement got its name after our family. This settlement became one of the more important branch settlements. The event must have taken place in the middle of the 16th century.

In gen. 63 we hear of 17 migrations, ten of which came from the family center, and most of these went into near-by villages. In only one of these cases do we hear that the founder "gave up the books" and became a farmer. Four of the secondary migrations went into other districts, while the rest were moves into near-by villages.

Of the nine migrations in gen. 64 only one is primary, and of all secondary migrations only one covered some distance. One of our secondary migrants came to the new place because of an undisclosed, but certainly unimportant job. He failed in his examinations and "became interested in farming".

In gen. 65, i.e. the time of the beginning of the Manchu dynasty, we hear of 19 migrations, six primary, and all into villages very close to the family home. One of the secondary migrants went into the city of Wu-chou in Kuanghsi. As this branch later is a family of businessmen, we might assume that the founder came as a merchant. Gen. 66 has nine migrations, only three primary. In most cases the migrants moved into near-by villages. Gen. 67 has again eleven migrations, three primary. It is now clear that for several generations the main center of migrations is the borderland between Kuangtung and Kuanghsi and the southernmost parts of the country.

TABLE 6. INTENSITY OF SETTLEMENT IN DIFFERENT PERIODS
(Lü-wei Branch)

Place	Number of settlements:	gen. 51-56	gen. 57-60	gen. 61-65	gen. 66-73	Total
1) T'ai-shan		4	21	21	27	73
2) Yang-chiang		1	2	1	3	7
3) Hsin-hsing		1	2	2	3	8
4) Kao-yao		4	7	9	—	20
5) Sha-pei		1	—	—	—	1
6) P'an-yü (Canton)		2	6	4	—	12
7) Shun-tê		5	5	1	—	11
8) Hsin-hui		1	5	2	—	8
9) Chung-shan		1	2	1	3	7

Place	Number of settlements:	gen. 51-56	gen. 57-60	gen. 61-65	gen. 66-73	Total
10) Hua		1	5	5	5	1
11) Feng-ch'uan		1	1	3	—	5
12) Hui-chou		2	3	—	—	5
13) K'ai-p'ing			3	—	—	3
14) En-p'ing			2	2	1	5
15) Nan-hai			2	—	1	3
16) Kuang-ning			7	3	7	17
17) Kiangsi Province			1	—	—	1
18) Kao-ming			1	—	—	1
19) Tung-wan			1	—	—	1
20) Kao-chou			2	—	—	2
21) Ho-p'u			1	—	—	1
22) Kui-hsien (Kuanghsi)			1	—	—	1
23) Tien-pai			2	—	—	2
24) Wu-chou			1	4	1	6
25) T'eng-hsien			1	3	—	4
26) Yang-ch'un			3	—	4	7
27) Pao-an			3	1	1	5
28) Hai-nan Island			1	—	—	1
29) Hao-shan			1	—	—	1
30) Ch'ing-yüan				2	1	3
31) Wen-ch'ang				1	—	1
32) Huai-chi				1	1	2
33) Jung-hsien				3	2	5
34) Ch'ao-an				1	—	1
35) Hsin-feng				1	—	1
36) Yü-nan				1	3	4
37) P'ing-nan				2	4	6
38) Sui-ch'i					1	1
39) Pei-liu					1	1
40) Chung-tu					1	1
41) P'ing-lo					1	1
42) Hsin-i					1	1
43) Yü-lin					1	1
44) Meng-shan					1	1
		24	87	69	69	249

In gen. 68 the trend seems to be reversed; of the 14 migrations (7 primary), 9 went into villages close to the family home. These 9 migrations included all seven primary migrations. We do not know the reason for this change.

In gen. 69, i.e. the middle of the 18th century, we have again 12 migrations. Three are primary and go into near-by places; most of the secondary migrations, too, do not go far from the secondary homes. One secondary migration goes into P'ing-lo city in Kuanghsi province. No reason is given.

In gen. 70 four of the five primary migrations went into places very close to the home; two of the four secondary moves also went into places close to the old home of the family. In one case we hear of a new reason: the area was overpopulated, there was not enough land left, so that the founder had to migrate to a near-by place. He died in 1817.

Information on gen. 71 is scant: only one secondary migration is mentioned, from a secondary home in the district of the primary home, to another near-by village. For gen. 72, however, we know of nine migrations, all secondary, and mostly into near-by places. One settlement of urban character is reported: that in Ch'ing-yüan city in Kuanghsi. Many of generation 73 are still alive. The genealogy mentions only three migrations (two of them secondary), but this may not represent the full picture.

In total: this family has settled in 44 different districts (hsien). It started out to settle within a circle which has its center in the family home and with Canton (first nine districts) on the perimeter. This was achieved before gen. 56. From then on the settlements can be said to be contained in an elliptic figure with a tendency toward Kuanghsi province. The 22nd district settled is the first one in Kuanghsi, settled in gen. 58. Settlement then penetrates farther into the interior of Kuanghsi, into areas in which, as we know, many natives still lived when our family immigrated. The intensity of settlement in different generations can be seen in Table 6. The table shows that the area around the original home is by far the best liked place, with almost one third of all new settlements; but the other settlements seem to follow closely the course of the Pearl River and its delta region, that is, areas of good irrigation.

9. The Jung-kui House

1. *Social Mobility*

The writers of the genealogy of this house believe that the Jung-kui and the Lü-wei houses are related to one another; they claim a common ancestor who lived in gen. 50. The Jung-kui house, however, began its first generation already at gen. 49. We know nothing more of this period, than that a man in gen. 52 had an office in Fukien.

In the next generations, new settlements took place, but we do not know enough about the social status of this group, other than to assume that this branch house is a Hakka family which is not really related to the Lü-wei house. The critical generation is gen. 56/4 in which, as genealogists say, the genealogy of the family members is "uncertain", and this is to say that there was a real break at that time.

We continue to have little information until the end of the Ming dynasty, when one member of the house was a commander of local soldiers. Then, in gen. 67/19 we find a man who was a magistrate; in gen. 69/21, around 1750, one man passed the *chü-jen*, and another was a *sui-kung*. All this information is too scant to allow conclusions beyond the guess that the family was probably not prominent until the middle of the 19th century. Only then, starting with gen. 72/24, do we get more details. The branch settlement in Hsing-ning produced a *chin-shih* in 1835 who held a court position; another *chin-shih* in 1847 who became a magistrate; two other persons also became magistrates, and two were *sui-kung*. There is still another *chih-shih* who became a censor (*yü-shih*). We cannot explain this cumulation of high positions in this generation. It may be that the genealogy which in general is pretty poor for the Jung-kui house has confused men who really belonged to several other generations. There is, contrary to our expectation, no prominent man in gen. 73/25, and only one *sui-kung* in gen. 74/26. He is the second man from Mei-hsien, the old branch house home, to get that high.

The Mei-hsien branch of the Jung-kui house exhibits a strange feature: while all other branches of the Wu clan are in gen. 72-74 in the years around 1930, this branch has members who are in gen. 85 at the same time. It is tempting to correct the genealogy by equating gen. 62/14, which is, according to another system of counting, the first official generation in Mei-hsien (gen. 62/14/1) with gen. 49, the first Jung-kui generation according to the official count. But the few data which we have, such as the statement that gen. 59/11 lived at the end of the Mongol time, fit into the chronology for the other houses. We therefore have to assume that during the 19th century this family married very early, so that the sequence of generations went on much faster. In gen. 74/26/13 we find a man who left home to go to Southeast Asia; he seems to have lived in the middle of the 19th century and is the first emigrant. He probably went out as a laborer. In gen. 78/30/17 we hear of a man who was a scholar and claimed that his ancestors through six generations had all been scholars, although we do not know anything about them. In gen. 79/31/18 the son of this man was also a scholar.

In gen. 79/31/18 two Mei-hsien men went overseas and both became very rich. One of them died in 1934 in Hong Kong; the other became famous as a builder of a school. In gen. 80/32/19 we find a student in Hong Kong and a businessman in Southeast Asia. In gen. 81/33/20 a laborer in Mei-hsien emigrated and became the owner of a famous wineshop in Bangkok and leader of the Chinese Community there. He helped his compatriots, made grants for hospitals, schools, bridges, roads, a clan school, a theatre and to the government. He died in 1921. Two of his sons (gen. 82/31/21) continued the business in Bangkok and their generous assistance to welfare activities. One of these men studied in Germany. Another man in this generation was a businessman in South Africa, Burma and Hong Kong. There is also in this generation a chief of a Chinese bank, a magistrate under the Republican regime, and a student. Gen. 83/35/22 has three students and one man in his father's business. These men were still young in 1930. The few members of gen. 84/36/23 and 85/37/24 who have reached adulthood became students.

The general picture of this house may be summarized as follows: the main settlement in Mei-hsien seems always to have been in modest circumstances, perhaps as farmers. Their upward mobility began only after the middle of the 19th century and only in connection with emigration into Southeast Asia. They may have left the country as hired laborers, but many became rich in various small businesses. This house did not settle in the United States; it had no persons in educational jobs, and very few students.

The Hsing-ning branch settlement (created in gen. 65/17/4) rose from ca. 1750 on, four generations after the settlement. It was most prominent around 1850 and attained position in the national capital. We do not hear much about them after the end of the 19th century. Perhaps they were involved in the T'ai-p'ing rebellion?

2) *Geographical Mobility*

It is intimated in the genealogy that already in gen. 52/4 a settlement in Fukien took place in connection with an office which a family member had there. In gen. 55/7 a first settlement in Mei-hsien is mentioned; but such a settlement is repeated in gen. 58/10. In gen. 59/11, in the late 14th century, two branch settlements nearby are mentioned.

Then, a branch emigrated back into Fukien, to "Stone wall Ward" in Ning-hua. Families of Hakka origin usually regard the "Stone wall Ward" as their home; therefore, the Jung-kui house may be a Hakka family. It is then said that a branch emigrated from there to Mei-hsien (gen. 62/14/1) and the present-day Mei-hsien clan is counting the generations from this moment on. Although emigration from Mei-hsien to the "Stone wall Ward" and later back to Mei-hsien is possible, it does not seem very likely, and even the authors of the genealogy are doubtful about it [1].

In gen. 63/15/2 we find a migration to San-shui close to Canton. In gen. 64/16/3 we hear of two migrations: another group from Fukien (Stone wall Ward?) settled in the Mei-hsien area, and a new settlement was created in Chiao-ling, a district close to Mei-hsien. The last wave of immigration from Fukien took place in gen. 66/18/5, when a new settlement in P'u-ning hsien, in the coastal area of Kuang-tung, was created. Thus, we hear about four migration waves from Fukien. Such a development is quite possible; in some other instances, similar successive migrations occur from one place to others close to those of the first settlers.

In gen. 65/17/4 the settlement in Hsing-ning (Kuangtung) was created; it is this settlement which produced a number of high officials.

In gen. 66/18/5 and 72/24/11 two places in Ho-yüan, farther south, were settled. The last reported settlement is in Kui-p'ing, in Kuanghsi Province (gen. 72/24/11). Thus, the following picture of the migrations of this house emerges: from a possible home in western Fukien, the family settled in and around Mei-hsien in several waves. They later moved farther south, even into Kuanghsi, but always kept inland, away from the ocean. In general, their center of distribution is farther to the northeast than that of the Lü-wei house.

10. The T'ien-hsiung (Ch'ing-hsiang) House
1) *Social Mobility*

The origin of this house and its relation to the other houses is unclear, and even the genealogists express their doubts [2]. The original

---

[1] 1a, 52a. In 2a, 15a, all settlements of this house are mentioned. Our hypothesis that this house may be a Hakka house is confirmed by the fact that the above-mentioned business leader in Bangkok is described as a Hakka by G. W. Skinner in his *Chinese Society in Thailand: an Analytic History*, Cornell University Press, 1957.

[2] 1b, 23a; 2a, 52a.

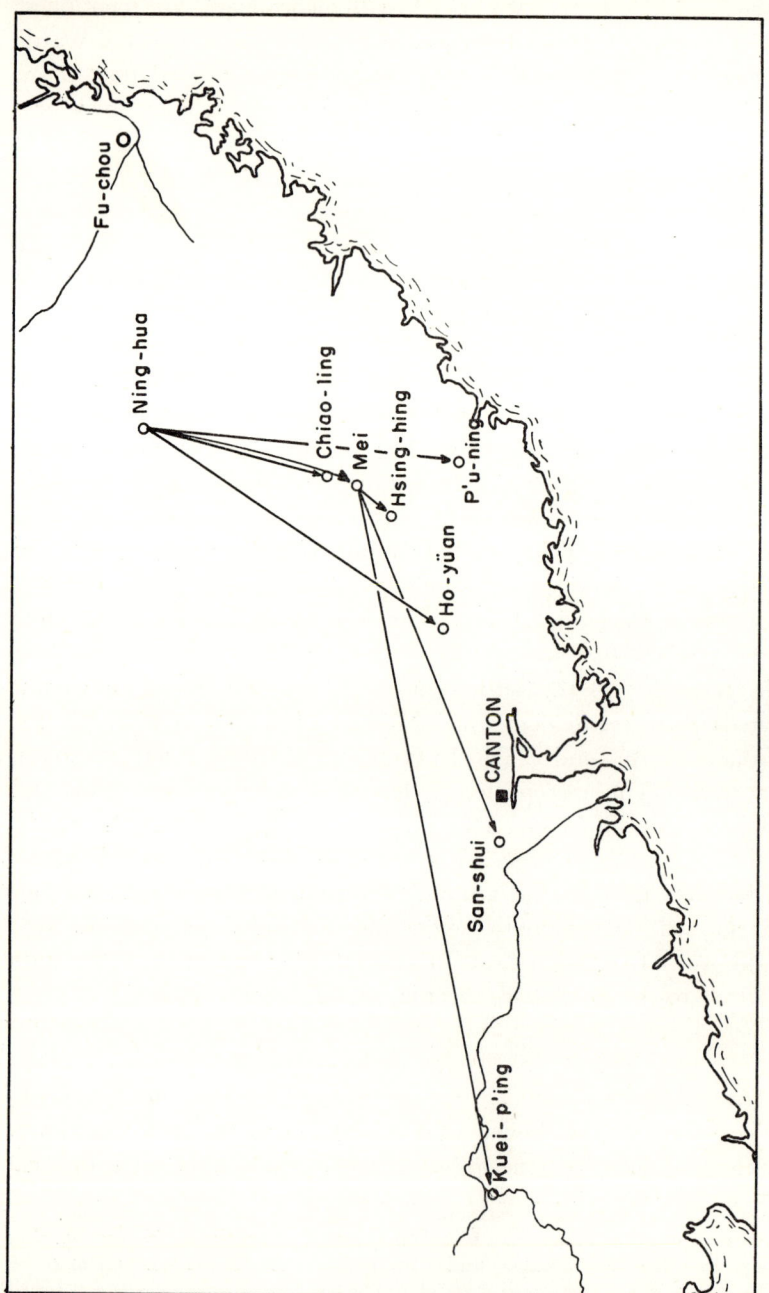

Map 5: Jung-kui house migrations.

home of this house is T'ai-ho in Chi-an (Kiangsi Province), and the founder (in gen. 53) is regarded as a brother (or cousin?) of the Lü-wei men. The family emigrated at that stage (ca. 1200) via Central Hunan into Kuanghsi. The first we learn about them is the fact that in gen. 55 the family produced a Han-lin academy student (1208-1273) who got some high court jobs. But the next item does not appear until gen. 58 (called 58/3; the son of the Han-lin student is the ancestor), where a scribe moved into near-by Kuan-yang with an army in 1369. He and other soldiers decided to settle there, and thus a new settlement was started. The son of this scribe (59/4) inherited his father's job. Again, there are no details for some generations; in gen. 61/6, probably in the early 16th century, we find a military man in Kuan-yang and a magistrate from the main house in Ch'üan-chou in Kuanghsi. Two sons of the magistrate were scholars (gen. 62/7). In the following generation (63/8) we know that two magistrates had a *chü-jen* degree, but about a third magistrate this is not reported. Two more magistrates are mentioned in addition to these, again one of them definitely with a *chü-jen* degree. The first three magistrates were Ch'üan-chou men; of the other two the same is very likely. The places in which these men served (all in the late 16th century) are interesting: one served in Nan-hsiung (northeast Kuangtung), the home of the Lü-wei house; one in Hsin-hui (S-Kuangtung), home of a main branch of the Lü-wei; and the third in Mao-ming (SW-Kuangtung), home of the Lü-wei and Lung-yen houses. One magistrate served in Yung-an (Central Fukien) at the same time his relative created a new settlement in Yung-an in Yung-fu district in Kuanghsi!

In this same generation (63/8) a young man in Kuan-yang showed military interests and led the local guard against bandits. It seems that from now on the family, now with a military tradition, moved higher up; in gen. 64/9 three brothers studied and increased the wealth of the family. One of them even composed poems. Another Kuan-yang man studied, but stressed economics and farming, and became very wealthy. Following tradition, he built roads and bridges for the population. In Ch'üan-chou the main house produced three magistrates in the early 17th century. One of these served in Ch'ing-yüan, seat of many Lü-wei men. The high position of the Ch'üan-chou house seems to have come to an end with the rise of the Manchu dynasty. Only one man, a student in the capital school (*Kuo-tzu-tien*) is mentioned in gen. 65. The Kuan-yang house produced

Map 6: Migrations of the T'ien-hsiung house

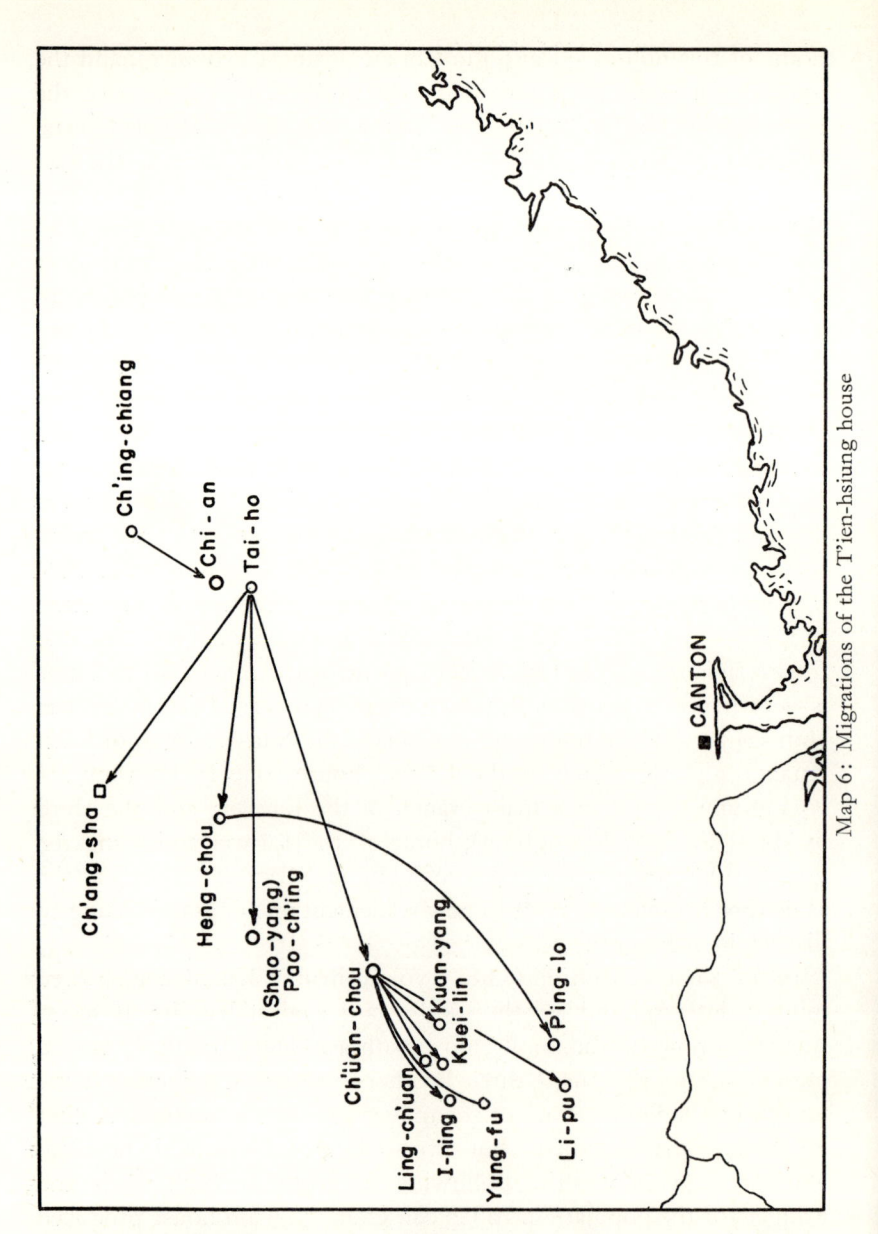

a man who studied but always failed, and another who studied but got a title only because of his famous son.

In gen. 66/9 three brothers passed the examinations between 1720 and 1735. One got an administrative job in the province, one took no job, and the most successful was a brother who was a hater of literature, who passed only the lower military examinations, but excelled in wars in the Kukunor area, against pirates in Chekiang and against the White Lotos rebels. Here, again, we see the military tradition of this branch house.

The next information is about a man in gen. 68 from Ch'üan-chou, who failed in his higher examinations, but who did much social work such as paying debts of poor people and otherwise helping the poor. From now on, the Ch'üan-chou house continued to rise, while the Kuan-yang house remained unimportant. In gen. 69 two men from Ch'üan-chou studied; one of them passed his higher examinations in 1766 and became an administrator in Kiangsi in the original family home area, famous mainly because of his dykes and sluices in an area in which the fields were lower than the level of the lake. In 1770 he served in Hsin-feng, close to the old home of the Lü-wei house and became famous by his fight against rowdyism and murderers. He then worked in Lin-ch'uan in Kiangsi, the home of Wang An-shih, again fighting bandits [1]. Finally we find him 1776 in Hsin-chien near the capital of Kiangsi as an administrator who favored merchants and invested in a large rice factory.

Three sons of this administrator played important roles in gen. 70: one did not study but simply bought a title; one studied, and one passed his *chü-jen* in 1779, became magistrate in Yung-p'ing (Yünnan), fought against the White Lotos rebels, wrote poems, philosophical essays and a study on grasshoppers. His wife was from Nan-ch'ang (Kiangsi), where his father had lived.

In Kuan-yang we hear of a man who got wealthy by marrying into a powerful local family, the T'ang family. During the T'ai-p'ing rebellion, i.e. after 1850, he supplied the refugees with food and coffins; he built bridges and roads and burned debt certificates.

One of his sons (in gen. 71) had to flee from the T'ai-p'ing. He also married a Miss T'ang, a powerful lady who ran the house, while he made educational grants, built bridges and regulated a river. He died as recently as 1921. One of his relatives was killed by the T'ai-p'ing in 1857.

---

[1] It should be mentioned here that a Sung source mentions a Wu family of hat makers and merchants in this place in the middle of the eleventh century (*Neng-kai-chai man-lu*, as quoted by Sh. Kato, *Studies in Chinese Econ. History*, Tokyo, 1952, vol. 1, p. 505). Whether these Wu were relatives of the early T'ien-hsiung house, cannot be established.

In this gen. 71 one man passed the *chü-jen* in 1804, got a position in the History Office, became examiner, and author of a book. But he was most famous for irrigation works in I-cheng in S-Kiangsu which irrigated 10,000 mou (after 1822). His brother was in the Public Works Department.

From now on, we hear only of the Kuan-yang house; some Ch'üan-chou men in later generations held small local jobs, but their position in the genealogy is unclear and their jobs without importance.

In gen. 72 one man in Kuan-yang also passed his military examination; another one failed in the military examination, lost his property by the T'ai-p'ing rebellion and went into farming and business, and became rich again. One man failed in the examinations but wrote poems; another one passed as *kung-sheng* and also wrote poetry; a third man passed in 1879 and got a position in Hopei and also wrote poems. Finally, one man was so poor that he had to weave; his clan-mates assisted him so that he could try to study.

In gen. 73 we find another poet, and among the young men in this and the following three generations a teacher and a few men in low local administrative offices. The family, in general, showed more interest in military jobs than in others; they stressed poetry and have established a position in irrigation. Since the late 18th century there were a few members who made investments in industry or in business, at least as a side line.

b) *Geographical Mobility*

From their original home in T'ai-ho near Chi-an in Central Kiangsi, the house spread in gen. 53, i.e. the first generation, towards the west: one settlement in Pao-ch'ing, one in Ch'ang-sha, and one in Heng-chou (all in Central Hunan). But two family members went farther west and one settled in Ch'üan-chou (northeast Kuanghsi) and the other in Yung-chou (Kuanghsi). The house has its main name after the founder, and the name Ch'ing-hsiang after the place where this man lived in Kiangsi. It is said that the Kiangsi settlement was the consequence of an office of the founder there.

In gen. 54 no new migration is known; there is no information at all about this generation, a fact which indicates a break in the genealogy. In gen. 55 there is a second migration from T'ai-ho to another settlement in Ch'üan-chou, and three settlements in Ch'üan-chou villages which came from the original settlement there. We also hear of a relative who came to Ch'üan-chou from Ch'ing-chiang in

Kiangsi. This place is north of T'ai-ho, and no settlement of the family there was reported in earlier generations.

The next report is from gen. 57: two settlements in villages near Ch'üan-chou, and two settlements in Kuan-yang (Kuanghsi), not far from Ch'üan-chou. One of the other Kuan-yang settlements (in En-ch'i) was created by a military official in gen. 58. There is a new settlement in gen. 58 in I-ning, by people from Ch'üan-chou, and a settlement in Shao-yang in south Hunan. The migratory tendency in general is towards the southwest, and the creation of settlements in villages, often in clan villages, indicates that most of the settlers were simple farmers.

The next migrations took place in the late 16th century: in gen. 63 a new settlement in I-ning is opened. A branch from I-ning's old settlement settled in Kui-lin. A man migrated to Yung-fu. Kuan-yang opened another settlement near Kuan-yang. And a new place in Ling-ch'uan was acquired. All these places still remain in northeast Kuanghsi. Following the general tendency of these migrations, we find a new settlement in Li-p'u (Kuanghsi) in gen. 66; a new village settlement near Kui-lin in gen. 67. The old Heng-shan branch from Hunan migrated into P'ing-lo (Kuanghsi) in gen. 70. Another village settlement was created in Kuan-yang as late as gen. 72. In this generation we hear that a man who settled in Kui-lin city had come from Fukien, the district of Lien-ch'eng, village Ch'üan-chou [1]. We have no report of a settlement of our family in Lien-ch'eng, although this place is in between the home areas of the Jung-kui and the Lung-yen houses. That a village there should have the same name as the big administrative center Ch'üan-chou is surprising. It would seem much more likely that the emigrant came from Ch'üan-chou, as did so many others.

It is typical of this family to migrate from village to village, to evade cities, to create clan villages, and to follow, basically, rivers and canals, i.e. fertile plains. They did not ever reach the coast.

11. The Lung-yen House

1) *Social Mobility*

This house owed its origin to a Wu Wen-yüan (therefore, it is also called Wen-yüan House). It is said that Wen-yüan's original

---

[1] T. Makino, in *Japanese Journal of Ethnology*, vol. 17, 1952, no. 3, p. 226, mentions that this place is inhabited by Fukienese-speaking people, who came to this area in Sung time as farmers.

Map 7: Migrations of the Lung-yen house

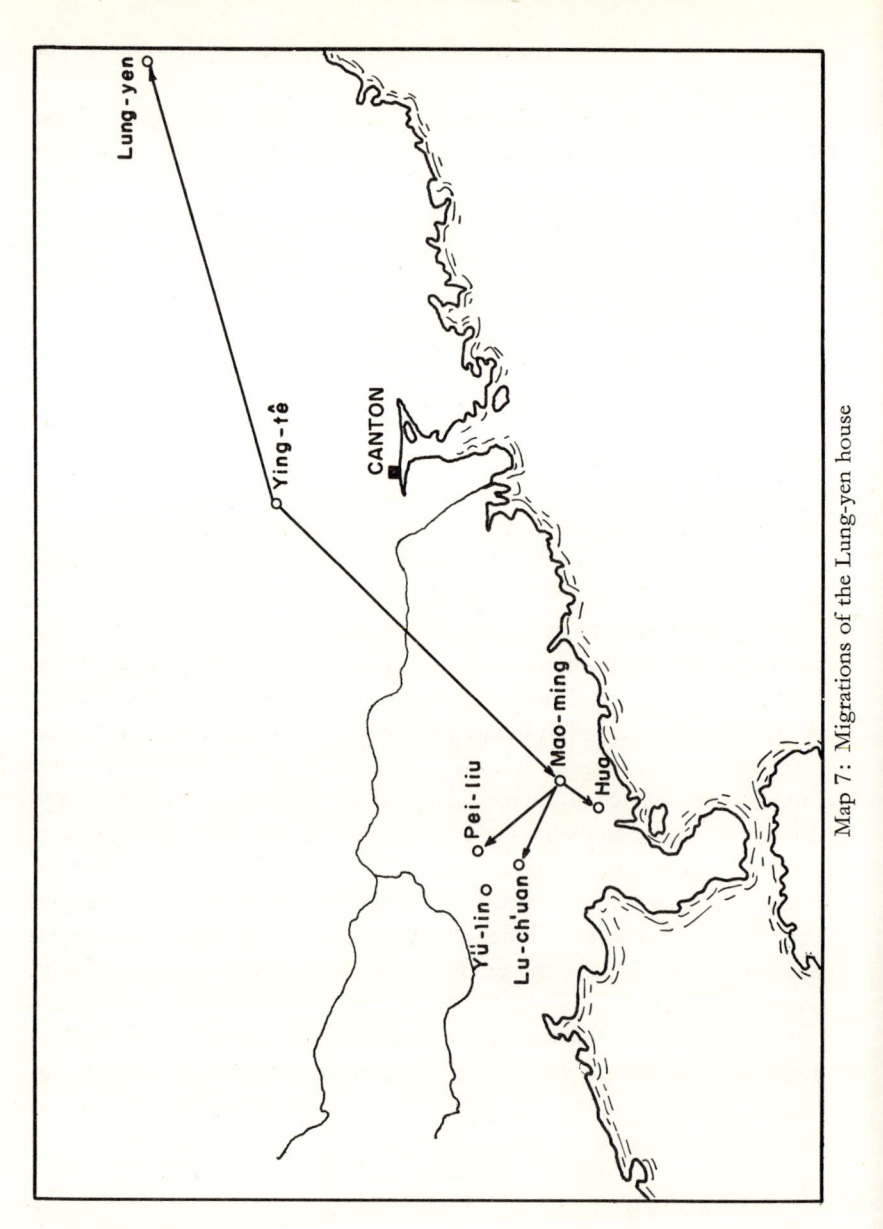

home was in Ying-tê (Central Kuangtung), but we have no record of an earlier settlement there. Ying-tê is on the river down which the ancestors of the whole clan must have gone from Nan-hsiung. It is thus possible that this tradition is correct. Wen-yüan was a *chü-jen* in the early 14th century and served as a magistrate in Lung-yen

(Fukien) (gen. 57). His house got its name from this place. It is indicated that already in gen. 58, a descendant, a student (ca. 1340) settled in Mao-ming (southwest-Kuangtung). His descendant (gen. 59) was also a student (ca. 1370) and later in the Department of Justice at the beginning of the Ming Dynasty.

From then on, there is no information until gen. 67 (early 18th century); one man in the Pei-liu settlement which had been created in gen. 60 by a son of the official in the Department of Justice, had some education. In gen. 68 we then find an essay writer in Pei-liu, and finally in gen. 69 two men who passed the examinations. One of them (who passed in 1744) became educational officer.

In gen. 70 the Pei-liu settlement had two students. One of these (born 1752) failed in the examinations and bought a rank by paying for a war in the South in 1787. A third man got posthumous honors because of his son's rank. In gen. 71 this son, a student, fought in 1857 against the T'ai-p'ing with his own, locally mobilized army. He was honored for this patriotic act, became a magistrate in 1862, helped the poor, punished bad officials and continued to have military interests. A relative got his *chü-jen* degree in 1867; a third one failed the examinations, but was passed because of his filial piety towards his mother. He set up moral rules for his village, helped clan people in wedding and burial costs, assisted widows of his clan and financed a temple.

The next generation (72) in Pei-liu is still involved in the T'ai-p'ing rebellion; four men studied. One of these became a file clerk and essay writer. He was quite wealthy, and defended his home by building, with his own money a fort for defense against the enemy; another clan mate had done the same in 1845. A third man fought the T'ai-p'ing and later became a magistrate, although he had failed in the examinations. In this generation we hear for the first time of a student who passed an examination (*kung-sheng*) in the Hua-hsien settlement of the family.

The gen. 73, some still living, has 13 educated men, nine of whom are from Pei-liu. Five of these Pei-liu scholars studied in the capital (as *Kuo-hsüeh-sheng*), and one in the Han-lin academy. In gen. 74 we again have three important men; one was a *chü-jen* who worked in the Department of History and later as educational officer and magistrate; the second one had a high post in the Central Secretariat (*Chung-shu*).

If we can trust these data, the Lung-yen house reached the status of a gentry family in the Mongol period. In the Ming dynasty it apparently lost its status and became a farming family, until the start of a slow rise from the early 18th century on. The real rise of the family, however, came only in the middle of the 19th century because of their attitude towards the T'ai-p'ing. We have to consider that their home was almost in the very heart of the T'ai-p'ing, and the reports indicate that a resistance against them was difficult and demanded courage. The government showed its appreciation by assisting the members of the house.

2) *Geographical Mobility*

We do not know how or why the son of the founder of the house in gen. 58 was already settled in Mao-ming: there seems to be no logical or geographical connection between Lung-yen in Fukien and this place in the extreme corner of Kuangtung; if we assume that the family formerly lived in Ying-tê, we must assume that the first settler in Mao-ming in its migrations passed right through the center of the Lü-wei and Han-yüan house settlements.

In gen. 60 the settlement in Na-ch'i in Pei-liu (southeast Kuanghsi) was created by a man who came to that place in a military function and who later joined the Department of Justice. In gen. 61, at the beginning of the Ming dynasty (end of 14th century) four new settlements were opened: three in villages in Lu-ch'uan and one in a village in Hua-hsien.

Not until gen. 68 (middle of the 18th century) did the Lu-ch'uan settlement establish a branch in Yü-lin. In gen. 69 four small settlements were opened in Na-ch'i (in Pei-liu district) and others in villages in Hua-hsien. In gen. 70 a new settlement in Pei-liu was opened by settlers from Hua-hsien.

This family seems to have remained from its first settlement around 1350, always in the border between Kuangtung and Kuanghsi provinces; it always settled in villages and avoided cities; it also did not reach the sea or send emigrants overseas.

12. General Conclusions: Migrations and Social Mobility of the Wu Clan

The study of the Wu clan and its traditions reveals that we have no reason to doubt that the clan originally lived somewhere between Anhui and Kiangsi, and that Kiangsi became its early home. It is still unclear whether the individual houses, some of which are Cantonese, others are Hakka and still others seem to be Fukienese-speaking, really all belong to one clan. If this were the case, we would have to conclude: a) that our Cantonese-speaking families developed this peculiarity as a consequence of living in Kuangtung and being mixed with native tribes and are not descendants of sinisized natives; b) that Fukienese-speaking branches of our clan acquired this trait in the period in which they lived in Fukien after their emigration from Kiangsi; c) that Hakka in our clan belong to the same Chinese stock as other families and acquired their peculiarities only secondarily as a consequence of their way of life in out-of-the-way mountain settlements. All these hypotheses are possible and have, in fact, been proposed by others in different connections [1], but we cannot prove them by our data.

Lines of Migration: The analysis of the Wu clan shows that the general tendency of migrations of the clan, if they are all combined, follow the general line of Chinese migrations, the "March to the Tropics" [2]. The line goes from Anhui to Kiangsi. From Kiangsi three of the existing routes have been taken: a) up the Kan river, then east over the mountains into South Fukien [3], from here along the coast farther to the south; b) up the Kan river, then south over the mountains into northeast Kuangtung (Nan-hsiung). From here to the Canton area, then into southwest Kuangtung and into east Kuanghsi; c) up the Kan river, then west into Hunan (Heng-shan, Ch'ang-sha), then farther to the southwest into northeast Kuanghsi, and from here into central Kuanghsi. The first steps in these migrations have generally been taken between 1100 and 1250. The move into Kuanghsi gained impetus from ca. 1400 on. This move has continued into the present time. The individual houses show different patterns of migration and distribution. The real farming families (Ch'iu-kuan

---

[1] For the Hakka, see Lo Hsiang-lin, *An Introduction to the Study of the Hakkas in its Ethnic, Historical, and Cultural Aspects* (in Chinese), Hsing-ning, 1933, 292 pages.

[2] H. J. Wiens, *China's March Towards the Tropics*, Hamden, 1954, 441 pages, studies the main lines of migration. Lo Hsiang-lin, *loc. cit.*, studies the lines of migration into Fukien and Kuangtung in detail and gives maps.

[3] For the Fukien migrations in early time see H. Bielenstein, "The Chinese Colonization of Fukien until the End of T'ang", in: *Studia Serica, B. Karlgren Dedicata*, Copenhagen, 1960, pp. 98-122. His article should be compared with Lo's book. Further study of these migrations will certainly throw new light upon the key position of a number of cities in this area, such as Chi-an (Kiangsi) and Hsin-an (Anhui). These cities were not only centers of business and centers of migrations, but also cultural centers of the greatest importance.

and T'ien-hsiung) moved along the river plains, usually avoiding cities. Hakka families move inland and do not avoid hilly areas. The wealthy landlord-scholar family of the Lü-wei shows a fan-shaped pattern with a strong concentration around the original family home. They seem to have no definite preference other than to remain not too far from the family home. The other landlord/scholar house of the Han-yüan, on the other hand, prefers to move not too far away from the coast.

Form of Migration: The form of the act of migration shows several patterns. Some persons move alone or with their closest family only, while others decide to make the move with friends or in-laws. Still others attach themselves to a larger emigrating group. Often, migrations are made in waves: after one nuclear family has successfully settled, other families follow in the same or in later generations. The form of a migration depends, of course, largely upon the reason for the migration.

Reasons for Migration: The earliest reported migration seems to have been a mass migration in which our Wu clan took part and which was the result of political persecution. Other settlements of farmers in areas inhabited by aboriginal tribes have a "colonial" character: an "underdeveloped area" is taken and put under cultivation. Still other settlements are close to the original clan home and indicate the growth of clan wealth and the need to administer the outlying farms. Officials in the family sometimes acquire land in the places in which they have served, probably because they had an opportunity to get the land easily or cheaply. There is also some movement into cities and towns, often in connection with small business—as one way to get ahead financially if farming showed no hope.

Social Mobility

a) *Family Traditions*: If we look at the houses as a whole, there is a good deal of stability: the An-hai and probably also the Sha-pei houses were connected with business as early as Sung time and still are business families. The Ch'iu-kuan, T'ien-hsiung and Lung-yen houses were always mainly farmers, and their families are characterized today as farmer families. Gentry families such as the Han-yüan and Lü-wei houses, try to stay in the same types of jobs over long periods; in both cases, the houses tried to get educational, provincial jobs. They seem to have shunned military, legal and economic positions.

If members of these houses did achieve higher rank they became magistrates, but again usually in their home areas.

This does not, of course, mean that the houses remained in these occupations over all the 800 years of our study, nor that all members remained in these occupations. There are some ups and down which affect whole houses. The Lü-wei house had a low between 1400 and 1500, the Han-yüan house from 1400 to 1650, and the Lung-yen house from 1400 to 1700. All houses show a rise in status from the early 19th century on. This rise seems to be in connection with foreign trade and its influence.

In general, the home of the house seems always to have been the most important center. In the Han-yüan house, the family home remained the leading one until ca. 1700, and in the Lü-wei house until the 17th century. After this time some of the other settlements began to take over, i.e. to produce important persons and to become the centers of family glory. However, none of the new centers gained any importance in the first generations after its creation; in many cases, it took ten generations before the daughter settlement began to produce important men.

b) *Downward Mobility*; If, as modern research seems to have proved, gentry families are larger than other families [1], these families would produce more than enough sons to fill all high positions which the father-generation had occupied. This would make upward mobility very difficult and would mean that we should find some downward mobility in gentry families. Indeed, we can find a considerable amount of downward social mobility in the development of the Wu clan; in the 249 settlements which the Lü-wei main house created over the last 800 years, and the 41 settlements of the Han-yüan house, many tens of thousands of members of the Wu clan live and many millions lived in these settlements over the centuries, yet most of these settlements never produced any leading personality. In most of these settlements, it seems, we find simple, poor farmers, if not tenants or agricultural laborers, certainly not members of gentry

---

[1] Fr. L. K. Hsu, *Under the Ancestor's Shadows*, New York, 1948, p. 214; *Yenching Journal of Social Studies*, vol. 3, p. 13. Chinese population census reports of earlier times do not count families but households. In most cases and areas, the size of the household always was around five persons, i.e. the normal size of a family, In cases in which the census mentions households with averages over eight, servants and slaves were, probably, included. In T'ang times, the expression "chia-jen" (people of the house) also meant all persons who lived in the household (*T'ang lü su-i*, chapter 8).

families. We have no reason to doubt the assertion of the genealogy that each of these settlements was created by a member of the main house, or a member of a known daughter settlement.

According to traditional values, any move into business by a gentry or landowning family was regarded as a downward move. The first reported case of a move into business in the Lü-wei house was around 1550; the next was around 1650; then more moves followed. Both of the first cases were moves into cities; in both cases, also, the new settlers remained in business over many generations and both seem to have flourished.

c) *Upward Social Mobility*: In spite of the loss of prestige and status which accompanied the move into business of even a poor farm boy, this move may in the long run prove to be one way to upward social mobility. In pre-modern China, a wealthy businessman could buy an official rank and sometimes even, if wealthy enough, get a small government post; simony was always practiced in China in times of financial need [1]. From 1453 on admission to the imperial academy could be bought by contribution of 800 *tan* rice (ca. 100,000 pound). In Manchu times, it cost only 108 *taels* silver (from 1827 on: 120 *taels*) to be admitted as "student". It is reported that around 1830 over 12% of the total provincial income of the province of Kuangtung came from the sale of titles or offices [2]. Even if a merchant could not by himself always get into the bureaucracy, he could by payment for a title open the road for the advancement of his son. If he himself tried to get into the bureaucracy, his best chance was by way of economic positions, for instance, the salt administration— jobs which at the same time held the greatest opportunity for further enrichment.

In the 20th century, access was easier: the businessman could make contributions to the Party (KMT) and he could move up into the leading elite as a party member. Or he could send his son to a foreign university for the study of law or, more recently, political science. The son, then, would be a natural candidate for all kinds of modern government positions. This way up was used by many members

---

[1] For the time of Wang Mang see *Han-shu* 99c, 5a; for the T'o-pa system of simony of 528 A.D. see *Wei-shu* 110: p. 2180c of the K'ai-ming edition; for the tenth century (944) see *Chiu Wu-tai-shih* 83: p. 4305a.

[2] *Nankai Weekly Statistical Service*, vol. 5, no. 12, pp. 49-52. General discussion of the 19th century practices in Chang Chung-li, *The Chinese Gentry*, Seattle, 1955, p. 139f.

of the Wu clan and was one of the main reasons for the high social position of some of its branches in the 20th century.

d) *Overseas Emigration*: Our genealogy does not give as much information on this point as we can get from other sources and studies. Only a few conclusions can be drawn. Our genealogy does not by any means mention all emigrants to foreign countries. Of the more than 70 people of our clan, who are buried in the four Chinese cemeteries at Colima near San Francisco, none is found in the genealogy; yet, by a study of the structure of their names, we can establish the fact that many, if not all, of them belonged to our clan. The 57 persons of our clan, whose tombs are in the Ning-yang cemetery of Colima, all were born in T'ai-shan; the three on the T'an-yin cemetery of Colima came from Chung-shan. The Chinese-Christian cemetery, the oldest of all, has been damaged by a forest fire and only 3 tombs of members of our clan are recognizable, but their home towns are not mentioned. The big Chinese Cemetery of the Six Companies in Colima has 6 Wu tombs; all these persons came from K'ai-p'ing. Tentatively we believe that two of these Wu members in Colima cemeteries belonged to gen. 72 of the Lü-wei house; 4 to gen. 73 and 14 to gen. 74. It seems also that gen. 72 and 73 of the Han-yüan house lived in San Francisco. The San Francisco telephone book of 1910 mentions only 4 Wu and one clan house, one family center; the February 1915 directory still has only 4 Wu names.

The Chinese temple in Marysville, California, has inscriptions and documents that date back to 1869. In these texts, 47 Wu are mentioned, probably all from K'ai-p'ing. They seem to have belonged to the gen. 72-74 of the Lü-wei house. I am informed that there are no longer Wu in Marysville. The temple in Weaverville, Calif., mentions 10 Wu, apparently belonging to the gen. 71-74 of the Lü-wei house and all from K'ai-p'ing. The earliest mention is from 1874, the year in which the present structure was built.

The "Old Kuan-yin Temple" in Rangoon (Burma) mentioned 73 Wu in its inscriptions of 1868 and 1871. While a few seem to belong to gen. 72, most of them are of gen. 73-74 of the Lü-wei house. Only one or two persons each in the inscriptions found in Marysville and Rangoon can tentatively be identified as persons mentioned in the genealogy; but the genealogy does not mention that these persons ever lived in foreign countries. This, unfortunately, is in keeping with the aim of the genealogies which characteristically mention only founders of new settlements or otherwise important persons.

We can establish, however, that the Han-yüan houses which always lived close to the coast, and the Lü-wei houses which also had many settlements close to the coast, did send emigrants overseas from the early 19th century on. The Sha-pei and An-hai houses, on the other hand, although they also always lived close to the coast and the ports, did not emigrate; they were well-settled businessmen in the cities of the coast. The inland houses of T'ien-hsiung and Lung-yen did not emigrate, so far as we now know, while the Hakka house Jung-kui emigrated inland, to Burma. Now that we have established the fact of differing attitudes and traditions in the various houses of the Wu clan, it would be interesting to investigate the degree of social mobility of the Wu emigrants of one, two, or even three generations living in the United States. We attempted such a study by sending questionnaires to all members of the Wu clan mentioned in the telephone books of San Francisco and the Bay Area. The returns were only 8% of the total sent out. Most of these were incomplete, partly because the respondents could no longer write Chinese fluently enough. Two of the persons who answered belonged to the Han-yüan and one to the Lü-wei house. This could be established on the basis of the name of the home village. No one knew the name of his house. The low percentage of returns indicates that a mailed questionnaire is not an adequate method in this case. But it is questionable whether personal interviews would have more success because the Chinese community seems to believe that research about families could be in connection with the Office of Immigration which attempts to track down illegal immigrants.

We hope that it will he possible to make a thorough study of social mobility in one of the communities outside China which could serve as a continuation of this study.

PART THREE

CHANGES IN THE STRUCTURE OF POPULATION

1. Systems of Intermarriage

It now seems necessary to study certain aspects of changes in the structure of the population during the last centuries in order to further clarify some of the problems raised above. As the material from the genealogy of the Wu clan is not sufficient for such inquiries, we have added material from the genealogy of the Jung clan. The Jung clan has its home close by the Wu clan, in Hsiang-shan (Kuang-tung), the home of Sun Yat-sen's family. Indeed, the Jung's even established some marriage relations with this famous family after it became famous. We are postponing a discussion of the general development of the Jung clan, its social status and other peculiarities. We are here merely using the rich data which the Jung genealogy provides: almost 10,000 persons are mentioned, and most of them with information sufficient for valid conclusions.

We know that some Chinese families, especially families in South China, had definite systems of intermarriage; others had no system at all. Our hypotheses are: a) If a family had a definite system of intermarriage, a decrease in the number of "preferential marriages", i.e. marriages with girls from the preferred family or families, would indicate a breakdown of the system and could be regarded as a "modernization". b) Since Sung time, a principle of hypergamy was known [1]: one should take a wife from a family which is slightly lower in status than one's own family; and one should give a daughter to a family with a slightly higher social status. If, therefore, more daughters are given to the "preferred" family than wives are taken from it, it would indicate that the family has a lower social status than the family with which it has marriage relations [2]. Any changes of the relation

---

[1] Wang Hui-chen in D. Nivison, *Confucianism in Action*, Stanford, 1959, p. 87.
[2] P'an Kuang-tan, pp. 92-3, Table 2, has drawn a kind of "sociogram" which shows the marriage relations between 91 gentry families in Chia-hsing (Chekiang) over time. This sociogram shows clearly the eminent importance of the Chu family from Hsiu-ning: it has family marriage ties with the largest number of other families. This type of analysis could be expanded to establish which family was a leading family in an area in a given time provided, of course, that the families of that area did not have a system of preferred marriages.

would indicate change in social status. c) We can expect that in families with an intermarriage system as well as in other "traditional" families most of the marriages take place within the village. An increase of out-of-village marriages then would indicate "modernization".

a) *The Marriages of the Wu Clan*

The genealogy reports on 397 cases of marriage only, and this number includes also the plural wives of some members of the family. Reporting of marriages is very uneven: the An-hai branch enumerated, especially in the later period, all wives of a person, while the Jung-kui and Lung-yen houses rarely report marriages, if at all.

The limited material can, however, indicate some traits: a) The Wu's did not have a strict marriage alliance with a limited number of families. There are 110 different clan names mentioned, from which Wu's have taken their wives, and this may indicate more than 110 different families.

b) Even individual branches of the Wu clan do not seem to have had a marriage alliance of any more permanent kind. We have only 28 clear cases of repeated marriage relations since gen. 50:

In 8 cases father and son took wives from the same family
In 10 cases brothers or cousins took wives from the same family
In 3 cases uncle and nephew took wives from the same family
In 4 cases grandfather or grand-uncle took wives from the same family as grandson
In 3 cases a man took two wives from the same family.

We do not have any data to clarify as to whether the Wu clan had a specific rule as to whom their daughters should marry.

Among the 110 different family names which are mentioned:
51 are mentioned only once
20 are mentioned twice.
10 are mentioned three times.

The most common partners are from the Li 李 (33 cases), Liang 梁 (32), Ch'en 陳 (19), Huang 黃 (19), Chang 張 (16), Ho 何 (16), and Wu 吳 (14) families. We find in this list some families which are usually identified with Fukien province, such as the Lin 林 and Ling 凌, or the Ch'en 陳 and Huang 黃; but all branch houses of the Wu take their wives from these clans. It might seem that the Lü-wei house has some preference for native Kuangtung wives (Punti), the An-hai house more for Fukienese, and the Han-yüan house more for gentry families, but these tendencies cannot be proved. The Lü-wei house seems to have preferred the local Liang 梁 clan as partner.

One more point should be mentioned in this connection. We have seen above that the Wu clan has a history of having immigrated into the Canton area from Nan-hsiung in the late 13th century. Together with them came 34 other clans. We should, *a priori*, expect that the Wu concluded more marriages with these 34 clans than with others who were local people or who came from other areas.

Indeed, our Wu clan members had—according to the limited data at our disposal—intermarriages with possibly 31 of these 34 clans. This fact cannot be established accurately, because there are many Li clans in the area, but only seven of these local Li clans were among the 97 families which constituted the 35 clans. And similarly for all other clans; if we make the daring assumption that *all* wives who were married by our Wu members and who had clan names which occur on the list, we find that over 60% of all reported marriages (239 out of 397) came from such families out of the 34 clans. (Marriage into the 35th clan, the Wu, is prohibited, of course.) And if we take only the marriages of the earlier periods, generations 49 to 63, the percentage of marriages rises to 66% (103 out of 157 marriages). Due to the very incomplete recording of marriages and the impossibility of safe identification of the clans, these calculations do not mean much. They may indicate that indeed the Wu preferred wives from the other 34 clans and that this preference was stronger in the early time than later. But the existence of a clear system of preferred marriages cannot be proved.

b) *The Marriages of the Jung Clan*

The Jung clan has an intermarriage system. The clan broke up into eight "houses" in the early 15th century. Of these houses, houses 3 and 8 died out so early that they are not considered in this study. Houses 1, 4, 5, 6 and 7 have marriage relations with the Yang clan, while house 2 has marriage relations with the Cheng clan. Initially, the Jung clan consisted of two families which belonged to one of two groups of ten families each. Group one contained also two families of the Yang clan. It is impossible, from our material, to differentiate between these two Jung and between these two Yang families. We think, however, that the descendants of the one Jung family established marriage relations with one or both Yang families of their original group, while the other Jung family probably established marriage relations with the Cheng family which did not belong to either of the groups of ten families.

We have arranged our data according to periods I to IV. Period I is from 1600 to 1699, period II from 1700 to 1799; period III from 1800 to 1849 and period IV from 1850 to 1899. The assignment of these groups, however, is made on the basis of generations. The data were arranged—as in the text—according to branch families (6 houses with a total of 19 branch families; 2 other houses extinct) and within the families according to generations. For each generation, the mean date of birth of the men was established. If in any case, the mean date of birth of men of one generation fell between 1600 and 1699, the whole generation was assigned to this period. This system of assignment involves some inaccuracy, because the variations within one generation are often quite wide. But the inaccuracy is not large as was revealed when the exact birth data were used and compared with the calculations according to periods.

The marriage pattern of those Jung houses which got their brides preferably from the Yang is presented in Table 7. There is a steady increase in preferential marriages until the third period; a decrease occurred in the last period.

TABLE 7. PREFERENTIAL MARRIAGES OF JUNG, COMBINED HOUSES 1, 4, 5, 6, 7.

Period	Yang	Group 1	Group 2	Cheng	Outsider	Total number
I	17.0%	27.8%	18.5%	6.2%	30.6%	324
II	32.2%	25.1%	16.6%	4.7%	21.4%	924
III	43.0%	15.7%	15.5%	4.6%	21.2%	586
IV	29.9%	17.4%	18.5%	11.1%	26.2%	940

Marriages with girls from the first group of ten families (to which the Yang's also belong) decreased during the three earlier periods and increased slightly in the post-1850 period; the same is true for the marriages with girls from the ten families of group 2. If these two groups are compared one with the other, one point should be taken into consideration: our statistics are biased in favor of group 1: five of the ten families of group 2 have the same family name as five of the ten families of group 1. In all cases, we have regarded these five families as belonging to group 1 and not to group 2, because it was impossible to find out to which of the two groups a family belonged. Marriage with women of the Cheng clan as well as with any outsiders was relatively frequent in Period I, decreased between 1700 and 1850, but increased again after 1850. The outside women (over-all average 24%) came from a total of 89 families.

The House 2 of the Jung clan married more exclusively women from the Cheng clan (overall average 55.9%) and has only very few marriages with the Yang clan. The tendency to take wives from the Cheng clan increased down to Period III and decreased only after 1850. Marriages with women from outsider families (over-all average 22.5%) increased steadily. Marriage with girls from both groups of ten families decreased steadily until Period III and tended to increase after 1850. The marriages with women from outsider families involved a total of 57 families (Table 8).

TABLE 8. PREFERENTIAL MARRIAGES OF JUNG HOUSE 2

Period	Yang	Group 1	Group 2	Cheng	Outsider	Total number
I	0.4%	17.9%	13.2%	57.0%	11.5%	235
II	0.6%	11.1%	8.0%	57.7%	22.5%	324
III	0.5%	5.4%	2.9%	70.0%	21.3%	207
IV	1.9%	10.6%	12.3%	43.6%	31.6%	310

Table 9, which combines both earlier tables, shows more clearly the slow increase of marriages with outsiders, but also shows the importance of marriages which are contracted within the two groups of ten families. As the Yang clan belongs to the ten families, 55.8% of all marriages over the whole 300-year period were contracted within the two ten-family groups. Outsiders came from 99 different families, with a strong preponderance of the Ch'en family (4.7% average over the whole period; other outsiders, combined, only 18.9%).

TABLE 9. MARRIAGES OF THE JUNG CLAN

Period	Yang	Group 1	Group 2	Cheng	Outsiders	No. of Families	% of Total Families
I	10.0%	23.6%	16.3%	27.6%	22.6%	41	40%
II	24.0%	21.5%	14.3%	18.4%	21.7%	60	60%
III	31.9%	13.0%	12.2%	21.7%	21.2%	52	52%
IV	23.0%	13.4%	17.0%	19.1%	27.5%	79	79%
Totals	23.3%	32.5%		20.6%	23.6%	99	100%

We found information for 24 of these outsider families, the Ch'en family included, indicating that they lived in the same villages as members of the Jung clan. Almost no brides were taken from seven of these 24 families (between 0 and 4 girls per family in 300 years). From Table 10 we see that over the whole period, 60% of all marriages with girls from outsider families were clearly in-village marriages. All marriages of Jung men taken together, 90% of all marriages over the whole period were marriages within the village.

TABLE 10. VILLAGE MARRIAGES

Period	In-Village Marriages	All Outside Marriages	% of In-Village Marriages
I	66	126	52.4%
II	162	271	59.8%
III	111	168	66.1%
IV	206	344	59.9%

Tendencies to change this system begin to appear after 1850, but are still so weak that we would not dare to stress this point. Perhaps the only safe conclusion is that the marriage pattern of the Jung men was stable and was temporarily disturbed only in periods of political revolution such as the 17th century (overthrow of Ming and establishment of Manchu government) and the later part of the 19th century (T'ai-p'ing rebellion). In order to evaluate the data accurately, a certain factor of insecurity should not be overloocked: it is possible that among the Yang, Cheng, and the other families in the two groups certain other families are hidden, which have the same clan name but are from different places. Our source material does not always give exact clues. But if there is such a bias in the data, it would be true for the data of all periods. Although I do not think that this bias is great, it might be that the percentage of marriages with women from the outside is in reality somewhat higher than we have indicated.

How old is this marriage pattern? Our period I which starts with 1600 corresponds to generation 21 of the Jung clan. We have some data covering generations 11 to 20, i.e. roughly the period between 1300 and 1600. For this period, 448 marriages are reported. 275 of these marriages occurred in branches which later had a preference for Yang brides. But in this early period only 10% (28 cases) of the men married Yang girls. The remaining 173 marriages occurred in branches which later had a preference for Cheng women. In this early period their preference for Cheng girls was already almost as strong as in later times: 36% (62 marriages) of their men married Cheng women. These branches, as in later periods, did not marry Yang girls at all; while the Yang-marrying branches had also some marriage relations with the Cheng clan (18 marriages). Although the material is scant, it seems that marriages with women from families of Group 1 may have started before generation 11, i.e. before 1300. Marriage with women of Group 2 started, if at all, not much later. Marriage with Cheng women started in 5 branch houses earlier, in 3 at the same time and in 3 houses later than marriage with Yang women. Neither marriages to Cheng women nor marriages to Yang women are reported before the generations 12 and 13. We can thus say that from about 1400 on, both marriage systems were practised. They have by now a history of over 500 years.

If a family regularly takes its wives from certain families, it should be expected that it also gives its daughters to the same families. This is, indeed, the case. Although the data for the sons-in-law are not as complete as those for the wives, they are extensive enough to allow comparisons (Tables 11 and 12).

TABLE 11. SONS-IN-LAW OF THE YANG-MARRYING BRANCHES OF THE JUNG CLAN

Period	Yang	Group 1	Group 2	Cheng	Other	Total Number of Cases
I	28.6%	34.5%	21.4%	4.8%	10.7%	84
II	42.9%	13.6%	20.1%	6.2%	17.0%	499
III	36.3%	13.4%	19.1%	10.5%	20.7%	507
IV	36.0%	13.5%	17.2%	7.5%	25.5%	400
Totals	38.0%	34.0%		7.9%	20.3%	1490

The branches of the Jung clan which take wives from the Yang clan have, with the exception of the period between 1800 and 1849, always given more girls to the Yang clan than they took wives from them; they gave about as many girls to families of the two groups as they took wives from them; and they gave fewer to the Cheng clan and other outsiders than they took wives from them. This might indicate that the Yang clan had over almost all of the last 300 years a higher social status than the Jung clan. The picture for the branches of the Jung clan which intermarry with the Cheng clan, is almost the same: they gave more girls to the Chengs and even to the Yangs than they took wives from them; they gave about as many girls to members of Groups 1 and 2 as they took from them, and gave fewer to outsiders than they took from them. We can here, too, assume that the social status of the Cheng clan was generally higher than that of the Jung clan.

TABLE 12. SONS-IN-LAW OF THE CHENG-MARRYING BRANCHES OF THE JUNG CLAN

Period	Yang	Group 1	Group 2	Cheng	Other	Total No. of Cases	Number of Families
I	0.0%	14.0%	0.0%	43.0%	43.0%	7	3
II	0.0%	10.4%	4.8%	64.8%	20.0%	125	13
III	1.6%	10.0%	8.3%	64.7%	15.6%	193	13
IV	4.1%	10.5%	12.8%	50.0%	22.7%	172	16
Totals	2.0%	19.1%		59.4%	19.5%	497	29

The combined figures for the whole Jung clan are in Table 13. Here, the picture changes somewhat: the Jung clan as a whole took as many girls from the Cheng clan as they gave, and almost as many from Groups 1 and 2 as they gave. But they took more outside wives than they gave girls to outsiders and they gave more girls to the Yang than they got wives from them.

TABLE 13. THE SONS-IN-LAW OF THE JUNG CLAN

Period	Yang	Group 1	Group 2	Cheng	Others	Total No. of Cases	No. of Outside Families
I	26.4%	33.0%	19.8%	7.7%	13.2%	91	9 (14%)
II	34.3%	12.9%	17.1%	18.0%	17.6%	624	37 (55%)
III	26.7%	12.4%	16.1%	25.4%	19.3%	700	38 (57%)
IV	26.4%	12.6%	15.9%	20.3%	24.8%	572	47 (70%)
Totals	29%	30.2%		20.8%	20.1%	1987	67 (100%)

The total number of families into which daughters were given by the Jung is much smaller than the total number of families from which they took their wives (67: 99), and the circle of families which were selected grew more slowly than the circle of families from which wives were taken (last column in Tables 9 and 13).

The percentage of sons-in-law from outsiders who live in the same village as the Jung (Table 14) is exactly the same as the percentage of wives from outsiders. And again, the most prominent family into which daughters were given and which at the same time did not belong to the Groups 1 and 2 was the Ch'en family (3.8% of all outside sons-in-law). There are 4 families which live in the same villages as do members of the Jung clan, but to whom no daughters were ever given; three of these were also not favored for daughters-in-law.

In conclusion, we can say that the principles according to which brides were selected corresponded closely to the principles according to which sons-in-law were selected. There is some indication that

TABLE 14. VILLAGE SONS-IN-LAW OF THE JUNG CLAN

Period	In-Village	All Outside Families	Percentage of In-Village Sons-in-Law
I	6	12	50%
II	73	110	66.4%
III	80	135	59.3%
IV	79	142	55.7%
Totals	238	399	59.7%

the Yang family as well as the Cheng family had a slightly higher social status than the Jung clan. There is some decline in the number of "preferential" brides, "preferential" sons-in-law and in-village marriages. We would, however, not dare to attribute this change to a process of dissolution of old customs and to "modernization", but rather to political disturbances between 1850 and 1899. Similar disturbances seem to be indicated by our material for the period between 1600 and 1699.

We may add here that, in all these discussions, we considered only marriage with the main wife and omitted all secondary wives (concubines). Secondary wives were taken for individual reasons rather than for family reasons, and the principles of selection were not as strict or formal as with main wives. The percentages of Yang-marrying Jungs who married Yang wives whether as main wives or as concubines is, over the whole 300-year period, 27.7% against 32% for main wives; and the percentage of Cheng-marrying Jungs who married Cheng wives as main wives or as concubines is 51.6% against 56% for main wives. This indicates that concubines were more often taken from families which were not prominent.

2) PLURAL MARRIAGES

The data for the Wu clan are too scant to analyze the question of plural marriages. Plural marriages can be of two types: a) After the death of the main wife, a man may take a second or third main wife. There can always be only one living main wife in a family. b) A man may take one or several secondary wives (concubines)[1]. According to the rules, a man should take a secondary wife only if his main wife is 40 years of age or older and has not yet given birth to a son. But this rule is rarely observed. Wealthy men and men with jobs in the bureaucracy often took concubines at earlier ages. There is a definite correlation between members of the bureaucracy and men with concubines (see Part 4, Chapter 3).

The over-all percentage of concubines in the total number of wives of the Jung clan is 7.7%. There is a definite increase through the years of the percentage of concubines, as shown in Table 15. The

TABLE 15. CONCUBINES OF THE JUNG CLAN

Period	% of Concubines	Total Wives
I	0.7%	547
II	4.8%	1238
III	10.9%	906
IV	11.1%	1321

increase might perhaps indicate that the economic position of the Jung clan from 1800 on was better than in the earlier two centuries before.

The average number of wives per husband, second main wives and concubines all included, remained almost the same over the whole period of 300 years (1.26 wives per husband) (see Table 16). This would seem to indicate that in the earlier periods, men more often took new main wives after the death of the main wife, while later they took more often concubines rather than second main wives.

If on the average 100 husbands have 126 wives, this can have

TABLE 16. NUMBER OF WIVES PER HUSBAND

Period	Number
I	1.16
II	1.22
III	1.35
IV	1.28

[1] According to S. Gamble, *Ting Hsien*, New York, 1954, less than 0.5% of all families had concubines. In our families, the percentage is much higher.

several reasons: a) more girls may have been born than boys. But this is contrary to fact. For we know that there were always more men than women in China. In some areas (especially Fukien) and some periods, female infanticide was practiced [1]. And always, patriarchal and patrilinear Chinese families preferred boys greatly to girls. We can, in such a situation, assume that more care was given to boys than to girls, so that infantile mortality was higher for girls than for boys. Our own material, incomplete as it is (Table 41) does not clearly indicate this; the ratio of daughters to sons is on the average 100: 105 [2]. b) a fairly large number of men may have remained unmarried, while almost all women were married. This hypothesis is difficult to test: we have no data concerning the numbers of married and unmarried women. On the other hand, we have 25.1% men of age 15 and above who had no sons. Four and three-tenths per cent of these had daughters but no sons. But we are not sure whether

---

[1] We cannot cite here the large literature on infanticide. We know that babies were killed for various reasons: a) pre-marital children and children of widows (S. M. Shirokogoroff, *Social Organization of the Manchus*, Shanghai, 1924, p. 108). b) The first child was killed, mainly among the border tribes of China (first documentation *Han-shu* 98, 3b, for the Ch'iang and Hu tribes), because it was often not a marital child. This custom was very common among South Chinese tribes. c) Children born in the 2nd and 5th month of the Chinese calendar and children born in the same month as their parents (*Hou-Han-shu* 95, 4b, for North-West China). Later, only children born on the 5th day of the 5th month were killed (J. J. M. De Groot, *Les fêtes annuellement célébrées à Émoui*, Paris, 1886, vol. 1, p. 320). But we have no proof that the first custom was ever practiced and we know of many men who were born on the fifth day of the fifth month. d) For economic reasons, either because in some periods of history (such as the Han time, according to *Yeh-k'o ts'ung shu* 25.4a), children of age three had to pay taxes, or because the family could not afford more than three children (i.e. two boys, one girl) (*Chien-hu-chi* 6, chapter 3, 3a; *Chung-hua ch'üan-kuo feng-su-chih*, part 1, ch. 5, p. 9). Female infanticide as a social institution is already mentioned by *Han Fei-tzu* (ch. 18, Liu-fan). In some areas all girls with the exception of one were killed (Chêkiang, around 1600; *Ling-nan Wu-shih tsung-p'u* 2a, p. 8b), in others only two girls at the most were raised (Fukien; Sung time; *Hou-tê-lu* 4, 6a and *Chien-hu-chi* 6, chap. 1, 3a).

[2] This ratio is lower than the ratio given by modern surveys. The Ministry of the Interior gave the ratio as 100: 124 in 1927 (Ch'en Ta, *Population in Modern China*, Chicago, 1946), the *Nankai Weekly Statistical Service*, vol. 7, no. 10, p. 49, gave 100: 125 for 1928. G. W. Skinner, "A Study in Miniature of Chinese Population" in *Population Studies*, vol. 5, 1951, p. 96, calculated a ratio of 119.6. Ch'en Ta's own survey gave a ratio of 111, and only for Ting-hsien in North China can a ratio of 106 be calculated (S. D. Gamble, *Ting Hsien*, New York, 1954). In our Taiwan sample the sex ratio is 100: 110. The extremely rich historical material for this problem has not yet been systematically explored. My impression is that for most areas and most of the more recent periods, a ratio of 110 and above would be found.

the remaining 20.8% really had no children at all or only no sons [1]; and we do not know whether they were married or not. We have data on 323 men who died at ages 15 and above and had never been married. This corresponds to some 12% of all men. But a good number of these men died before the normal marriage age and it is likely that just as many girls died before reaching the age of marriage. c) A number of wives may have been married twice, i.e. some of our second main wives or concubines or perhaps even first main wives may have been widows. Some discussion of this problem will follow below. d) Finally, if the age difference between husband and wife is large enough, mortality may have reduced the number of men so much that there are enough or more than enough wives available for them, so that they do not have to remain unmarried even though the number of men may be higher than the number of women in each cohort. The following discussion will show that this may well be one of the contributing factors.

3) Age Difference Between Husband and Wives

Normally, the main wife is some 5 years younger than her husband; but there are cases in which the wife is older than her husband. If we study such cases, we usually find that the man was younger at the time of the birth of his first son than is normally the case, while the wife was as old at the time of the birth of her first son as was normal. The reason, then, for such marriages, was that the family was very eager to have a daughter-in-law who would immediately bear a child [2]. Such considerations play a role in periods of crisis, when it can be expected that the son may meet an untimely death.

---

[1] We have no data on the extent of infertility in China. Tuan Chi-hsien, "Reproductive Histories of Chinese Women in Rural Taiwan", in *Population Studies*, vol. 12, 1958, p. 46, found that about 4% of all women with completed reproductive periods were barren. Our Taiwan data seem to indicate that roughly 10% of all married women at the end of their reproductive period had no children; assuming that in about half of all cases the husband may have been infertile, we come to results which are comparable to those of Tuan.

[2] In the Yeh clan on Formosa the average age difference between husband and wife is 2.9 years for generations 1-8 (n = 99). Generation 8 lived around 1800-1820. In about 20% of all cases, the wife was older than the husband. Huang Tien-ch'üan (in *T'ai-nan wen-hua*, vol. 5, no. 2, 1956, p. 40; the raw data are given on this page and converted by ourselves) in his discussion also explains the older wives as an indication of crisis: poor families take a "live-in daughter-in-law", i.e. a poor girl who in the first years does the work of a servant and later, as soon as the son has reached puberty, becomes his wife. This seems to be a good explanation for many cases.

Table 17 can, therefore, be regarded as an index of crises periods. Husbands born between 1820-1829 were at marriageable age at the time of the Opium War, a definite period of crisis for our area [1].

TABLE 17. PERCENTAGE OF WIVES WHO WERE OLDER
THAN HUSBANDS (JUNG CLAN)

Husband Born	Per Cent
1690-1720	7.5%
1720-1749	6.1%
1750-1779	3.1%
1780-1809	4.9%
1810-1819	4.9%
1820-1829	8.1%
1830-1839	4.3%
1840-1849	4.9%
1850-1859	4.3%
1860-1869	3.6%
1870-1879	6.4%
1880-1889	9.0%
1890-1899	9.7%

We will, from now on, add some recent data to facilitate comparisons with present-day conditions. As it is impossible to get the type of data which we need from Mainland China at this moment, I am using a sample from the small district of T'ao-yüan in Taiwan, collected in 1960 [2]. The sample contains all women born between 1911 and 1946 and their husbands, if they are married. It is taken from 7 wards of the town and contains 4714 women. The data were copied from the local official registers. We are aware of the fact that the Taiwanese population has, for quite a period, lived under conditions which differ from those under which our families in the Kuangtung province lived; according to their origin, most of the T'ao-yüan families are from Fukien, although a number of them came from Kuangtung. But most of them have been so long, often for many generations, in Taiwan that it cannot be assumed that they preserved the attitudes of their old homes, although the T'ao-yüan families

---

[1] In a Yünnan survey (Ch'en Ta, *Population in Modern China*, Chicago, 1946) 11% of all wives were older than their husbands. In Ting-hsien (Gamble, *Ting Hsien*, New York, 1954) 69.2% of all wives were older. This seems, to all our knowledge, an unusually high figure.

[2] Some of the data are published by W. and Alide Eberhard, *Family Planning in a Taiwanese Town*, U. of California, Berkeley, Center of Chinese Studies, 1962, mimeogr.

are, to some extent, conservative. Thus, the data from T'ao-yüan (Taiwan) should not be regarded as data which indicate a straight line of development continuing the line of development studied in this book. They should rather be used to put the data presented by our texts into proper perspective. In T'ao-yüan, the percentage of women who are from one to twelve years older than their husbands is 5.8% (n = 2365).

Over the whole time studied there is a gradual, but slow and irregular decrease in the age differences between husband and wife. While it is 4.4 years now in T'ao-yüan (n = 2365), it was according to the texts some 5.5 years between 1600 and 1699; 5.4 in the 18th century, 5.2 in the first half of the 19th century and 4.9 in the last half of the century [1]. Table 18 gives the more exact data.

TABLE 18. AGE DIFFERENCE BETWEEN HUSBAND AND MAIN WIFE (JUNG CLAN)

Husband Born	Average
1600-1689	5.5 years
1690-1719	5.6
1720-1749	6.4
1750-1779	5.2
1780-1809	4.9
1810-1819	4.9
1820-1829	5.1
1830-1839	5.2
1840-1849	4.9
1850-1859	6.4
1860-1869	5.4
1870-1879	4.8
1880-1889	4.8
1890-1899	4.1

For second or later main wives as well as for concubines, the age differences are much higher. A later main wife is on the average 11.3 years younger than her husband, while a concubine is 18.6 years younger than the husband. As far as the limited material in Table 19 allows us to judge, there has been no change in these attitudes over the last 300 years. The data for the period between 1900 and 1930 are naturally fewer, because many men were too young to have second main wives or concubines who were considerably younger than they themselves were.

[1] Tun-huang data give an average age difference of 5 years (16 cases analyzed; Texts in Niida Noboru, *Legal Documents*, pp. 669-747).

TABLE 19. AGE DIFFERENCE BETWEEN HUSBAND AND SECOND MAIN WIFE AND CONCUBINES

Period	Second Wives, Number	Age Difference	Concubines, Number	Age Difference
I	22	10.78	2	25.50
II	97	10.80	43	19.65
III	114	10.68	92	18.40
IV	129	12.43	125	18.61
V (after 1900)	11	10.46	9	14.67

4) DIVORCE AND REMARRIAGE

It is very difficult to get information on divorces. The Wu genealogy has no data; the Jung gnealogy mentions only 6 cases between 1803 and 1890. In three of these 6 cases, it is indicated that the main wife "re-married" before the death of her husband; in one case it is said that she was "expelled". If more divorces occurred, we do not hear of them. In any case, divorce seems to have been quite unusual [1].

Ideally, a widow should never remarry after the death of her husband; this rule, although valid also for concubines, was never so strictly applied to them.

If a wife were widowed before she reached the Chinese age of 31 (i.e., according to the Western calculation 30) and never married again, she was specially honored as a "chaste widow" at the time of her death. Such honor reflected back upon the family of her husband and raised the social status of his family. Therefore, some pressure was exercised upon young widows not to marry again. On the other

---

[1] There are no modern *statistical* data available (O. Lang, *Chinese Family and Society*, New York, 1946, pp. 217-218; in general H. Lamson, *Social Pathology in China*, Shanghai, 1935, pp. 526-549). Our Taiwan data indicate that 3% of the once married women were divorced. Classical literature mentions a number of cases of divorce, from Chou time on (*Li-chi, T'an-kung*; transl. Wilhelm, p. 269). There were 7 official reasons for divorce (*Ta Tai Li-chi* 13, transl. Wilhelm, p. 248): if the wife had no children, committed adultery, did not serve the in-laws, committed theft, was stricken with certain diseases, or was overly jealous and too talkative. During T'ang time a divorce on the basis of mutual agreement was allowed (Niida Noboru, *Legal Documents*, p. 484). In T'ang and Sung times, special divorce agreements were set up in written form (Niida, *Legal Documents*, p. 62 and 507), but such documents occurred also during the Manchu time (S. M. Shirokogoroff, *Social Organization of the Manchu*, p. 91). A wife could initiate a divorce only if her husband had killed a member of her own clan or if he had cursed her ancestors (Niida, *loc. cit.*, p. 487) or if the husband left her and did not return within the next 3 years (p. 486). In rare cases, she was allowed to take her daughters with her (p. 497), but not her sons.

hand, a widow is a definite burden for a poor family; therefore, in poor families, the pressure toward remarriage was more often strong. A widow who remarried lost her children; they remained in the house of her husband. Emotionally, therefore, remarriage for a widow was a painful step. We may assume that it was more often the family of her husband which pressed for a remarriage than the widow herself.

The fact that "chaste widows", i.e. widows of 30 or less years of age, were specially honored, while older widows were not, indicates: a) that it was more common for a young widow to remarry, and b) that remarriage of widows over 30 was regarded as unusual.

The Jung genealogy reports clearly 42 cases of "chaste widows" whose husbands were born between 1660 and 1843; the fact that no later "chaste widows" are mentioned may simply indicate that at the time of their death, the system of official honor had broken down. Of these widows, only one was 19 years of age when her husband died; 7 were between 20 and 22; 4 between 23 and 25, 21 between 26 and 29, and 9 between 30 and 31. These cases of chaste widows of age 31 are really "borderline" cases. Of the 42 "chaste widows" two were concubines, the others were main wives. Eighteen of these widows had children; the others probably not. To remain a widow with child was certainly easier than to remain alone in the husband's family [1].

The genealogies clearly show their indignation about widows who remarry. If a wife remarried after she had children, her family name is usually mentioned, but never her birth and death dates; if she remarried without having had children, we usually find only the remark "wife remarried". In all these cases, it is, therefore, impossible to find out exactly how old the wife was when she became a widow. On the basis of our earlier discussions, we assume (on the basis of the information given on Table 30) that she was 5 years younger than her husband. Thus, if the husband of a remarrying widow died at an age below 35, she was presumably below 30 years of age when she became a widow; in such a case, she would have become a "chaste"

---

[1] There are no comparable data available for modern China. Tuan Chi-hsien, "Reproductive Histories of Chinese Women in Rural Taiwan", in *Population Studies*, vol. 12, 1958, p. 44 reports for Taiwanese Chinese around 1905 that 6.9% of all wives became widows before the age of 30, and another 9.4% between 30 and 34. Our Taiwan data indicate that about 2% of the married women had remarried after the death of their husbands.

widow, had she not remarried. If the husband was 35 or older at the time of his death, we assume that his wife was 30 or older when she became a widow. In such a situation, she was not expected to remarry. We have information on 186 remarrying widows between 1600 and 1892. In at least 30% of all cases, they had children which they had to give up when they remarried.

TABLE 20. REMARRYING WIDOWS

Period	Number of Cases	(Number of Concubines)	Husband Died When Below 35	Husband Died When 35 Plus	?
1600-99	5	(1)	20%	40%	40%
1700-49	20	(2)	53%	47%	
1750-99	48	(4)	53%	47%	
1800-49	66	(4)	57%	43%	
1850-92	47	(2)	60%	40%	

Table 20 shows that the percentage of older widows decreased. Although, as we will discuss later, the life expectancy of women declined, I think that this decrease can be explained fully perhaps only by assuming a) that the clan reached a higher social status over time, and b), concurrently with this, that the clan stressed Confucian values more than in earlier times. But it should be kept in mind, that this interpretation is highly hypothetical, because it is based upon an assumption (see above).

If a number of widows of men of the Jung clan remarried, and if this—as we assume—is largely a result of poverty of some branches of the clan, we should also assume that a number of poor Jung men marry wives who had been married before. There is no way to find out whether a first wife had ever been married before. Only in some individual cases, we think it is possible. But, normally, to judge from modern conditions, even a poor Chinese will try to marry a virgin as his first wife; after her death, however, if he decided to remarry, he could afford the high bride price only if he was relatively well off. If he were poor, he could probably only marry a widow whose bride price naturally was quite low.

In fact, practically all men who became widowers remarried. Table 21 shows the men who later remarried and their age at the time of the deaths of their wives.

Of the 6 husbands who became widowers between the ages 13 and 19, some were engaged only. The percentages of men widowed

TABLE 21. AGE OF HUSBANDS WHEN THEY BECAME
WIDOWERS (JUNG CLAN)

Period	Below 20	20-24	25-29	30-39	40-49	50-73	Number of Cases
1600/99	0	6%	17%	17%	44%	17%	18
1700/49	0	15%	19%	26%	22%	19%	27
1750/99	0	3%	15%	40%	26%	17%	66
1800/49	2%	16%	11%	39%	19%	12%	145
1850/99	2%	17%	27%	33%	20%	2%	147

at ages 20-24 and 30-39 have remained more or less unchanged, while more and more men became widowers between the ages 25-29 and fewer and fewer after age 40. We may conclude, then, that there was an increasing tendency of those men who became widowers after age 40 either not to take another main wife or to take a concubine only. This, of course, limited the chances of widows of ages higher than 30 to remarry. This tendency also appears in the next analysis.

We now assume arbitrarily that the widower took a second wife a year after the loss of his first wife; such behavior has often been observed for many civilizations, although I do not have statistical proof for it for any period of Chinese history. Such an early remarriage was certainly not practised in *all* cases. We have, for instance, one case in which the wife died nine years before the second wife was born; in one other case, the second wife was one year old when the first wife died. But in the overwhelming majority of cases, the second wife was at the time of the death of the first one at a marriageable age (Table 22).

TABLE 22. THE AGE OF THE SECOND WIFE AT THE TIME OF
THE DEATH OF THE FIRST WIFE

Period	Below 20	20-24	25-29	30-39	40-49	50 plus	Number of Cases
1600/99	6%	28%	6%	33%	20%	6%	18
1700/49	8%	30%	15%	26%	22%	—	27
1750/00	12%	29%	29%	26%	3%	1%	66
1800/49	28%	27%	21%	19%	1%	4%	145
1850/99	47%	34%	10%	7%	2%	—	147

Table 22 shows that after 1750 almost no woman over 41 (assuming that they married a year after the death of the first wife) married a widower. The tendency is clearly to marry younger wives as second wives. From the discussion below it will be seen that most women were married before they reached the age of 25. Those women, then, who married after age 25 and became the second wife of a widower, probably were, themselves, widows who remarried. The table therefore agrees with the earlier Table 20, indicating that remarriage of widows became rarer with time [1]. On the other hand, we can assume that most women at age 20 or less, who married a widower, were never married before. Our widowers, then, increasingly preferred never-married young girls as second wives. This indicates that they must have been economically better off, so that they could pay the higher bride price, and that, at the same time they paid more attention to the rules of Confucianism.

There is, especially after 1800, a large number of women who were between 17 and 19 when the first wife of their future husband died. Assuming that they were married a year after the death of the first wife, the ages between 18 and 20 seem to have been favored ages for their getting married.

On the average, husbands were five years older than their first wives (see Table 30). If, as it seems from the last paragraph, the ages between 18 and 20 were preferred ages for a girl to marry for the first time, then most husbands should marry between the ages 23 and 25. Table 23 shows some data to elucidate this hypothesis. With

TABLE 23. PERCENTAGE OF UNMARRIED MEN IN ALL MEN WHO DIED AT AN AGE BELOW 30

Period	Below 20	20-22	23-25	26-29	Number of Cases
1700-1749	40%	66%	50%	13%	22
1750-1799	60%	22%	18%	17%	49
1800-1849	90%	59%	42%	40%	105
1850/1869	28%	22%	9%	18%	192
Totals:	52%	37%	21%	23%	368

the exception of men who were born after 1850, about 50% of the men in the age group, "below 20" and 20-22 were unmarried and 50% married.

---

[1] *Li-chi, Chiao-t'e-sheng* 3 (Couvreur I, 607; in general see J. J. M. de Groot, *Religious System* II, pp. 744-745) prohibited remarriage. But we know of many cases of remarriage in classical texts. From the Sung time on, Confucians tended to be stricter in their attitudes (Wang Hui-chen in D. Nivison, *Confucianism in Action*, Stanford, 1959, p. 93). But remarriage of poor widows was always condoned (de Groot, *loc. cit.*, pp. 758-761), and is, at least for some parts of modern China, reported as a general custom (*Chung-hua ch'üan-kuo feng-su-chih*, I, ch. 4, p. 13 for Fukien; II, ch. 2, p. 30 for Shensi). For Kuangtung, the province in

From our Taiwan data, we cannot make any direct statements about the age of men at the time of marriage. However, we could determine that the average age of marriage of women was 20.7 years (n = 483). No woman was married before the age of 15 and only one married a month before she became 16. As men are 4.4 years older than their wives in this Taiwanese sample, we can conclude that they were 24.1 years of age when they married.

5) Age of Marriage

The genealogies do not indicate the date of marriage. We can try to determine this date by several methods, all of them inaccurate. One of the ways to determine the age of men at marriage was shown in Table 23. It seemed to indicate the ages between 23 and 25 as the most popular ages for men; for the recent period, however, it seemed to point to an earlier age.

One other, limited, way was to start from the end of the Jung genealogy. The Jung genealogy contains no information later than 1930. We can therefore try to find out who was married by 1930 and who was not yet married. The results are given in Table 24.

TABLE 24. PERCENTAGES OF MEN MARRIED BY 1930 (JUNG CLAN)

Date of Birth	Age in 1930	Percentage of Married Men to All Men	Number
1912	18	2%	1
1911	19	5%	2
1910	20	5%	2
1909	21	15%	7
1908	22	22%	8
1907	23	15%	5
1906	24	31%	11
1905	25	20%	8
1904	26	41%	17
1903	27	22%	9
1902	28	32%	13
1901	29	46%	15
1900	30	53%	23

which our clans lived, it is said that nobody would marry a widow, because they are believed to be always accompanied by the soul of their first husband (*ibid.*, II, ch. 7, p. 97; earliest reference in *Lieh-tzu* 5, 7; transl. Wilhelm p. 55). As our data show, this custom had no basis in fact. Confucians were especially against levirate (Wang Hui-chen, p. 93); yet, since the Manchu time, the laws against levirate disappeared (Ch'ü T'ung-tsu, p. 74 f.), and levirate occurs in present-day villages (Niida, *Chinese Rural Families*, p. 194).

No man, born after 1912, i.e. no man under 17 at the time of the completion of the genealogy was married. Although the data are quite small (for each year, around 40 persons are mentioned), they seem to indicate that only from age 24 on is a larger percentage of men married [1].

We are not able to give the percentage of girls who were married by 1930. But only one girl born in 1917 was married by 1930, i.e. she had been 13 or younger when she was married. Three girls each had been 16 and 17 years or younger when they got married. Only at the ages of 22 and above do we find many girls married.

A third way to calculate the age at the time of marriage is to assume that a year after marriage the first child was born; although this certainly was not always the case, it was clearly desired by both parents to have a child as quickly as possible. Here, again, we meet with great difficulties: a) although the Jung genealogy (for one) mentions a number of children who died at very early age, we believe that not all cases of infant mortality are mentioned. It is, therefore, possible that the son who is mentioned as "first son" may in reality not be the first son, b) the birth date of daughters is never given. Thus, we do not know whether and how many daughters were born before the birth of the first son, c) for the Wu genealogy, the total number of cases reported is too small. If we take these observations into consideration, we can construct the following tables (Table 25 and Table 26).

TABLE 25. AGE OF FATHER AT TIME OF BIRTH OF FIRST LIVING SON (WU CLAN)

Gen. 50-59	21 Cases	33 Years
Gen. 60-69	7 Cases	31 Years
Gen. 70-72	23 Cases	23 Years
Total	51 Cases	24.8 Years

---

[1] This result differs strongly from S. D. Gamble, *Ting Hsien*, New York, 1954, p. 5, who stated that in Ting-Hsien, near Peking, 93% of all men and 79% of all women above the age of 14 were married. Ch'en Ta, *Population in Modern China*, Chicago, 1946, stated that only 10% of the total population of 15 and above were unmarried. On Taiwan the average marriage age in 1906 seems to have been 24 for men and 18 for women; in 1940 it was 22 for men and 19 for women (Tuan Chi-hsien in *Geography and Industries*, vol. 1, no.1, Taipei, July, 1956, p. 47). In a fishing village in North Taiwan men concluded the first marriage at 22.5, women at 18.8 years (*Pa-tou-tzu*, p. 8).

TABLE 26. AGE OF FATHER AT TIME OF BIRTH OF
FIRST LIVING SON (JUNG CLAN)

Period	Number of Cases	Mean Age	Median Age	Modal Ages
1600-1699	165	31.4	30.8	24 (7.3%), 27 (7.3%)
1700-1799	716	31.6	31.0	28 (7.7%)
1800-1849	528	30.9	30.4	26 (8%), 30 (7.2%)
1850-1899	732	29.6	28.9	25 (6.1%), 28 (6%), 30 (6%)
after 1900	60	28.0	—	—
Totals:	2141	30.7		
Taiwan	1920	26.9	25 years	23 and 25

In both tables, the most recent data are distorted, because many men were still quite young when the genealogies were written and many who might have married at later ages were not included. Thus, the age was unduly depressed. Otherwise the tables show closely related results; the age of the father at the time of the birth of his first living son was always over 29 [1]. There is a decrease of the age over the last 300 years: fathers now are younger than in earlier times. The changes which have occurred can be more clearly seen in the following table (Table 27). Here, it is obvious that the percentages of fathers below 25 are steadily increasing, while the percentages of fathers of 35 and above are similarly decreasing. Even in the middle group between 25 and 35, the shift is towards a lower age.

TABLE 27. AGE OF FATHER AT TIME OF BIRTH OF FIRST LIVING SON,
ACC. TO AGE GROUPS (JUNG CLAN)

Period	Below 20	20-24	25-29	30-34	35-39	40 and over	Number
1600-1699	0.6%	16.4%	27.3%	28.5%	11.5%	15.8%	165
1700-1799	1.3%	13.1%	30.9%	25.9%	16.2%	12.8%	716
1800-1849	2.1%	13.8%	31.4%	27.5%	14.4%	10.8%	528
1850-1899	4.1%	22.7%	29.5%	23.3%	10.8%	10.0%	732

[1] It may be remarked that the early Tun-huang texts do not contain enough data for such calculations (W. Eberhard, "Notes on the Population of the Tun-huang Area", in *Sinologica*, vol. 4, 1954, p. 81); the data for T'ang and Sung times (as reported by Niida, *Legal Documents*, pp. 144 to 747; 28 cases) show an average of 29.6 for men and 25.7 for women. The similarity with our data is surprising. Modern studies report 17.6 years as mean marriage age for women (Ch'en Ta, *Population*).

In a similar way, we can study the age of the mother at the time of the birth of her first son, but we have data only for the Jung clan (Table 28).

TABLE 28. AGE OF MOTHER AT TIME OF BIRTH OF FIRST LIVING SON (JUNG CLAN)

Period	No. of Cases	Mean Age	Median Age	Modal Ages
1600-1699	133	26.2	24.4	24 (10%), 25 (10%)
1700-1799	632	25.3	24.9	22 (10%)
1800-1849	482	25.3	24.9	21 (10%)
1850-1899	665	24.1	22.4	20 (10%), 22 (10%)
(after 1900	61	23.9)	—	—
totals	1912	25.0	—	—
Taiwan	2161	22.8	21.5	20

Here, too, women are younger in recent times at the time of the birth of their first recorded son than in earlier times. The shift can be more clearly seen in Table 29:

TABLE 29. AGE OF MOTHER AT TIME OF BIRTH OF FIRST LIVING SON, ACC. TO AGE GROUPS

Period	Below 20	20-24	25-29	30-34	35-39	40 plus	Number
1600-1699	10.0%	36.9%	35.6%	15.1%	9.0%	3.8%	133
1700-1799	11.4%	39.6%	28.5%	14.3%	4.7%	1.6%	632
1800-1849	11.2%	40.3%	26.8%	15.6%	4.6%	1.7%	482
1850-1899	18.6%	43.8%	21.1%	10.7%	4.5%	1.4%	665

In is interesting to compare the age difference between father and mother at the time of the birth of their first son with the age difference between the husband and his wife, calculated on the basis of their birth dates (Table 30). The similarities between the two sets of data

TABLE 30. AGE DIFFERENCE BETWEEN HUSBAND AND WIFE (JUNG CLAN)

Period	Difference in Birth Data	Difference at Time of Birth of Son
1600-1699	5.7	5.20
1700-1749	5.6	{6.28}
1750-1799	5.3	{ — }
1800-1849	5.0	5.59
1850-1899	5.1	5.49
(after 1900)	—	(4.05)
Averages	5.2	5.6
Taiwan	4.4	4.1

are great, and might be even greater if the periods of comparison were cut into smaller units; for instance, for the years 1720-1749 the difference in birth dates is 6.4 years, and for 1870-1889 it is 4.8 years. The first date comes close to the 6.28 years of the difference in ages at the time of the birth of the first son; the second date makes the low difference after 1900 more understandable.

Let us now study the age of the parents at the time of the birth of the second son. For the Wu clan, we have only 23 cases, mainly from the most recent period. On the basis of these few cases, the father was 30.0 years old at the age of the birth of the second son, i.e. some 7 years older than at the time of the birth of the first son. The material for the Jung clan, on the other hand, is fairly extensive (Table 31).

TABLE 31. AGE OF PARENTS AT THE TIME OF BIRTH OF SECOND SON (JUNG CLAN)

Period	Age of Father	Age Difference First/Second Son	Age of Mother	Age Difference First/Second Son
1600-1699	36.70 (n: 96)	5.28	30.97 (n: 74)	4.75
1700-1799	36.94 (n: 403)	5.34	30.42 (n: 344)	5.10
1800-1849	35.88 (n: 313)	4.95	26.65 (n: 260)	4.31
1850-1899	34.46 (n: 455)	4.90	28.20 (n: 367)	4.13
(after 1900)	32.04 (n: 29)	4.06	27.88 (n: 26)	3.95
Averages	35.69 (n: 1296)	5.04	29.45 (n: 1071)	4.52

The difference between the father's first and second son and the mother's first and second son should be the same; but it should be taken into consideration that the age at the time of the birth of the first son was calculated on the basis of all parents, including those who had only one son; the second calculation, therefore, does not include the same parents. The table shows, however, several points clearly: a) even though we have to assume that on the average there will be at least one daughter between the first and the second son, and that there may be one or even more unregistered babies between the first and the second son who died in earliest childhood, children were spaced [1]. b) The age of the parents at the time of their second son decreases in the last 300 years even slightly more than the age of parents at the time of the birth of their first son has: children came not only earlier but also followed one another more quickly. c) In the 18th century fathers (but not mothers) had their sons slightly later than in the 17th century. This might indicate that in the 17th century, because of the insecurity of the times (change of dynasties), some men married earlier than they would otherwise have, in order to be sure to have a son. With settled times, in the 18th century, they preferred to wait.

If between the first and the second sons the time difference is some 5 years we can very tentatively say that parents were 2.5 years younger at the time of the birth of their first child than they were at the time of the birth of their first son. This would give us 27.5 years for fathers and 22.5 for mothers. Ideally, then, the average marriage could be around 26 for men and 20 for women. These data, however, should be regarded as very hypothetical. Our Taiwan data give the distance between first child and first son for both parents as only 1.3 years. Our Jung clan data seen to indicate a higher marriage age than the marriage age tentatively calculated with the other methods above. The main and most important finding is that Chinese did not have their children at unusually early ages, and that the age at childbirth has been decreasing over the centuries. We would like to remark here that the material found in genealogies could be subjected to still further studies. In the case of intermarriage systems for instance, a detailed study of cross-cousin marriages could easily be made. Here, we wish to indicate only two areas of research. The Jung genealogy gives not only the year of birth, but also the day and month of birth. In a test run (n: 635) we found that more than the expected number of births occurred in the 8th to tenth Chinese months, and less than the expected number in the second and third Chinese months. This indicates that more pregnancies occurred during the winter months (January to March) and fewer during the oppressive heat and moisture of summer [2]. A similar test run (n: 439) for the

---

[1] If we assume that there was always a girl between the first and the second son, we would have an interval of 2.5 years between each two children. Tuan Chi-hsien, "Reproductive Histories of Chinese Women in Rural Taiwan" in *PopulationStudies*, vol. 12, 1958, p. 48 reports the interval in modern Taiwanese-Chinese families as 2.7 years.

[2] According to Ch'en Ta, weddings occur normally between November and February and therefore more births took place in the winter (Ch'en Ta, *Population*).

months of death did not lead to a clear result, but we believe that possibly a full-range study might show that the death rate in certain months is higher than in others.

A second area of research is the study of twin births. As no birth data for daughters are given, no study of twins of different sex or of female twins can be made. But a study of male twins might still be rewarding. Folk belief regards the birth of twins as an unlucky event [1] and the birth of triplets as extremely unlucky [2]. Although the Jung genealogy mentions twins in 1624, records of twin births become more common only after 1825 (10 cases between 1826 and 1927). The information which we have thus far is not extensive enough to allow the conclusion that a change in the attitude towards twins has occurred in the 19th century.

6) Duration of a Generation

If we define, as the genealogies do, a generation as *all* sons born by all fathers, a generation naturally is longer than the time between father and first son. We have calculated the mean date of birth of all fathers and compared it with the mean data of birth of all sons. In the Wu clan, the duration of a generation in this sense is 33 years for the generations 50-59 and 31 years for the generations 60-69. The results for the Jung clan (Table 32) with its much richer material, are similar: the duration of a generation became shorter over the

TABLE 32. Duration of a Generation (Jung Clan)

1600-1699	35.03 years
1700-1799	34.31
1800-1849	32.96
1850-1899	27.37
Average	33.3

This is confirmed by our study. Classical texts (such as the *Po-hu-t'ung*, quoted in *T'ai-p'ing yü-lan* 541, 5a) state that marriage should take place in the Spring, but according to the Chinese calendar, the first month of the year is the first month of Spring and the first month began during the period in question between late January and late February. The custom is, therefore, quite old.

[1] J. Frick, in *Anthropos*, vol. 50, 1955, p. 690. If the twins were of different sex, they were even more feared. The main problem of twins of the same sex for Chinese is to determine which one is the older one, because in the hierarchically structured Chinese family no two persons can be of absolutely the same rank.

[2] According to an old popular belief of the first centuries A.D., triplets should not be kept (*Feng-su-t'ung*, quoted in *I-lin* 4, 1b). We found no cases of triplets.

last 300 years—another indication that men had their children at earlier ages. The duration of a generation after 1850 refers to one single generation only and is, therefore, not very reliable [1].

Within the individual families of the Jung clan, the duration of a generation differs. The clan split into 8 houses in generation 11; as already remarked, two houses quickly died out. The remaining houses split again in generation 16. By the beginning of the 17th century, there were already marked differences between different houses and families, and these differences had a tendency to increase over time, as shown in Table 33, which shows the mean year for each generation in each family. As already stated, these data are the basis for our large periods, if not otherwise indicated.

We will later see that there is some correlation between social status and duration of a generation: in general, the higher the social status of a family, the shorter the duration of a generation [2].

7) Life Expectancy

We cannot calculate the average life expectancy, mainly because the data for infantile and juvenile mortality are not complete enough (see below). We can, however, make some statements which have a relatively high degree of reliability. The genealogies mention for the earlier times with full data only such persons who achieved an age of 15 or above. For persons who died earlier, only the names are mentioned. From about 1800 on, juvenile deaths are more often mentioned, but not always. We can assume, therefore, that information on persons who reached the age of 15 or above, is fairly complete, and we can calculate the mean age at death of such persons. The Wu genealogy offers only 167 dates, and the majority of these is for the latter part of the 19th century. Such late data may be distorted because some very old persons may still have been alive at the time of the completion of the genealogy and, therefore, the mean age (Table 34) may be distorted. The data for the Jung genealogy are quite extensive; information for 2697 men who were born before

---

[1] Classical texts define a generation as 30 years (*Shuo-wen* 3a, 2b). In his analysis of leading families of Chia-hsing (Chekiang) P'an Kuang-tan, *l.c.*, p. 95, found that the average length of a generation between about 1400 and 1850 was around 26 years. His analysis is, however, not based upon a thorough study of all data.

[2] S. Gamble, *Ting Hsien* (pp. 42-43) also pointed out that wealthier families marry earlier and poorer families postpone marriage; earlier marriage means, on the average, earlier children and shorter duration of a generation. In Ting-hsien, according to Gamble, girls marry at 17.5 years.

TABLE 33. MEAN YEAR OF EACH GENERATION OF EACH HOUSE OF THE JUNG CLAN

Period	gen.	1	2	3	4	5	6	7	8	9	10	11	12	13	14	15	16	17	18	19
I	20	—	—	—	—	—	1616	1590	—	—	—	—	—	—	—	—	—	—	—	—
	21	—	1667	1625	1639	1642	1651	1617	—	—	1667	1658	1664	1692	1699	1622	1638	1639	1621	1636
	22	1645	1684	1654	1683	1686	1681	1670	—	—	—	1697	—	—	—	1658	1675	1679	1657	1695
	23	1686	—	1682	—	—	—	1688	—	1655	—	—	—	—	—	1689	1695	—	1690	—
	24	—	—	—	—	—	—	—	—	1698	—	—	—	—	—	—	—	—	—	—
II	22	—	—	—	—	—	—	—	—	—	1704	—	1702	1730	1739	—	—	1710	—	—
	23	—	1718	—	1709	1716	1710	—	—	—	1738	1733	1711	1764	1775	—	1716	1745	1732	1720
	24	1723	1754	1722	1748	1752	1760	1726	—	—	1768	1765	1763	—	—	1724	1749	1772	1769	1747
	25	1751	1791	1762	1781	1784	1794	1755	—	1730	—	1796	1773	—	—	1758	1780	—	—	1786
	26	1787	—	1791	—	—	—	1788	—	1765	—	—	—	—	—	1796	—	—	—	—
	27	—	—	—	—	—	—	—	—	1798	—	—	—	—	—	—	—	—	—	—
III	24	—	—	—	—	—	—	—	—	—	1801	—	—	1800	1815	—	—	—	—	—
	25	—	—	—	—	—	—	—	1828	—	1836	1832	1817	1836	—	—	—	—	—	—
	26	—	1823	—	1817	1814	1833	—	—	—	—	—	—	—	—	—	—	1809	1802	1820
	27	1824	1838	1832	1845	1846	—	1830	—	—	—	—	—	—	—	1828	1814	1846	—	1847
	28	—	—	—	—	—	—	—	—	1837	—	—	—	—	—	—	1847	—	—	—
IV	25	—	—	—	—	—	—	—	—	—	—	—	—	—	1853	—	—	—	—	—
	26	—	—	—	—	—	—	—	—	—	—	—	—	1864	1884	—	—	—	—	—
	27	—	—	—	—	—	1863	—	1866	—	1863	1872	1851	1892	—	1866	1882	1875	1857	—
	28	1853	1862	1867	1878	1890	1891	1859	1896	1859	1891	1892	1883	—	—	1887	—	—	1896	1894
	29	1873	1881	1899	1894	—	—	1889	—	1885	—	—	—	—	—	—	—	—	—	—
	30	1898	—	—	—	—	—	—	—	—	—	—	—	—	—	—	—	—	—	—
V	27	—	—	—	—	—	—	—	—	—	—	—	—	—	1909	—	—	—	—	—
	28	—	—	—	—	—	—	—	—	—	—	—	—	1911	—	—	—	—	—	—
	29	—	1907	—	—	1915	—	—	—	—	1908	1906	—	—	—	—	1902	—	—
	30	—	—	—	—	—	—	—	—	—	—	—	—	—	—	1908	—	—	1912
	31	—	—	—	—	—	—	1912	—	1927	—	—	—	—	—	—	—	—	—	—

1869 and for 2323 of their wives are given. Tables 34, 35, and 36 give the resulsts of our analysis [1].

TABLE 34. AVERAGE AGE AT DEATH OF MEN AGE 15 OR ABOVE (WU CLAN)

Gen. 50-59	33 cases	60.8 years
Gen. 60-69	24 cases	58.2 years
Gen. 70 plus	110 cases	46.8 years
	167 cases	51.2 years

TABLE 35. AVERAGE AGE AT DEATH OF MEN AGE 15 OR ABOVE (Jung Clan)

1600-1699	61.1
1700-1749	56.2
1750-1809	53.9
1810-1869	50.8
Average	53.3 years; decrease 10.3 years

TABLE 36. SPECULATED AVERAGE AGE AT DEATH OF WOMEN AGE 15 OR ABOVE (JUNG CLAN)

1600-1699	62.0
1700-1749	60.7
1750-1809	58.7
1810-1859	55.7
Average	58.0 years; decrease 6.3 years

For the wives, we had to use the year of birth of their husbands, not their own birth year. It has to be taken into consideration that

---

[1] An analysis of data from Chinese Central Asia from the time between 500 and 750 gave an average age at death of 64 years (W. Eberhard, "Notes on the Population of the Tun-huang Area" in *Sinologica*, vol. 4, 1954, p. 78). In the Yeh clan on Formosa, the average age at the time of death was 50.3 years among 105 males above 14 years of age in generations 1-9 (generation 9 lived around 1850). These date are calculated in a rough way on the basis of Huang Tien-ch'üan (in *T'ai-nan wen-hua*, vol. 15, no. 2, 1956, p. 45): we took his categories 20-30, 30-40 and changed them into averages of 25, 35, etc.; his category "below 20" was understood as 15, and his category "above 90" as 95, although the one average is certainly too low, the other too high. These approximations may have influenced our average of 50.3 years; the actual average may be slightly lower. In general, such a low average may be the result of the unhealthy climate and unsafe conditions which prevailed in Formosa before 1850.

main wives were, on the average, some 5 years younger than their husbands, and secondary wives and concubines, taken together, some 14 years younger. For this reason, we ended the survey with wives whose husbands were born before 1860. The Wu genealogy contains dates for a total of 22 wives over the whole period; they preferred to mention mainly wives who reached a very high age and were, therefore, specially honored by the government.

It may be interesting to give a more detailed break-down for the changes in the Jung clan, in order to show the regularity of the decline, as well as the influence of the T'ai-p'ing rebellion, upon the tendency of the curve. In Table 37 we have adjusted the data for

TABLE 37. AVERAGE AGE AT DEATH OF MEN AND WOMEN OF AGE 15 AND ABOVE (JUNG CLAN)

1600-1699	61.1	62.0
1700-1719	57.7	62.3
1720-1749	56.7	60.0
1750-1779	54.8	59.2
1780-1809	53.1	58.3
1810-1819	52.2	57.8
1820-1829	52.7	56.0
1830-1839	48.2	56.9
1840-1849	51.6	53.3
1850-1859	(49.9)	(54.2)
1860-1869	(50.6)	—

men born between 1850 and 1869 and for their wives; as by 1930 some of these men and women probably were still alive, we adjusted the data by adding to them the same percentages of very old people as we found in the preceding period. By doing so, we may have come out with an average death age which is slightly too high, because the percentages of very old people show over the last 300 years a tendency to decrease. Yet, we think that the error is not too high.

If we examine the data in more detail (Tables 38 and 39), we see that the decrease in longevity is really the result of more deaths at younger ages (below 40) and concomitantly the fact that fewer people reached a high age. Admittedly, these conclusions, based as they are on a study of only two clans, can hardly be used for generalizations. However, a study for Chung-shan, an area in which many of our clan members lived, and which covers the period between 1365 and

1914 [1] also showed that mortality was on the increase, and that after 1599 it was higher in China than in England. Life expectancy at birth in the early 20th century in China has been calculated as 34.85 for males and 34.63 for females [2] and at 40.7 or 40.1 for persons who had reached the age of 20 [3].

TABLE 38. PERCENTAGES OF MALE DEATHS, ACCORDING TO AGE GROUPS (JUNG CLAN)

Age Groups	1600-1699	1700-1749	1750-1799	1800-1849	1850-1869
15-19	0.42	0.52	1.13	2.04	2.72
20-24	0.00	3.41	1.77	4.90	6.00
25-29	2.52	2.88	5.16	5.82	4.26
30-34	2.52	3.15	6.13	7.35	9.11
35-39	5.03	5.76	6.94	7.65	7.37
40-44	5.86	8.64	7.58	8.47	7.95
45-49	5.03	9.95	8.87	9.19	9.50
50-54	9.62	12.31	11.62	8.98	8.14
55-59	10.46	7.59	11.94	9.80	8.92
60-64	12.97	13.10	10.33	10.21	
65-69	13.39	12.05	9.37	7.55	
70-74	14.23	7.59	7.42	7.55	(36.0%)
75-79	8.40	4.97	6.13	5.92	
80 plus	9.62	8.12	5.66	4.49	
Number of Cases	239	382	620	980	516 (adj. from 489)

A comparison of Tables 38 and 39 shows that death during childbirth took its toll among women between the ages 20 and 30, but that women who survived the age of childbirth, lived much longer then their husbands.

---

[1] *Nankai Weekly Statistical Service*, vol. 5, 1932.

[2] G. F. Winfield, *China; the Land and the People*, New York, 1948, pp. 105-106. According to him, the yearly death rate is 27.1. On Formosa, the death rate has been calculated at 31.0 for the period 1906-1915 and at 16.1 for the period 1950-1952 (Chang Te-tsui, *Agricultural Economics in Taiwan*, mimeogr. Taipei, 1960). On the other hand, a 1959 survey of villages in Taiwan found a yearly death rate of 7.4 (*Second Socio-Economic Report on Rural Taiwan*, ms, chapter 2), while at the same time the city of Taipei claimed the lowest death rate ever, 0.48% (*China Post*, Feb. 9, 1960).

[3] Ch. L. Chang, *Chinese Gentry*, Seattle, 1955, pp. 96-97. On Formosa life expectancy for men who had reached an age between 15-19 years was 30 years in 1906 and 41.7 years in 1939/41; for women the ages were 34.2 and 47.1 (Tuan Chi-hsien in *Geography and Industries*, vol. 1, no. 1, Taipei, July, 1956, p. 46).

TABLE 39. PERCENTAGES OF FEMALE DEATHS, ACCORDING TO AGE GROUPS (JUNG CLAN)

Age Groups	1600-1699	1700-1749	1750-1799	1800-1849
15-19	0.87	1.43	0.83	2.04
20-24	2.63	2.00	3.16	4.58
25-29	3.49	2.86	5.82	4.58
30-34	1.75	4.00	3.99	6.31
35-39	4.81	3.43	5.65	5.81
40-44	4.81	6.57	7.15	6.42
45-49	4.81	4.29	5.65	6.11
50-54	7.43	7.43	6.32	7.84
55-59	9.20	10.30	9.31	7.74
60-64	8.30	10.57	9.81	8.45
65-69	15.28	12.00	10.63	9.47
70-74	13.11	12.29	9.48	9.47
75-79	9.61	10.30	9.15	11.10
80 plus	14.51	12.57	13.13	10.08
Number of Cases	229	350	602	982

The critical problem, of course, is the mortality of persons younger than 15. Table 41 shows a row "Early death" which shows that on the average 11% of the persons (all male) mentioned died before reaching the age of 15 [1]. The low percentage for the period between 1600 and 1699 can be explained by the high percentage of "unknowns": we are quite sure that most of the "unknowns" were persons who either died at an early age or had no sons. If the "unknowns" are reduced to a number comparable to that of the later periods and redistributed among the categories of "early death" and "no sons", both items in the early period become quite similar to the same items in later periods. Yet some 11% of infant and child mortality is certainly much less than we should expect. From the fact that from after 1800 the Jung genealogy occasionally gives the full life data even for persons who died early, we can conclude that "early death" means not all infantile and child mortality, but only mortality of males who had lived at least one year and less than 15 years. This would correspond to an attitude which is widely spread in Asia, namely that nobody really counts a baby before it has reached

---

[1] In the generations 1-9 of the Yeh clan in Formosa in 45.20% of all known cases the men died "at young age" (*yao*), i.e. before the age of 15. This is an unusually high percentage and may reflect the hygienic conditions of the island at that time. (Data according to Huang Tien-ch'üan in *T'ai-nan wen-hua*, vol. 5, no. 2, 1956, p. 45. Number of cases 189).

its first full year. If this is true, we should add to the 11% something like 24% for the first year of life [1] and then may hypothesize that about 35% of all males died before they reached the age of 15. Such speculations are, however, highly hypothetical, because we have no way of determining whether the mortality rate for children during their first year was always as high as 24%. The stability of the figure of 11%, on the other hand, is surprising.

8) The Number of Children

Only for the Jung clan, we have some data on fathers who had no sons (Table 41): after 1800 over 30% of all those males who could have become fathers (i.e. who had reached the age of 15 or above) had no sons. Unfortunately, we do not always know whether they perhaps had daughters, though they had no sons; we believe that our row "no sons, but daughters" does not include all such cases and we are afraid that some of the men who had "no sons" had daughters. The majority of these, however, probably had no children at all. According to Confucian standards, every father should have at least one son, so that the ancestral offerings could be given after his death. The fact, then, that almost a third of all men of marriageable age had no sons (either never had any or, at least, never had any who survived the first year) is surprising. Even if we take some under-representation into consideration, the number of potential fathers who had no sons seems to have increased over the last 300 years. One of the reasons for this was certainly the gradual increase of men who never married. We found between 1600 and 1899, 323 men over 15 in the Jung clan of whom we are certain that they were never married, and 40% of these were over 30 years old when they died. But also the percentage of men who were married and had no sons increased over time. If we first study those men who we know had at least one son (called "sons of actual fathers", Table 41), we find that they had just over 2 sons on the average; the number of their children is slowly increasing over time [2]. The

---

[1] G. F. Winfield, *China, the Land the People*, New York, 1948, pp. 105-106. Ch'en Ta, *Population*, gives an estimate of 27.5%. The actual birth rate for China is unknown. Ch'en Ta quotes P. Buck who gives the rate as 42.2, C. M. Chiao with 35.7, and a partial census from Yünnan with 24.9; S. Gamble, *Ting Hsien* p. 46 gives 40.1. Taiwan data are between 39.9 and 46.8.

[2] This would mean, that they had a total of slightly over 4 children. It is not known how many children are born by a mother in modern China. Tuan Chi-hsien, "Reproductive Histories of Chinese Women in Rural Taiwan", in *Population*

small decrease in period IV (1850-1899) has its main reason in the fact that by the end of the compilation of the Jung clan genealogy (1930) not all fathers born before 1899 had already had all their sons. In actuality, there was no decrease in period IV. This result is confirmed by the data which the Wu genealogy supplies (Table 40).

TABLE 40. AVERAGE NUMBER OF SONS OF PARENTS WITH ONE OR MORE SONS (WU CLAN)

House	gen. 50-59	gen. 60-69	Total
Ch'iu-kuan	1.63		1.84
Han-yuan	2.48		2.48
Lu-wei	2.10		2.17
Sha-pei		1.88	1.93
Ch'ing-hsiang		2.25	2.24
Lung-yen		2.16	2.87
Others			1.77
Averages	2.09	2.16	2.19

Here, too, the number of sons of actual fathers shows an increase, and for the 19th century the numbers are almost identical. In this table, the column "total" includes all known cases over all periods; it is, therefore, slightly higher than the individual columns. This table also shows that different houses have different birth rates. This

---

Studies, vol. 12, 1958, p. 50 came to the conclusion that Taiwanese Chinese women had on the average 7.1 children. (We found 6.1 children on the average). He gives the size of the family (not the household) as 7.6 (p. 47). A comparison of both data seems to indicate a fairly high infant mortality, if we assume that most families will have a father and one mother. The data concerning the size of the family represent certain difficulties as not always a biological family, but sometimes a household may be meant. This must be kept in mind when the greatly varying estimates are compared. For example, a small Yünnan community had an average size of 4.6 persons (G. W. Skinner, "A Study in Miniature of Chinese Population" in *Population Studies*, vol. 5, 1951, p. 100), Ch'en Ta, *Population in Modern China*, Chicago, 1946, calculated a Chinese average of 4.84. An estimate for South China in 1930 came to 4.9 (*Yenching Journal of Social Studies*, vol. 3, p. 13) and for an all-China average of 5.2. The North-China average was calculated in the 1920's as 5.24 (*China Internat. Famine Relief Commission*, Pub. Series B, no. 10, 1924, p. 14). Fr. L. F, Hsü, *Under the Ancestor's Shadows*, p. 113, found in Yünnan an average of 5.3. Fei Hsiao-t'ung *Earthbound China*, p. 64, found 5.4. O. Lang, *Family and Society*, p. 147, calculated a general average of 5.5. S. D. Gamble, *Ting Hsien*, p. 4, found for his rural area an average of 5.83, and O. Lattimore, *Pivot of Asia*, p. 169 reports for a place near Ting-hsien an average of 6.0 and for Kansu province 6.8 (p. 169). In my own historical research I found for the first centuries A.D. a general average of 5.1 for the tax-paying unit. Most of these data would seem to indicate a nuclear family with slightly over 3 living children.

point will be discussed later [1]. In spite of the fact that other studies indicate a rising mortality in the area in which our clans lived [2], there must also have been an increase in the number of children, because the population increased.

When we consider that studies of this type are very time-consuming and difficult, it is reasonable to expect that few other clans have been so thoroughly studied. The only comparable study known to me is by P'an Kuang-tan [3], a study of a clan in Chia-hsing (Chekiang) over 11 generations (between about 1450 and 1750). The study covers 3035 males and indicates that 7.6% died at an early age, i.e. a percentage lower than ours, but that 28.4% males had no children and 4.3% males did not marry. P'an's percentages of early deaths increase greatly over time, while the percentage of men who had no children was highest in his 7th to 9th generations. If we add to our men with no sons (Table 41: 20.8%) those with daughters but no sons (4.3%) and those men about whose descendants nothing is known (8.0%) and of whom probably a good number had no children, our results come quite close to those of P'an [4]. Further research is necessary in order to allow us to generalize.

If a couple with children has an average of 2 sons (reported), we should expect that they then have an average of 4 children. We cannot prove this, because of the inaccurate method of recording in our source material: We have a good number of data which indicate how many daughters a couple had. In all these cases, all sons are also mentioned. When only sons and no daughters were reported, we have to guess whether there were also daughters. The texts never says: "So and So had three sons and no daughters", but only "So and so had three sons". The data in the last row of Table 41 are, therefore, to some degree distorted. There were certainly at least slightly more daughters. For an assessment of the rate of population growth—if we may hypothesize that our Jung clan is so tome degree representative for the whole area—the rows 2 and 3 of Table 41 are more important. The one row shows the number of sons which could have been the sons of all men of an age at which these

---

[1] Ch'en Ta, *l.c.*, mentions differential fertility.
[2] *Nankai Weekly Statistical Service*, vol. 5, 1932.
[3] P'an Kuang-tan, p. 133; we calculated from his table the percentages.
[4] In generations 1-8 of the Formosan Yeh clan, 30.8% of 198 men had no sons. Information about daughters is too scanty to be acceptable. (Huang Tien-ch'üan in *T'ai-nan wen-hua*, vol. 5, no. 2, 1956, pp. 46-47 gives the data on which these calculations are made.)

men could have become fathers (i.e. this row includes row 1); the other row excludes the "unknown" cases.

TABLE 41. THE CHILDREN OF THE JUNG CLAN

Period	1	2	3	4	5	average
% of unknown	21.8	8.11	4.4	4.9	—	8.8
no. of sons of all males	1.31	1.26	1.20	1.09	—	
no. of sons of known fathers (excl. "unknown")	1.67	1.37	1.20	1.15	—	
no. of sons of actual fathers	1.90	2.00	2.20	2.15	—	2.05
no sons	5.0	17.6	27.9	27.8		20.8
no sons, but daughters	1.3	2.6	5.6	7.2	—	4.3
early death	5.8	11.4	11.9	11.6	—	11.0
ratio f: m	100:108	100:108	100:105	100:98.3	100:72.8	100:105
Taiwan ratio						100:112
No. of children of parents with daughters	4.13	3.74	4.09	3.90	3.25	3.93

Both rows similarly show a gradual decrease of fertility over the last 300 years. We can, therefore, say that over the whole period the number of persons who ever had children (and who were ever married) decreased, while those persons who had children increasingly had more children. The explanation of this phenomenon is not difficult; we will come back to it later, but want to point out here that just as the percentage of persons "never married" increased, the percentage of men with a number of wives (concurrently or successively) increased also. These men with several wives usually had more children than men with one wife only. The basic force behind this whole mechanism is, probably, economics: only wealthier men could marry more than one wife; very poor men either could not marry or had to postpone marriage. They may also not have been in a position to keep as many of their children alive as wealthier families could.

The distribution of children, as shown in Table 42 for the Jung clan and in Table 45 for the Wu clan, confirms the picture which has already been given: families with only one or two sons are on

TABLE 42. DISTRIBUTION OF CHILDREN IN FAMILIES WITH CHILDREN

	Sons					
	1	2	3	4	5	over
Period						
1:	46.4%	28.6%	14.5%	8.7%	2.2%	0.6%
2:	42.0%	30.8%	15.7%	8.3%	2.1%	1.1%
3:	38.4%	28.4%	16.2%	8.9%	5.2%	3.0%
4:	40.0%	27.9%	15.0%	10.3%	3.6%	3.2%

	Daughters					
	1	2	3	4	5	over
Period						
1:	37.3%	38.8%	14.9%	5.9%	3.0%	0
2:	47.7%	27.4%	17.1%	5.1%	2.2%	0.5%
3:	44.9%	29.8%	15.6%	5.2%	3.0%	1.5%
4:	47.5%	26.4%	15.5%	6.6%	2.3%	1.7%

TABLE 43. DISTRIBUTION OF CHILDREN IN FAMILIES WITH CHILDREN, ACC. TO GROUPS, JUNG CLAN

Sons 1-2	3-4	5 and above	daughters 1-2	3-4	5 and above
Period					
1: 75.0%	22.2%	2.8%	76.1%	20.8%	3.0%
2: 72.8%	24.0%	3.2%	75.1%	22.2%	2.7%
3: 66.8%	25.1%	8.3%	74.7%	20.8%	4.5%
4: 67.9%	25.3%	6.6%	73.9%	22.1%	4.0%

TABLE 44. GENERAL SEX RATIO, JUNG CLAN

Period	Sons	Daughters	Ratio f/m
1:	518	67	100 : 773
2:	1042	369	100 : 282
3:	574	403	100 : 142
4:	807	573	100 : 141

the decrease, while families with three or more sons are on the increase [1]. In the Wu clan, the increase is more spectacular than in the Jung clan, especially in the most recent period, although the data are based on a relatively small number of cases. These tables cannot, without adjustment, be compared with similar tables for other countries, because they do not contain all those children who died in their infancy, i.e. an estimated 24% of children is omitted.

The number of daughters in the Jung clan is on the increase, just as is the number of sons; but in general, there are fewer daughters than sons. If we look at Table 44 we see that in the early period, daughters were grossly underreported, as has already been mentioned. From 1800 on, however, we believe that while registration was probably as complete for daughters as it was for sons, more attention must have been devoted to raising baby boys than baby girls, so that after one year of age, there were many more boys alive than girls (141: 100). But because in general women lived longer than men, the sex ratio for the whole population was not as extreme. Statistics for recent periods show that men outnumbered women often by as much as 124: 100 [2]. The difference may have been greater in earlier periods.

TABLE 45. DISTRIBUTION OF SONS IN FAMILIES WITH AT LEAST ONE SON, WU CLAN

Period	1	2	3	4	5	Over	n
gen. 50-59	44%	28%	15%	7%	4.5%	1.5%	513
gen. 60-69	43.4%	23%	19.5%	6.6%	4.2%	3.3%	333
gen. 70-72	21%	24%	22%	12%	12%	9%	67
Average	42%	26%	17%	7%	5%	3%	913

Families with an unusually high number of either sons or daughters are very rare, in spite of polygyny. Among the 2941 sons which we studied in the Jung clan, there are only one case each of a family with ten and with eleven sons and three cases of families with nine

---

[1] In the generations 1-8 of the Formosan Yeh clan, i.e. in the 8 generations before approximately 1800 to 1820, the first sons were 34.8% of all sons (n = 137), the second sons 27.5%, third sons 15.2%, and the rest of 22.4 included all later sons (calculated on the basis of Huang Tien-ch'üan in *T'ai-nan wen-hua*, vol. 5, no. 2, 1956, pp. 46-47). Huang calculated that all known fathers had an average of 1.7 sons; if we take only those of whom we know that they had at least one son, such actual fathers had 2.4 sons. Both data are higher than those for the Jung clan (according to Table 41).

[2] According to Ch'en Ta, see also p. 131, note 2. In a Formosan fishing village the sex ratio was 110 (*Pa-tou-tzu*, p. 5).

sons. Among the 1412 daughters which we studied there is only one case each of families with eight and nine daughters and four with seven daughters.

9) Adoptions

According to Confucian standards, a man without a son should adopt a son, so that the ancestral sacrifices can be continued. Such an adoption can, if not made in time, also be made posthumously, i.e. the "adopted son" does not necessarily have to leave his parental home and move into the household of his adopted parents. Such a son should, if possible, be taken from a close relative, possibly a brother. Adoption of the son of a cousin was also acceptable. The adopted son always had to be a member of the following generation; he could not be a member of his adopting father's generation. This was one limitation. The second limitation was that he should be a member at least of one's own clan. If no suitable son could be found in the clan, an "outsider" could then be selected. In such cases (in which a different term for "adoption" is used!) a son of a brother or other relative of the wife was the best possible solution [1]. We found such cases in the Jung genealogy. But we also found that for a good number of persons, no adoption was ever made. Although we did not attempt to analyze these questions statistically, we found that a) as a rule, an adoption was made only for a man who lived up to an age at which he could have been the father, i.e. as a rule no "son" was adopted for a child who died before the age of 15. b) An adoption was more important for the oldest living son than for other sons, i.e. if the oldest living son had no son of his own, he would adopt a son, preferably a younger brother's son, even if the brother had only one single son. In such cases, then, the younger brother died without a son, because he had to give his only son to his older brother. This

---

[1] In T'ang time, special laws prohibited adoption of children from the lower social classes by members of the higher classes (texts and discussion in Niida, *Legal Documents*, p. 516; Tamai Korehiro, *Shina Shakai Keizai-shi Kenkyu*, Tokyo, 1937, pp. 148-149) and in general of non-related children (Sh. Kato, *Studies in Chinese Economic History*, vol. 2, 1953, pp. 766-767 and Niida, p. 513; an early Chinese discussion of the subject is in the *Yeh-k'o ts'ung-shu* 15, 3a-b). However, adoption of non-related children seems to have occurred not too rarely. Special conditions stimulated this custom on Formosa, because until around 1720, the settlers were not allowed to bring relatives with them to the island. As men needed cheap labor and wanted to have sons, they adopted non-related boys (Yang Ch'ing-mei, "T'ai-wan-ti min-su", in *Hsin-shê-hui*, vol. 12, no. 4, April, 1960, p. 15). We will return later to this point.

is an interesting highlight on the importance of primogeniture for clan and sacrificial purposes. c) In some cases of the type just mentioned, an intermediate solution was made: the only son of the younger brother was "split" and was counted as the son of the older as well as of the younger brother. We have no indication as to whether the sons of such a "split heir" were later equally distributed among both branches; it seems that this was not the case. d) There are cases in which a son was adopted from a family not related to the clan by blood or by marriage, but such cases are quite rare. No cases of adoption of daughters are reported. If a family wanted to have a girl in the house, they would use the system which is widely practiced in Asia [1].

Our Taiwan data mention 337 cases in which a girl daughter was given away before reaching the age of 14: in 265 cases it was mentioned that she was given away as *"sung yang"* = sent away for being brought up by somebody other than family, in the other cases it was simply said that she "went away". These cases represent 6.5% of all girl daughters. Some of these were given away within a month after birth, but the average age was 3 years and one month. Most frequently, these girls (29.2%) were second daughters and they came from families which had an average of 7.6 children.

The same Taiwanese data mention only 62 cases of boys given away before reaching the age of 14. In 28 cases it was stated that the boy was "sent away for being brought up by somebody", while in the other cases it was said that he "went away". These cases

---

[1] In Turkey, girls from poor families are taken into the family and are educated with the other children (called "besleme"), but have to serve as baby-sitters and to do other light services. In some cases, the parents of the girl get some gift—which can, legally, be regarded as an advance payment of wages—and in all cases the adopting family has to give the girl away in marriage and supply her with a dowry—which also can be regarded as a payment of wages. For Japan, see R. J. Smith, *Kurusu* (in *Occasional Papers*, no. 5, 1956, p. 67; University of Michigan Press). Earlier studies often describe such agreements as "slavery". In other cases, an adopted girl is a cheap bride for the young son of the family or is only adopted in order to be later sold into a house of prostitution. According to an estimate made before 1956, the year in which this custom was forbidden, about 60% of all prostitutes of Taiwan were "adopted girls" (Yang Ch'ing-mei, "T'ai-wan-ti min-su", in *Hsin-shê-hui*, vol. 12, no. 4, April, 1960, p. 15). Sun Te-hsiung (in *Pa-tou-tzu*, pp. 21-22) gives some additional reasons: poor families cannot afford to "buy" an adopted son, but can get cheaply a girl as adopted daughter. Later, they take a son-in-law into their family as husband for this daughter. If the male children of a family die, the family might adopt a girl in order to change the bad luck into good luck. Finally, a woman whose baby died shortly after birth, may adopt a girl baby to nurse.

represent only a little more than 1% of all boys. They were an average of 5 years and 1 month of age when given away, although some were given away within a month after birth. Most frequently these boys were 4th sons (24.2%), but 17.7% of them were first sons. The families from which they came had an average of 7.0 children.

We see that the percentage of boys given away in modern Taiwan is much lower than the percentage which we find in our texts (see Table 46). This need not indicate a sharp change in the custom of

TABLE 46. PERCENTAGE OF SONS GIVEN AWAY IN ADOPTION (JUNG CLAN)

Period	% Given Away	Number of Adoptions
I	2.7%	25
II	8.7%	189
III	13.0%	180
IV	12.6%	237
Average	10%	631 Sons out of 6335

adoption. We have to consider the fact that often adoptions were made when the childless man died and in such a case the child "adopted" for him may have been a mature man himself. And even if he was a young child when "adopted", he continued to live with his parents and was "given away" only for ceremonial purposes. We cannot find in our source the percentage of such "ceremonial" adoptions. Thus present-day "real" adoptions cannot be compared with adoptions mentioned in the texts.

Leaving aside the question as to whether the adoption was a "real" one, i.e. whether the child actually moved to the home of the other family and lived there, or whether it was a "ceremonial" adoption for ritual purposes only which did not involve a change of domicile, we must now answer the question: how many sons were "given away" to be "adopted" by members of our Wu and Jung clans? And which son has the highest chance to be "given away" in adoption? For the Wu clan, we have information for only 63 cases, for the Jung clan ten times as much. The percentages are calculated for the Jung clan only. Table 46 indicates a surprisingly high percentage of adoptions. The overwhelming majority of these sons were given to close relatives. We said above (Table 41) that some 35% of men who could have been fathers had no sons and often no children at all. It is clear that even with this number of sons given in adoption, and even if some "outside" sons are added, high as this percentage seems to be, still a fair number of men had *no* sons when they died. Realities were apparently more important than Confucian values. If we study the question whether poor families give away more children than rich families, we do not find great differences. Because of the lack of other criteria, we regard as "poor" a family which over the last 300 years had a lower than the average number of official jobs, and as "rich" a family with relatively many jobs. If these admittedly inaccurate and questionable standards are accepted, rich families give more children away than the middle range of families and poor families give exactly 10% away. But, as stated previously, the wealthier families have more children, and can therefore more easily give a son away, and a wealthy family will, if they have to adopt a son, first try to adopt a son of a close relative from the same family, and take a distant relative only if no close relative is available. Therefore, there is more demand for sons of rich families. But, as stated, the differences are small.

While there seems to be a general increase in the number of sons given away in adoption, which can roughly be compared with the general increase in the number of men without sons, a further breakdown of the ages of children who were given away reveals an even more interesting change. According to Table 47 the percentage of

TABLE 47. SONS GIVEN IN ADOPTION (JUNG CLAN)

Period	Oldest Son	Only Son	Youngest Son	Middle Sons
I	8%	12%	48%	32%
II	18.7%	0.5%	46%	34.8%
III	26.7%	5.0%	32.8%	35.6%
IV	29.5%	6.6%	29.5%	33.4%
Averages	24.8%	4.6%	36.3%	34.3%
	(n: 156)	(n: 29)	(n: 228)	(n: 216)

middle children given away remains always the same, but the percentage of youngest children decreases as steadily as the percentage of first sons increases. Among the first sons, the percentage of "only" sons given away in adoption is specially high in periods of unrest (Period I, establishment of the Manchu Dynasty; Period IV, T'ai-p'ing rebellion). We can assume that no father will easily be prepared to give his only son away; but even if he has more than one son, he will probably prefer to keep the oldest at home. The oldest son is, according to custom, the natural and correct person to continue the sacrifices [1]. And at the time when the question of adoption comes up, his younger brother may still be so young that he might fall victim to infantile mortality, while the oldest son may already have passed the critical age. When a father decides to give away his only son, great poverty or great moral pressure may have moved him to do so. The moral pressure would be involved in the case of a younger brother who could hardly refuse the request of his oldest brother, or (if the older brother is already dead when the decision is made to adopt a son for him) the request of the clan. Our data on social status are, as we said, not exact enough to establish whether economic or moral pressures were more important. It seems, impressionistically, that cases in which the only son is given away are more common in poorer families, and cases in which the first son is given away more common in wealthier families. We know that wealthier families paid more attention to the rules of the dogma than others. For the Wu clan, the oldest or only son is given away in 9.5% of all cases, the youngest in 40%, and other sons in 50.5% of the cases.

As families with sons have an average of about 2 sons, as we found above, the "youngest son" quite often is also the second son. Thus,

TABLE 48. SONS GIVEN AWAY IN ADOPTION (JUNG CLAN)

Period	\	\	Sequence of Sons \	\	\	Other	Number of Cases
	1	2	3	4	5		
I	20%	48%	28%	4%	—	—	25
II	19.3%	52.9%	19.8%	7%	0.5%	0.5%	187
III	31.7%	40.6%	18.9%	6.2%	1.1%	1.7%	180
IV	37%	34.2%	19.0%	8%	1.3%	0.8%	237
Average	29.4%	42.1%	19.6%	7%	1%	1%	629

in the Wu clan, in 71.4% of all adoptions the second son is given away. In the Jung clan, the situation is not as extreme, but comparable (Table 48). While the fourth and later sons have a less than average chance to be given away, and the first son has much less than average chance, the second son has almost twice the normal chance to be given away. We can, therefore, say that the second son, and to a

---

[1] The importance of the first son and the question of primogeniture has been discussed by M. Freedman, *Lineage Organization in Southeastern China*, London, 1958, p. 82 f.

much smaller degree also the third son, experiences a much higher degree of insecurity than the first or the fourth son. He can always expect to be the one who has to be given away if a member of the clan is in need of a son. It would be interesting to know whether this institution had significant psychological consequences.

10) Birth Rate

A calculation of the birth rate on the basis of our material seems almost impossible: a) we do not know the actual number of live births, and b) the data for women are insufficient. We can only attempt to calculate the population increase, and the results of this attempt are, naturally, highly hypothetical. The first, very crude, way is a comparison of increase over long periods (Table 49). The second

TABLE 49. INCREASE OF POPULATION, BASED UPON THE NUMBER OF SONS BORN (JUNG CLAN)

Period	Sons Born	
I (1600-1699)	913	
II (1700-1799)	2166	Increase 237%
III (1800-1849)	1382	Increase 128% if calculated for 100 years
IV (1850-1899)	1874	Increase 136% for the 50 year period
	6335	

way is to take all men born in a period of 5 or of 10 years and then to calculate the increase (Table 50). In this Table, only those men are mentioned for whom we have birth data. This means that we take into consideration only some 35% of the persons mentioned for Period I in Table 49, some 50%, 80% and 85% for the later periods.

Table 50, therefore, certainly strongly underestimates the rate of population increase, especially for the early periods. Yet if it shows anything, it indicates that a) the rate of population increase seems to show a slow decline, b) periods of crisis (1850/1859, T'ai-p'ing rebellion) seem to influence the rate of population increase, c) the rate of increase, even if allowance is made for the incompletemess of our data, never reached even 2% per year. Only further research and comparison of data from genealogies with census data can determine whether the low rate of increase is a special trait of the Jung clan.

TABLE 50. Men's Birth Years (Including All Known Data)

1600/4	4	1625/9	7	1650/4	11
1605/9	2	1630/4	4	1655/9	11
1610/4	5	1635/9	9	1660/4	11
1615/9	6	1640/4	17	1665/9	18
1620/4	6	1645/9	11	1670/4	16

1675/9	14		
1680/4	26		
1685/9	18		
1690/4	33		
1695/9	29	1690/1699	62

(260)

	1700/09	57	Increase in 10 years	92%	Average
	1710/19	61		107.1%	
	1720/29	84		137.7%	
	1730/39	95		113.1%	
	1740/49	117 (188.7%)		123.2%	114.6%
	1750/59	105		89.8%	
	1760/69	152		144.8%	
	1770/79	122		80.3%	
	1780/89	152		124.6%	
	1790/99	166 (142.0%)		109.2%	109.7%

average 1700/1799 (268% increase) average 1.22 p/y
(1111)

1800/09	169	101.9%	
1810/19	211	124.9%	
1820/29	223	105.7%	
1830/39	266	119.3%	
1840/49	282 (166.9%)	106.0%	111.5%

(1151)

1850/59	281	99.3%	
1860/69	293	104.3%	
1870/79	355	121.2%	
1800/89	350	98.6%	
1890/99	326 (116.0%)	93.1%	103.3%

(1605)

average 1800/99 (196.4% increase) average 0.74 p/y

1900/09	393	120.6%	
1910/19	396	100.8%	
1920/29	356	89.9%	104.3%

average 1900/29 (109.2% increase) average 0.43 p/y

P'an-Kuang-tan in his study of a prominent family in Chia-hsing (Chekiang) [1] over 11 generations, gives some comparable materials. He calculated the average duration of a generation as 26 years. How accurate this figure is, and whether or not the duration of a generation changed over time, we cannot know. But between his 5th and his 11th generations, each generation showed an average of 21% which might indicate an increase of 0.8% per year. Between his second and his fifth generations, the average increase is 57% which would point to a 2.2% increase per year. While this percentage is much higher than our figure (although his generations 2-5 cover a period for which we did not calculate yearly increases), his data for the later period, which comes to an end before 1880, are at least comparable with ours.

Two facts must be mentioned here, because they too influence the rate of population increase if data from genealogies are used: a) emigration and b) expulsions from the clan. Emigration will be discussed presently. Expulsion is one of the punishments which can be given by the clan elders to disobedient or criminal members of the clan. We know that in extreme cases the clan could and did execute a member, although this was an illegal act. The clan should, in such cases, hand the man over to the authorities. Expulsion from the clan is a punishment which is allowed and which has harsh consequences for the afflicted. His name is taken out of the clan registers when he is expelled. We must, therefore, assume that most cases of expulsion are not noticeable when we use genealogies: the person simply would not appear in the book. But if he had one or several sons and if his wife was not implicated in the crime or offense, children and wife would not be omitted. The Jung genealogy mentions seven cases (roughly between 1760 and 1900) of expulsion, reporting the expelled man's name, but not his birth date nor the date of his death. However, the birth date of his wife is given. We tend to believe that

---

[1] P'an Kuang-tan, p. 133, calculated according to his data. Taeuber and Wang pointed out that a reconstruction of growth trends on the basis of Chinese official population statistics is always problematic. Yet if these statistics are taken they indicate a yearly growth of one percent or 0.9% for the period between, 1749-1767, and between 0.8 and 0.9% yearly for the period between 1776-1812; an exception are the years between 1767-1771 with only 0.6% and 1771-1776 with as much as 4.5% increase per year. A comparison of these results with ours is difficult, because we are dealing with *one* clan, while Taeuber and Wang's data include all strata of society (see I. Taeuber and Wang Nai-chi, "Population Reports in the Ch'ing Dynasty" in *Journal of Asian Studies*, vol. 19, no. 4, August 1960, p. 403-417). On the unreliability of census data see recently Ch'ü T'ung-tsu, *Local Government in China*, 1962, p. 147f.

in general the percentage of persons expelled was always extremely low and statistically negligible, even though we would admit that over the 300 years studied more than 7 persons may have been expelled. In addition to these, one man who was born in 1789 [1], was sent to Ili in Central Asia. Ili was a well-known place of exile in that time. This man, therefore, must have committed some act which was regarded as criminal.

11) Overseas Emigration

The Jung clan, as the Wu clan, sent many of its members into foreign countries. Unfortunately, however, the genealogies do not mention such an emigration if the writers can assume that the man was only temporarily in foreign countries and would return some day. That a man lived in a foreign country, therefore, is reported only if he died in that country. But we are sure that not even all cases such as these are reported, because at least the remains of the deceased would some day come back to the family home and then the genealogist might have felt that no real emigration ever took place.

Out of 5985 cases which could be used for this purpose, the Jung genealogy mentions 101 cases of emigration (1.7%). Cases of emigration increased and reached a peak between 1800 and 1849: Period I: one case (0.1%); Period II: twenty-five cases (1.4%); Period III: thirty-five cases (2.9%); Period IV: forty cases (1.7%). For the earlier times, normally no place names are given. However, a man who was born in 1772 emigrated to the Philippines and another one born in 1796 to Hong Kong. Two men, born in 1808 and 1818, were the first persons to migrate to San Francisco, and many others from different houses of the clan followed. A man born in 1838 migrated to Japan. Migrations to Annam started with a man born in 1844 and to Hawaii with a man born 1847.

Who were these emigrants? We do not know at what age they left home, but it seems logical to assume that they were fairly young when they left. We do not know what they did in the foreign country: the Jung genealogy never mentions their work. From all we know of later emigrants and of those that arrived in the United States, it is the poorer families who sent their sons away in the hope that they might become wealthy. While emigration to California and Hawaii in the 19th century often meant digging gold or work on railroads or in planta-

---

[1] He belonged to gen. 25 of the family 2/Ju-chin.

tions, emigration to Annam, Japan and the Philippines most likely meant business. In any case, not only was the Chinese government against emigration, and for long periods declared it illegal, but also the family seemed not to have been in favor of emigration, since a loss of status must have been the consequence of a son's leaving, if emigration carried the implication of poverty. The number of cases known to us from the genealogy (101) is too low to allow us to attempt any correlation between number of emigrants and status of the family. But one problem can be studied in this connection for both clans: which of the sons is most likely to emigrate? Hypothetically, we should assume that it is not the first son who emigrates, because he is the future leader of the family. Our data are in Table 51 and Table 52. Both Tables show roughly the same tendency at least in Periods III and IV: as a rule, more second sons emigrate than one would expect (the percentage of second sons is in brackets on Table 51 and 52),

TABLE 51. EMIGRANT SONS (WU CLAN)

First Son	35% (42%)	34 Cases
Second Son	38% (26%)	37
Third Son	12% (17%)	12
Later Sons	15% (15%)	15

TABLE 52. EMIGRANT SONS (JUNG CLAN)

Period	II	III	IV
First Son	55.0% (42%)	36.1% (38.4%)	37.2% (40%)
Second Son	20.0% (30.8%)	41.6% (28.4%)	28.6% (27.9%)
Third Son	10.0% (15.3%)	13.9% (16.2%)	17.2% (15.0%)
Fourth Son	5.0% (8.3%)	2.8% (8.9%)	17.2% (10.3%)
Fifth Son	10.0% (2.1%)	2.8% (5.2%)	— (3.6%)
Later Sons	— (1.1%)	2.8 (3.0%)	— (3.2%)

and fewer first sons than one would expect. In the 18th century, more first and more fifth sons emigrate, and after 1850 more third and fourth sons, but considering the small size of our sample, no conclusions can be drawn.

12) SUMMARY OF RESULTS

We may now briefly summarize the results of our analysis of changes in the structure of population, which was based upon data from the Jung clan and some from the Wu clan.

The material from the Jung clan is quite impressive, as almost 10,000 persons are mentioned between 1600 and 1930, and a good number more for the time before 1600. The data are not all reliable, as we pointed out. In the earlier periods, it seems that people who reached a relatively greater age and who were socially important, had a greater chance to be accepted into the genealogy than others; or, in other words, the genealogy became more complete in the later periods, especially after 1800. The incompleteness of data introduced a bias into some parts of our analysis; but other parts of the analysis probably remain unaffected by a potential bias, such as the analysis of the age difference between husband and wife, or the age of father or mother at the time of the birth of their children. In general, however, we have refrained from interpreting very small numerical differences that might have been produced merely by the incompleteness of data. Yet we believe that a potential bias of this type did not distort the results because there were sets of data showing no change over time. Secondly, a potential bias due to incompleteness of data may be expected to influence different sets of material in the same direction. Yet we found sets of data showing tendencies different from the tendencies in other sets, and therefore we believe that these were true differences. In these cases where we felt that a strong bias might be involved, we have made special mention of the relevant conditions.

We found that there is no trace of "modernization", i.e. of changes which can be explained *only* as the result of contact with the West or its ideas. Emigration into foreign countries, it is true, did increase, and Western demand for labor and Western means of communication certainly have facilitated emigration, at least in the 19th century, but emigration had already started before any substantial Western impact. It seems, as we have seen in the study of the Wu clan, that emigration into foreign countries was simply one of the results of the fact that there was no more land available for an increasing population in in Kuangtung province after 1800. We can safely say that all changes which occurred can be easily explained as the result of long-term developments which have nothing to do with foreign impact. Modernization, then, seems to have begun to affect our clans only in the 20th century.

Our study reveals a number of long-term changes. Only one of these changes could be explained as a change in attitudes: there are more reports on twins since 1800 than for the earlier periods, i.e.

more twins remained alive. This might be the result of a change in in the earlier attitude which regarded twins as an unlucky omen. But our data are so small, that such a conclusion can hardly be proved. In the more recent periods, daughters are more often mentioned in the Jung genealogy. But in some branches of the clan, daughters were always mentioned; the richer the family, the earlier are daughters mentioned. The reason for this seems to be that for rich families, which practiced a system of preferential marriages, a good record of intermarriages was important; poorer families did not bother as much. The mentioning of daughters, then, cannot be taken as an indication that the position of women has tended to become higher in recent times. Most changes which we observed can be easily explained by the assumption that over time the clan's economic status became more diversified. In the early times the differences in economic (and, concomitantly, social) status between the individual houses were small; in more recent times, some families became wealthier and others became poorer. For the Jung clan, the data to prove this follow below; for the Wu clan, data have been given above in the discussion of individual houses.

If a family became wealthier and/or achieved higher social status, it identified, as we know, more with the Confucian values [1]. We find, therefore, in our data a tendency towards stricter observance of Confucian values.

We found that in recent times there are 1) more wives per husband; and 2) a higher percentage of concubines; 3) the second wife was more often a "never-married" woman, and 4) widows after age 40 usually rarely remarried; 5) the remarriage of older widows declined. All these five changes indicate an increase in wealth. But the latter three changes also indicate stricter adherence to Confucian values: nobody should marry a widow, especially not one of an age above 30. Furthermore, we found for recent times that 6) men and women marry earlier; 7) the duration of a generation becomes shorter; 8) parents have their first and 9) their second sons at earlier ages; 10) families who have children have on the average more children. Finally, 11), the age difference between husband and wife and 12) husband and concubines decreases. The percentage of wives who are older than their husbands remains unchanged; only periods of war and crisis tend to increase the percentage. The changes all

---

[1] See Wang Hui-chen, "An Analysis of Chinese Clan Rules: Confucian Theories in Action", in D. S. Nivison, *Confucianism in Action*, Stanford, 1959, pp. 63-96.

indicate greater wealth: only rich people can give their children in marriage at an early age. Poor people cannot easily bring together the money which marriages usually involve [1]. Earlier marriage also means that the children tend to come earlier, and logically also means that the age difference between husband and wife decreases, because there is a lower limit for the marriage age of women. Greater wealth also means that a family can afford to have more children and that it can give its children food and care of a quality which keeps more children alive than is possible in poor families. It had been noted by earlier observers that rich families have, on the average, more children [2]; an exception of this rule are foreign-trained upper-class families which marry later and have fewer children than average families [3]. Wealthier people also can afford to buy concubines at an earlier age than less wealthy families; poor families, of course, cannot have concubines at all. According to Confucian values, early—but not too early—marriage is desirable, and many sons are desirable, but a concubine should not be taken at too early an age.

These changes which point towards an increase of wealth are counterbalanced by a number of other changes which point towards an increase of poverty: 1) the duration of life of persons of both sexes decreases, 2) although mortality between the ages of 1 and 14 remains the same, mortality between 15 and 35 increases in both sexes, 3) although the number of sons of families with sons increased,

---

[1] H. T. Fei, *Earthbound China*, New York, 1945, p. 256 f. calculated that at that time, a wedding in Yünnan cost $ 1,205 for the groom's family and $ 4,195 for the bride's family (Chinese dollars).

[2] Fr. L. K. Hsu, *Under the Ancestor's Shadows*, New York, 1948, pp. 113 and 214; O. Lang, *Family and Society in China*, p. 147; *Yenching Journal of Social Studies*, vol. 3, p. 13; H. T. Fei, *Earthbound China*, p. 64. It should be understood, however, that all these references refer to the size of the family, not exactly to the number of children. Methods to prevent conception were known in China (*Folklore Studies*, vol. 6, no. 2, p. 96 and J. Frick in *Anthropos*, vol. 50, 1955, pp. 675-676, both for the Kansu area), but abortion was more common (O. Lang, *loc. cit.*, p. 153; J. Frick, *loc. cit.*, p. 675; F. D. K. Hsu, *Under the Ancestor's Shadows*, pp. 109-110 and earlier texts). Confucian scholars were against abortion (*Ch'üan-shan yao-yen*, p. 38b of the Manchu language text). The most important limitation, reported by F. Hsu, is that parents cease to have intercourse as soon as a grandchild is born. The one reason for this is, of course, to prevent overlapping of different generations. According to our data, the average age of grandfathers when a grandson is born would be around 60, since marriages took place comparatively late. In fact, we did not notice cases in which the youngest son is younger than the oldest grandchild, although we did not systematically test our material.

[3] Ch'en Ta, *Population*.

the number of sons of all males, whether married or not, declines. Correspondingly, 4) the percentages of men with no children or with no sons increase, and 5) the percentage of men who never marry increases, 6) the percentage of children given away for adoption also increases because more families were without sons [1], and 7) the general birth rate seems to decline. 9) Even if daughters are fully reported, their average number is lower than the average number of sons, i.e. daughters seemed to receive less care and tended to die more often at an earlier age than sons, if they were not, indeed, even consciously done away with. 10) Emigration into foreign countries increased greatly up to 1850. In view of prejudice against emigration, an increase of emigration indicates growing economic difficulties. If emigration towards the end of the 19th century seems to decrease, this may be a) because some of the emigrants were still alive and the genealogy mentions emigrants as such only if they die in a foreign country, b) some legal restrictions, set up by a number of countries toward the end of the century, may have reduced emigration, although we do not think that this factor affected our material in any important way.

The two tendencies, changes due to increase in wealth and/or social status, and changes due to an increase in poverty and/or loss of social status, are not contradictory, as can easily be seen. For example: while on the one hand the number of persons who never marry and/or who never had sons, increased due to poverty, on the other hand those who married and who had children, could marry earlier and could have more children, due to wealth.

Two changes do not fall into the pattern of wealth versus poverty: 1) recently more often the oldest son is given away for adoption. The strong pressure which is necessary to induce a family to give the away their only or their oldest son, can come from strongly Confucian high-status families and be exercised upon families of the same status with the same values, but it can also be exercised upon poor families which find some relief by giving away a son, even if he is the only one. 2) The percentage of in-village marriages decreases, especially for the sons-in-law. This change could indicate a higher

---

[1] Another change seems to be that death-marriages increased from about 1800 on. A death marriage is a marriage ceremony in which a man who died before marriage is married to a girl who also died before marriage. Such marriages were, according to Yü Yüeh, *Yü Ch'ü-yüan pi-chi* 1, p. 22 (with texts), always prohibited but always occurred.

degree of mobility and such a change could mean a "modernization". But another explanation is equally possible. A high-status family can stabilize its position by "political marriages": by giving daughters to other high-status and influential families, connections may be created which may prove useful for the family; the same can be achieved by taking a wife from an outside [1], influential family. In any case, this tendency of change was not great enough to change the general intermarriage pattern which had existed for at least 500 years.

Balancing the changes one against the other, we come to the conclusion that changes induced by a decrease in the general standard of living had a wider and deeper general influence upon the clan than changes induced by greater wealth. As expected, the number of wealthy persons may have increased, but the number of poor persons always remained larger.

The discussion in the following chapter will further confirm these conclusions.

---

[1] Some old texts (such as *Lü-shih ch'un-ch'iu* 26; transl. Wilhelm p. 453) stated that all marriages should take place within the village; this rule was never generally observed.

PART FOUR

SOCIAL MOBILITY OF THE JUNG CLAN OF SOUTH CHINA

1) Early History of the Jung

By now, we have heard much about the Jung clan. The material is from the Jung genealogy, the *Jung-shih p'u-tieh* (容氏譜牒), which was compiled shortly after 1930 and printed in 16 Chinese fascicules containing 16 Chinese chapters of normally around 100 double pages [1]. The genealogy is in the form of a list of persons and, therefore, contains little information other than personal life data. Some 10,000 persons at least are mentioned in one way or another, sometimes only by name. In addition to these clan members, a fair number of sons-in-law are also mentioned. The Jung do not know too much about their ancestors. There is an old tradition that they originally lived in Tun-huang, in the extreme north-west of China [2], but in a catalogue of many thousands of names from Tun-huang documents, covering the first 1000 years A.D., I found no mention of a Jung clan member. The same text admits that there are no data before the T'ang period, and not much was known before 1200. The first genealogy, it is said, was composed in 1446 [3]. In the Spring of 1386 there was a meeting of all eight houses of the clan, and clan sacrifices were initiated [4]. According to our calculations, the family at that time must have been in the 13th generation. It was called probably by the son of Mr. Jung T'i-yü, a man who, it is reported, had passed the lowest examination, was interested in local history, and brought the clan closer together. At that time, the clan was already living in Hsiang-shan.

The present genealogy states [5] that the ancestors came from Fukien province to Nan-hsiung, and that they counted as first generation the first settlers in Nan-hsiung (Kuangtung province).

---

[1] University of California Library No. 2252.9/3022.
[2] I, 8a.
[3] I, 11b.
[4] I, 5a-b.
[5] I, 81a.

No data are given for the first generation, but these first settlers must, according to our calculations, have been living there shortly before 1000 A.D. Although Nan-hsiung had a population of over 20,000 families around 1080 [1], we know [2] that all Cantonese families claim to have come from Nan-hsiung, so that such a claim does not necessarily have to be historically true. The first settler in Nan-hsiung may have had, it is stated [3], a very low governmental position there; though this information is admittedly doubtful, it is stated that a man in the 7th generation passed the lowest examination and got a title which corresponded to the 9th rank. He lived between 1122 and 1183 [4]. His oldest son held an even higher rank. But in generation 8, a second son left home in his early years, moved into the Canton area and settled there in Hsin-hui. He liked the place, it is reported [5], because there was no malaria, and no droughts nor floods ever occurred. So he built a grass hut, cleared a homestead and bought land from the local Hu clan. Shortly after 1200, however, his descendants, for reasons which are not given, left Hsin-hui and moved to Hsiang-shan [6], and soon the property in Hsin-hui was lost. According to this story, an adventure-loving young man started the new settlement close to Canton, but for unknown reasons his descendants moved over to the present-day clan home in Hsiang-shan. The clan split into eight houses in gen. 11, probably around 1300, and it would seem that this split came at the same time as the move from Hsin-hui to Hsiang-shan.

If we believe this story, the clan was not a clan belonging to the upper class. The emigrant son seems to have been fairly poor, and this may even have been the reason for his migration. But there are serious doubts concerning the whole report. At the very end of the Jung genealogy [7] we find a very different story. It begins with a statement that Hsiang-shan is a seashore district in which many people made a living by making salt from sea water. From Sung and Yüan time on, it attracted more and more people, and at the very beginning of the Ming Dynasty (i.e. shortly after 1368) the government opened a salt plant in Hsiang-shan. Twenty families were attached to it in two

---

[1] Lo Hsiang-lin, *K'o-chia*, p. 58.
[2] T. Makino, *Jap. Journ. Ethnology*, 14, 1950, no. 3, p. 212.
[3] I, 81a.
[4] I, 82b.
[5] I, 83a.
[6] I, 8a.
[7] XIV, 21a ff.

groups of ten families each; they were called "Upper" and "Lower Tent". Among the ten families of the "Upper Tent" (Shang p'eng) were two Jung. Both groups together (we have called them "Group I" and "Group II" above) were called "the ten *p'ai*". *P'ai* means a small group of soldiers or similar persons. All *p'ai* members called one another "*P'ai* brother" (actually P'ai-ch'in 排親). They lived in their own separate settlements, built their own "City God Temple" and organized regular temple fairs in honor of their gods. The text then continues with the statement that in the course of time the area dried up and the salty marsh became good land, so that the saltmakers became farmers and paid taxes based on the former salt dues. Their dues were heavy and hard to pay. Only shortly before 1620 could they interest the magistrate of the city to investigate their condition and he got a reduction in payments for them. They could from then on collect some capital among themselves and created a local village market, of the type which is so typical for the area: it is normally between villages, sometimes attached to a village (or a village may grow out of such a market), and every 5 days or so, there is a market day. Locally, such markets are called "Malaria Markets", because their pattern of holding market is similar to the attacks of *malaria tertiana*.

They soon acquired much money from market income, which was divided according to a well-defined system among the 20 families, while a part was used to pay the government dues, to finance the yearly temple fair, and to keep the temple in repair. During the fair, many guests were invited. When the farmer's market began to give a good income, the city leaders of the district city Hsiang-shan appropriated the market fees. When the P'ai families planned to sue the city leaders, they are supposed to have said that they would return the farmers' market income to the P'ai as soon as one of them passed the examination. This happened in 1705, and from then on, the market income again came into the hands of the P'ai; as the lucky candidate was a member of the first family of the "Upper Tent", he received special honors at the fairs. Although, the text concludes, there is hardly anybody who still knows about the salt-making, the P'ai and their festivals are still alive. This refers to the time around 1800.

There can hardly be any doubt that this report is much closer to the truth than the first one. We have the report only because it was felt important to mention the Jung clan's rights in the yearly ceremonies of the God.

Ch'en Shih-ch'i, in his study of the position of state craftsmen and artisans during the Ming time [1], has shown that the production of salt was under the control of the Ministry of Finance. The salt workers were hereditarily attached to the Ministry and their status was the third highest of the state workers, i.e. even in their social class, they were not high. Their organization while they were working was comparable to a military organization, usually five workers under a foreman.

Several interpretations can now be made: it is possible that the report about the move from Nan-hsiung to Hsin-hui is true; if so, we would have to assume that some clan member or members committed some crime so that the family was reduced from the status of free citizens to the status of state craftsmen, and were moved by force from Hsin-hui [2] to Hsiang-shan, where they had to make salt, as members of a 20-family gang. It is, of course, also possible that the family from earliest times on was in the low condition of salt workers, and that the introduction of the genealogy was not made up until later. In any case, our Jung clan had a very modest origin.

Secondly, because the Jung belonged to a labor gang, they intermarried among themselves. Intermarriages of bonded workers with free people were at the early time not allowed. This explains easily the high percentage of intermarriages with members of Group I ("Upper Tent") and Group II ("Lower Tent") and especially with the Yang clan, which also belonged to the "Upper Tent".

Thirdly, although it is mentioned that the P'ai families, after they gave up saltmaking, became farmers, their main interest seems to have been in business, especially in the development of a farmer's market. The Jung, then, developed from a worker's clan, active in saltmaking, to a business clan which pooled its resources with a number of similar, related families.

At this point, we would like to make an interesting observation: M. Granet and C. Levy-Strauss have studied what they believed to be ancient intermarriage patterns in China. The story of the Jung clan, as it is here developed, should caution us against certain quick conclusions. The intermarriage pattern of the Jung, which—if studied in more detail—might reveal a cross-cousin marriage pattern, or at least a system close to cross-cousin marriage, is a pattern which

---

[1] Ch'en Shih-ch'i, *Ming-tai kuan-shou-kung-yeh-ti yen-chiu*, Wu-han, 1958, 183 p.
[2] Around 1150, the Jung intermarried once with the Wu clan in Hsin-hui—one of the few cases in which both clans had contacts.

was the result of unique historical circumstances. Intermarriage with the Yang clan—i.e. a clan belonging to the saltmakers—began, as we have seen, around 1400, the time at which the salt-worker gangs were organized. Intermarriage was not, then, in the general culture, but was the result of being thrown together, of belonging to a caste with low social status; only later did it become an institution which was continued. It seems dangerous to combine such cases with cases incompletely reported in the early literature, or to speak of general marriage customs without first having made a number of very detailed studies into their beginnings in fact.

2) Divisions and the Early History of the Eight Houses

As already stated, in gen. 11, i.e. around 1300, the clan divided itself into 8 houses. Each house professes to come from one member of the generation [1], and according to the names, the houses are called "Chao 1", "Chao 2", etc., because the ancestors were numbered.

For the house Chao 3, only one member of gen. 12 is given, no further data. For the house Chao 8 it is said that in gen. 13 one man went to Peking as a soldier and never returned. The genealogists did not know what became of him. The time when he went to Peking, corresponds roughly to the beginning of the Ming Dynasty. He may have participated in the fights against the Mongols, and it is quite possible that he was ordered to become a soldier which could happen to members of the lower classes to which the Jung belonged at that time.

The first house ("*fang*") suffered only one further split: with gen. 16, the Heng-mou branch (*chih*) developed into an independent branch. According to Confucian rules, a family can establish its independence after 5 generations. We had seen a similar process in the Wu clan. The main "Chao 1" (Chao-i) house became the house with the greatest number of members, and its branch, the Chao-i Heng-mou branch, was also quite numerous (Table 53).

While not much more is known about house Chao-1 than that it was already in early times a large house, house Chao-2 is much more interesting. We remember that this house intermarried with the Cheng clan, and that the Cheng did not belong to the saltmaker gangs. Chao-2 has intermarried with the Cheng clan since at least 1350 (gen. 13). It also had marriage connections with the local Ch'en

---

[1] Two brothers had 5 and 3 sons.

TABLE 53. NUMBER OF MALES MENTIONED BETWEEN GEN. 21 AND 30 IN INDIVIDUAL HOUSES

(1)	Chao 1 House		967 (full name: Chao-i)
(2)		Heng-mou	395 (full name: Chao-i house, Heng-mou branch)
(3)	Chao 2 House		383 (full name: Chao-erh house, Ju-hsin branch, K'o-chang claw)
(4)		2 K'uan	456 (full name: Chao-erh house, Ju-chin branch, K'o-k'uan claw)
(5)		2 Side	101 (full name: Chao-erh house, Ju-ch'in branch)
(6)		2 Ju-ch'in	183 (full name: Chao-erh house, Ju-ch'in branch)
(7)		2 Ju-chia	694 (full name: Chao-erh house, Ju-chia branch)
(8)		2 Ju-ch'ang	29
	Chao 4		(full name: Chao-szu)
(9)		4 Ti-wen	112
(10)		4 Chi-wen	167
(11)		4 Yen-wen	860
(12)	Chao 5		127 (full name: Chao-wu)
(13)	Chao 6		
		6 Liang	447 (full name: Chao-liu house, Liang-kung branch)
(14)		6 Shan	202 (Chao-liu house, Shan-kung branch)
(15)		6 Pi-luan	689 (Chao-liu house, Sen-kung branch, Pi-luan claw)
(16)		6 Pi-ch'i	321 (Chao-liu house, Sen-kung branch, Pi-ch'i claw)
(17)		6 Ching	279 (Chao-liu house, Ching-kung branch)
(18)		6 Pi-han	54 (Chao-liu house, Sen-kung branch, Pi-han claw)
(19)	Chao 7		191 (Chao-ch'i)

	House 1	1362
	2	1846
	3	1
	4	1139
	5	127
	6	1992
	7	191
	8	3
	Total	6861

clan, as we pointed out; of course, there were also other houses that married into the Ch'en clan, and the first Ch'en marriage was in gen. 5, i.e. before the division into houses. But a man of gen. 16 in the house Chao-2 was a student of Ch'en Po-sha, a famous local Confucian and scholar (born 1428, in Hsin-hui, the old Jung home). We remember that the Wu clan also was influenced by Ch'en Po-sha.

The Chao-2 house has a more scholarly tradition than this: Mr. Jung T'i-yü, who passed the lowest examinations and won a post, already had a good education (1361-1436; gen. 13). Three of his sons had education; the third son (1404-1459) was interested in the clan genealogy, and the fourth son had a low, local job in which, it is reported, he was successful. Among the 15 male members of the gen. 15, we find four who had local jobs. Two of these men had been in the state school, while a third man also studied but nothing is known about any job he may have held. One of the local administrators was also interested in genealogy. In this generation, roughly during the later half of the 15th century, the Chao-2 house moved to a new clan home. The student of Ch'en Po-sha in gen. 16 is counted as the leader of the Ju-hsin branch and K'o-chang claw, after his name (Jung K'o-chang, 1453-1517). He had an honorary title. His son, Jung Shih-ch'eng (born 1487), reached the highest distinction which the house attained: he passed the *chü-jen* examination (gen. 17). After this, the Ju-hsin branch went downward again.

The Ju-chin branch of house Chao-2 came from Jung K'o-k'uan, a brother of Jung K'o-chang. K'o-k'uan's son, it is stated, was interested in increasing the family's wealth. In gen. 19 the K'o-k'uan family had two members with a low title, and one in gen. 20.

The Ju-ch'in branch (no. 5 of all branch houses; called by us "Side branch") had four cousins of Jung K'o-chang as founders. Most of these cousins had no more descendants after gen. 17. Among the later descendants, one had a low title (in gen. 20).

The Ju-ch'in branch (written differently from the one just mentioned) had also 2 cousins of Jung K'o-chang as ancestors. Down to gen. 21, they had no honored member except for Jung Shih, (1497-1517) who cared well for his sick father, and when bandits caught them, he let himself be burned to death in order to save his father. This deed brought his clan official recognition.

The Ju-chia branch house had many members but none of these down to gen. 21 was famous or honored. And the Ju-ch'ang house which started out with 7 cousins as ancestors, never had any honored member at all, in its entire history.

If we compare the Chao-2 house with all other houses, we find that it occupied a different position: by around 1350, it already had educated members. And it intermarried with a family with which the remaining branches did not intermarry. We might conclude that the Chao-2 house was not affected by the order to become saltmakers, and that this house retained at least the status of "free citizens". Except for a brief period, the house never attained a really high position.

The house Chao-4 had two soldiers in gen. 12 and one in gen. 13. There are no data given, but these men must have served under the Mongol dynasty (Yüan). Military service was then and later an unfortunate and socially degrading job. The status of the family at that time (early 14th century?) certainly was not high. In gen. 16 the house split into 4 branches, one of which soon died out. Down to gen. 21, no member of any branch had any job or title. Only in the Yen-wen branch, a man in gen. 19 "loved books", and the daughter of a man in gen. 20 married an educated man—but this was already in the late 17th century! No member of the house Chao-5 between gen. 11 and 21 had a government job.

House Chao-6 is very closely related to the House Chao-4, because its ancestor in gen. 11 had no sons and adopted a son from the newly formed Chao-4 house. Similar to the Chao-4 house, we find in the Chao-6 house in gen. 12 a man who became a soldier. None of the branch houses which started with gen. 16 achieved fame, except a man in gen. 18 in the Pi-luan family, who was honored, probably only because he reached an unusually great age (1520-1619); in gen. 20 another member of the family was similarly honored, when he was 78 years old. Otherwise, a certain geographic mobility is noticeable: it seems that Mr. Jung Chao-k'uan (1570-1627) of the Chao-6 house, Shan-kung branch (gen. 18), accompanied his famous clan uncle Jung Shih-ch'eng (Chao-2; gen. 17) to Peking when he went up after his degree, and remained there. One of his sons settled then in Peking. Similarly, five men of gen. 19 of the Ching branch of Chao-6 moved to Canton and never returned, i.e. they settled there.

No person in the house Chao-7 was famous until gen. 21. But it is clearly stated here that one of the members of gen. 16 was the ancestor of the "Upper Tent" salt gang. This may be factually true, but the time does not seem to be correct; according to our calculations, this so-called ancestor should have lived around 1510, a 120 years later than the creation of the saltmaker gangs.

In any case, no house except house Chao-2 had any prominent ancestors between gen. 11 and 21. On the contrary, our findings seem to indicate that their status was quite low; and as they all intermarried with the Yang clan, which definitely belonged to the saltmakers, we are probably not mistaken if we accept the saltmaker

182   SOCIAL MOBILITY OF THE JUNG CLAN OF SOUTH CHINA

report, and regard all branches, with the exception of Chao-2, as saltmakers, at least from gen. 13 or 14 on.

3) SOCIAL MOBILITY OF THE JUNG CLAN

The data for the history of the Jung clan before gen. 20/21, i.e. before 1600, are not detailed enough to describe the mobility of the clan with any degree of accuracy. We saw that the clan in seven of its 8 branches was of a status lower than that of free citizens and that it seemed to develop into a clan of business people. One house even achieved national fame, because one of its members passed the *chü-jen* examination.

For the time between 1600 and 1900 we will now attempt a dual analysis: according to time periods as well as according to families. Table 54 shows that the Jung clan as a whole had a low status in the 17th century; only 4.6% of its members had any kind of relation with the bureaucracy. We utilized for this table the following data: a) degree holders who had received their degrees by examination; b) men who had been admitted to the state schools which means that they had passed the initial examinations; c) men who bought titles; d) men who got a job by any means: examination or purchase; e) men who got a title after their death because they had famous sons; f) men who got a title only because they lived abnormally long. The only class which, perhaps, had better be excluded here is that of persons who got a title posthumously because of the achievements of their sons; the text, however, does not always indicate whether a title was given for such a reason or not. Thus our total (over the whole period), namely that 8% of the men who reached an age in which they could have received title and actually got one, is slightly too high. The data indicate, however, that between 1700 and 1850

TABLE 54. HOLDERS OF TITLES IN THE JUNG CLAN, AS PERCENTAGES OF TOTAL MEN (1600-1899)

Period	All Branches numbers	%	Chao-2 House Only numbers	%	All Other Houses numbers	%
I	36 (757)	4.6%	26 (292)	8.9%	10 (465)	2.2%
II	199 (1716)	11.6%	72 (431)	16.7%	127 (1285)	9.9%
III	138 (1187)	11.3%	34 (322)	10.6%	104 (865)	12.0%
IV	115 (2325)	4.9%	12 (705)	1.7%	103 (1620)	6.3%
	488 (5985)	8.2%	144 (1750)	8.2%	344 (4235)	8.1%

the clan had more than twice as many degree- or title-holders as either between 1600 and 1700 on the one hand, or between 1850 and 1900 on the other.

The low percentage of men who got recognition of a kind which conferred high social status upon them (at least in their local community, if not in the community as a whole), is in agreement with what we already know of the clan. In the 18th century, as we have seen, the clan got richer because of the income from market activities. After 1850, the percentage of men with honors again became very low. This time many men were still fairly young when the whole system of honors broke down, and when new educational ideas came into China. Others may never have developed an interest in imperial honors at a time when revolutionary, anti-dynastic ideas began to spread in this part of China.

In the attempt to describe changes in social status, we used titles as a measure—though not a completely satisfactory one—of the status of the clan in different periods. Our list of titles (Appendix to Part 2, ch. 3) contains three types of titles: persons in a training situation (Group A), persons in educational positions (Group B), and persons with active or honorary positions in the administration (C). Of these titles, these of Groups B and C are classified by the Chinese into 9 groups (ranks), each with 2 classes. We assigned the numbers 1 to 18 to each rank of groups B and C and added the numbers 19 and 20 for two more titles which are just below this level. By adding all title numbers of all title-bearers in a certain period and by calculating the average rank number, we can establish the "position" of the clan in a given period. Titles of Group A do not carry rank grades. These have to be excluded and calculated separately. There are 430 title-bearers from 1600 to 1889 for whom enough, as well as classifiable, information is available [1]. The results of this test are given in Table 55. We see that the clan slowly but steadily rose in status by gaining, on the average, higher and higher positions (as expressed by falling numbers). The number of "students", enrolled in government schools and working for some degree, or the number of students who already had a degree but did not have a rank or job increased first slowly, then rapidly in the 19th century. The more this group increased, the more the other group decreased. To be a "student" in the national school (*kuo-hsüeh*) certainly gave as

---

[1] The sample is the same as the one mentioned in note 1, p. 187 minus 16 men whose position could not be tabulated.

much status as to have a rank between our points 13-16 (rank 7A-8B), and the possibility of reaching still much higher positions.

TABLE 55. RANK POSITION OF THE JUNG CLAN, WITHIN THE SYSTEM OF 9 RANKS

	Mean rank position	percentage of persons of all men in gvt. schools
-1699	16.5	5.0%
1700-1749	16.3	8.8%
1750-1799	15.4	9.4%
1800-1849	14.5	17.2%
1850-1889	14.0	61.5%

It is hard to estimate correctly the national average of men with some kind of official recognition. As soon as we adopt as a definition of "upper class" only persons with a higher degree, the percentage of such persons within the total population is very low [1]; but as we included probably even more "titled" men than Ho did in his study [2], something like 5% of the total male population of over 15 years of age might not be too far off. If this were correct, our Jung clan would be "average" except for the period between 1700 and 1850 in which it was above average. If we now break down the data on the basis of our earlier finding concerning the Chao-2 house, we find that most of the titled men in the 17th century came from the Chao-2 house, and that the Chao-2 house had a status higher than all other houses up to the time around 1800. The other houses slowly gained in status until they surpassed the Chao-2 house after 1800. Their fall after 1850, however, was by far not as spectacular as the downfall of the Chao-2 house.

The study of persons with some kind of title or job reveals then, that the fate of the clan changed a over long period: from the time they were saltmakers around 1400 to 1850, the position of the clan *as a whole* improved steadily. But in individual houses and individual families within the clan, other tendencies may have been at work: the Chao-2 house rose only until 1800 and then moved downward.

Before we analyze the titles further, we will turn to another question. The conventional study of social mobility usually includes a

---

[1] Chang Chung-li, *The Chinese Gentry*, Seattle, 1955, uses a narrow definition.
[2] Ho Ping-ti, "Aspects of Social Mobility in China, 1369-1911", in *Comparative Studies in Society and History*, Vol. 1, No. 4, 1959, pp. 330-359.

comparison of the status of the father with the status of the son. Most scholars who have studied social mobility in China have taken an even broader view and have studied the fathers and grandfathers [1] of men with official titles. We found between 1600 and 1899, as mentioned in Table 54, 488 men with some title. As the whole system of giving titles broke down from 1904 on, many men in the last period (1850-1899) may no longer have had an opportunity to get any traditional title. We included in this group, however, some men who held modern-type University titles and modern-type official positions. In the following calculations, we analyzed 446 title-bearers, of whom 2 were born before 1600 and none was born after 1889.

TABLE 56. TITLE-BEARERS WITH TITLE-BEARING FATHERS

	Father	Brother	Total Title-Bearers
-1699	7 (17.5%)	2	40
1700-1749	15 (26.3%)	8	57
1750-1799	59 (46.0%)	4	129
1800-1849	120 (77.5%)	6	155
1850-1889	56 (86.0%)	0	65
	257 (57.7%)	20 (4.5%)	446 (100%)

We also excluded men about whom data are too incomplete to be useful for calculations. In this sample we found that 57.7% of title-bearers had fathers who also had titles (and an additional 4.5% had brothers who had a title). Here, a significant change can be seen over time (Table 56).

The percentage of title-bearers with title-bearing fathers grew

---

[1] Some even included the 3 preceding generations. I am referring here to the studies by Ed. Kracke, P. T. Ho and the unpublished thesis by Robert M. Marsch, *Mandarin and Executive*, University of Michigan, 1959. Marsh's study is based upon an analysis of some 570 persons who occur in A. Hummel's *Eminent Chinese*. In methodological respects, P'an Kuang-tan's study of the prominent Chia-hsing clans in Chekiang is interesting. With his method he established that between about 1400 and 1900 there were 91 prominent clans in Chia-hsing. He then asks: if these were the prominent men, how many of them do I find in the list of successful examination candidates? His result is 67.5% (p. 99). This number would be much higher still, if successful candidates who belonged to these clans but did not actually reside in Chia-hsing had been added. Moreover, many of the successful candidates who did not belong to the 91 clans (they belonged to 60 other clans) got their titles because of filial piety or old age and not because of merit (Table on p. 107-110). Thus, the method of using lists of sucessful candidates for a study of gentry mobility is not ideal.

continuously over the last 300 years. In other words, it became more and more common to have a father who also had a title—or: social mobility became more and more restricted.

Our percentages are, on the one hand, slightly biased: there are some sons who reached positions which were so high that the Emperor gave post-humous honors to their fathers, and sometimes even to their grandfathers, although during their lives these fathers and grandfathers had had no title. Such cases are, we believe, rare, because only few Jung ever got positions which were high enough to warrant such an honor. On the other hand, our percentages deviate from those of Ho [1], because Ho includes three generations. Of course, if our percentages are compared with those of Ho, his "transitional group" (B) should be added to his final percentages, because in the Jung family, such "transitional" persons, i.e. persons who had only the lowest titles or jobs either by examination or, more often, by purchase, are the majority of cases. In general, although both sets of data are difficult to compare because of still other differences, both sets of data had surprising similarities (Table 57). The table

TABLE 57. SOCIAL MOBILITY ACCORDING TO HO PING-TI AND EBERHARD

Ho	Eberhard
52.4% (for 1371-1610)	?
61.0 plus 15.4 = 76.4% (1652-1703)	17.5% (1586-1699)
62.4 plus 22.7 = 85.1% (1822-1868)	77.5 (1800-1849)
64.7 plus 18.6 = 83.3% (1871-1904)	86.0% (1850-1889)

shows the percentages of title-bearers whose ancestors also had a title. According to one's personal convictions, one might regard the fact that in the late 19th century, 16.7% of the title-bearers did not come from the upper class or its fringe (if we follow Ho), as "high mobility" or, considering that these 16.7% were recruited from some 95% of the population one might speak of "low mobility".

It may now be interesting to study the question: did fathers prefer their oldest sons, by doing more for their education or by being more willing to buy a title for them? Or did fathers tend to treat their sons equally, or, perhaps, according to their ability? Here, we can introduce some material from the Wu and the Jung (Tables 58, 59). In the Wu clan, first sons had percentagewise almost the same chance to

---

[1] See note 2, p. 184.

get a title as second sons. We receive the impression that in earlier generations fathers showed more preference for their first sons in this respect than was true later. In later times, it seems, fathers gave

TABLE 58. EDUCATION AND SONS, WU CLAN

The Title is Held by	n	%
First Sons	72	46.8
Second Sons	45	28.8
Third Sons	21	13.5
Later Sons	18	10.9

TABLE 59. EDUCATION AND SONS, JUNG CLAN [1]

Title is Held by:	1	2	3	Later Sons
to 1699	45.0% (46.4%)	40.0% (28.6%)	5.0% (14.5%)	10.0%
1700-1749	54.4%	24.6%	10.5%	10.5%
	(42.0%)	(30.8%)	(15.7%)	
1750-1799	58.2%	24.0%	11.6%	6.2%
1800-1849	48.3% (38.4%)	27.1% (28.4%)	12.9% (16.2%)	11.6%
1850-1889	54.0% (40.0%)	20.0% (27.9%)	12.3% (15.0%)	13.8%
Averages	52.5%	26.0%	11.4%	10.1%

an education to (or tried to get a title for) those sons who showed the most promise. In the Jung clan, after 1700 first sons always had a better chance to get a title than they could otherwise expect. The tendency to give preference to the first son is greatest between 1700 and 1800. The discrimination seems to work mainly against the second son, because we have seen that if a son emigrates, it is more often the second son, and that if a son is given away for adoption, it is also more often the second son. The preference for the first son might indicate that fathers thought it important that the future leader and possible head of the family had the highest possible position. This would reinforce his status and enable him to help the whole family by his contacts with the leading elite. If we study only those men with titles whose fathers also had titles, the discrimination against the second son becomes even more marked. In the 263 cases

[1] In brackets the percentages for *all* Jung men, as far as data are known. The data do not correspond completely, as the general data include the years 1890-1899 and the title-holders do not occur in these years. Total n = 446.

of this type which can be analyzed, 50.6% were first sons, 22.4% second and 12.6% third sons [1].

We now ask: does the difference in social status which—according to all we know—can roughly be defined as the percentage of persons in a family who have titles or jobs in the government, cause any other differences between families? There is one very obvious and understandable correlation between the percentage of titles a family has and the number of concubines, expressed in the percentage of concubines in the total number of wives. The average percentage of males with titles or jobs is 8%, and the average percentage of concubines is 7.7%. For a closer comparison we divide our 19 families of the Jung clan into 3 classes: 6 families with 0 to 5% jobs; 6 families in the middle range with 6 to 8.7% jobs; 7 families in the upper range with 8.9 to 15.0% jobs. We can, if we study Table 62, clearly state: the higher the social status, i.e. the more jobs or titles a family had, the more concubines it had. To keep a concubine is an extra expense which only a fairly well-to-do family can afford. We know that a wealthy man felt socially almost obliged to have at least one concubine, just as a wealthy man in our society may feel obliged to have a Cadillac.

TABLE 60. NUMBER OF WIVES OF THE TITLE-BEARERS, JUNG CLAN [2]

	Husbands	Wives	%
-1699	40 (509)	49 (589)	1.23 (1.16)
1700-1749	57 ⎫	75 ⎫	1.31 ⎫
	⎬ 186 (1070)	⎬ 249 (1283)	⎬ 1.34 (1.20)
1750-1799	129 ⎭	174 ⎭	1.35 ⎭
1800-1849	155 (643)	289 (788)	1.87 (1.23)
1850-1889	65 (1187)	112 (1488)	1.72 (1.25)
Totals	446 (3389)	699 (4148)	1.57 (1.22)

If we study only the title-bearers of the Jung clan (n = 446), we find (Table 60) that they had more wives than common Jung men: every other title-bearer had 2 wives. Some of these second wives

---

[1] For a comparison: in 1954 in the United States of all children born alive to a mother, 27.8% were first children, 26.7% second and 18.7% were third children and 26.9% were later children (U.S. National Office of Vital Statistics, *Vital Statistics, Special Reports*, Vol. 44, No. 8, Table 1, p. 162).

[2] In brackets the numbers and percentages for non-titled persons. The data do not completely correspond to one another, as the group of non-titled includes the years 1890-99, while there are no title-holders in these 10 years.

were second main wives, married after the death of the first wife. Such a second marriage was quite expensive and a poor man had difficulties in getting a second wife except a widow. Other wives were concubines. In the common population, only one out of 5 men had more than one wife.

It we study concubines only, it is interesting to compare the percentage of wives who are concubines among the wives of the titlebearers with the percentage of concubines among the non-titled (Table 61). Here, we see that the titled had more than 3 times as

TABLE 61. THE NUMBER OF CONCUBINES AMONG THE WIVES OF TITLED (NON-TITLED) JUNG CLAN MEMBERS

	All Wives	Concubines	%
-1699	49 (498)	3 (1)	6.2% (0.2%)
1700-1799	249 (989)	26 (34)	10.4% (3.4%)
1800-1849	289 (617)	72 (27)	24.9% (4.4%)
1850-1889 (1899)	112 (1209)	27 (120)	24.2% (9.9%)
	699 (3313)	128 (182)	18.3 (5.5%)

many concubines as ordinary clan members. There is, at the same time, and connected with the first correlation, a second one: the higher the social status of a family, the higher the average number of sons; this correlation, as can be seen, is not as high as the first one (Table 62). As we have seen above, in families with titles (high status), those persons with titles and their direct relatives have more than the normal number of sons; but each such family also has a large number of persons who have no sons at all, so that the average will be depressed.

There is some, but not a strong, association between the status of a family and the duration of a generation: the higher the status, the shorter the generation (i.e. the earlier the children are born).

Further potential associations are put together in Table 63, in which we have grouped the families into 3 groups, as we did in Table 62.

The only obvious association is Table 63 is that the higher the status of a family, the lower is the percentage of persons about whom it is unknown whether or not they had sons. We might mention here that the higher the status of the family, the more detailed are the genealogies. We have said above, however, that most of the "unknowns" were probably persons who either died at an early age or had no sons. If this group of "unknowns" were to be distributed among the other classes in Table 63, there would probably remain no correlation between status and percentage of persons with sons, without sons, or with early death. But as we cannot safely dissolve the "unknown" category, this hypothesis cannot be tested. Some other

TABLE 62. RELATION BETWEEN HIGH STATUS AND NUMBER OF CONCUBINES AND SONS

Name of Family	% with Titles	% of Concubines	Average Number of Sons
2 Ju-ch'ang			2.00
4 Ti-wen		2.5	1.64
6 Pi-han		2.5	2.05
1 Heng-mou	2.0	3.2	1.88
6 Ching	4.6	6.8	1.99
2	5.0	3.2	2.16
Averages Group 1:		3.0	1.95
2 Ju-chia	6.6	3.4	1.98
1 Main house	7.0	(not counted)	1.99
6 Pi-luan	7.2	5.2	2.10
7	7.6	8.5	1.94
6 Pi-chi	8.0	6.8	2.05
2 Ju-ch'in	8.7	2.8	2.10
Averages Group 2:		5.3	2.03
2 Side	8.9	2.5	1.95
4 Chi-wen	9.0	5.3	2.27
5	9.0	16.7	2.09
4 Yen-wen	9.4	12.7	2.22
2 K'uan	12.1	12.3	2.10
6 Liang	13.7	14.1	2.10
6 Shan	15.0	11.7	2.29
Averages Group 3:		10.7	2.21
Average All Families		7.7	2.05

TABLE 63. INFLUENCE OF THE SOCIAL STATUS UPON THE FAMILY

Group:	1 (low)	2 (middle)	3 (high status)
% of Men with Sons	66.3	64.4	64.1
% of Early Deaths	11.3	10.2	10.5
% of Men Without Sons	19.2	20.5	21.3
% of Fathers with Only Daughters, no Sons	3.9	4.5	4.2
% of Unknown Persons	15.0	9.8	7.4
% of Adopted	9.8	8.7	10.8

correlations, which are not so much influenced by the character of these data seem to be more important (Table 64). As we already

TABLE 64. INFLUENCE OF SOCIAL STATUS UPON THE FAMILY, 2

Group:	1 (low)	2 (middle)	3 (high)
Aver. Life, Men	54.3	53.7	53.5
Aver. Life, Women	57.7	57.8	57.7
Age Diff. H/Wife	5.6	5.5	5.2
Age Diff. F/Son	31.6	30.6	30.4
Age Diff. M/Son	25.1	24.7	25.1
Number of Wives	1.15	1.22	1.28
% of Preferred Wives	35.3	36.7	34.2
% Preferred Sons-in-law	42.7	37.2	48.8

know, the men of higher status have more concubines. Naturally, then, they have also a higher average of total wives, including second main wives. They also marry earlier (as expressed by their lower age at the time of the birth of the first son), and although their wives do not give birth to a son earlier than in the other families, the age difference between husband and wife is smaller, because of earlier marriage. While the average duration of life of women is the same in all classes, the men of the upper family status group seem to meet an earlier death, though the differences are very small. Families of middle status give almost as many daughters in marriage to the family they prefer as they take from that family; low status and high status families give more daughters than they take daughters as wives.

These correlations become much clearer, if not whole families, but individuals are compared. The first point is: men with titles have a much higher life expectancy than men without titles (Table 65).

TABLE 65. AGE AT DEATH OF TITLED (UN-TITLED) MEN, JUNG CLAN [1]

	number	Average Age	Difference t:n-t
-1699	39 (197)	74.9 (58.4)	16.5 years
1700-1749	53 (324)	76.4 (52.9)	23.5
1750-1799	123 (501)	71.0 (49.8)	21.2
1800-1849	150 (826)	60.3 (47.0)	13.3
	365 (1848)	67.8 (50.5)	17.3

[1] Here and in the following tables, the non-titled are in brackets. The two sets of data are not fully comparable, because the first group includes 2 title-holders born before 1600 and the last group stops at 1889 for the title-holders and at 1899 for the non-titled. The total number of titled men is always 446, but often data are not complete for all of these.

The difference of 17 years is enormous and can have two main explanations: a) Men received titles very often *because* they reached a high age [1]. Certain titles were more or less exclusively reserved for men who reached more than 70, and others for ages of over 80, and others for men over 90 years of age. The high average age of the titled men may, therefore, indicate only what we already knew. But the hypothesis can be made that these men could reach such high age only because they were economically better off in the first place. They had better food and lived longer. Although they got the title because of their age, they reached the age only because of wealth. Thus, titles may indicate wealth (and status) even if they were given mainly because of age. This hypothesis is weak and can be contested. b) If it is correct that men with titles lived longer because of better living conditions women who were married to titled men should also have a higher average age. Their husbands did not get the title because the wives reached high age, but if the husbands were well off, their wives also had better than average food. To a considerable degree this is proved by Table 66. The wives of

TABLE 66. AGE AT DEATH OF WIVES OF TITLED (UN-TITLED) MEN, JUNG CLAN

	number	Average Age	Difference t: n-t
-1699	41 (181)	63.9 (61.5)	2.4 years
1700-1749	61 (288)	66.3 (59.5)	6.8
1750-1799	144 (450)	65.0 (57.1)	7.9
1800-1849	242 (723)	57.8 (55.9)	1.9
	488 (1652)	61.5 (57.5)	4.0 years

the titled men also lived longer than the wives of ordinary men, although among them there were quite a number who died quite early, presumably during the birth of a child. Both facts, that men as well as their wives live longer if they belong to the titled group than do those who belong to the rest of the clan, do not come out clearly in Table 64 which analyzes whole branches of the clan: here, the few long-lived balance the many short-lived, so that no significant differences appear. This table indicates also that high-standard families show a smaller age difference between husband and first wife. This

---

[1] P'an Kuang-tan, pp. 131-132, mentions that old age and high family status are traditionally connected in China.

difference becomes quite marked, if we compare titled individuals with non-titled men (Table 67). A possible explanation, which we

TABLE 67. THE AGE DIFFERENCE BETWEEN HUSBAND AND FIRST WIFE AMONG TITLED (NON-TITLED) PERSONS, JUNG CLAN

	number	Age Difference, Average	Difference t: n-t
-1699	35 (149)	7.3 (5.3)	-2.0
1700-1749	54 (269)	5.3 (5.5)	0.2
1750-1799	118 (429)	5.0 (5.4)	0.4
1800-1849	148 (694)	3.2 (5.5)	2.3
1850-1889	61 (744)	2.2 (5.6)	3.4 [1]
	416 (2325)	4.2 (5.4)	1.2

cannot prove, is that persons with title were economically so much better off that they could marry at an earlier age. In such a case, they might have had to marry a girl not much younger than they were, because otherwise the girl might be too young for marriage. On the other hand, we know that poor men often had to postpone marriage until quite late, because they could not afford to pay the bride price. In such a case, men may have tried to get as young a wife as possible, which might explain the greater difference in age between husband and wife in the common population.

A comparison of high status versus low status families in relation to their preferred marriages (Table 64) does not give a clear picture. A comparison of the titled individuals with the rest of the population does not reveal striking differences (Table 68). It seems as if at first

TABLE 68. THE PREFERRED MARRIAGES AMONG THE TOTAL NUMBER OF FIRST MARRIAGES OF TITLED (NON-TITLED) MEMBERS OF THE JUNG CLAN

Wife from:	Cheng	Yang	Both Clans (in percentage of total marriages)
1699	38.4 (26.7)	10.3 (10.0)	48.7 (36.7)
1700-1749	28.9 ⎫	21.2 ⎫	50.1 ⎫
	⎬ 17.3)	⎬ 24.0)	⎬ 41.3)
1750-1799	25.3 ⎭	18.9 ⎭	44.2 ⎭
1800-1849	20.9 (21.8)	31.1 (32.1)	52.0 (52.9)
1850-1889	4.1 (19.7)	26.5 (22.8)	30.6 (42.5)
n	87	89	all marriages 380
Totals	22.9 (20.4)	23.4 (23.3)	46.3 (43.7)

[1] Data for the non-titled cover the years to 1889 only, as those for the titled

the titled men married more Cheng girls than ordinary men, and later many fewer than did ordinary men. In recent times the titled men seem to show a somewhat greater preference for Yang girls than do ordinary men. It seems to be safe to assume that these changes in the type of preferred marriages are in connection with short-range political or other changes which we do not know, and thus we cannot say that titled men *a priori* follow the system of preferred marriages more or less strictly.

4. General Conclusions: Migrations and Mobility of the Jung Clan

The Jung clan genealogy contains only very few and scattered remarks about where the clan members lived, to which places they went and even what they did. We can develop the following picture concerning its migrations and its mobility: the clan, which perhaps originally was a farming clan, after a southward migration had settled around Hsiang-shan at some time and remained there. One branch perhaps always remained a farmer's clan, while the other branches became saltmakers. Later they became merchants, and they seem to have remained in business until recent times. Some members of the clan were drafted as soldiers, and were moved into distant places. Some of these seem to have survived the military service and to have settled in places outside South China. Few moved into cities. We know of one man who, around 1670, moved into the city of Hsiang-shan—and this was unusual.

A study of the official titles which clan members got, indicates a further upward mobility. Yet if we look deeper into what titles they had, some interesting details begin to emerge. In the 17th century there was only one clan member who had studied so that he was accepted into the local official school, i.e. so that he could be a candidate for higher examinations. Another clan member attained shortly before his death an honorary *chin-shih* degree—he did not get it by study. The other titles are titles which can and usually are bought, but which also can be and often were given posthumously by the government to people who reached exceptionally high age or were otherwise prominent though not educated. In the 17th century 25 persons got the "Teng-shih-lang" title, which confers no office (and equals rank 9A)—the second lowest in the rank order. Others had the title of "Hsiu-chih-lang" which is rank 8A; only one had

had the title Wen-lin-lang, which confers rank 7A. Military ranks or offices were not sought for in the 17th century; only one man had an honorary military rank. We know that a military career was one of the ways of upward mobility—and the easiest one. Yet, the Jung clan did not select this way in the 17th century and preferred the civil honorary titles which could be bought. This indicates that they were a business clan which got status by buying titles rather than by studying.

In the 18th century, the interest of clan members began to shift more to the field of education. Three members were accepted into the local school and 13 into the national school in the capital city. One man, on the other hand, passed a military examination. Yet none of the students achieved literary fame or passed one of the highest examinations. The majority of clan members stuck to the honorary titles which conferred rank: 85 had the Teng-shih-lang title (rank 9A), 36 the Hsiu-chih-lang title (rank 8A), 4 were Wen-lin-lang (rank 7A), one was Ju-lin-lang (rank 6B), etc. Thus we can see that the general tendency is still the same: the family tried to get titles which conferred status and which could be got by paying money, or by simply reaching old age.

In the first half of the 19th century, the first member of the clan passed the *chin-shih* degree (in 1835), 66 others were in local schools and 20 in the national school. It is interesting, however, that two of the national school students were businessmen and one later became a poor teacher. In this period we find some clan members in real governmental positions, mainly in the provincial administration. Otherwise, the majority of clan members continued to buy titles as before.

Only between 1850 and 1889 do we see a further change towards active participation in government. One clan member achieved high rank and became an ambassador and an international figure. Others had less important government posts. Twenty-two members were in the national school, only 3 in the local school. But this decline was more than made up, especially after 1890, by a great number of young men who went to universities in China or in the United States. We find university graduates in the fields of medicine, engineering, business administration, commerce, transportation and communications, and chemistry. Some clan members joined the modern armies or entered the Whampoa Military Academy, joined the Kuo-min-tang Party in later life, and are found in the Ministry of Railways, the

Telegraph Administration or the Ministry of Communications. Yet, again, even among the national school students we find merchants, as among the men with military titles. In general, however, the interest in titles which are bought diminished—together with the general breakdown of the old system and its values.

Emigration into foreign countries, as we have seen, began early and continued. It indicates only that the upward social mobility was not shared by all clan members.

A difference from the Wu clan is that none of the main houses retained throughout the whole time or for longer periods, a status higher than the branches. This seems to us again an indication that the Jung clan was a business clan in which possession of land was not the decisive element.

The Jung clan, then, in general presents the picture of a rising clan with a slow tendency to acquire higher education and to move into actual government posts.

PART FIVE

GENERAL REMARKS ON SOCIAL MOBILITY

1) Introduction

We have seen that Chinese philosophers, over the course of centuries, adopted an increasingly rigid attitude towards freedom of social mobility. While in the early time they believed that with proper education all men can reach the same position in society, they later came to believe that basic differences between men existed from birth on, and that these differences to a high degree determined people's positions in society. We pointed out that the whole subject needs further investigation, especially as the attitudes of philosophers after Sung time towards the problem of social mobility have not yet been sufficiently studied. Our conclusions should, therefore, be regarded as only tentative—a kind of outline of what is known today about the problem.

We have further seen that over the course of Chinese history, the government tried more and more to stabilize society by assigning to each class its definite position in that society, and by enacting laws to make the status of each person clearly recognizable by his personal appearance as well as by the appearance of his house. In addition, each class had certain privileges and obligations to the extent that even intermarriage between different classes was prevented. These attempts to stabilize society reached their institutional peak in Sung time—the same period in which the attitude of philosophers was most deterministic. After Sung time, especially between 1450 and 1720, a number of restrictions were removed. As far as these relaxations dealt with craftsmen, the reason seems to have been purely economic: the old system of conscript artisan labor proved inefficient. Relaxation of restrictions for merchants, on the other hand, seems to have been a result of some pressure towards recognizing a situation which had developed over time: from Sung time, merchants gained increasing importance; they gained wealth and often power, and by all kinds of more or less illegal means they moved gradually toward the gentry class. In the 18th century, finally, they were given the legal right to move up, although they remained under a quota system which limited their chances greatly. And from the 18th century on, restrictions against descendants of slaves and of aborigines were relaxed. We are not yet able to state exactly the reasons for this relaxation in the 18th century. It is not impossible to relate the changes to increased contact with the West, although final proof awaits further study.

In our analysis of the Wu and the Jung clans, we have seen that there was a great deal of social mobility in both. Although our data include over 10,000 individuals, objections may still be raised that after all the development of these two clans may not be typical. Granted that it would be ideal to subject several hundred genealogies to the same method of study, yet we doubt that the general picture would be much different—providing only that the area under research is similarly restricted to coastal South China. We have studied, in addition to the Wu and Jung clans, a fair number of other clans in a non-statistical way and found basically the same development. Some of these data from other genealogies will be mentioned below.

In South China, many of the genealogies which we have studied begin in T'ang time, some even much earlier (e.g. the Wu clan genealogy); but for any statistical analysis, genealogies from this area can in general be useful only from about 1500 on. We know from official texts that during the period between 1500 and 1930 some social mobility was legally possible. For the periods before 1500, our genealogies usually mention only a few family members, not all; and among those mentioned are more often the prominent men or those who became ancestors of new branch families. This type of information can be used for a general, impressionistic study of mobility, though it does not lend itself to statistical analyses. It seems that even before 1500, mobility was relatively high, perhaps not much lower than after 1500.

Before we analyze the types of social mobility in more detail, some general questions bear discussion.

From historical texts we know beyond any doubt that very early in history the whole of South China—i.e. the area of Fukien, Kuangtung and Kuanghsi provinces in which the clans here under study now live—once was inhabited by aboriginal tribes only. Several different aboriginal cultures can be found [1] and studied. Chinese sources give enough data to identify these tribes, and in some cases

---

[1] See my *Kultur und Siedlung der Randvölker Chinas,* Leiden, 1942.

remnants of the tribes are today still living in the area. We know that Chinese peoples immigrated into the Kuangtung area probably around 400 B.C., and into Fukien and Kuanghsi at a slightly later time. The immigrants accepted some traits of the aboriginal cultures [1], but almost nothing of their languages [2]. Archeology presents us with a picture which is more or less Chinese. None of the genealogies which I know traces any one of the clans back to an aboriginal group. We suspect, however, that in the Wu clan there might be one branch which originally did not belong to the main Wu clan, but connected itself with it at a later time. This branch might be of aboriginal origin, but there is no way of proving it; in fact, the line of migration which is given for this branch fits very well into the picture of general lines of migration which we have for the Wu clan. It is, therefore, not possible to state that here we may have a case of "passing".

On the other hand, we have numerous texts which state that certain tribal leaders accepted certain Chinese clan names [3]. In many other cases, we know that by imperial decree some tribal leaders got the privilege to take Chinese clan names [4], and in these cases the genealogies of these men are available for, often, a period of more than 500 years [5]. Some of these Chinese clan names taken by tribal leaders betray their "barbarian" origin by their unusual form, but they by no means all do. Many could easily "pass". Yet, from at least the T'ang period on, it was strictly forbidden to adopt any child from the lower classes, even if the child was a foundling [6], and in most cases descendants of "barbarians" would be classified as lower class people. But laws equally prohibited adoption of children from "good"

---

[1] See my *Lokalkulturen im alten China*, Peking, 1943.

[2] Thus we know that Ch'u, a state along the middle part of the Yangtse River, had its own culture and its own language which perhaps belonged to the T'ai language group, but almost nothing of Ch'u language has remained. On the contrary, early documents found in the Ch'u area recently, are written in "Chinese" language, although with a fairly high percentage of strange, unusual words.

[3] See my *Kultur und Siedlung der Randvölker Chinas*, Leiden, 1942, pp. 275-300.

[4] Examples in *Frontier Affairs* (in Chinese), vol. 4, no. 7/8, p. 36 and other books on the aborigines.

[5] The An clan in Yünnan claims a genealogy which starts in 1252 (*Frontier Affairs*, vol. 4, no. 5/6, p. 14). The Wen clan in Yünnan claims to have had its 6th generation in 1344 (*ibid.*, vol. 4, no. 7/8, pp. 20-24). The Mu, a clan of the Moso tribes in Yünnan, received the right to have this Chinese name in 1382 (Chang Yin-t'ang in *Tsing Hua Journal*, new series no. 2, 1960, p. 252).

[6] *T'ang-lü su-i*, as quoted by *Niida*, p. 516, and *K. Tamai*, pp. 148-149.

families if they had a different clan name [1]. And even if the clan name of an aboriginal was the same as that of a Chinese family, it would still, legally, and especially by the Chinese clan itself, be regarded as "different". Thus, the only way by which a native could claim to be "in reality" a Chinese would be to connect his own genealogy with that of a Chinese family of the same name at such an early time that the Chinese family could not later disprove the connection. On an *a priori* basis we and Chinese writers have often assumed that this happened fairly often, so that, in reality, many so-called Chinese clans of South China are aboriginal clans who manufactured a tie to some Chinese clan genealogy and thus managed to "pass". But is this really so? In many cases the tribal leaders who carried Chinese names and at some time got the legal right to use the name, assert that their clan was originally Chinese: their ancestors at some early time in history immigrated from Chinese territory into the territory of the natives and set themselves up as leaders of the natives. For all we know, this could very well be the case. In fact, I tend to propose as a hypothesis that before approximately 500 B.C. most of the tribes south of the Yangtse River had a loose and relatively unstructured social organization (similar to that of the Liao tribes which retained this type of organization until relatively late) [2], and that immigrants, mainly from the area of Ch'u [3], set themselves up as rulers in areas in which native tribes lived. This led to the formation of tribes with chieftains and later to the *t'u-szu* system [4].

But whatever the situation was, what happened to the natives if all clans which we now study can more or less convincingly prove their Chinese origin? I think the answer depends upon the period in question. In feudal China (i.e. before approximately 300 B.C.) when every person below the aristocracy was "low", integration of non-Chinese at the lower levels was easy. We even know of integration at the level of the aristocracy. In gentry China (i.e. approximately

---

[1] *Niida*, p. 516.

[2] See my *Kultur und Siedlung der Randvölker Chinas*, under "Liao".

[3] In our terminology, as introduced in *Kultur und Siedlung*, these would be members of the Pa culture or Chinese from this area.

[4] This system by which local non-Chinese leaders were to some degree integrated into the Chinese bureaucracy is well described by N. Kanda, "On the Establishment of the T'u-szu in the Sino-Burmese Frontier in Early Ming Dynasty" in *Tôyô Gakuhô*, 35, no. 3, 1953, pp. 64-80, in *Frontier Affairs*, Vol. 2, 1943, no. 11 and 12 and Vol. 3, 1944, no. 1-2; in *Yü-kung*, vol. 4, no. 11, pp. 1-9; in H. Wiens, *China's March Towards the Tropics*, Hamden, 1954, p. 214 ff., and for the northern borders of China by H. Serruys, *The Mongols in China*, 1959, pp. 232-233.

after 100 B.C.) integration became more difficult, especially in areas where the technical and cultural superiority of the Chinese was great. In such areas—and this includes much of the area here under discussion—Chinese immigrants pressed the natives back into the mountains and took over the valleys and plains. In the mountains, the culture of the natives degenerated and the difference in level became even greater. Some natives then emigrated farther south into Southeast Asia. Others became economically more and more depressed, became dependent upon Chinese merchants (by indebtedness) or officials, occasionally supplied girls to the Chinese as concubines, or servants and day laborers to the landowners, and slowly disappeared as a result of an ever-decreasing birth rate. Few wives were available because of the competition by Chinese; men could not marry early because of indebtedness or because they were kept as servants and prevented from marrying; mortality was high because of depressed economic conditions; general moral decay which led to loss of interest in having many children (I am thinking here of processes similar to those which went on in the Central American area after the conquest) [1].

Naturally, we would not deny that a number of natives succeeded in "passing", but it seems safer to accept statements of genealogies, if we cannot prove that they are wrong. On the basis of such considerations, then, we conclude that the majority of the clans of South China which have genealogies in fact came from Central China, following the main trade routes which have, in part, been established by H. Bielenstein [2] and Lo Hsiang-lin [3] on the basis of data different from our data. In many cases, mainly of Fukien clans, the original home is said to have been in Honan province, and immigration took place via Kiangsi into Fukien. In other cases, the original home seems to have been on the lower Yangtze, and migration took place via Kiangsi into northeastern Kuangtung towards Canton, or into southern Hunan towards northeastern Kuanghsi. There was additional migration from southern Fukien into Kuangtung, and from Kuangtung into Kuanghsi. Finally, there is migration from southern Fukien into Taiwan and southeast Asia, as there was migration from

---

[1] Compare, for instance, the development of the conditions of the aborigines on Taiwan.

[2] "The Chinese Colonization of Fukien until the End of T'ang", in *Studia Serica, Bernhard Karlgren Dedicata*, Copenhagen, 1960, pp. 98-122.

[3] Lo Hsiang-lin, *K'o-chia yen-chiu t'ao-lun*, Hsing-ning (Kuangtung Province) 1933 (this rare book is in the Harvard University Library 2200/6124).

the Canton area into southeast Asia and other continents. In this book, we do not attempt to establish the geography of migrations, nor the strength of population movements along different geographical routes. It is greatly to be hoped that more research will be done in this field. Several different research approaches are possible.

From what has been said it is clear that the area covered by our research is a "colonial" area, i.e. an area which was sparsely inhabited and, indeed, partly empty when the Chinese settlers came. They had, therefore, opportunities similar to those of European immigrants in the Americas. Not all parts of China offered the same opportunities at all times. Let us take, as an illustration, some moments in history and analyze the situation in general.

Around the time of the birth of Christ, for instance, population along the Wei and Yellow Rivers was quite dense. But migration into the dryer parts of Shensi and Shansi, and especially into Kansu, was possible and frequently occurred. In the east, migration into Hopei province [1] and Korea was very promising. But perhaps the greatest chance at the time was offered by migration toward southern Shantung, Kiangsu, Anhui, Hupei. More daring persons even moved still farther south.

When North China came under the rule of non-Chinese nomadic tribes (approximately 300 A.D.), migration northward was not tempting, though it apparently occurred. But with the shift of Chinese dynasties into the "colonial" South (the area of the lower Yangtze), great numbers of Chinese moved with them into the South and a whole period of "colonial society" began around the Yangtze basin [2]. Although later in the re-unified empire (approximately 600 A.D.) migration into Central Asia and the north again became possible and tempting, most of the period until 800 A.D. seems to have been a time in which the space already settled in the earlier centuries was thoroughly filled up, while Fukien and the South: Kuangtung, Kuanghsi, Kuichou, Yünnan, even parts of Hunan and Szuch'uan remained thinly inhabited.

When, around 800, the T'ang empire began to dissolve and, in the 10th century, bandits and military leaders established their own little states, new centers developed, which attracted immigrants. Often these immigrants were the families of soldiers and their leaders who

---

[1] We are using here the modern names of areas, not the contemporary ones.
[2] See the descriptions in my *History of China*, Second edition, London, 1960, p. 152 f.

came to this region. Thus, there was a first rush into Fukien and Kuangtung in the 10th century. When the Sung dynasty was finally driven out of the Yellow River basin (around 1200) and the refugee Chinese government set itself up farther south than ever (in Hangchou), southern Chekiang and Fukien became the immediate hinterland of the capital and gained in economic importance. This apparently induced a flood of immigrants into Fukien, southern Chekiang, southern Kiangsi, and soon into Kuangtung. Many of the clans which we studied state that they came into the South during this period.

By around 1500, most of the central and southern parts of China were already quite densely populated; but parts of Kuangtung, the whole of Kuanghsi, Kuichou and Yünnan were still relatively unpopulated and attracted many settlers. In the north, however, there was not the same opportunity for emigration. This situation held in general until the late 19th century. At this time, firstly the Manchu government opened Manchuria for immigration, so that people in North China, mainly in Shantung, could again emigrate, and secondly, emigration overseas became easier, so that Southern Chinese had new opportunity.

Thus, there was always some opportunity for emigration in China, even if that opportunity for men in the central provinces was not too great in the last centuries and even though emigration into the areas north of China or into Central Asia in the periods between 1700 and 1890 was not too enticing. If we say, as we do say, that "colonial" settlement offers new chances for upward social mobility, then we might say that our conclusions from material of Kuangtung and Fukien provinces might be similarly valid for provinces like Kuanghsi, Hunan, Szuch'uan and perhaps Kiangsi for the period between 1600 and 1930, but they may not be valid for provinces north of these. Special research should be devoted to the northern parts of China during this period.

A number of studies have shown, and I think convincingly, that in the course of Chinese history the place of origin of "prominent" political leaders has shifted from Shensi and Honan first to East Honan and Shantung, later to Kiangsu and Chekiang, and that finally there seemed an indication that South China, at least in some fields, would have produced the highest percentage of leaders if the Manchu government had not set up special quotas. This shift, it has been found, took place although the capital was usually situated outside the area of origin of the highest number of leaders. The capital, naturally, attracted many leaders and sons of leaders, but never—in the last centuries before the end of the Manchu government—was productive of many leaders. It seems that the "colonial" situation and its opportunities had something to do with the supply of leaders. This problem might deserve further study.

2) The Gentry

We have defined "gentry" here as the leading sector of Chinese society from about 300 B.C. on, and we are speaking in terms of families, not of individuals. Gentry families normally were landed families and had their family home outside the cities. In each generation, ideally, at least one member of a gentry family would be a member of the bureaucracy and, at least during the time of his office, would live in a city or in the capital. By the fact of having either an official rank or an official title, the official and his family would have the legal privileges which accrue to gentry families (see Part 1, Chapter 2). These privileges were hereditary, so that the status of the family was not changed even if in one generation no member of the family held a rank or a title.

There is no Chinese term which completely covers this concept [1]. All terms, like *chin-shen* or others, mean only *persons* with certain characteristics, not a social class [1]. The term *ju-hu* (儒戶) is perhaps fairly close to our term "gentry", because it speaks of "families" and includes actual officials as well as persons without a position but with a title, and persons who studied for an examination but who may not actually have passed any of the higher examinations which give access to positions in the higher bureaucracy. It even includes persons who were granted the title of "students" because they had paid for this title.

Two points puzzled earlier researchers. One is the apparent fact that there is only a very limited number of family names in China and that families with the same family name are not allowed to intermarry [2] because, supposedly, they are all related. With such a limited number of "basic" families, then, one would expect to come up with a gentry clan for every genealogy studied. This is not quite true.

---

[1] Authors like Ch'ü T'ung-tsu and Chang Chung-li define "gentry" as a translation of one or the other Chinese terms. As long as an author clarifies what he means, there should be no discussion as to who is using a term correctly or incorrectly. The term "wang-tsu" (望族), "prominent clans", stresses another aspect, but in practice is very close to Ju-hu.

[2] With very few, comparatively recent exceptions.

A family, if it is asked to describe itself, does not simply say: "We are the Li family"; they qualify this by saying, for instance: "We are the Ch'ing-ho Li". This clearly separates this (gentry) Li family family from other, possibly non-gentry families with the same name. Although perhaps many, but certainly not all Li may go back to common ancestors of some almost prehistoric time, in Chinese consciousness they are separate families. Secondly, a good number of genealogies do not show any prominent ancestor. These are usually genealogies which do not date back very far, or genealogies in which there are great and obvious gaps between a supposed high-ranking ancestor, and the first ancestor for whom documentation is known, and whose descendants can be clearly established. As a special case, genealogies of Taiwan-Chinese families often refer back to ancestors who were not prominent at all.

The other point is the observation that a gentry family often holds its position over many centuries. Do all the prominent members of this family really belong to the same line and does this point to an unusually high degree of nepotism or favoritism? How can a family keep its economic and social standards up for such a long time? It was said, for instance, that continuous equal division of property among all sons would obviously bring about the end even of the largest property in a few generations. And proverbs were cited to prove that families show a cycle of upward and downward mobility which covers about five generations [1]. In my earlier studies on the gentry which were limited to the period before 1000 A.D., I found myself unable to answer this question. There was simply not enough detailed material available to provide an answer. Only a study of each individual in each branch of a family can provide the information. To this has to be added information as to inheritance and property which we do not have for the earlier periods.

The new picture which evolves out of our data as presented above, out of additional data from other genealogies, from a study of clan rules, and from the work of British and Japanese colleagues, differs strongly from the traditional picture of gentry families.

Gentry families consist of main houses and branch houses. At certain times, a branch house may split off altogether and become a new, independent house. It seems that such splits which created

---

[1] P'an Kuang-tao, p. 94, cited the proverbs and found that his 91 famous families in Chia-hsing (Chekiang) remained within the top level of importance from between 4 to 21 generations with an average of 8.3 generations or 210-220 years.

new houses were more common in earlier times, i.e. prior to 1600. The creation of a new house means that this part of the family has to register as an independent unit in the new location; this usually means that the new family is fairly far away from the old family. The new family has to get the permission of the old family to erect its own family and/or ancestral clan temple and to keep their own, separate genealogy. This new genealogy has to show at what place the new family broke from the old house. The break often (though probably not always) seems also to mean that the new family starts a new code for the names of the family members (see Appendix), or uses the family code in a different way. For instance in a two-word personal name the code word in the one main house may be the first word, and in the other main house the second word. In the Wu clan, houses like the Lü-wei or the Ch'iu-kuan houses are independent main houses. There is no connection between the two houses except a general courtesy in mutual contacts. No property is in common, no documents; if one house becomes involved in legal affairs, it would not affect the other house.

But as a rule, the main house controls a number of branch houses. The main house is the ritual and economic center of the family. Any charitable institutions for the welfare or the education of clan members are under the administration and control of the main house. For the main house the clan rules which have been mentioned above (Part 2, Chapter 4) are set up, and, as we have seen, these rules control also the relations between the main house and the branch houses. The branches of the main house are living on what in some periods is called a "manor" (*chuang*). Texts like the following are quite typical and enlightening:

> In a case of splitting up the property of the Ch'en clan in 1062 A.D. among new families, 291 manors and another group of 43 manors connected with offices belonging to members of the house were involved. But according to a report to the court from the year 1025, there were even more manors which had not been reported: "Those (manors) in the Chiang-nan districts could still be reached within a day; but those far-away manors in Yang-chou, Ching-chou, Huang-chou, Su-chou, Ch'üan-chou, Hui-chou, Ting-chou, Chin-hua, T'ai-p'ing, Wu-ch'ang, K'ang-chou and others involved travel of a thousand *li*. There was always the fear that notices would not reach them, and that distant members might not come to the festivals; lucky and unlucky (family) events would not be heard by them...." [1]

---

[1] *T'ai-wan Ch'en Ta-tsung-szu Tê-hsing-t'ang chung-hsiu chi-nien t'ê-k'an*, Taipei 1958, p. 100.

This shows that in 1062 the main house controlled more than 334 manors. On all of these were branch families. They all had to be served notice when there was a festival, a birth or a death, or when there were meetings in which decisions about the family had to be made. The manors consisted of two groups: one group fairly close to the main house—a travel of a day was involved. The other group of manors' was far away. A thousand *li* is not meant as an accurate measure, but may indicate distances of 200 miles and more. It was found impossible—if we interpret the words—to keep in contact with these distant manors. And this was the reason for the split which was considered. Indeed, in the next generation several hundred persons are mentioned, and each entry has a form like: "Mr. X took charge of 50 family members and went to live in Su-chou", "Mr. Y took charge of 30 family members and went to live in Wu-chou" [1] which shows that from now on the branches in Su-chou or Wu-chou, which already consisted of 50 and 30 persons, were independent from the main house.

But up to 1062, to stay with this example, the main house controlled and administrated all these more than 300 manors. The main house dealt with the government and in the tenth century, for instance, received regularly every year a government grant of 2000 *shih* grain because the clan was so large and relatively poor at that time. Around 1000 A.D. the main house got exemption from forced labor service obligations [2]. Again, later, the main house got a tax reduction of 2700 *shih* per year. All these things required skill and experience, but also gave the main house prestige over the branch houses and increased its power over the branches. Although, theoretically, division of property among male family members was equal, it was understood that the eldest son of the main house got more, because he had so many social obligations towards the branch houses. He also had charge of the property close to the main house and other brothers had to take property in the outlying manors unless they preferred to reject the idea of division of property and remained, legally as joint owners, in the main house with their older brother. In this case, they always remained under his rule as even their children were, so long as they were in the house. "Joint ownership" meant in practice that the management of the property was in the hands of the head of the family. From the management of the temple land,

---
[1] *Ibid.*, p. 117.
[2] *Ibid.*, p. 114.

the school land or the charitable foundation which the clan may possess, the main house can draw special benefits—and this is regarded as their "natural" right. If in an above-quoted clan rule it is said that everybody, "without consideration of the degree of relationship", i.e. every clan member, can use the clan study, this rule indicates that there was a tendency to restrict the use of the study to members of the main house and its favorites.

On the days of family festivals or other celebrations (like New Year's) the branch houses sent delegates. These, naturally, had to bring gifts to the main house. And the income and expenditure of the manors were controlled by the main house. All these institutions made the main house strong and wealthy. With this background, the main house could have its sons study for the examinations and could get into the official bureaucracy. This, again, could mean that the main house got the privileges of gentry families—privileges which only in rare, special cases were also automatically given to members of the branch house. Thus, the main house was typically a gentry house with all privileges, and its branch houses were common houses of free farmers. The clan, in such a case, belonged to two social classes.

We have no clear statistical data, but we can safely assume that the branch houses had to supply the main house with all it needed; free labor if the main house needed extra labor for the preparation of ceremonies; paid agricultural labor if the main house needed it for the harvest; and free household service (servants, maids) if necessary. The branch houses could get some extra income by farm labor, if their own manors were small. Otherwise, the branch houses profited in a different way from the main house: the prestige and power of the main house could protect them. In cases in which the branch house got involved in a law suit, the main house would try to straighten the case out; or the prestige of the main house alone would frighten the other side enough to make them stop action. Thus, main house and branch houses were a unit in which both partners got some benefits. If, however, the branch houses were too far away, benefits for both sides decreased quickly and the situation was favorable for a split.

With its prestige and its economic strength, the main house could acquire new land and set up new manors. If a member of the main house became a magistrate or higher official, he would hear of opportunities where good or promising land was for sale; he could, in some cases, perhaps even exercise a certain amount of pressure to get the piece of land he wanted. The new manor would, legally, belong to the main house, although we find a good number of cases in which the official who acquired the land took it himself and started a settlement which often soon became independent. More often, we hear of men who set up welfare institutions for the clan members; this is an act of merit and is, therefore, much more often mentioned than the mere acquisition of land for the clan. As an example:

> Mr. Ch'eng Chih-ho, born in 1320 A.D., later gave 500 *mou* land for the construction of the Chien-an Welfare School, and still later he gave 40 mou land for a Buddhist Sung-shen Temple at the tomb of one of the ancestors [1].

Thus, in general, the main house had possibilities to acquire more land and could, if brothers wanted to separate, give them a share without the danger that the property of the main house would become so small that the main house itself would become poor. In the less well-situated branch houses, the situation was different: if there the sons wanted their shares, the property of each became smaller and smaller in succeeding generations and the economic position of the branch house became more and more precarious. Thus, there was no danger, if the main house had many sons; on the contrary, many sons could become many influential men and raise the status and wealth of the main house even higher. Therefore, on the average, the wealthy (main) houses report more children than the poor (branch) houses.

Clearly, the head of the main house is a little king and has to be a good politician, if he wants to be successful. He has, for instance, to decide what to do with his sons. We found that perhaps in the earlier periods (before 1790) he may have shown some preference for his eldest son, but later certainly he did not show much restraint in helping through the examinations that son whom he regarded as the best. Or he bought a title for the best son. It was on this capable son that the fate of the main house in future generations hinged. Those sons who did not go to school because they either did not want to or were not capable enough to succeed, could choose to remain in the main house and, after the death of the head of the household, live under the control of their successful brother or the brother who became the new head (which was not *a priori* the success-

---

[1] *Hsin-an Ch'eng-shih t'ung-tsung shih-p'u* (Ming edition, printed after 1720), 4, 14a.

ful brother), or they could ask for their shares. In this case, the head of the family would settle them on a manor. We see further, especially in the Wu clan genealogy, that such branches which were settled on manors and whose heads were sons who had not shown special abilities, normally did not produce any capable child within at least the next 5 generations; often never. As we cannot assume that all sons in such manors were stupid, we can assume that the economic situation of the branch in the next generations was so precarious that all sons had to work as farmers, or even as tenants or laborers, to make a living. There was, for an exceptionally able child in one of these branch families, the theoretical chance that he could go to the clan school in the main house. This depended upon many factors: whether the father could spare the son; whether the main house wanted the boy; whether the main house was willing to pay his living expenses. There was also the possibility that he could get lost to the branch family by being adopted into the main house as a son. We have seen that there is a fairly high number of adoptions. The main house, if it had no son, would adopt a son, and preferably an able son, from one of the branches. This would drain talent away from the branch and into the main house—another factor which guaranteed the high position of the main house over long periods. But even if the main house had sons, they still could adopt an able son from a branch house. We have found cases in which there was a son and yet the family adopted a child. Seen from the point of view of families, a gentry family could relatively easily retain its social status and its economic strength over centuries. Whether the family moved into the top level of bureaucrats or whether it was content to remain a locally influential, "provincial gentry family" depended upon the decision of the house and factors outside their power.

In the course of time, branch families split off from the main house. These branch families are normally created by the less able members of the main house. There is not much chance for the branch house to expand its property (although we know of such cases) and, therefore, in general, the branch family shows a downward social mobility. Normally, even at the start it did not have the gentry privileges of the main house, but had the status of "farmers", i.e. free, full citizens. The branch house has to support the main house, but is protected, and to some extent assisted by the main house.

Under certain conditions split-off houses may become new main houses. The normal case is that a famous member of the main house in his activity as official acquires land, registers in the place where the land is located, and later he or his descendants make the separation official. In such a case, the new main house starts out with considerable wealth, or even with gentry status. It then can, under normal conditions, retain this gentry status and later create its own branch houses for further support.

This pattern is interrupted only in the case of a dynastic change. The most disruptive change was, as far as our texts show, the Mongol invasion of China; but the emergence of the Ming and then the Manchu invasion, too, influenced the fate of many main houses. At a certain moment, the head of the main house must decide whether he wants to stay with the old regime as well as whether he *can* stay with it, or whether he wants to and can go with the new regime. If he selects the wrong side—the one which later loses—misfortune overtakes the main house, and perhaps even some of the branch houses near-by: the male members of the house may be executed or exiled, they may lose all their land, or the like. In the Wu clan, as we saw, one house decided to go with the Mongols and rose to very high positions; the other houses were against the Mongols and suffered.

In such periods of turmoil, the main house might decide to move into a city for more protection: "... Because bandits oppressed the big families, he moved from... to...."[1] As a result of such moves, the house may lose its property: " He had left many fields, but because there was nobody to take care of the land, powerful bad persons took away almost everything.... (When the Ming Dynasty had again established order, around 1400), his son (who had lost his father and had been reared by a faithful tenant) went around under the instructions of the tenant, and collected all his old land back, over 10 ch'ing...."[2] This text also shows another danger for the main house: involvement with other, equally powerful houses[3].

We know, for instance, that our Wu clan had intermarriages, on the basis of their common origin from "Pearl Ward", with the T'an clan. We surmise from the data about the Lü-wei house of the Wu clan that something seems to have happened in generation 58, i.e. around 1400, but the Wu genealogy does not say much about it.

---

[1] *T'an-shih chih*, vol. 1, p. 337b; late 14th century.
[2] *Ibid.*, p. 338a.
[3] Such clan fights are well known also in Chinese communities outside China proper, even in San Francisco's Chinatown.

We know that at the end of the 14th century, two female members of this house were married to T'an; one of the girls was born in 1371 [1]. The husband of one of these girls became involved in a battle with neighboring clans over some burial ground. He and others were brought to Peking where they committed suicide in order to avoid public execution. This indicates that in the fight several persons had been killed, local court action had taken place, and the T'an men had been convicted. This, certainly, was a heavy blow for the T'an clan, and we can be sure that it was also a blow for the Lü-wei house of the Wu, even if the Lü-wei house did not participate directly in the fight. It is possible that the decline of the Lü-wei in this generation was in connection with the lost fight of the T'an.

Developments may also go the other way, as a text from about 100 years later, also concerning the T'an clan, shows:

> ... he then moved to Ts'ang-tou and lived there, together with the Tsou, Cheng, and other clans. Then, his descendants increased day after day and lived separately in all near-by villages. The clan made the Tu-ch'eng fort [2]. Now the Tsou, Cheng and other families felt that people were too numerous and land too scarce, so that the food decreased every day. Therefore, they selected a (new) place and moved away....[3]

Here we see that a house established branch houses all around its territory and fortified its position militarily, whereupon the neighboring, nonrelated clans found life unbearable and moved away.

The best method to retain power in this competition of clans for land was to establish sound and long-lasting marriage relations, so that a whole network of clans came into existence. These clans could exercise pressure as a group, and they could cooperatively defend themselves. We saw that the Wu clan belonged to a group of 35 clans bound together by the ties of common immigration. The Jung clan also belonged to a group of clans who at some time were sharing the same fate. There is a group of eight Fukien clans reporting that they all together immigrated into Fukien in the 4th century [4]. On Taiwan there is a group, the "Six United Clans" all of which came

---

[1] *T'an-shih chih*, vol. 1, p. 334a.
[2] Such forts(*pao*) were typical attempts towards self-defense of colonial settlements in this area; similar developments could be observed in T'ai-wan.
[3] *T'an-shih chih*, vol. 1, p. 338b.
[4] *Lin-hsing tsung-ch'in lu*, Taipei, 1937, p. 11, quoting a text from 1088. These clans were led by the famous Lin. The other clans are the Huang, Ch'en, Ch'eng, Tan, Ch'iu, Ho, and Hu.

from P'u-t'ien in Fukien and later all immigrated into Taiwan [1]. As far as I was able to study intermarriages, the preferential marriage is always within such a group. Marriages outside the group can be explained either as marriages which were concluded because no preferred partner was available, or as political marriages [2]: in order to tie another family to one's own family for a short-term period, such as for one generation. But we find within these immigrant groups some families who developed still narrower marriage relations, by selecting their partners, as far as possible, from only one other clan. The policy of the Jung clan is an example of this. Such a system, which is not rare in South China, looks to the outside, like a cross-cousin marriage system. But it should not be confounded with the intermarriage system which M. Granet tried to reconstruct for ancient China. I am not at all sure whether Granet's interpretations [3] are correct; it could well be that conditions similar to those which we found in South China prevailed also in ancient China and led to similar consequences, i.e. to the picture that some, but not all, families had preferential marriage systems which may have approached cross-cousin or similar systems. Under no conditions, however, can the preferential marriage systems of our South Chinese clans be regarded as a "survival" of ancient Chinese customs.

---

[1] *Liu-Kui ts'ung-k'an*, Taichung, 1957, p. 19. This clan federation exists also in the Philippines (J. Amyot, *The Chinese Community of Manila, a Study of Adaptation of Chinese Familism to the Philippine Environment*, Philipp. Studies Program, Research Series no. 2, mimeogr., Univ. of Chicago 1960, p. 34 et al.). Amyot points out that in some federations endogamic marriages were forbidden, because the clans, although they have different clan names, believe that they had common ancestors. Other federations were set up on the basis of an "artificial brotherhood" bond which again excluded marriages within such a group. I found no comparable data from Mainland China yet.

[2] There are, of course, cases of marriages with still other motivations. I want to mention here, as an example, a case of "eugenic" marriage: a member of the gentry notices on a children's playground a boy with remarkable features and takes him as a husband for his daughter. As it happens, the father of the boy was a cloth dealer and objected against the marriage because he felt socially too low to become associated with a gentry family (P'an Kuang-tan, *loc. cit.*, p. 125). Normally cases of "inter-class" marriages have to be checked closely. In a case reported by P'an (*loc. cit.*, p. 125-6), a gentry member marries the daughter of a cloth dealer, but it turns out that the man had been an official, i.e. a member of the gentry, who had been so honest during his period of office that he had lost all his means and had to try to make a living by selling cloth.

[3] M. Granet, "Catégories matrimoniales et relations de proximité dans la Chine ancienne", in *Annales sociologiques*, serie B, Paris, 1939, 254 pages, and his earlier books and articles. His theory has been taken up by Lévy-Strauss.

They can all be satisfactorily explained as a result of an immigration situation and concomitant power struggles among clans.

The alliances between clans by marriage are often, though apparently not always, strengthened by common religious worship. Clearly, for instance, the cult of the deity T'ien-hou (Heavenly Queen) is connected with the Fukienese Lin clan; according to the tradition of the Lin clan [1], she was a daughter of the Lin clan, born in 999 A.D. Her cult, which spread as far as California, migrated together with clans of Fukienese who originally were allied with the Lin clan. This subject of the connection of cults with clans has not yet been extensively studied [2], but some data from Taiwan may indicate the connections:

> On the days of sacrifices in the Kuang-chi temple in Pang-liao and the Fu-ho temple in Miao-mei, the 14 villages near Pang-liao all celebrate, and people from these villages come to the festival, creating an unusual crowd. At this time there are great feasts for relatives and friends. Statistically, each farm family spends on such a day as much for food as a family of five persons needs in a month [3].

Such festivals, called "pai-pai" in Taiwan, may cost the community as much as 80 million NT [4]. So we read:

> The residents of Shihlin in suburban Taipei spent an estimated NT 6,000,000 last Tuesday in an extravagant "pai-pai" honoring a local deity. According to statistics, they consumed in a single day about 500 heads of hogs, 20,000 chickens, 12,000 ducks, 10,000 catties of fish, 36,000 bottles of liquor, 60,000 bottles of soda water and 12,000 packs of cigarettes. The number of people who gathered from other places for "pai-pai" dinners was estimated at over 50,000 [5].

Now, in the area mentioned above, there were twenty villages with 3,603 families. Only two villages had ancestral temples, which indicates that there were only two established main houses in this area, the rest being branch houses. There were a total of five other temples in this area, two of which are mentioned above. On the

---

[1] According to Lou Tzu-k'uang in *Wen-shih hui-k'an*, vol. 1, Taipei, 1959, p. 1; others give her birth date as 960 (Texts in *T'oung Pao*, vol. 34, p. 344 f.) or 961 (*Lin-shih tsung-p'u*, Taichung, 1935, p. 53a-b and *China Post*, Taipei, of April 15, 1960) and some even as 742 (H. C. Li in *Tôyô gakuhô*, vol. 39, 1956, no. 1, p. 76).

[2] A detailed study along these lines is under preparation.

[3] *T'ai-pei hsien, Chung-ho ch'ü-chih yen-chiu*, anonymous B. A. thesis, Taipei, 1951, Nat. Taiwan University Library, no. 589449, p. 55.

[4] *China Post*, Taipei, June 5, 1960. One US $ corresponded roughtly to 40 NT. $

[5] *China Post*, May 19, 1960.

average each village had one Earth God temple [1]. But Earth God temples serve a very special function, and do not concern us here. Of the five temples, two were connected with 14 of the twenty villages and served a total of 15,362 persons, while another temple served only three villages with 3,643 persons [2]. The Kuang-chi temple, mentioned above, is devoted to the T'ien-hou, and this, again, indicates that the worshippers in these 14 villages were Fukienese from the group related to the Lin clan. Thus:

> The old Taiwanese temple was not only a center of the life of villagers; it was also an institution which bound the villagers together, and a center which connected villagers with the officials. These temples were not only functioning as an institution of self-government in the villages, they were also institutions for social contact and entertainment, and sometimes they were even organizations for culture and education.... [3]

Similarly, the famous Lung-shan temple in the Wan-hua quarter of Taipei, was

> since the Middle of the Manchu period the meeting place of the guilds from Ch'üan-chou (in Fukien) and the affairs and meetings of the Ch'üan-chou people were all handled there. Also, the Ch'üan-chou people had the obligation of caring for the reconstruction of the temple and had to carry all costs for its operation [4].

Those Taiwanese immigrants who came from Chang-chou, by preference worship the K'ai-Chang temples, devoted to Ch'en Yüan-kuang, who created the city of Chang-chou in Fukien and who was killed 711 A.D. in a fight with natives. His descendants ruled more or less independently over the city down to about 1000 A.D. Later, the Ch'en clan together with a group of other Chang-chou clans emigrated to Formosa and the K'ai-Chang temples ("Temples for the Opener of Chang-chou") are the common center for this group of clans [5].

For branch families such temples were institutions which bound them together and served their emotional needs. For main families they were a symbol of strength, status and pride. I know a number

---

[1] *T'ai-pei hsien Chung-ho ch'ü-chih yen-chiu*, p. 44.
[2] *ibid.*, p. 56-7.
[3] Mrs. Yang Ch'ing-yü, "T'ai-wan-ti min-su" in *Hsin-shê-hui*, Taipei, Febr. 1960, vol. 12, no. 2, p. 5b-c.
[4] *ibid.*, p. 5c
[5] *T'ai-wan Ch'en Ta-tsung-szu*, p. 310 gives the connection between the temples and the clan.

of Taiwanese temples which were built by families whose descendants are today very proud of them. Through the temple organization and administration (by way of committees), the founding family may gain extra strength. And through the use of the temple as a meeting place of the family and its allied families, the temple may become the political center of the clan. Temples served also as places where interclan troubles (among allied clans) were settled [1].

So much for the relations between the main house and its branch houses and the relations between different clans; so much also for the ways by which the main house attempts to keep up its status as a gentry family, and the reasons that it was so difficult for branch families who had a lower status to begin with to move up. There are some individual cases which are highly interesting. Usually, such persons are described in the genealogies by phrases like: "He threw away the books and went away" [2]. We guess that here we have sons who were supposed to study and to enter the official career, but who, for some reason, felt unwilling to go through the long rigmarole of studying and memorizing, and who, also, were not willing to settle down on some manor, pick up the plough and work hard without much hope of ever achieving a satisfactory standard of living or of seeing any other part of the world. These young men, then, the "maladjusted", went away, apparently often with some money from their fathers, and entered the world of business. Typically,

---

[1] Disputes within the clan were settled in the clan's ancestral temple. Cases of dispute between clans were often settled in the Kuan-ti temple (Makino, *l.c.*, p. 148). Of course, clans can also temporarily collaborate in religious ceremonies, for instance in a rain sacrifice when no rain is falling (Makino, *l.c.*, p. 147). —Two other connections between gentry families and certain deities should be studied: On large religious paintings in Taiwan I have seen accompanying figures who carry names which make it clear that they were thought of as deified ancestors of clans still living in the area. In one temple, for instance, I met a deified ancestor of the Wu clan on such a painting. It seems clear that the clan in such cases has a special relationship to this temple and to the other deified ancestors on the same painting. But it remains unclear what type of relationship is indicated here. Are these figures perhaps the mythical ancestors of persons who immigrated together as a group? Secondly, we know that some of the side figures on large religious paintings are actual portraits of donors. We know this from frescoes in Central Asia, but we can prove that this custom also existed in Ming time China, although art historians usually claim that the Chinese had no interest in portraits except for ancestral worship made after the death of the person. Here again, we believe, that the portrait of the donor on a particular painting in a particular temple might provide clues for clarification of the connections between clans and deities.

[2] Huang Tien-ch'üan in *T'ai-nan wen-hua*, vol. 5, no. 2, 1956, p. 34.

they went quite far, at least a hundred miles. They seem not to have started small business, but usually went into large-scale (later, often export-import) business. And then, at the end of their biographies, we often read: "He became quite wealthy". He would then typically buy land and create a new settlement far away from the home settlement. Or he would buy a title for himself and/or his son(s), and in the next generation we may see our "maladjusted" family on the level of the main house. There is considerable crossing the lines from gentry families into business, in spite of the regulations which forbade this, and in spite of the prejudices against business preached by the philosophers. It seems plausible that the regulations could easily be circumvented as long as the "run-away" son remained legally attached to the main house and remained, legally, either a gentry member or a free farmer (member of classes 1 or 2). From experience in Formosa, we might conclude that the main house was not always as unhappy about these "maladjusted" individuals as one might think; such a large house which controlled branch houses had a lot of business to do: selling and exporting of rice and other farm products, as well as buying of luxury goods and other farm needs. It might be very advantageous to have this type of business conducted by a family member who is known, and under family control rather than by a stranger of low class whom one had no reason to trust.[1] Popular opinion in Taiwan believes that among the new settlers the strongest sons became soldiers who guarded the land against attack by the aborigines; the most clever and active ones became merchants who sold the produce on the mainland; the other sons became farmers. Such "division of labor" was regarded as very advantageous. In modern times, since the impact of trade with the West, more and more of these family businessmen became independent and lifetime businessmen. This career of a family-businessman was, then, a third possibility for a son from the gentry, or main house.

We will later, in the discussion of the merchants, talk more about these "gentleman-merchants". As an example, we would like to give here some data from the Yeh clan on Formosa which has been studied so ably by Huang Tien-ch'üan [2].

The Yeh clan from the coast of Fukien could boast of members

---

[1] The same development could be observed among Southeastern Turkish landlord families.
[2] Huang Tien-ch'üan in *T'ai-nan wen-hua*, vol. 5, no. 2, 1956, p. 20-48; our texts below are from pages 39-40; 32, 33.

from gen. 4 (the first man lived from 1634-1694) who received titles of the lowest rank, and from gen. 5 (the first man lived from 1656-1730) of men who were admitted to government schools, i.e. who were *Ju-hu*, gentry members.

But from this same 5th generation on, clan members also showed other inclinations. One man in this generation "had from birth a leg disease. Therefore, he did not attempt to compete for the examinations (invalids or cripples were not admitted) and studied medicine". Until the present day, the clan still has a pharmacy and sells a special drug discovered by this ancestor. This type of activity and its importance will be described later in more detail.

More typical are other clan members: Yeh Feng-ch'un, of gen. 3 (1588-1677), "was an unusual man, way above ordinary men. But he did not succeed in the examinations. So, he went away and into business. When not yet 30 years of age, he became the head of the big merchants of An-p'ing".

Yeh Sen of gen. 4 (1618-1674) "was intelligent and studied hard. He had a broad knowledge of classical and historical texts. But after 1644 there were troubles along the sea coast. Thus he learned business and went to sea to do business. He made 13 trips to foreign countries.... Later he settled inland, and started again in business with Kuangtung and Kuanghsi provinces...."

A member of gen. 5 (1687-1760) "did business in Taiwan... and got rich. He returned home, built a house and served his ancestors".

Yeh I-chang (gen. 6, 1686-1765) in his younger years travelled on business. Later he lived at home and became a music lover and was a good singer. A cousin of this man (gen. 6, 1690-1721) first studied, but then, because his family was poor, and because he felt that he should raise their standard of living, he "learned business in the atelier of Ch'en Wen-i in Taiwan". Because of his honesty, he was commissioned to trade with Japan.

Yeh Wen-chih, (gen. 7, 1726-1785) "studied for the examination but because his parents were old, he gave up and went into business in Formosa. As soon as he had some capital, he returned and took care of the parents. From time to time, he had credit agreements with the foreign merchants in Amoy and again achieved wealth...."

Yeh Tun-hsiao (gen. 8, 1745-1770) at 18 years of age gave up studying to go into business with his uncles in Jun-chou. Incidentally, this man rejected a concubine. He was the first family member who, with an uncle, moved into Shanghai for business.

The clan genealogy offers still more examples. This clan had gentry status at the same time that other members went into business. Some became gentleman-merchants because they failed the examinations and rejected a life of study. Others were poor and had not much hope of becoming rich by virtue of officialdom. It should be kept in mind that the home town of the Yeh in Fukien was in an area in which investment in land was difficult and unprofitable; the place was close to the coast and mountainous. Thus, large-scale business as gentlemen-businessmen was the best solution.

As we then see, most of these gentlemen, towards the end of their lives, and sometimes earlier, retired to their homes, lived according to their inclinations, served their family and their ancestors—and changed back from businessmen to "gentlemen".

3) The Farmer

Let us now look into the pattern of social mobility in the second of the four traditional social classes of the Chinese, the farmers (*nung*). This term includes individual, independent farm families as well as families of tenants, part-tenants and even families of agricultural laborers, under some conditions. We are excluding from this definition the above-mentioned gentry families even if the main house might, if asked in modern times, classify itself as "farmers".

We have already seen that farm families are often branches of families with gentry status, who were settled on one of the gentry family's manors. As the newly settled branch family started with land only, and no capital, it could not quickly enlarge its property. Normally, then, with the growing size of the family, the economic position would become more and more depressed. This decline could be slowed down by two developments: a) The limitation of the size of families. Each survey shows again, that small cultivators have smaller families than large cultivators:

> "The average size of each household is 8.44 persons.... Our study shows that the average size of households of small cultivators is smaller than those of households of the medium and large cultivators. ... In the northern section of Taiwan, the average size of households of small cultivators is 7.07 persons, in the central section it it 7.65 persons, and in the southern section it is 7.45 persons. ... In the small-cultivator families the average number of earners is 3.24 of

7.42 persons, the average number of earning dependents is 0.39, and the average number of dependents is 3.79" [1].

b) The farmer can keep the land together by joint ownership. Here is a report from modern Taiwan describing a custom which has existed in the same form on the Mainland for a long time. Actually, during the Ming time (1368-1644) it was punishable by law to divide the land among sons as long as their parents and grandparents lived [2]. We doubt whether actual practice was always so and suspect that a separation could take place and yet be legal.

> "A few words about the joint ownership of land. This is a rather common phenomenon in Taiwan. It means that the land is jointly owned by brothers, close relatives, or other kinship-related people.... The number of joint-owner families is even larger than the number of individual-owner families. The causes that have given rise to joint ownership are three: reclamation of land through common efforts in the early history of Taiwan; joint purchase of land; and inheritance of ancestral landed property by brothers. The Taiwan landowners themselves preferred joint ownership in order to avoid incidental troubles of sub-division, surveying, and the red tape of transfers. Under such circumstances, it frequently happened that a piece of land originally under individual ownership might come to be jointly owned when it was transferred or inherited; and that a piece of land originally under joint ownership might have a larger number of joint owners as time went on. The number of joint owners of a plot of land varies from 3 or 5 to scores or hundreds of persons. This state of affairs not only is a positive hindrance to cadastral management, but also obstructs land improvement and gives rise to innumerable disputes" [3].

Note that in Taiwan at the time of this survey (1958), the average area of farm land per family was 1.1 hectares [4].

Joint operation, even if the owners do not live together in one household (which they not often do), may cut down the cost of operations under traditional agricultural techniques, and if the owners live in one household, the cost of operation of households may be cut considerably. Yet, with growing population, in spite of attempts towards limitation, the standard of living of these farmers over time could not improve much, if at all. Technical improvements or improved varieties of crops mean an increased risk; and we know

---

[1] *Preliminary Report: A Study on the Impact of Farmer's Associations and Extension Program on the Development of Agriculture in Taiwan*, Taipei, June 15, 1959, pp. 71-72.
[2] N. Niida, *Legal Documents*, p. 559.
[3] *Preliminary Report*, p. 35.
[4] *Preliminary Report*, p. 34.

from farmers all over the world that poor farmers often think they cannot afford extra risks in their already precarious situation.

Now what could farm families do? Emigration is not easy, because the emigrant has to have enough capital to be able to finance his first year until the time of his first harvest. Usually, in South China, successful settlement meant the installation of irrigation works which is a big capital outlay. Our above-mentioned officials who bought land at the places where they once had a job, usually had enough money and thus we see them building irrigation facilities and quickly getting rich. But even in areas like Taiwan where, in the 18th century, much land could give high yields without irrigation, simple farmers had not too much chance: they had to pay the fare on the boat; had to homestead land, to clear it and to wait. Homesteading was not easy, as officials immediately interfered and as the aborigines set up sales contracts which cost the Chinese dearly. One way which was apparently often used was to accompany a colonial party. Such parties were organized by influential and wealthy men (occasionally by bandits, as well) who conquered or otherwise claimed land in the new place, and who then settled the farmers, who had to work for the organizers, i.e. who became tenants. The organizer paid for the move and kept the future tenants alive during the first year. He also helped them with implements and, if necessary, with animals. He put in irrigation where this was regarded by him as necessary, but only after the tenants had cleared the jungle. Finally, he made all arrangements with the local authorities in the new place or organized out of his tenants or out of a special group a military force which could keep the aborigines in check. The farmer who joined such an enterprise may—and we think that this was relatively often the case—have been a tenant of the organizer in the first place and induced by him to join the expedition. Or he may have joined the organizer just for the purpose of emigration. His hope was always that in the new country he and his family would have so much more land that even as a tenant he could live better than before. Usually, as an added attraction, there was a promise of low or no rent in the first years. The farmer may also have hoped that he either could make some surpluses and then acquire land of his own or that tenancy conditions would be loose so that he could soon regard himself as an owner. Developments of this type can be studied in the history of the settlement of Taiwan. There, some organizers finally had little kingdoms under their control, and what developed here—and apparently in other places as well—were conditions which looked exactly like some type of feudalism. We should add here that we gained the impression that in some cases even craftsmen and artisan families were added to the emigrating party so that "full" settlements could be created in the new country immediately. From the scant information about the earliest settlement of people from mainland Asia in Japan, it seems that here processes of this type were carried out, i.e. immigration of already structured groups, consisting of an organizer and his family or clan, farmers who would become tenants, soldiers and craftsmen. The organizer at the same time seems to have been the owner (or renter?) of the ship. As for the immigration into Formosa which went on mainly in the 18th and 19th centuries [1], we do not yet know who owned the ships. A special study of the details of immigration into Formosa seems to be highly desirable.

Another similar process could perhaps be described as "seepage". It occurs typically in thinly inhabited areas just outside the area of Chinese sovereignty, or in areas in which Chinese sovereignty is so weak that it is not an important factor. Farmers close to these areas could muster the courage and go on a march of several days or more until they reached a landowner outside the borders, or a settler in the jungle. If he was a relatively recent settler who had claimed a large area but had not yet been able to develop the place because of lack of manpower, he might be willing to accept the newcomers as tenants under relatively good conditions. Such processes—in which not only Chinese were involved (the newcomers could belong to any other group as well) are known from the Southeast Asian countries [2]. A variant of this type is the case in which a Chinese farmer leaves the country and puts himself under the authority of an aboriginal landowner. There are large groups of tribes in China's Southwest in which the chiefs assert that many of the "serfs" or slaves which they have in their group were originally Chinese [3]. Often, it is difficult to say whether these people, if they really originally

---

[1] After 1683 all Chinese living on Formosa had to return. From 1710 on Fukienese settlers began to make contracts with aborigines and settled. Emigrants had to check in in Amoy and were not allowed to take relatives over. 1723 began a period in which sometimes emigration was allowed, sometimes not. Only from 1760 on, immigration into Taiwan became free (*An-p'ing Kao-shih tsu-p'u chih-lüeh*, p. 1 of Appendix).

[2] J. Cuisinier, *Les Mu'o'ng, géographie humaine et sociologie*, Paris, 1948, 618 pages, Travaux et mémoires de l'Institute d'Ethnologie, vol. 45, is a good example of this type of settlement.

[3] Brief discussion in my *Kultur und Siedlung der Randvölker*, p. 324.

had been Chinese, came of their own free will, or were prisoners of war who had been forced to stay. A better, clearer example of this type of settlement is found in the North of China, in Manchuria or Mongolia [1]. The Chinese farmer who subordinates himself to a native hopes to get tenancy conditions which are better than those at home, and perhaps a landlord who treats him better than his own landlords or his own government officials did. This "seepage" migration of farmers is illegal according to Chinese law; thus, there is the added difficulty for seepage migrations that they have to be done secretly. As in the organized migrations, seepage migrations can produce social structures which look like feudal societies.

Another variant of this "seepage" migration occurred not rarely within China: farmers who had lived as tenants under some landlord whom they regarded as specially oppressive, could leave him and try to find another, better landlord and become his tenants. This act was also illegal, because each family was registered in its home area and was not allowed simply to leave to move into another district. Moreover, the former landlord could use his influence or power to recover the fugitive tenants. Finally, the new landlord, if he had power or influence enough to protect the newcomers, might try to keep them without having them registered. In such a case, they were completely dependent upon him, and he could use them in whatever way he saw fit. When a landlord wanted to start some industry, he typically used such unregistered tenants as industrial workers. He also could use them as his private army in case he planned some military action [2]. Chinese official terminology calls such farmers who left their homes (where they were impoverished, marginal landowners or tenants) and put themselves under the protection of another landlord, "vagrants" (*liu-min*). While the first two variants of "seepage" migration may lead to serfdom, this third type may and often did lead to the status of industrial laborer in small, rural factories or mines.

Although no statistics are available or possible, it would seem that neither organized nor seepage migrations ever offered the farmer much of a future: at best, he could hope to become a small landowner, if he had been a tenant before; or he could hope to have enough to

---

[1] A good analysis in O. Lattimore, *Mongols of Manchuria*, New York, 1934; also in his *Inner Asian Frontiers of China*, New York, 1940.

[2] See the story of an industrialist (W. Eberhard, "Wang K'o, an early Industrialist" in *Oriens*, vol. 10, 1957, pp. 248-252).

eat as a tenant in the new country. But access into the gentry class was only a distant hope for future generations.

If, at this point, we turn back to the discussion of the gentry, we see now that there is a second circle which surrounds the main house of a gentry family. The first circle are the branch families which may be landowner families tied to the main house by legal and/or ritual ties or which may be quasi-tenants tied to the main house by special ties. The next circle, then, are the real tenants of the main house: non-related families who have received part of the land (and/or houses) of the main house for the purpose of cultivation, and who return to the main house a contractually defined percentage of the produce. They receive a treatment which differs from that of the branch family tenants, because the basis of the mutual relations is only a contract; no ritual, emotional or familistic ties exist. Some clan rules indicate that landowners were quite aware of the difference, and stipulated that certain parts of the clan land, especially temple land (i.e. land belonging to the clan, the income of which serves to pay for the costs of one or more family shrines or temples) or school land (i.e. land the income from which serves to pay for the cost of the clan school) should never be rented out to relatives (i.e. branch families), but only to strangers, because of the difficulty in collecting rents from such land which the branch families would regard as at least in part their own land, and because of the added difficulty in evicting blood-related tenants should they prove to be unfit. Income from tenants would add financial strength to the main house. Tenants could much more often be asked to perform unpaid labor services than branch families who could be asked only to perform unpaid services which were in some way related to clan affairs of ritual character and who would otherwise have to be paid for their services. In special cases, landlords could organize their tenants as a military corps and use them for that purpose. Tenants were an important factor for the landlord and he did not want to lose them. As a result of all these conditions, it can be seen clearly that farmers who were tenants had practically no hope for much upward social mobility.

Now, what possibilities other than organized or seepage migration did a farmer have? One way which especially in the Ming time was quite common was government-sponsored migration. Here, again, we can see several variants: a) Farmers who had committed some crime were sent in groups to the Southern provinces and were settled as a criminal colony. Except for the restriction that they were not allowed to return home [1], they were practically free landowners. b) Farmers who had been drafted into the armed forces, had participated in some military activity, were settled in the newly conquered or "pacified" place as a military, colony (*ying*) [2]. Such a settlement may be forced but it also could be a reward for good service. Such settlers were, in practice, free landowners. c) The government transported farmers from one place to another either to break their power (if the farmers had constituted a political force) or to supply the government or government officials with some product, such as rice, in areas where supply was scarce [3], or to fill up an underpopulated area. All three variant forms of government-sponsored migrations are extremely common through almost all of Chinese history; thus far no systematic study of these processes has been made.

If we regard the story of the Pearl Ward settlers (see above, Part 2, chapter 2) as historical truth, we could try to interpret it as a form of variant "a" above: because the government assumed that the farmers in Nan-hsiung planned a revolt, they were sent away to the south as a group. The report which we have represents the embellished story of this. But we could also try to interpret the text as a form of variant "c": the government was interested in filling up some district in South China and sent this group of farmers down. In the history of the Jung clan we can perhaps see more clearly a migration of form "a": for some reason, probably a crime, farmers were sent to the South to work in the salt fields. Later, they regained their freedom.

---

[1] A text, from Han time, mentions 379 convicts as farm laborers in a military settlement in Central Asia (*Bull. Academia Sinica*, vol. 11, p. 66). From this time on, we find many texts on convicts. Laws of 719 and 737 determined that a deported convict could get 20 days vacation to visit his parents once every 3 years, if they were still alive and if his place of exile was more than 3000 *li* away from home. Travel time was not included (N. Niida, *T'ang Law*, p. 736).

[2] The system was called the *t'un-t'ien* system and existed in various forms from the 2nd century B.C. on (in general see Ōshima Toshikazu in *Tōyōshi Kenkyu*, vol. 14, 1955, p 1 ff, and Sadao Nishijima in *Memoirs Inst. Orient. Culture*, vol. 10, 1956, p. 1-84). A thorough study of forms of settlement in China is an urgent desideratum. At the moment, the Ph. D. thesis by H. D. Scholz, *Die Formen der ländlichen Siedlung in China*, Universität Bonn 1949, 185 pages, is the only work on this topic which tries to generalize. See also H. D. Scholz's short note in *Sinologica*, vol. 3, 1953, p. 40 f.

[3] As one example in many: the Mongols resettled farmers from Chekiang province near Peking in order to have more rice there (texts in *Yü-kung*, vol. 7, 1937, no. 1/3, p. 231; the same article discusses the settlement policy of the Ming dynasty, p. 232 ff).

The settlers of type "a" are not necessarily always farmers; punishment of this type could happen to members of gentry families, especially if the family head had been executed. Then other members of his family (main house) could be sent away into exile as were criminals, or they could be put into the army. In such cases, the exile meant a legal loss of gentry status, and the exile's family, stripped of their wealth, was in more or less the same position as other exiles. In other cases, a gentry member was exiled for a more or less definite period and without permanent legal loss of status. We know, for instance, from the Wu genealogy that such gentry members were not entirely without means, and also had status enough to be able to marry into local influential families [1], so that soon they reappeared as local landowners of considerable status.

Government-sponsored migration, especially of forms "a" and "b", is not regarded as very glamorous; thus, genealogies are not too explicit about them. Yet it seems that such migrations gave much better opportunity to the settlers than the other types of migration, if we think in terms of families and of generations, rather than in terms of individuals. Before we conclude the discussion of rural migrations of farmers, we should add here the modern, i.e. 19th century, type of labor migration into overseas areas, including the United States. Here, we typically find the foreign labor recruiter, assisted by local recruiters. In spite of several studies of this problem of labor migration [2] we do not know too much about the local recruiters. We know from other countries that a labor recruiter is really efficient if he is 1) well known in the area in which he recruits and trusted by the local population, 2) trusted by his customer, the foreign labor recruiter, the factory owner (if he recruits for factory labor) or other customers, and 3) if he has some capital so that he can pay advances on the salaries of the men he recruits to the families

---

[1] This is not the "living-in son-in-law" custom. But Chinese settlers all over South China and Southeast Asia have, since early times, liked to marry into local families, and have by this act often gained considerable power. For a Chinese, any woman becomes a Chinese woman after marriage. For some of the aboriginal tribes with matrilineal organization or tendency towards such a form of organization, it was proper to marry a man, even a stranger, who then would be the manager of the family property, though not the owner. Thus, such a marriage, was "good" for both parties, especially if the Chinese husband could arrange so that after his death the property would go to his children.

[2] For instance, see K. J. Pelzer, *Die Arbeiterwanderungen in Südostasien*, Hamburg, 1935, or his later *Pioneer Settlement in the Asiatic Tropics*, New York, 1945, or many other books.

of these men, can pay the travel expenses or at least part of them, and does not have to ask his customer immediately for payment of his expenses. We hypothesize that many labor recruiters in China who worked for foreign labor recruiters and supplied them with "coolies" were members of gentry families who lived temporarily in the sea ports of China or were businessmen who still had kinship ties to local gentry families and could, in either event, use their influence in the family home area to recruit sons of tenants or sons of impoverished marginal landowners. Experience all over Southeast Asia and the Americas show that this type of migration opened excellent chances for upward social mobility, if again we think in terms of families and generations, not in terms of individuals.

There is yet another possibility for an impoverished farmer to change his condition: migration into cities. This is an extremely interesting problem about which we know almost nothing, and research is urgently needed to clarify essential, general questions. Not even some of the fundamental questions are clear. We know, for instance, that in Japan under the Tokugawa regime philosophers were against migration of farmers into the cities, and proclaimed city life as "bad". Following them, the government tried to prevent movement into the cities by legislation. We think that similar attitudes and laws existed in China as well, but we are not aware of any special study of this question. It is surprising to note how little the city was discussed by Chinese philosophers, essayists or even poets in the time between 300 B.C. and 1300, with which the author is fairly familiar. We find quite a number of descriptions of buildings, mainly palaces and temples, in cities; and these descriptions are usually in praise of the construction, unless the object is to criticize an extravagant ruler. We find, especially from 1000 A.D. on, quite lively descriptions of city life: different shops, amusement centers, parks, temples, fairs, festivals, etc. Such descriptions continue to be written down to the 19th century and are almost totally positive. The city is a wonderful, exciting place. I have not yet found texts which complain about the noises, the smells, the crowds in cities. If persons leave the city to live in their villas in the surrounding hills, they do so for personal reasons, usually because they are tired of the life of a government official, but not primarily because they hate the city. I want to propose as a hypothesis that the writers, i.e. gentry members, never felt caught in the cities: their family always kept the family home in the countryside, and whenever they wanted, at least for all festivals and ceremonies, they could and did return to the country house. They knew they had to stay in the city only so long as they wanted to.

The main problem which we encounter if we want to study the Chinese city [1] is that, perhaps out of the conditions which we just indicated, Chinese administrators did not regard the city as an administrative unit (the capital district excepted) but as a part of a regional area which was largely rural. It is extremely difficult to decide whether a certain text, especially one which contains statistical data, speaks of the whole district of, let us say, Chiu-chiang, or only of Chiu-chiang which is the administrative center of the district.

For these reasons, the following remarks are more or less impressionistic, i.e. they cannot yet be put on a statistical basis.

The city offered several possibilities to the farmer. The first one—to start at the bottom—was to become a *beggar*. By definition a beggar is a person whose whole family and clan are so poor that they cannot take care of this person any more. Or, a beggar is a person who by some bad luck has lost all contact with his family and clan; for instance, if as a soldier he had been transported into a place far away from his home and then had been discharged or had run away from the army. Finally, a beggar can be a man who has been excommunicated from his clan. We discussed some such cases of excommunication above [2]. It is not true that beggars in China are a result of contact with the West. We have enough texts to prove that even before any real impact of the West upon China there were places in which masses of beggars rotted together and bothered the citizens [3]. And we know that the government periodically supported the poor by free distribution of food, that poor houses and old age homes were created [4], or poor people were picked up and sent away as settlers. Beggars even had their own guildlike organization [5]. An intensive study of social welfare institutions in pre-modern China would, I believe, give much new insight and is a highly desirable research project.

Once a person had become a beggar, chances for upward social

---

[1] Preliminary remarks in my article "Data on the Structure of the Chinese City in the pre-industrial Period", in *Economic Development and Cultural Change*, 1956, pp. 253-268.

[2] In general see Makino, p. 140.

[3] *Yang-chou hua-fang lu*, 4, p. 81 (18th century).

[4] The creation and organization of poor-houses is much discussed in Chinese texts. The best general article in Chinese is by Hsü I-t'ang in the *Bull. of Chinese Studies*, vol. 8, 1948, pp. 65-82; but see also *Bull. Chinese Studies*, vol. 4a, 194 pp. 231-288 and vol. 5a, pp. 33-49. In general on reasons for poverty and types of poverty see H. Lamson, *Social Pathology in China*, Shanghai, 1935, p. 14 f.

[5] P. Maybon, *Essay sur les associations en Chine*, Paris, 1925, p. 179 f.

mobility were extremely slim, according to all we know now. This was more or less the end of the line.

Secondly, a farmer could become a *servant*. If he was already a tenant of a landowner who had gentry status and who had one branch in the city as an official, this official might hire him or his son as a servant, and this was an honor which one could reject only with difficulty. Besides, a young village boy could come to the city, approach the official from his village and ask him for a job. The official often would either take him or find a job with some other city gentry family. Of course, the city official also needed female servants and would find them in the same way. Beautiful daughters of farmers even had the chance to become mistresses and later concubines of their masters. Some of the glory which was theirs would then, normally, also fall upon her family, especially her brothers. The servants usually had fairly good security in the houses of the gentry in town, could marry and raise families which always would have enough to eat. They could by "squeeze" or other means, save some capital, perhaps in time even so much that they could acquire some land and finally become landowners. A good number of cases of servants to foreign families are known in which the servants in time became real landlords. Thus, the career of a servant in a gentry family in town, especially in a family whose home was in the village from which the servant came, offered good prospects if the master was decent and the servant intelligent and willing to settle in a place other than his home village.

A farmer could also become office servant in some government office [1] Such positions were normally part of the forced labor requirements of Chinese citizens; but it was good luck if the person became an office boy or an office clerk instead of a road-worker, or was assigned other menial jobs. His term of service was legally limited, but we know of cases in which an office clerk remained of his own free will or otherwise, because special ties between him and the official whom he served had developed. As an experienced office boy, the young man, in course of time, would have some possibility of saving money, as by "squeezing" persons who wanted to see the official, by outright bribes or other means. Especially, if such a man had some training, for instance, if he could read and write, his chances became quite good. We have cases in the genealogies in which young men from branch families followed an official on his tours and, finally, found ways and means to acquire some land—perhaps even

---

[1] see the excellent discussion by Ch'ü T'ung-tsu, *Local Government in China*, Cambridge 1962, p. 74-92.

the official helped him as a reward for years of faithful service. In general, this career was not quite as promising as the first one, because the tie was primarily to the office and not primarily to the person.

Here, we should mention the "half-educated", i.e. the man from a farmer's family, who had had some chance to learn something, though not enough to be able to compete in the official examination. He could become, for instance, a shaman, i.e. a practician of folk religion, or a doctor, i.e. a practician of folk medicine, not an officially recognized government doctor who had to pass through a set of government examinations. Or he could become a geomancer, i.e. a person who had some knowledge about where to bury a dead person so that the descendants of the dead would have good luck; or where and how to build a house so that the inhabitants would have good luck. As we saw from the clan rules, a shaman or a doctor could be employed by a gentry family as clan servant. Because of his special training, he was higher than ordinary servants, though lower than a teacher who also was a clan employee. As a geomancer he would be self-employed, but many of his customers would be gentry members. In all these cases, he had the opportunity to establish quite close and personal ties with gentry members, closer than any other non-gentry person, and such ties could (and apparently often did) pay off either in terms of cash and wealth, or in terms of opportunities and protection: the gentry protector might help the son of his doctor or geomancer to go to a real school; or he might help him to acquire a good piece of land perhaps at a low price. This is one of the best and almost the only avenue for farmers' sons to move up into the gentry within two or three generations. But the starting level of these "half-educated" was already above that of the others.

We know from Tokugawa Japan that farmers, often successfully, tried to have their sons accepted as apprentices of craftsmen in the cities. We have, to my knowledge, not yet any knowledge about this question in China. We know that craftsmen were organized in guilds and that they tried to restrict access to the guild and preferred as apprentices the sons of craftsmen. But whether they accepted farm boys, we do not know. When we read passages such as this:

> "Hung Shou-ch'un... migrated from Fukien to Formosa... and earned his living by making ricepaper. Whenever he got money, he bought books and read from morning to evening.... (and finally left a collection of poems) [1],

---

[1] *Liu-Kui ts'ung-k'an*, Taichung, 1957, p. 64.

we may assume that ricepaper making in the 18th century in Formosa was not yet so organized that it was in the hands of a guild which could keep out outsiders. Moreover, the young man belonged to a family of some standing, and had learned to read and write before he emigrated to Formosa. His status may have made his life as a craftsman easier.

Impressionistically, we believe that mobility from farmer to merchant was not common. Here, we have to define "merchant": this is everything between the peddler who owns nothing else than the board which he carries and the merchandise on this board, with a total investment of about US $ 1.00, and the grocer or owner of the "general store" who has a shop and several lines of merchandise with an investment which may reach more than US $ 1000.00. Although Chinese terminology seems not to be consistent, this type of merchant is usually meant by the term "ku". The "shang", however, seems to define the large-scale businessman, wholesaler, or export/import merchant. This second category is excluded from our present discussion, because his operations involve the availability of large sums of liquid assets, while the small merchant usually has hardly any.

A farmer's son, then, could move into a town with some farm products such as vegetables or fruits (fruits are a luxury item, bought for children by wealthier families) try to sell them and thus make a living [1]. He may start out as an itinerant peddler. This would circumvent the necessity of registering in the city as a resident. He could always claim that he was a resident on the farm. He could also erect with almost no cost a small mud hut or a tent—taking the chance that a watchful official would not have his tent or hut torn down as an illegal structure; a chance, which by payment of some bribes could be reduced considerably. And the merchant would regard the bribes as a kind of tax. In the long run, and if fairly successful, the young man would probably try to settle more permanently by erecting a mud hut directly outside the city walls. Though not outside the jurisdiction of the officials in the city, the officials would not care much about these squatters outside the gates, often would not even see them because they would not leave the city too often on official business. City families and city merchants who were organized would

---

[1] We do not consider here the case of a farmer who became a small merchant when he was too old to continue farming. Such cases, apparently, were not rare. But such cases do not usually involve migration of the family into town; the sons of such a man often remain in the village as farmers.

also not care too much about the squatters as long as they remained outside the city and, therefore, without the protection the walls gave against attacks by bandits, robbers or soldiers. Outside the city gates, then, our small merchant could settle; other people from his village or neighboring villages would join him; soon there is a whole "suburb" outside the city gates. Business here is relatively fine: our merchant is supplied by his family and other farmers with farm products. Merchants inside the city may buy from him. As the city gates were closed during the night, latecomers would try to stay in an inn outside the gates and would buy from the merchants there; persons who went to start very early, may stay the last night in the inn and buy their breakfast. City people would come out to visit the cheaper houses of prostitution in which they would find the village girls; they also would enjoy village amusements, and would buy. As long as there was peace and as long as the officials in the city would not interfere—*and* as long as our merchant remained small and unimportant, he could continue, uninterrupted. But further moves upward were quite difficult: then our merchant had to fight the competition and resist the power of the city's big merchants. Then, too, the officials would get quite interested in his activities, and he might find that his son could not participate in the examinations because of the father's occupation.

Thus, the outlook for the farmer who went to town and became a peddler or small merchant was good, but not splendid: he could achieve with good luck a standard of living higher than he had in the village and could enjoy certain freedoms which he did not have at home, but to move up into big business or into the gentry was quite difficult and, as far as we can see, quite rare. There are exceptional cases such as the following:

> "The oldest son... , born in 1717, went to Taiwan and settled in Wan-hua, where he cleared fields. He understood something about medicine, especially about bladder diseases, and his fame became known to the Emperor. By Imperial grace, he got the title Teng-shih-lang. He died at the age of 80" [1].

This man was not an independent emigrant: more than ten others of his generation moved to Taiwan. In Wan-hua, which at that time

---

[1] *An-p'ing Kao-shih tsu-p'u chih-lüeh*, 1955 edition, p. 67b; Teng-shih-lang is rank 9A, the second-lowest rank. This rank was also given to people of over 70 years of age. This man may have received the rank for his age, as well. Wan-hua is the first settlement out of which modern Taipei grew. It is today a quarter of the city.

was already a town and not a village, he may have had a small medicine shop in addition to his fields outside of town. He must have helped some officials who then reported about him to the Court. Otherwise the Court would not have known about him. Selling medicines and helping officials with bladder diseases gave him a special chance; he got a title at the end of his life. In the following generation, then, we find already several members of this clan with titles, and some with an education. The family was now on the move upward.

One could get *titles* and *ranks* simply by buying them; but few of these small merchants had the money and few would have dared to approach high local officials to negotiate the title for them—this approach would also have cost additional "gifts". Without some personal "connection" it was even difficult to get a title because of great age. A family also could get recognition by producing a "chaste widow", i.e. a woman who became a widow before she was 30 years old and who refused to remarry. But the case had to be reported to the government, a committee had to be set up and had to investigate the situation and to make a recommendation [1]. And only if the case was positive, could the widow be honored—and this honor would reflect back upon the whole family. This case, as we see, did not evolve automatically, and we can be sure that there were many "chaste widows" who never came to be known or who never passed the committees. After all, this "title" was not free of charge: after the report of the committee, the government would erect a monument for the widow for which the family around 1860 had to pay 30 *liang* of silver; then there had to be a ceremony the cost of which was 17 *yuan* and 7,920 cash [2]. Not everybody had so much money. Three more chances existed for fortunate individuals: families who had no sons and only daughters sometimes did not adopt a nephew as adopted son, but preferred to "adopt" an unrelated boy as "live-in son-in-law" (*chi* 贅). The boy later on had to marry the daughter and was supposed to carry her family name and to give up his own family name. This regulation went against established tradition [3]

---

[1] Huang Tien-ch'üan has published the text of such a report in *T'ai-wan shih-shih yen-chiu*, no. 2, pp. 48-50.

[2] For comparison: the cost of one *chin* ("pound") of oil for kitchen use was at that time 0.071 *yüan* (Huang Tien-ch'üan, *loc. cit.*, p. 88), and 1,000 cash were one *yüan*.

[3] It seems, however, to have been a local custom of aboriginal tribes, see my *Lokalkulturen im alten China*, vol. 2, pp. 91-92.

and was regarded as dishonorable for men [1]. Those interested in this type of arrangement were usually wealthier landowners. Because of the prejudice against the custom, they would, normally, induce only sons from poor families to come as "live-in son-in-law". The boy, then, moved up economically by this marriage arrangement, but he lost social status and often the tie to his own clan, although we know of cases where he retained or regained his own name later or where his descendants switched back to their natural clan. Naturally, such marriages were not always happy; the husbands later typically took a second wife according to their own tastes:

> "... his brother moved in as "living-in son-in-law" to a family whose daughter he then had to marry, but he took a second, additional wife...." [2]

Secondly, in spite of all rules against it, men could be adopted into nonrelated families. The "excusable" form is to adopt a nephew of the wife instead of adopting a nephew of the husband. But I know of families in which many adoptions from completely non-related families occurred [3]. In a fishing village close to Keelung on Taiwan, 26.3% of persons who leave the village go because they have been adopted, and of those who are adopted, 70% are less than 4 years old. 50% of those who are adopted leave the village and go to the city of Keelung [4]. Such an abnormally high percentage of adoptions points to a custom which is reported often from Taiwan and which, it seems, also existed on the coastal Mainland: if a fisher or a seaman goes to sea, he hands his small son(s) over to a friend. If he should not return, the friend would adopt the child(ren) as his own. The friend is interested in this adoption because he needs for his own fishing and sailing business additional male help, and such an adoption cannot cause any loss of land or property to his family or clan, because he has no land and no property to speak of. The extent of this custom should be studied further, and it should be found out whether it may still have other reasons than this one. To my knowledge, it has not been discussed in Western, nor in Chinese modern literature.

Thirdly, a son might become a Buddhist or Taoist monk, although clan rules speak out against this. In fact, the situation is different for a

---

[1] According to Fr. L. K. Hsu, *Under the Ancestor's Shadows*, p. 99, a third of all marriages in a small town in Yünnan was of this type.

[2] *T'an-shih chih*, vol. 1, p. 327b.

[3] *T'ai-pei Lu-chou t'ien-yeh mei-pen chih-shih-hsi tsu-p'u*, manuscript written from 1911 on.

[4] *Pa-tou-tzu yü-ts'un t'iao-ch'a pao-kao*, pp. 24-27.

son of a wealthy or gentry family from what it is for a son of a poor family. If a son of a wealthy family enters a monastery for non-political reasons [1], he obliges his own family not only to feed him, but also to contribute to the upkeep of the monastery and to make appropriate donations. But he may, on the positive side, become an influential monk or abbott. If a poor boy becomes a monk, the monastery knows that his family cannot pay. But he will be a useful servant in the monastery, will do the menial work while the others do the spiritual work. In the course of time, if he is intelligent and interested, he may rise to a higher rank in the hierarchy and achieve prestige in the local community. But as he is not supposed to marry, any social status ends with his death.

It has often been said that the best way to achieve upward mobility was to try to get a military degree. Because of the lower prestige of the military, competition for military degrees was not very high. Yet even a military degree could not be obtained without spending much money: study and examinations cost a great deal, especially as the boy was not always living at home, and thus the father lost one man's labor. From our data, we should guess that most military titles were bought rather than earned by members of houses which were already economically better off.

However, non-gentry members could be drafted into the army, and in case of war they had some chance for quick promotions. On the other hand, members of gentry families could be drafted into the army only because of some crime they or their relatives had committed. In such cases, the family became registered as an "army family" and had to supply one man in each generation. In the T'an clan we have a typical case of this kind: shortly before 1400, a man of this clan, whose grandfather had been an official and whose father had been a rich landowner, got involved in some affair and had to join the army [2]. At about the same time, another relative of his also had to join the army and became an arsenal guardian. This man died around 1400. Nobody cared about his successor, until some 40 years after his death, the army sent a notice to the clan, telling them that their name was still on the lists and that they had to replace the dead officer. A poor boy was, indeed, enrolled and only later succeeded in getting demobilized and having his name taken from

---

[1] I.e. if he does not use the monastery as a temporary hiding place.
[2] *T'an-shih chih*, vol. 1, p. 338b.

the lists [1]. Such men from gentry families did not try to move up in the ranks of the army; they tried to get out quickly.

As we have seen, farmers have a number of possibilities for social mobility, even for upward mobility. If they belong to a branch house and if their main house is interested in them, their chances are quite high. But, on the whole, for most farm boys the future was hard work and a frugal life.

4) Artisans and Craftsmen

In the traditional and legal classification, artisans and craftsmen (*kung*) represent the third class. We have, above, heard about the restrictions to which this class was subjected. These restrictions were relaxed from 1485 on, yet not completely removed. More detailed studies concerning the artisans during the Ming time (1368-1644) have shown that artisans were under the jurisdiction of several government offices. Most were under the Ministry of Labor, and worked there in four of its sections. Artisans in the Building Section were in charge of palace, temple and wall constructions for the imperial offices and houses, as well as the palaces of the princes. They also produced the chariots for the imperial family. In order to supply the necessary materials, artisans worked all over the country in a number of state factories producing bricks, tiles, mortar, glass, pottery, etc. Artisans in the "Mountain Department" of the Ministry of Labor were in mining and metal industries; they produced the metals and made ceremonial as well as military implements; they also produced feathers, skins, hides, etc. for the use of the army and made money, pottery, and paper for government use. They also were in charge of road and canal construction. Workers in the "Water Department" of the Ministry of Labor produced materials for the Ministry of Receptions and the Ministry of Imperial Sacrifices, i.e. objects for the tombs, weddings and funerals of the imperial house, objects which were to be given to foreign ambassadors as gifts, and ceremonial clothes, including the weaving and dying of textiles for the court. This department controlled the canals near Peking and the granaries there.

Workers in the Department of Military Colonies produced all housing and furniture for these settlements, built the imperial tombs and produced firewood and charcoal. Many craftsmen were under

---

[3] *T'an-shih chih*, vol. 1, p. 344a.

the jurisdiction of the Palace Administration and worked there in over 10 departments, producing imperial beds, tables, desks, chests; the objects for the dowry of princesses, luxury objects for the emperor made of lacquer, ivory and teak-wood; dresses and hats, shoes for the emperor as well as for eunuchs and other palace personnel; there was a dyeing and weaving plant in the palace and one outside of it. Special paper and silver ornaments were made for the emperor and also knives and weapons.

The Ministry of Finance also employed craftsmen. They produced salt, while a special department produced weapons for the provincial armies.

The Ministry of Ceremonies used craftsmen in its printing presses. And many craftsmen were in the provincial administration. They were under the supervision of weaving offices in all places where textiles were produced; under the supervision of the mints which controlled 321 workshops; they worked in local porcelain factories, and they produced iron and mercury.

Artisans in the Ministry of Labor had the highest status, because they were civil workers. The military workers in the Ministry of Finance had the second-highest status, and those who were salt workers had the lowest status. The Ministry of Labor kept the lists of registered artisans. In the late 14th century, their total number is given as 232,089 men; with their families, this would point to over one million persons. We tend to believe, however, that this number did not include all artisans, especially not all military craftsmen. Moreover, each craftsman ideally controlled 5 workers (apprentices??). Though this certainly was not always the case, the total number of persons legally belonging to the artisan class was definitely well over one million.

We hear that in the Ming time some craftsman families were old families who always had been artisans. Others were members of families of criminals who had been assigned to this class. It seems, for instance, that somehow our Jung clan had this fate at one time. And it is indicated that, when there were not enough craftsmen, sons of tenants were conscripted [1].

As to social mobility: we have already seen that some people can become craftsmen by misfortune, i.e. they move socially downward.

---

[1] We took this information largely from Ch'en Shih-ch'i, *Ming-tai kuan shou-kung-yeh-ti yen-chiu*, Hupei 1958 (Wu-han), 183 pages. This topic deserves more detail studies like this one.

But what are the chances for craftsmen to move up into the other classes? Our Jung clan seems to indicate one way of upward mobility: from salt producers they became traders, because salt production had stopped and the government had not taken the trouble to move them to another place. Cases of men who slipped out of the files of registered craftsmen seemed to be fairly common, as were cases of registered soldiers who "disappeared". The way into small business was probably the easiest because the control of such men was difficult. Farmers who had land could be much more easily controlled.

On the basis of our own data, then, we would say that changes from the upper two classes into the craftsmen class were rare and taken only if forced. We have no case in which a poor farmer became a craftsman by his own choice [1]. And apart from the cases in which craftsmen succeeded in slipping through and engaging in trade and, if they had much luck, into farming, there are few "normal" cases of upward mobility known.

H. Friese has been able to find cases in which artisans under the Ministry of Labor, who had been in responsible positions as carpenters for the emperor, or as stone-cutters and (perhaps) sculptors for the court, got honorific titles and finally official positions in the technical offices of the Ministry of Labor [2]. One man even became president of the Ministry in the 16th century. The number of such cases is small. It seems that these craftsmen of high skill and good connections got into some jobs which were so technical that ordinary scholars from the gentry disliked them because they lacked the knowledge, and did not want to take the responsibility. In general, we gain the impression that the class of artisans and craftsmen had the smallest chances for upward mobility.

5) Merchants

We have already discussed several ways by which individuals or families can enter the merchant class. Now we turn our attention to a discussion of the merchant group itself in an attempt to find out what chance there was for a merchant in pre-modern China to change his position. This is an extremely difficult topic. Research of the type

---

[1] P'an Kuang-tan, p. 125, mentions a gentry man who as a consequence of his scrupulous honesty became so poor that the took up weaving. But: a) he did not think of registering as a craftsman, b) he went into the cloth business, i.e. became an unregistered merchant, c) his daughter married a gentry member.

[2] H. Friese, „Zum Aufstieg von Handwerkern ins Beamtentum während der Ming-Zeit", in *Oriens Extremus*, vol. 7, 1959, pp. 160-175.

which, according to our opinion, needs to be done, has not really started yet. This chapter is an attempt to bring together all that can be said at this moment.

The difficulties begin—as already pointed out—with the terminology. Merchants as one of the four "classes" of Chinese social structure, are called "*shang*", but, in practice, texts often make a difference between *shang*, i.e. the large, wholesale or traveling merchants, and *ku*, i.e. the small, settled grocery store or general-store operators in cities and towns. This difference, however, is not always made nor is it always clear in the texts which group is referred to. One of the "reasons" the Chinese thinkers discriminated against merchants was the belief that they (*shang*) cannot be good sons because they travel constantly and cannot perform the services to the living or dead parents, as settled persons can. This clearly points to the *shang* only. *Ku* do not travel around. We are led to assume, then, that the laws governing merchants which we discussed in Part 1 are against *shang* and not against *ku*. And along the same line of reasoning, we tend to assume that *ku* might have been treated similarly to the *kung*, the craftsmen, mainly because a good deal of what they sell is their own product, and therefore it is often not easy to differentiate clearly between craftsman and shopkeeper. We must admit, however, that this is a somewhat hypothetical line of reasoning. To take, as an illustration, a modern example: the city of Taipei (pop. 813,825) in 1958 had 11,764 shops; 1247 processing and finishing works with shops; 954 operation or service undertakings; 138 pawnshops and 108 other shops of various types. Here, it is a question whether the processing and finishing works are operated by *ku*, because they had a shop, or by *kung* because they involved a craft. If we decide in the first way, we find 14,211 operations of *ku* in this city, i.e. one shop for 57 persons. The city further had 3709 processing and finishing works without shops, 359 technical undertakings, 211 printing houses, 38 publishing houses. These all would be classified as *kung*, craftsmen enterprises in the old terminology, a total of 4317 workshops, i.e. one for every 189 persons. Finally, the city had 236 trade establishments, 92 brokerage firms, 53 borrowing institutions, 12 agents, 1 storage firm and 48 operations in the transportation business. These would probably all be classified under *shang*, merchant enterprises in classical terminology; 442 operations, i.e. one for every 1,840 persons [1]. Unfortunately, we do not have similar data

---

[1] As a comparison: In 1949 there was a working population of 147,279 persons

for early periods of Chinese history, not even for the 19th century. The difficulty of separating the *shang* from the *ku* appears also in the Western sources. The West had many close contacts with Chinese merchants, as well as with shopkeepers. There are many reports about Chinese merchants, but because the Western merchant was not clear about the social structure of the Chinese, we cannot find out from their reports what the men with whom they did business really were. Thus, their reports do not help us as much as they perhaps could. Once we know more about merchants from Chinese sources, we will, I believe, be able to interpret Western reports better and, through such additional information, round out our picture of Chinese business and its development.

We now try to treat shopkeepers (*ku*) and merchants (*shang*) separately.

a) *shopkeepers*

We have already indicated that many farm boys tried to set up small shops at the outskirts of cities or towns, or to peddle some merchandise in the city [1]. And we think that such persons were normally not classified as either merchants or craftsmen, but remained in the classification of "farmers" if they did not fall under the category of vagrants or migrants (*liu-min*). We pointed out further that such men normally did not have much opportunity of leading a life much better than that of a poor farmer. Farmers who already in their villages had some technical skills, could in the city continue along the same line and open something which in modern terminology then would be called "processing and finishing works with shop". But here I am not sure as to how such persons would be registered if they decided to stay in the city for good. Perhaps, they would fall under the category "craftsmen".

As far as we can see, such men normally did not have much of a chance to move up socially or economically. The exception is the emigrant. It seems to have been fairly common for farmers to join an emigration group (see above, Chapter 3) and then, after they were

---

in Taipei city. Of these, 28.5% were in trade, 22.9% in industry, 20.9% in office work, 6.9% in free occupations, 7.3% in services, 5.2% in agriculture. (C. S. Chen and C. H. Tuan, *Population of Taiwan*, Inst. of Agric. Geography, Taipei, 1951, p. 28).

[1] Lo Hsiang-lin, *K'o-chia*, p. 57 (with source references) mentions that farmers became merchants because of lack of land. These references refer to the 13th century.

settled on new land where they were supposed to work as tenants of the organizer, somehow to slip away and set up their own little businesses in the new area. In such cases they could utilize the differences in cultural and/or technical level and introduce new skills into an area inhabited by primitives. They also could exploit the aborigines, buy up their products and sell them to wholesalers. Frequently colonial settler-farmers conducted businesses while farming. In the late 19th century many of the contract laborers who were shipped to Southeast Asia made the transition from plantation or mine worker to shopkeeper and often later to big merchant. This "colonial chance" seems to be the greatest opportunity a small shopkeeper can have.

Another possibility seems to be indicated by the Jung clan's history. The clan succeeded in setting up a farmer's market on a collective basis. The members were probably soon able to extend loans or to give credit to farmers until eventually they were able to go into bigger business themselves. To judge whether such a development is exceptional or not would require a knowledge about the organization of farmer's markets and county fairs in China, a problem about which we do not know much more than that there were many such farmer's markets and fairs all over China [1].

But let us return to the shopkeeper or small businessman in town. He had to have a shop. While we might assume that he could fairly easily build a shack outside the city gates, we cannot assume that he could easily do the same in town. How did he get his shop?

We know that gentry families, often government officials, constructed shops and than rented them out to shopkeepers [2], but the

---

[1] E. Balazs, *Les Foires en Chine*, Editions de la Libr. Encycloped., Bruxelles, 1953, 15 pages, mentions only a few, and not the most important characteristics of markets and fairs. A good, short description of modern farmer's markets is by J. E. Spencer, "The Szechwan Village Fair", in *Economic Geography*, vol. 16, 1940, pp. 48-58. H. Fei, *Earthbound China*, New York, 1945, p. 47 f describes markets in Yünnan. Sh. Kato, *Studies in Chinese Economic History*, vol. 2, 1953, pp. 508-520 and 538-539, gives much detail. He found that in present-day Hopei province a farmer's market served almost 17,000 persons on the average in the late 19th century, while in Kuangtung province a market served only 8,149 and in Fukien 5,849 persons. The only study of market towns of rural character is by H. D. Scholz, *Formen der ländlichen Siedlung in China*, Bonn, 1949, p. 119 f. He pointed out that such a settlement can have 20-30 families, that it usually has a religious center and often a theater, pawnshop, tea house and restaurants. More research is needed. Hsiao Kung-chuan, *Rural China*, Seattle 1960, p. 20-24, mentions the problem.

[2] The rental should not be higher than 500 coppers per month in 720 A.D.

government regulated the rents. And even quite early texts indicate that the government also regulated the number of shops [1]. Correspondingly, we hear also that at very early times the government gave state land to a citizen with the permission to erect shops on that land [2].

While some shops always belonged to gentry families, others belonged to the state and the privilege to control them and to collect the rents from them could be given to deserving persons [3]. Finally, temples also owned shops [4] just as they owned houses which they rented out to tenants. We do not know the legal status of the shopkeepers in such shops. We doubt whether they were classified as "*shang*", and would tend to assume that some were classified as *kung*, craftsmen, while others were perhaps classified as members of the servant or other unfree classes, and were directly dependent upon the shopowners. In any case, it was not in the interest of the owners of these shops, whether it was the state, a temple, or a gentry family, to let the shopkeepers get too wealthy. Again, their big chance would be to be accepted into an emigrant group, if the group decided in the first place to accept nonfarmers.

b) *Itinerant merchants*

While admittedly our data on shopkeepers are poor and there is not too much hope of uncovering much new information, we could get more information on one sector of the merchants, the "itinerant merchants". We mean by this term the small, independant merchants who travel from one market to the other, from one fair to the other— those who are permanently on the move. It is clear that the legislation about *shang* (merchants) refers mainly to these men, yet texts often call them *ku*. To this group also belongs the *ya*, the middleman, agent or broker.

Typically, such *shang* or itinerant merchants, would be found in farmer's markets, to which they would bring such merchandise as farmers need: knives, agricultural implements of metal; pots and pans and porcelain. Other important market items were horses, donkeys and cows; brushes, seals, books, and paintings. And, most

---

(*Ch'üan T'ang wen* 32, as quoted by Sh. Kato, *Studies in Chin. Econ. History*, vol. 1, 1952, p. 328).

[1] Already mentioned in *Kuan-tzu*, chapter 78, Maverick translation, p. 153.
[2] Text from early post-Christian time in *Hou-Han-shu* 41 as quoted by Sh. Kato, *loc. cit.*, vol. 2, p. 768.
[3] Texts for the year 813 quoted in Sh. Kato, *loc. cit.*, vol. 2, p. 768.
[4] Korehiro Tamai, *loc. cit.*, p. 122, quotes texts for the T'ang period.

of all, textiles[1]. All these things had to be brought into the local markets, often from quite far-away places.

The Chinese government since pre-Christian times has had controlled markets in cities. These markets were open places surrounded by a mud wall, operating in the mornings and closed in the evenings. Sellers could offer their merchandise there, squatting on the ground, or they could have tents or stalls made of more or less impermanent materials. No doubt many were local farmers who brought their products, which they themselves sold. Some, however, were specialized merchants who would buy up merchandise in villages or in other cities and sell them on the market. Every merchant in such a market was obliged to pay fees to the government.

The ideal spot, of course, for these merchants was not so much the regular market place, but the fair. Fairs were normally organized by temples and took place at certain definite times, usually in connection with the birthday of a deity, or with a similar religious festival. There are many temples and many deities, and sometimes even the birthday of the deity is celebrated on one day in this place and on another day in the next place so that all these roving merchants keep on the move, from one to another temple. In the temple fair we meet not only townspeople, but also the villagers from all around, who come to worship in the temple and to buy at the fair. Some such fairs are outside towns—in the temple area, but many temple fairs are in the cities. City people, even the members of the upper classes, go to these fairs, even if they are not at all interested in religion, because here they can make good buys—often "discoveries". We have hundreds of descriptions in the literature of how a scholar walked over the fair ground and discovered in the stall of a bookseller a rare manuscript or a valuable painting, which he bought at a ridiculously low price. At these fairs, one colorful type could be found which stimulated Chinese phantasy greatly: the "Mohammedan peddler" [2]—the foreign merchant. He is physically different and has

---

[1] J. K. Fairbank, A. Eckstein and L. S. Yang, "Economic Change in Early Modern China: an Analytic Frame-work", in *Economic Development and Cultural Change*, vol. 9, no. 1, 1960, p. 7A. See also note 1, page 241.

[2] The reflection of this trade on Chinese folk tales is studied in W. Eberhard, *Typen chinesischer Volksmärchen*, Helsinki, 1937, Typ no. 169 and *Volksmärchen aus Südost-China*, Helsinki, 1941, p. 193 f. See also M. Köymen, *Der Einfluss des Handels mit Zentral- und Vorderasien in der T'ang-Zeit auf die chinesischen Märchen* (Dil ve Tarih-Coğrafya Fakültesi, Sinoloji Enstitüsü neşriyatı no. 5, Istanbul, 1941, pp. 774-832; Turkish with abstract in German).

all kinds of rare foreign objects, usually luxury items. He buys as well as sells, with a knowledge the local Chinese does not have. Thus, he may buy at an "exorbitant" price an object which, to the local Chinese has no value at all and sells it as a rare object in distant markets and thus becomes extremely rich—if he is not cheated by a Chinese [1]. We guess that these foreigners as well as the other merchants at the markets and fairs were registered as "merchants" (*shang*). They often formed small organizations centering around temples, and not rarely the temples were directly involved in serving as hotels, as loan institutions, or as storage houses for these merchants.

We do not know about the origins of these roving merchants. Certainly, a fair number of them were foreigners, i.e. either persons from foreign countries or persons from other parts of China who for generations had been in this business [2]. I am thinking here of castelike social groups. For instance, we guess that many ironworkers and blacksmiths (also typical figures of markets and fairs) were originally members of specialized, semi-nomadic tribes, such as can still be observed in many parts of Central, South and West Asia and in Africa [3]. Bronzesmiths, tinsmiths, and tinkers seem to have belonged originally to similar tribes. Horse and cattle dealers too belong, in many parts of Asia and even Europe (gypsies), to a special group, often of foreigners, of semi-nomadic habits. Similarly, there are potter tribes. From China proper we know the To-min in Chekiang [4] who clearly were originally a tribal group belonging to an aboriginal culture, and who later became a "caste" specializing in the production of lanterns made of the horns of cattle. In discussing the "commoners"—the non-free members of Chinese society—Chinese legal documents refer to quite a number of similar groups, including fishermen and fishsellers, who could and did become itinerant merchants in our sense. Here again, much more research is necessary to clarify details of this outline. But it is clear that such persons had no blood connections with the gentry.

To this group also belong the agents or middlemen in the markets

---

[1] The usual pattern is that the Chinese believes to have found the secret and by his ignorance destroys the value of the object.

[2] The concept of a "trade frontier" (as developed by F. G. Bailey, *Caste and the Economic Frontier*, p. 233) is a valuable tool for an understanding of these processes.

[3] W. Ruben, *Eisenschmiede und Dämonen*, Internat. Archiv f. Ethnologie, Leiden, 1939, brings the data together well.

[4] Data collected in W. Eberhard, *Kultur und Siedlung der Randvölker Chinas*, Leiden, 1942, pp. 206-207.

(*ya*): those men who may act as "towncriers", as auctioneers, or as go-betweens who could be approached for such discreet transactions as the purchase of a slave girl or concubines [1]. The *ya* were the ideal "contact men" for a member of the gentry who had business which should remain secret, either because it was illegal or because his good standing stood to suffer were his connections with these merchants to become known. The *ya* might negotiate a loan, a mortgage, or a rental agreement for a gentryman, just as they might locate a rare painting or a fine horse, and try to get it for a good price, upon his request.

The chance which these men, these *shang*, had to move socially up, was not too good in China proper. After all, they were registered and under discriminatory laws [2]. On the other hand, they were the only class which was allowed to move around—though with passports and permits only—and the only group which would go into foreign countries or outside the borders of China. There, they could acquire land, even settle permanently and set up large-scale businesses, exploiting the cultural lag between them and the aborigines. Many of them certainly had enough capital to operate a pawnshop or a restaurant, if they did not set up other types of businesses. We know that some of them in the late 19th century followed the labor emigrants and set up stores near the camps of the laborers, catering to their countrymen. It is this group which in foreign countries likes to organize itself, often around a temple, or around a club.

c) *Big merchants*

We have already met this last group of "gentleman-merchants"; they are members of gentry families, who start out with much capital. Sometimes their capital is a loan from a cash endowment of a school [3], and this school is probably often a clan school or at least financed by the clan. The principal job of the gentleman-merchant is to sell clan products and to buy for the clan; but then any profitable big

---

[1] On *ya* in general see Sh. Kato, Studies in *Chin. Econ. Hist.*, vol. 1, 1952, p. 482 f and vol. 2, p. 226. Briefly also N. Niida, *Legal Documents*, p. 434. The *Hou-tê-lu* 1, 7a mentions a *ya* whose business it was to sell servant girls. The broker and harbor agents were more important than these ordinary *ya*. According to an edict of 1397 they had to be "persons of substance", i.e. landowners (Ch. W. MacSherry, *The Impairment of the Ming Tributary System*, Unpubl. Ph. D. thesis, Berkeley, chapter 2).

[2] P'an Kuang-tan, *loc. cit.*, p. 119, states that merchants from Anhui province became citizens in Chia-hsing (Chêkiang) by registering formally there. Does this mean that they quit the *shang* class?

[3] According to J. Nakamura in *Tōhōgaku*, vol. 11, 1955, pp. 100-109.

business is good, because at least a part of that income will return to the clan either directly or as new endowment for another school, an academy (*shu-yüan*), temple land, or as a foundation to sustain poor clan members. If not in clan business, we find our gentleman-merchants typically in the salt monopoly: positions could be bought and as about half of the salt went into illegal smuggling channels [1] in the 19th century, gains could be very high. Another typical activity is in the grain transport business. Similar to the salt administration, grain collection and transportation was a semi-governmental activity of great importance, and an activity which guaranteed a safe and steady income because of the inelasticity of consumption, so long as some opponent of our gentleman-merchant was not able to close the illegal channels. Normally, such a gentleman-merchant would, towards the end of his life, return and settle down on the clan land or on land of his own, and his sons would try to get into positions in the bureaucracy; he would behave just as any other gentry member would. He might also retire and leave the business to a manager—who was not necessarily a relative. And some of them continued to the end of their lives, when their sons took over. Apparently some of the big "Hong" merchants of the 18th and early 19th centuries in Canton were from such families, though the earlier history of our Wu house is not too clear. But when Western books speak of merchants who do not have the "real" business spirit, they seem to allude to this type of gentleman-merchant who is a merchant only for a part of his life. He is, of course, not registered as a merchant (*shang*), although technically he is a *shang*. He is very much sought after by other merchants, because he has "connections": he may be related to the local governor or magistrate; he may know him personally and will, therefore, be received by him and get all the facilities which others could not get or at least not without great expenditures in bribes. Men like Jung Hung of our Jung clan, one of the five earliest textile industrialists in the 19th century, is a good model [2] insofar as he was in politics as well as in business and insofar as he hired an American textile expert for his factory; he did not himself worry about how a factory should work. Probably Chang Ch'ien, who created the Ta-sheng Cotton Mill in 1898, might be another example: he approached the highest

---

[1] J. K. Fairbank, *loc. cit.*, p. 7.
[2] Wu Hsiang-hsiang (ed.), *Chung-kuo chin-tai-shih lun-ts'ung*, Series 2, vol. 2, Taipei, 1958, p. 255.

government circles for financial support [1]. The state-controlled or state-sponsored industries of the late 19th century, and men like Tso Tsung-t'ang and others who have recently been studied, could probably be classified as gentleman-merchants or—as a later type—gentleman-industrialists. They were, of course, interested in making money; but they felt even stronger as members of the bureaucracy, as representatives of the government. Building up big business and new industries for them was also a political necessity, a national necessity—whether these industries made much money or not was of secondary importance to them. It seems to me that such a classification of merchants might explain some of the problems which have been put forth by analysts. Max Weber and others thought that government and family were too strong in China, so that no business spirit could come up; merchants would always tend to enter government posts and if not, they would not really be efficient because they were too much restricted by family ties. But, on the other hand, we knew of extremely efficient and successful merchants, specially outside of China. The government ties are strong only in those individuals who anyhow come from this background; family ties are strong again only in such cases in which the family is a gentry clan. Merchant families (*shang*, i.e. our "itinerant merchants") did not represent the Confucian type of family organization, though later they often adopted Confucian ways, when they had climbed up the social ladder. Confucian values were not, originally, meant for *shang*. On the contrary, Confucians recognized that *shang* by the very fact of their work, cannot be good Confucians.

d) *Merchant ethics*

Does this, then, mean that merchants (*shang*) had their own business ethics? Apparently this was so. There was an ethical code of *shang*, made for the "itinerant merchant", not for the little *ku*, the shopkeeper, and not for the gentleman-merchant. We have recently found three codes for merchants; the earliest thus far is from 1782, but we suspect that there were earlier codes which are not preserved, or not yet found. The other two codes are from 1792 and 1854. We here give a few excerpts in condensed form [2] in order to show the business spirit.

---

[1] See Samuel Chu in *Tsing Hua Journal*, N.S., vol. 2, 1960, pp. 301-316.
[2] Texts first published in *Shih-huo*, no. 18, 19, 21 in 1937, reprinted in Wu Hsiang-hsiang, *Chung-kuo chin-tai-shih lun-ts'ung*, Series 2, no. 2, Taipei, 1958, p. 205-244. We summarized the main points of these codes.

If these rules are read with our above classification of merchants in mind, it is clear that they do not apply to the gentleman-merchant.

If a merchant travels, he should always make contacts with his co-travellers and should travel in company, if he has much money. If he has only little money with him, he may travel alone, with haste. He should not inform his servants or concubines of his departure. He should not look out of the boat, so that nobody guesses who he is and recognizes him. He should take care of his baggage himself and not rely upon others. During the trip, he should not have relations with girls and should not become friendly with strangers. He should watch carefully whomever he meets and never rely on hearsay.

These are the basic ten rules for merchants: 1) Get a travel pass, so that you can pass the tolls and customs stations. 2) Do not travel by night. And during the night, do not take off your undergarments. 3) Close all windows and doors carefully. Your shop should not look luxurious. 4) Do not visit tea or music houses at the end of the month. Do not drink much. 5) Always be friendly, never be harsh. Honor the old and do not cheat the young. 6) Immediately check all payments and make the entry into your books. 7) Watch your words. 8) Always make firm decisions in word and action. 9) When you are an invited guest, do not make noise or talk nonsense. 10) Keep away from gamblers and whores.

For the shopkeeper:

You should act like a gentleman: do not criticize or ridicule others and do not talk too much.

Do not flirt with female customers. This gives your shop a bad reputation. If she does not buy, tell her in elegant words to buy in another shop. But do not belittle your own shop.

If an educated man comes, first ask his name, where he lives and what the reason for his visit is. Also ask him the names of all persons who came with him. They might pose as his men but might in reality be thieves.

Give good change for silver, slightly above the market price. Give good weight to a person who might sell to you; understate the weight, when you sell. Check and recheck money, cash and receipts when you receive them. Do not be in a hurry when you accept money.

If somebody wants to buy, first ask what he wants to buy; then say the price; then only look at his money and weigh the money. If a person goes away without buying and then comes back in order to buy, count his money again and do not say: "I have already counted it". He may have exchanged his silver for copper.

Count the money even of good customers; they never give too much. "In these days people with human faces and animal hearts are numerous". Business now is not as in the old days, when people still were honest. If you should behave as in the old days, not even ghosts would come to you.

Treat the rich and the poor equally—money from the rich is hard to get. Otherwise they would not be rich. Be polite to the middle class: they are grateful and do not expect that you bow down to them in subservience.

Only one salesman should talk to a customer.

React to your customer's personality. If he is straight and upright, you should be straight and upright. If he talks a coarse language, you talk coarsely. If he thinks that you are frightened by him, he will become increasingly harsh.

Be always nice, elegant, speak calmly. If you start cursing, the customer will too, and a fight might ensue.

Never be nervous; never speak loosely. You cannot take back your words.

Do not get nervous when many customers come at once. Treat all alike, give them all the same price. Do not be too hard, but also not too soft: if you are too soft, you go bankrupt. If you are too hard, you have no customers.

Talk to customers, if they like it. If they criticize your merchandise, do not disprove them. Always agree with them.

First show the cheap merchandise, then the better. Finally say that still better merchandise is expensive. The customer then is willing to pay a high price. If you first show the high-priced stuff, he does not believe the price.

Set the price high, so that you can go down. If you immediately state the honest price, the customer will not believe it.

If a customer just wants to find out a price, give him too low a statement: he will not buy anyway.

If one wants to buy something, one should not say how much of it one wants.

If a customer hesitates too long after the price is finally reached, he will not buy. If a customer is undecided before the price is reached, do not let him go. You can even be too soft and not attempt to make money on him this time: he will come back. Be kind to him....

Do not ask a price which is higher than that of the other shops nearby. The customer will find out.

Do not write high prices on the sign boards. Explain to the customer that high prices are the result of draught or flood. He will then understand.

If prices go up, try to raise them later than others; if they go down, try to be earlier.

If somebody gives you too much money, return it. Do not keep it.

Show your best merchandise in the doorway.

Give the merchandise only after the price has been agreed upon. Otherwise, the customer will continue to talk, he will say the stuff is poor or the weight is poor. If you specialize in small business, do not go into big business. The methods differ. Give credit only after you have checked the person.

If you want to get back your money, ask the debtor three, four times. Go to his place and ask for a definite date. Go on that date, and tighten up until he pays. But do not be extreme: "If a dog is brought to extremes, he jumps a wall; if a man is brought to extremes, he hangs himself". Loss of life means trouble.

Study supply and demand before you buy merchandise.

Calculate even the tiny extras; they add up.

If prices are extreme, they will change. If one buys when prices are at the bottom, one prevents them from getting up again.

If the market is becoming soft, try to get rid of your stock. If prices go up, hold on. Quick changes of prices are not real, only slow changes show a tendency.

If one opens a shop, one has to visit the neighbors to find out about the market situation.

If one opens a shop, he should not show off. Be not expensively dressed, be simple.

No girls, drinks, opium, gambling. If others are extravagant, let them be so. Do not talk about it.

A big, powerful merchant should never show this; be modest.

Treat your employees with trust. Discuss with them problems, as between host and guest.

An employee must be honest in money matters. Study the employee's household and finances. Warn him, if he spends too much. Give him a good salary; pay him well.

An employee should not be lazy. He should do the necessary work automatically and should not say: "This is not my job".

Write bills out clearly.

Do not smoke in bed, lest a fire might start. Do not smoke on the street. But smoke when you go to the toilet in the morning to dampen the stench. But do not go too early. It is not healthy.

Do not drink alcoholic beverages during the daytime, and never after midnight. Do not drink more than 40 or 50 per cent of your capacity. You might talk too much.

Have no contacts with gamblers. No contacts with vagabonds either. Small merchants should not be tough towards others.

If someone gives you copper instead of silver, do not say this directly, but say that the color of the silver is not right. If he insists, offer to cut it and tell him to look for himself.

Be very careful with persons who, instead of money, offer their silver hairpins as payment.

A big merchant should never brag about his shop and his importance. People will be afraid to enter his shop.

One should be equally friendly with all neighbors, whether rich or poor. It is said: "Relatives in the distance are not as good as neighbors nearby".

In your personal relations, you should keep away from low people and those who have bad habits. There are, today, many bad people and few honest ones. If you eat and drink with them daily, if you have business with them, it will be said that you are their good friend.

Big and small businessmen should not gamble. Company with low people means that there is no longer a difference between high and low. Whoever makes the day night and the night day, will get in trouble with the officials.

Never buy useless things or playthings.

One should personally check the doors, candles, drawers and chests during the night. Do not let others do this.

No money should be left in sight. Somebody might see it and with his companions come and crowd in, or they may entice you out of the shop.

Even to your closest friends you should not tell the whole story. Relations with them may change. And if people are bad towards you, do not tell them to their face. Keep up conversation.

If the government wants taxes, pay what they want; then you do not have trouble.

If you hide merchandise, or if you cheat on taxes—and this becomes known, the consequences are not small.

The style of these texts, including the frequent use of proverbs, indicates that they are written for the *shang* merchant, not for the gentleman-merchant. The ethics these texts proclaim is quite similar to Western codes for merchants. Whatever one does—it is done in order to do good business or to avoid trouble, not for high Confucian principles. Everybody tries to cheat merchants; so a merchant should be very circumspect in all his dealings. But he should not cheat, because it would, in the long run, be bad business. He should not have contacts with whores or gamblers and should not drink much—not for moral reasons, but because he might fall into a trap and lose money. A merchant may have much power but should not show it. He should pay no attention to class differences and treat everybody equally; it is good business.

I think the differences between this *shang* ethics and the code for Confucians (i.e. gentleman-merchants and their relatives) are quite clear and very great. After all, we should be aware that China for many centuries has been a multi-value society: Confucianism and the Taoism which structurally belongs to Confucianism as its counterbalance [1] were for the highest class only. Merchant ethics were for the *shang* merchant class. M. Granet has tried to uncover the value system of the farmers and recently civilized aborigines [2].

Biographies of businessmen in clan genealogies stress the same ethical principles. They also always try to show that the merchants were extremely civic-minded: that they repaired bridges, built temples, made donations, helped the poor. Although these are desirable virtues for a member of the gentry, too, such actions have much more weight in the case of a businessman, because the official biographer (a Confucian himself) has nothing else to say about him. For a member of the gentry, the biographer can usually find other laudable accomplishments: he wrote a collection of essays; he made fine poems; he knew the great scholars and was the student of one of them; he memorialized the emperor; he got this or that job. So a businessman's biography has to be filled with social activities; and we have the right to assume that, in fact, such activities were what he wanted to do or did, because through them he could aspire to a title (by paying for it) or to get the benevolence of the officials in his town.

At another place, the life of this man is described in more detail:

---

[1] See my *A History of China*, 2nd edition, London, 1960, pp. 46-48.
[2] Mainly in his *Danses et légendes de la Chine ancienne*, Paris, 1926.

"When (Hung Chia) did business with somebody, he was always deferential and reliable. He himself was frugal. His dress just covered his body, his food just relieved the hunger.... From his middle years to his old age he always walked barefoot on the streets and never rode a cart or a horse. He had some education and wrote Chinese very exactly. Even when he was very busy, he never wrote one word in cursive script...." [1].

"Hung Sung (an ancestor of Hung Chia) became rich through business. He repaired the (road on) Niu-shih-ling and built the Yang-t'ou bridge, and the travellers enjoyed this greatly" [2].

"His parents died one soon after the other, so that he became so poor that he could not live. He went into An-chi's village Hu-t'ou. When the market people saw that his stature was strong, poor people competed with one another in feeding him. Later, a merchant gave him a place to live, and as he realized that he could draw well, and that he was honest, he esteemed him even more. In the market, there was a physiognomist who said that he would not remain poor. Then, there was an old lady Lan, who let him live with her and treated him as her own son. At this time, he borrowed capital from the rich family Yin, and his wealth began as he 'counted and calculated' (i.e. went into business). He accumulated, planted trees and kept animals. He lent money on interest and collected the profits, so that by and by he became well-to-do. Then he returned to Ch'ien-yü (his home), gave his parents proper burial, assisted his clansmen when they were poor, repaid all those who had fed him formerly by giving each of them several tens of pieces of gold. The physiognomist was already dead, but he found his tomb and honored him posthumously, and rewarded Madam Lan well and took care of her all his life. He spent several thousands of strings of money and repaired Niu-shih-ling, built the Yang-t'ou bridge, so that travelers had comfort. When there was an epidemic, he gave over a hundred dollars...." [3].

"Hung T'eng-yün... went in 1824 with his father to Formosa and lived in Tan-shui. At 13 years of age, he learned business and became a rice dealer.... He learned business administration and traded with Ch'üan-chou and Amoy, and in due time he became rich. When in 1881 governor Ts'en Min-ying wanted to build the Ta-chia bridge and asked all gentry members to make contributions, T'eng-yün provided 70 workers and the bridge could be built.... Later he made contributions for the construction of a public granary in Meng-chia; he also made possible a public cemetery...." [4]

Mr. Li Huo-tê was quite rich, but he loved social work:

"Whenever there were in his neighborhood weddings or funerals for which the people, because of their poverty, could not carry the

---

[1] *Liu-kui ts'ung-k'an*, Taichung, 1957, p. 57.
[2] *Liu-kui ts'ung-k'an*, p. 54.
[3] *Liu-kui ts'ung-k'an*, pp. 58-59.
[4] *Liu-kui ts'ung-k'an*, p. 64.

cost, he always gave money to help them. In hunger years, people in his neighborhood closed their shops, but he opened his and sold at reduced princes. When there were vagrants in his quarter, he admonished them to go into business and gave them loans and they all became settled. Therefore, there was nobody in his neighborhood or quarter who was not moved by gratitude...." [1]

Mr. Li is from a clan of tea merchants. Stories like his and the others are typical, and many more examples could be given. Actually, we believe that if an inquiry could be made, we would find that these *shang* merchants were the main carriers of social welfare, and therefore, the main supporters of Buddhist temples, while the gentry more often acted through the government, and only partially with their own money. The connections between Buddhism and the business world and active social work should be studied in more detail.

e) *Financial organization*

Gentleman-merchants did not need much capital—not more than they could find within their own clan. They had only to buy themselves into the salt administration or into grain transportation, and they then could operate, increasing their working capital by the gains they made. They could also, if necessary, easily get credit from itinerant merchants with whom their social position and influence counted as good security, so that there was no question of high interest.

The situation of the itinerant merchant (*shang*) was not so simple. He probably often did not have enough capital to finance larger operations on his own. If he approached usurers from his own social class, he had to pay their high interest rates. He could also be financed by the gentry, and we have the impression that more often than not, this "assistance" was in reality a burden more than a help. We know that the officials, when in need of funds, liked to make levies upon merchants [2], i.e. upon the *shang*, perhaps also upon the *ku*, though not upon the gentleman-merchants. Such levies were common all over Asia for thousands of years. One has to have experienced such a levy as an observer to know that the chips fall pretty irregularly: there are merchants who, somehow, have to pay almost nothing, while their neighbor has to pay more than his total capital and investment worth. The one man had "protection", the other did not [3].

---

[1] *Li-chia tsu kuang shih tsu-p'u*, generation 13. This happened in the late 13th century.

[2] J. K. Fairbank, *loc. cit.*, p. 12.

[3] I think of the so-called *varlik vergisi* in Turkey during World War II.

One typical way to get "protection" was to offer an official "partnership". The official, or a member of this gentry family, would invest some money in the merchant's business and would thus acquire some kind of "preferred stock", i.e. he would get returns of often not less than 100% per year on his investment, even if the merchant himself did not earn so much. Most famous were such arrangements during the Mongol period (14th century) under the name *"ortaq"* (Partnership arrangement) [1]. Several parties, among them even members of the Imperial Mongol family, would invest capital in overland caravans going to Western Asia. The caravans would be en route for at least one, more often two, years, and upon return, the partners would get their share in the profits. They expected 100% interest per year. Another type of business of this kind was investment in a ship voyage. A ship had to be hired, together with a captain who, in turn, hired his crew. Merchants sailed on board with their merchandise, although assignments were possible and common. The ship would export Chinese products such as porcelain or silk and would return with products of the South Seas [2]. With the safe return of the ship, the venture often was over: each partner received his share in the profits, and might or might not decide to try another venture of this type. Such enterprises had, then, two characteristics: because of the financial contributions by the gentry, these ventures were relatively safe from levies, confiscations and all other annoyances by the officials. But the type of business was often not selected on the basis of good business calculation, but on the basis of the wishes of the gentry. Such wishes could be politically determined or could be just poor business calculations. Secondly, as the gentry investor was not dependent upon income from such arrangements, there was no continuity in these enterprises. Bankruptcies and short duration of such enterprises seem to have been typical.

On the other hand, the *shang* merchants had developed organizations on the basis of which modern, capitalistic industry could have been built up. It is true that the Chinese "banks" were not banks in our

---

[1] See *Monumenta Serica*, vol. 9, pp. 275-276; *Tōyō gakuhō*, vol. 13, no. 1, 1942; *Harvard Journal of As. Studies*, vol. 13, 1950, pp. 222-225; L. S. Yang, *Money and Credit in China*, Cambridge, 1952, pp. 57-58; F. Schurmann, *Economic Structure of the Yuan Dynasty*, Cambridge, 1956, p. 214 and p. 4; Zeki V. Togan, *Umumî Türk Tarihine Giriş*, Istanbul, 1946, p. 119.

[2] See Ch'üan Han-sheng in *Bulletin of Chinese Studies*, vol. 5, 1945, pp. 49-84 on the organization of sea trade in the Sung period.

modern sense [1]. But the form of organization which has the name "*kung-szu*"—a word with the present meaning of "Ltd."—was quite able to handle the financial and other problems of the merchants. Originally, a *kung-szu* was a group organized for any purpose, political, social, or economic [2]. The famous *lan-fang* organization of Chinese merchants on Borneo [3] which developed into a kind of oligarchio-colonial regime controlling Chinese and local natives is one of these *kung-szu*. Members of a *kung-szu*, typically, were merchants who organized themselves under a contract for certain activities. For instance, eight persons from eight different clans set up a sugar factory in southern Taiwan in 1760. Each person had a share in the factory and contributed money towards its construction and operation. The contract contains five main clauses:

1) If any of the oxen which are needed to turn the cylinders which squeeze the juice out of the cane are stolen, each member has the obligation to catch the thief, not only the owner of the oxen. If the robber is caught, he should be brought to court and the court costs will be paid by all members.

2) Workers have to get a fair deal. If any trouble occurs, the employer is liable.

3) Anybody, including soldiers, is allowed to take away from the sugar cane fields up to 3 canes. But if any person takes more, he should be caught and brought to trial.

4) If the cane fields burn down, this must be an act of sabotage. If the criminal is known, the owner of the plantation which was burnt down should bring him to court. But all shareholders will pay the costs.

5) If there is any incident in the factory, all shareholders have to pay. All such cases will be settled in the Buddhist temple in the city in which there is also the office of the *kung-szu* [4].

In another instructive case, a sugar factory was created in 1725 on a piece of land which belonged to a temple. In 1818 the factory was destroyed by a flood. A military official wanted to erect a big new factory. The owners of the old factory approached him and asked

---

[1] J. K. Fairbank, *loc. cit.*, pp. 9-10.
[2] B. E. Ward in *Journal of Orient. Studies*, Hong Kong, vol. 1, no. 2, 1954, p. 359.
[3] See note 12 and especially Lo Hsiang-lin in *Yü-kung*, vol. 6, 1936, no. 8, p. 19 f.
[4] Chiang Chia-chin, "Taiwan's Sugar Industry before the War of 1894, Part 2" in *T'ai-nan wen-hua*, vol. 5, no. 2, 1956, p. 72.

him to buy their old machines. Thus, a new factory was built on higher ground with the old machines. The old shareholders, seven men from different families with a total of eight shares, in turn managed the operations. Each shareholder had to supply a certain number of ox teams (each team consists of three oxen) and work the machine for about 12 hours a day. The contract determines the rights of the manager, his financial responsibilities, the obligations of a man who does not supply the promised oxpower, and the right to hire outside oxen if needed for the operation [1].

Instructive in these cases and in many others is: a) capital is supplied not on the basis of relationships, but by individuals from different, non-related families; b) operation and management obligations are all contractually stated; c) the main idea of the contract is to make sure that all shareholders do their duty and share responsibilities; d) the high cost of bribes (so-called costs of court action); e) the importance of temples in such industrial enterprises. Important here also is the fact that a *kung-szu* can deal with purely commercial activities as well as with industrial enterprises, or with mixed agricultural-industrial enterprises, as in the 1760 case which included cane plantations as well as a sugar factory. Taiwan's sugar factories numbered 1275 in 1890 [2], and were operated under several types of organization, not only the straight *kung-szu* type: a group of cane producers, for instance, may band together and rent a factory. They cut the cane, but the factory owner supplies the machines and factory labor. The cane producers receive 45% of the sugar. The factory is often managed not by the owner, but by a hired manager. Yet another form is one whereby the producers individually supply the cane and the ox-power and buy or rent the rest according to individual shares. Or five or ten planters organize a kind of cooperative to make their own sugar as well as sugar for others. Each ox team constitutes a share. Whoever has 12 shares (i.e. 36 oxen or cash of the value of 36 oxen) is a big boss. The shareholders hire a manager and divide the profits according to the shares [3]. We know that this sugar was then often transported to Shanghai from which place it was moved farther to the north. In North China, Formosan sugar in the early 19th century competed with sugar from Szuch'uan.

---

[1] Chiang Chia-chin, *loc. cit.*, p. 73.
[2] Ch'en Cheng-hsiang, *Place Names of Taiwan*, Taipei, 1960, p. 15 (Res. Report no. 104, Fu-min Geogr. Inst. of Econ. Development).
[3] Chiang Chia-chin, *loc. cit.*, pp. 71-72.

Transportation to Shanghai was by Taiwanese merchants (usually of Fukienese origin) who then bought textiles or raw cotton in Shanghai for Formosa [1]. We have indications which seem to show that this business was also organized on a *kung-szu* or similar basis, but we do not know whether there were organizations which included planters, sugar factory operators and shipping merchants all together. In any case, the Formosan examples show how *shang* merchants easily could get the capital and the organization, including the managerial personnel for industry.

Why, then, did China's industrialization take such a long time? We already pointed out that the *shang* who had capital and spirit could have built up industries, but a) the great involvement of the gentry always threatened their businesses or drained the profits away, so that no large scale investment took place; b) we believe that the development of modern industry really hinged on the invention of the steam engine. It is only with this invention that Western industry got an impetus by which it was soon far ahead of Eastern industry which, in the early 18th century, had been hardly inferior to Western industry. At this point we want to indicate that we regard the other differences which have been pointed out by Max Weber and many others after him as of less importance mainly because the more our knowledge of China increases, the more we see that such elements as a business spirit, organizational forms, labor supply, etc., all existed in China [2]. At least it seems that in the light of our increased knowledge, a thorough reevaluation of all earlier sociological theories concerning differences of sociological type between China and the West is necessary. In any case, the steam engine was not invented in China. With this invention, industrial products really could become so much cheaper and so much more numerous that they could threaten Asian markets. The Chinese *shang* now

---

[1] Ch'üan Han-sheng in *Tsing Hua Journal*, N.S., vol. 1, 1958, no. 3, p. 37.

[2] However, most authors believe that there was no "free city", and only a relatively small amount of foreign trade in China, and these two elements are often regarded as decisive elements for the development of modern society (see discussion in J. K. Fairbank, *loc. cit.*, p. 14). The point of the "free city" could to some degree be disputed. If we admit that in many of the so-called "free" European Hansa cities a large percentage of the population was "foreign", i.e. businessmen from other places who had settled more or less permanently, we could make the same point for Chinese coastal cities like Ch'üan-chou, Canton, and others in which at least the foreign communities lived under their own laws and their own elected leaders with their own religion. More research in the social structure of such coastal cities in the Far East might be rewarding.

saw the influx of cheap textiles and other Western products much earlier than the machines by which they were produced. How could a *shang* get a steam engine or other machines which operated with steam for power? The foreign merchant in the earlier part of the 19th century was not exporting steam engines to the Far East. The *shang* could not even easily find out how these machines looked. He had no possibility of asking the foreign merchant to bring such a machine over, and he could not go to England, look over the machines and buy them. He had no such possibilities, and he did not have sufficient credit.

While, in our opinion, foreign machines were out of the reach of the *shang* even at the time when the foreigners opened their own foreign factories with modern machines in China, the gentleman-merchant could have obtained them. He could and did travel to Europe. If he came as a government representative, he could get into factories and see how these machines worked. He could, with government authority behind him, find ways to finance the purchase and transportation of such machines. He, then, could have built the factories China needed. Some of the gentleman-merchants, as we know, went into this business, but not with great success. The *shang* could have been successful—but he could not get the machines.

It would transgress the scope of this book to delve deeper into this problem. It interests us here only insofar as we can assess the chances for social mobility within the merchant class. But we hope that further research on this question of availability of foreign machines will be done.

f) *Was there a bourgeois culture in China?*

At a certain point of development in Europe we see that the big city families of businessmen, the "patricians", developed a type of culture of their own, a culture which differed in many ways from the court culture of the nobility, although in many of its details it was an imitation of the culture of that nobility [1]; a culture which we call "bourgeois" culture. The development of this sub-culture was the result of the success of the businessman; it grew rapidly in strength, and its members became the middle class of the West.

In Japan, we know that in cities like Osaka and Edo, a culture

---

[1] See the discussions about "gesunkenes Kulturgut" in Hans Naumann, *Primitive Gemeinschaftskultur*, Jena, 1921.

existed which was carried by the businessmen and merchants and which differed from the Confucian culture of the court and the nobility. In fact, officially the nobility looked down on this bourgeois culture, though secretly, they liked it.

Did something of this type exist in China? To our knowledge, this subject has not yet been studied in sufficient detail. Yet, in our opinion the answer should be "yes". We contend that there was a specific style of culture in China, from perhaps the middle of the 15th century on, which flourished in the trade and industry centers of Central China and which was carried and promoted by wealthy merchants. The data needed to prove this contention are still very scant, but we believe that much more can be found once the search is begun.

We know that in the 16th century, the city of Hsin-an was a famous center for the production of Chinese ink [1]—the lifeblood of the scholar and official, and a high-priced quality product. Hsin-an was also, as early as the Sung period, the center of salt trade, and from the 15th century on became the center of the silver trade. Merchants from Hsin-an brought the supplies for the armies along the Mongolian borders and, indeed, carried on trade all over China in salt, rice, cotton, silk and tea [2]. The place was so famous that already in the 14th century a special book containing the names of Hsin-an's famous clans, the *Hsin-an ming-tsu chih* [3] had been compiled. Now, in this city we find—much to the dismay of scholars—merchants who buy rare manuscripts at high prices for their collections of unica [4].

Often, instead of Hsin-an merchants, the term Hui-chou merchants is used with exactly the same connotation. Hui-chou in Anhui is the district in which Hsin-an is situated. We now hear that Hui-chou merchants bought valuable manuscripts [5], old paintings [6] or expensive

---

[1] *Wan-li yeh-huo pien* 26: p. 660.

[2] H. Fujii, "A Study of the Hsin-an Merchants" in *Tōyō gakuhō*, vol. 36, 1953, no. 2, pp. 32-60; *Li-shih yen-chiu*, no. 3, 1955, p. 110, and Ch. L. Chang, *Chinese Gentry*, Seattle, 1955, p. 85. Ch. MacSherry, *The Impairment of the Ming Tributary System*, unpubl. Ph. D. thesis, Berkeley, chapter 3, points out that Hui-chou was the home of two men who around 1540 made themselves "kings" of the coast of Fukien and engaged in smuggling activities in collaboration with influential gentry families. The smuggling was mainly with Japan. It seems that in this way many Japanese products came into Central China in spite of government measures against Japan trade.

[3] P'an Kuang-tan, *loc. cit.*, p. 2, mentions this book as preserved in the Peking National Library. It was not accessible to me, unfortunately.

[4] *Wan-li yeh-huo pien* 26: p. 655; 26: p. 657; 26: p. 658.

[5] *Wan-li yeh-huo pien* 26: p. 657.

[6] *Ibid.*, 26: p. 658.

rare seals [1]. In Yang-chou, in the 18th century, there was a salt merchant who had a big house built and became a painter [2]; at the same time the salt merchant Hsü in Yang-chou is introduced to us as a collector of bronzes of the Chou period [3], while the salt merchant Mr. An in Yang-chou ordered pieces of art for his house [4]. Mr. Pao, a salt merchant originally from Hui-chou, moved to Yang-chou; he was a well educated man who introduced modern customs into Yang-chou society: in his house men and women ate together and not separated as usual [5]. In his time, also, an educated man who understood about rare Sung and Yüan prints, became a bookstore owner in Yang-chou [6]. Yang-chou was the Kiangsu center of merchants and culturally important since at least the 15th century. Here, merchants gave funds for an academy in 1665—though not for purely scholarly reasons: a local high official had petitioned for a lowering of trade taxes and they thanked him by giving him this academy [7].

Shen Wan-san, the famous Croesus of the Ming period, figure of many stories and tales [8], got his money from a Kiangsu merchant, Mr. Lu, who in his later years became a Taoist [9]. These scattered notes about the Anhui (Hui-chou, Hsin-an) and Kiangsu (Yang-chou) merchants show that here were men who wanted to be more than merchants: they were collectors, men of good taste, men of high education and even men with philosophical aspirations. Such men could compare themselves with the scholars of gentry origin. Actually, they could do what gentry members could not very well do: they seem to have patronized (as did their Japanese colleagues) the arts; we find paintings of famous courtesans who had attained high repute, erotic paintings and erotic sculpture. It seems also that they fostered the block print, especially the multicolored block print which later became so famous in Japan. We suspect that the famous painters Ch'iu Ying and T'ang Yin were really painters for this class rather than for the scholarly class. We have reason to believe that these

---

[1] *Ibid.*, 26: p. 660.
[2] *Yang-chou hua-fang lu* 4: p. 91.
[3] *Ibid.*, 1: p. 5a.
[4] *Ibid.*, 1: p. 11a.
[5] *Ibid.*, 6: pp. 148-149.
[6] *Ibid.*, 4: p. 94.
[7] *Ibid.*, 3: p. 64.
[8] W. Eberhard, *Volksmärchen aus Südost-China*, p. 202. His name is sometimes given as Shen Wan-shan.
[9] *Jung-t'ung hsiao-p'in* 17, 12a.

merchants also fostered the writing of novels. China's most famous romantic novel, *Chin P'ing Mei*, has a merchant as the hero and defends the "middle class" against the corrupt officials. Li Yü's novel *Jou Pu Tuan* [1] seems to have had its setting around Nanking in Kiangsu. We know well that geisha houses in Japan as well as in China were intimately connected with business life. The Kiangsu houses were famous; here we find praise of courtesans for their art, their songs, their dress, their intelligence, even scholarly praise. Here began the glorification of the tea-house courtesans, and their biographies were written up.

But perhaps most important of all, Kiangsu and Anhui became centers of China's musical and theatrical activities. The so-called "*k'un*" style was a Kiangsu style, and we know that a merchant of Yang-chou in the 18th century started a whole new style within the *k'un* style by calling the famous troupe of Hsü from Hui-chou to Yang-chou [2].

It is perhaps not mere chance that in 1777 the government which believed that the plays were too vulgar, sent a salt commissary to Yang-chou to "improve" the texts of the plays. A scholar from Shê accompanied him [3]. Shê is just another name for Hui-chou, the merchant center. A man from a gentry family with the same name as the scholar—we do not know whether they were related—and who was well known as a poet and calligrapher, became so enthusiastic over the theater that he joined a troupe in Yang-chou [4], although this meant loss of gentry status. We know that merchants always financed theater productions, usually in connection with thanksgiving ceremonies organized by temples. But it might turn out that they not only financed and stimulated the theater but were even instrumental in the production of plays. The whole theatrical world seems to be a merchant's world, with homosexuals and prostitutes on the outer fringe. Actors and prostitutes created the new dress styles for which the merchants supplied the materials or organized the production of the materials. And from Ming time on—if not earlier—this Chinese class was very style-conscious [5]. If these condi-

---

[1] In German adaptation as Li Yü, *Jou Pu Tuan*, by Franz Kuhn, Zürich, 1959.
[2] *Yang-chou hua-fang lu* 5: p. 107.
[3] *Ibid.*, 5: pp. 107-108.
[4] *Ibid.*, 5: p. 132.
[5] See the discussions about quick changes in fashions in the *Yün-chien chü-mu-ch'ao*, ch. 2, an important text for the study of attitudes towards change in Ming China.

tions were widely spread, and if the impressions suggested by the available material were true, we had an early Chinese bourgeois culture in which some artistic elements, such as the novel and theater, are as typical as they are for the same type of culture in Europe and Japan.

There seems to be one important unanswered question: who were these wealthy merchants? We saw that some members of the gentry entered this society: the bookseller and the actor (mentioned above). We know from our earlier discussion that salt merchants often were gentleman merchants. It seems, then, possible that this whole "merchant culture" was a sub-culture of China's "gentry culture". This would explain the fact that some famous gentry scholars worked also with this group—for example, the above-mentioned Li Yü (1611-1680). Li Yü, incidentally, was not only a novel writer, the author of a book on beauty treatment for women [1], of a cook book [2], of several plays, but also China's first great theater critic. Other gentry scholars were T'ang Yin, the above-mentioned painter, and Ch'iu Ying, famous for the same accomplishment. Many novels were written by scholars, but under a pseudonym, and many plays were composed by scholars, but also often anonymously.

It is to be hoped that this line of thinking will be followed up, so that the possibilities here suggested may be proved. Only then would we be able to decide whether this "bourgeois" culture was a direct development of the ordinary merchant class (*shang*) or whether it emerged as a sub-culture of the gentry, modified and reinforced through the gentleman merchant.

---

[1] Some translations in W. Eberhard, "Die Vollkommene Frau" in *Ostasiatische Zeitschrift*, N.F. 15, 1939, no. 3/6.

[2] A few translations in W. Eberhard, "Die chinesische Küche" in *Sinica*, vol. 15, 1940.

PART SIX

CONCLUDING OBSERVATIONS

1) General Observations on Mobility

We believe we have shown that there was social mobility in China in the last thousand years, contrary to some earlier theories. Yet not every individual had the same chance of moving up into the top level of society. If the whole process of mobility is conceived of as a movement of families rather than a movement of individuals, a long-term social rise can be seen. Within these long-term movements, individual changes are in part a consequence of the individual's family membership, and in part a consequence of the individual's own abilities and psychological makeup. Ability is not enough to succeed, but it is one factor of importance.

Movements of families within the social framework were conditioned by Chinese social theory and legislation. Law assigned to each family a definite position and generally tried to prevent changes of status. Where the law permitted change of status, as in the examination system, it limited the number of those who could succeed so strictly that in the competition the families of high status had to use every means to maintain their own status, i.e. they had to try to keep others out.

In addition, upper-class families had a larger number of children than lower-class families—partly as a consequence of their better economic situation, partly because of the need for using the family or the clan as a political power group. But while, on the one hand, a family or clan of high status needed many sons to be able to conclude alliances with other families through marriage (to bring as many sons into key positions as possible in order to consolidate the power and security of the family, and in order to administrate family or clan properties), on the other hand, this meant that some sons had to move socially downward because the generation of high-status sons was much larger than the generation of high-status fathers, while the number of jobs increased more slowly, at best in proportion to the growth of the general population. Only in industrial societies do we find a general shift of the job market: percentagewise, the number of persons needed in low-class positions decreases steadily, while the number of persons in skilled jobs and in high-class positions increases much more than the population increases.

We find, therefore, among the Chinese elite, the "gentry families" a downward social mobility of individuals. Family policy attempts and usually succeeds in retaining the social level of the main house over a long period, but many branch families move down into the next level, that of farmers.

Farmer families can, structurally, be branch families of gentry families or actual farmer families. In the first case, their chances to move up are greater than in the second case, though in all cases upward movement is slow and difficult. Farmers can also move down socially; but this lowering of the social status may mean a subsequent improvement of their economic status. Situations of this type are connected with a migration of the farmer into the city.

The merchant class in the strict, Chinese sense (i.e. the *shang*) seems to exhibit more upward than downward movement, and economic strength was their main tool of social advancement. Small shopkeepers and peddlers did not really belong to the merchant class, and their chances of changing their status were quite limited, probably as much as those of the craftsmen class. Finally, we find among the merchants a sector which we called the "gentleman merchant"; these men are legally not *shang* but are a special sector of the gentry, assigned a slightly lower status than "real" gentry. These gentlemen merchants, the carriers of a kind of "bourgeois" city culture, normally moved back into the gentry within a generation or two.

We have not discussed in detail the fate of the unfree citizens of classical China. We know that their legal status had improved over the last centuries, but we do not have concise data to find out by which means such families actually changed their status.

Although our data are not sufficiently large to permit definite conclusions, it seems that social mobility in China was strong—and perhaps as strong as in Western countries in the same centuries. It seems to have differed in intensity; periods of dynastic change were also periods of the greatest change. It is, then, certainly incorrect to regard Chinese society as "static" in comparison to "mobile" Western society and to attempt to explain differences in the development of both societies as results of differences in social mobility.

Let us now follow up with some further results of our general study of social mobility in China. We should point out here again that we can speak with some authority only for South China, perhaps also for Central China, but we do not dare to generalize so as to include all of China.

2) Village and City

The backbone of European medieval nobility was the countryside. Here, they had their manors; here, many also had their fortified castles. Only later did they move into the cities or the cities located themselves around the castles.

The Chinese leading class, the gentry, did not have "castles", although some of their compounds were strong and could be defended [1]. The base of the gentry family also was the village and around the village was the family land. Gentry families kept their village homes over centuries as European aristocrats kept their castles; gentry families often carry names which are taken from the countryside where they live or give their names to the places where they live [2], just as Western aristocratic families did.

But the Western nobleman remained a nobleman over generations, except if he happened to be an illegitimate child. A Chinese gentryman often moved down and became a farmer even if he was a child of the main, legitimate wife. A Chinese village because of these and other peculiarities of clan development, has a structure different from a medieval European village. It is on the average small [3], and may contain only about 50 families [4]. The large majority of hamlets consists of only one clan. This indicates that the village was once founded by one family which eventually grew and split. The main house might have continued being a gentry family; the branch houses around it might have become farmer's families. Even in villages inhabited by more than one clan, one clan usually dominates. About half of all village families may belong to a single clan [5], and in over half of a number of mixed villages the main clan had more than 70% of the village population [6].

While in medieval Europe the seat of the aristocrat was surrounded by miserable villages in which lived the serfs who worked the land

---

[1] For the Canton area villages with high towers which could be defended were characteristic. They indicated the home of a landlord and/or moneylender.
[2] Such as "Wang-chia chuang" (Manor of the Wang Family), etc.
[3] See below for more detail; Makino, *loc. cit.*, pp. 185-191 indicated that the population was around 240 in Chekiang villages.
[4] Makino, *loc. cit.*, p. 210 gives 54 as an average for Chekiang.
[5] 47% according to Makino, *loc. cit.*, p. 210.
[6] Makino, *loc. cit.*, p. 221.

of the nobleman, the Chinese gentry family was surrounded by farm families to which, most often, it was connected by ties of blood. The gentry family protected the farm families against pressures from the government and often assisted them financially; occasionally individuals were assisted so that they could move up into the gentry. The farm families in turn assisted the gentry family economically by supplying cheap or free farm labor, or at least with labor in peak work periods, as well as with many other kinds of services. The farm families could be free farmers or tenants, but this changed their economic status, not their function.

Villages with more than one clan can have different structures. The other clan(s) may have come to the place together with the main clan. In this case all co-migrating clans would normally have the same, or at least almost the same status as the main clan. Or a clan may have come later than the main clan, and its people started out as tenants of the main clan. In this event the new clan's status would always remain relatively lower.

As the Chinese conceived of marriage as a political act tying families and clans together, exogamy was always the rule. A special constellation in the village may lead to special arrangements of "preferential marriages". Such arrangements may be structurally more or less perfect cross-cousin marriage systems or other systems well known in comparative anthropology; they can be proved to be not a survival of a general custom, but a result of historical accidents of settlement.

The city in China does not show the traits of cities in dual societies. While we certainly can find some "trade cities" in China, in the minds of the Chinese the city is an administrative center of an area and not an entity of its own. It is, in its ideal form, a place in which gentry members who are administrators reside temporarily to exercise the necessary functions of government. In practice, this "temporary residence" may often become a residence for a lifetime or for more than one generation. But we know also that in certain periods of Chinese history, the capital of the country had thousands of large properties reserved for gentry members who lived in the provinces and came to live in the capital only when there was a special temporary need to live there. A house in the city might be the place to which one could retreat when there was unrest in the countryside [1]. The city

---

[1] Although the opposite could also happen: a gentryman would try to retreat to the village if the situation within the administration became too threatening to him.

also contained the silos where grain was stored and protected against attacks by bandits or other enemies.

The active officials, who had to live in the city, surrounded themselves with the necessary personnel. There was an army in the city—ready to defend the villages if necessary, but not living in the villages. An army was in fact akin to a group of bandits, and no farmer wanted to have it too near. There were all the craftsmen in the city, to build and fabricate whatever the office and its occupants needed. And there were peddlers and merchants ready to provide food and luxuries for the officials. Social competition between the different officials stimulated business and led to the growth of cities. Thus, the various ancient capitals of China were usually very large and some reached or even surpassed a million inhabitants, but typically, the other cities of classical China stopped growing when they had reached an "optimum" size [1] because the government would need, in a heavily inhabited area, to create a new administrative center which would draw population away from the older center.

As a consequence of a set of changes which began in the 8th century A.D. and became very influential by the 11th century, cities began to grow greatly from the 11th century on, and many of them gradually lost their character as administrative centers and "temporary" residence of officials. They became centers of a new "urban" or "bourgeois" culture which was carried by a new social group, gentleman-merchants, imitated on a simpler level by ordinary merchants, and which was accepted by the gentry officials. This development certainly appears similar to the contemporary development in Japan (and probably *is* similar), but also similar to the developments in Europe in the same centuries, though the similarities here are perhaps more superficial. Such development did not lead to the "free city" of Western Europe nor to the industrial city of the West [2]. This should not be interpreted to mean that we regard the "free" city as a necessary stage in the development of modern society, nor

---

[1] Obviously, the Chinese government found it difficult to administrate very large units adequately. It broke up units which had grown too much, creating two districts out of one. We do not yet know where, in terms of population, the "optimum" was. Over time, Chinese skill in administration grew (especially since Sung time), but at the same time, higher efficiency was desired.

[2] Before Western influence. Yet, a city like Ching-tê-chên in Kiangsi, a center of porcelain production, had 200-300 kilns and over 70% of the population of more than 10,000 families were craftsmen and merchants (*Li-shih yen-chiu*, Peking, 1955, no. 3, p. 93).

that we believe that modern industry could not have originated in some other manner than in cities which became industrial cities.

3) Population Changes

Social mobility depends to a certain degree upon the general tendency of population movements. We had, therefore, to study some aspects of population changes in the period in which we are interested. While the population of China had been relatively stable in the first millenium A.D., we observe a great growth of population in the last millenium. We think that this growth contributed much to the increased social mobility which we believe has existed since the 11th cnetury. Let us very briefly summarize the general lines and factors of China's population movement so far as it is now known.

We do not know the size of China's population in 1000 or in 500 B.C. Some later sources, which may rely upon older information, estimate the population at that time at about 10 million. We do not have data for the next 500 years, but the population must have quite suddenly increased greatly between 400 and 200 B.C. We guess this from the change of the size of armies and war casualties in this period. Armies before 400 B.C. were always small; after that time, they were astonishingly large. We also know that the area inhabited by Chinese began to grow quickly in this period. We further know that in this period many new cities were created. And—most important—we know that from about 400 on, great changes in food production occurred:

1) The iron plow began to replace the old wooden plow. A farmer could, from then on, produce more than before.

2) Cattle were used to pull the plow and replaced earlier human power. Although the animals had to be provided for, there was enough unused land to graze on, so that replacement of human power by animal power meant higher production of food for human beings.

3) China definitely changed from millet to wheat as the main grain. Wheat needs more care, but has higher yields per acre.

4) The Chinese changed their meat-eating habits. First, over-all meat consumption was greatly reduced. Secondly, sheep and cattle which need large pasturage were slowly replaced by dogs and pigs which eat refuse and need no pasturage.

All these changes made it possible that the average man could produce more food and feed more persons than before. Therefore, he could afford to have more children. This is the first population explosion of China. The population went up from perhaps 10 million to 50 million.

In the following period the population of China remained almost static at the 50 million level for a thousand years at least. It did not make much difference—if we take a long-term view—whether the whole of North China was under foreign rule or whether China was the allpowerful nation which ruled even over distant Central Asia. There are short-term changes in this period, but the over-all picture is that of a population stable at 50 million. At the end of the period, at 1000 A.D., the average farmer even seems to have had a little more land than the average farmer at the beginning of the period, i.e. cultivation seems to have become more extensive. This was possible because politically China proper was now much larger than it was in the beginning of the period; more land was available. The population did not immediately increase, because the new land was not as fertile as the old land [1]: it needs a great deal of labor and capital to install a perfect irrigation system, and good knowledge of climate and soil to get the most out of new land.

The next population change had its roots appearently as early as the tenth and twelfth centuries. As far as we know, however, it did not develop into a real explosion until the sixteenth century. From perhaps 1550 to 1830 the population increased almost regularly, and at a high rate. It is difficult to determine at this time more exactly the date at which the strong increase began, mainly because of difficulties in evaluating the census reports: in the Sung period (the time between 960 and 1278) at first the part of China north of the Yellow River, but later an area almost down to the Yangtze River, came under foreign, non-Chinese rule. The statistics in the two states which ruled successively over the north, are quite poor. Wittfogel came to the conclusion that the north had a total population of 3.8 million, of which only 2.4 million were Chinese [2]. If this should be correct, the majority of Chinese who originally lived in the north, must have migrated into the south. As we, for our comparisons, need the total number of Chinese, whether under Chinese or, temporarily,

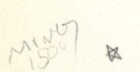

---

[1] This refers to irrigated land and its problems like development of salinity, etc. Virgin land usually has some high initial harvests; then the nitrogen level goes constantly down and with it the fertility. After some 50 years of cultivation, a new nitrogen level, much lower than the original one, is re-established. At which level this will happen depends very much upon the techniques of fertilizing the fields and irrigating them.

[2] K. A. Wittfogel, *Liao*, p. 58.

under foreign rule, it is quite difficult to calculate the Sung population. We know that the population in Sung China, i.e. South China, increased a great deal, but we cannot yet decide whether this increase was due to an immigration of refugee Chinese from the north. In any case, by about 1500 the total population of united China was already at the 100 million level; i.e. it had doubled in 400 years, and from then on it increased 4 times in 300 years, to 400 million around 1800.

Now, how did this happen? There are a great number of developments which made this change possible. Let us start with technological and agricultural changes Already by 1000 A.D. the Chinese had slowly changed their food habits once again: the population of Central and South China had changed from wheat to rice, and even in the North the upper class, especially the government officials, all ate rice and no longer wheat. If rice culture is done in the Chinese way, i.e. in a very intensive type of wet-culture, a rice field produces more food than a wheat field. But in addition, irrigated rice fields, if irrigation is done with river water and not with rain water, can be cultivated every year. Wheat fields until that time had to have periods of fallow, so that actually every year only some 50 to 60 per cent of the agricultural land was under cultivation; the rest was fallow. In the rice areas, the land was 100 per cent under cultivation. This means that the area under cultivation automatically increased by some 40 to 50 per cent.

If the rice farmer is able to get so much more from his land than the wheat farmer, the latter—even in those areas where rice cultivation is impossible— certainly must have felt this competition. Indeed, a number of agrarian projects in the eleventh and twelfth centuries attempted to strengthen economically the northern parts of the Sung empire. It is in this time that these farmers began to change from a wheat monoculture to a continuous cultivation of wheat and cotton without fallow at all. Cotton as a summer crop brought high prices; wheat as a winter crop provided the farmer with food. Cotton was the more important in the north, as silk cultivation in the north is marginal, so that the northern areas had depended upon silk imports from the south. They could now give up the production of hemp or hemplike fibers which could not be cultivated in crop rotation with wheat. Increased income from cotton—even though the cotton crop was bought up by southern wholesalers and was sold to the factories in the south—increased the standard of living of the northern farmer, too [1]. He, too, by immediately abolishing the fallow system, had an increase in agricultural surface of at least 40 to 50 per cent, and by crop rotation and double-cropping he had another increase. Moreover his cotton crop fetched much higher prices than his wheat had formerly fetched.

In 1012 Chinese merchants imported rice seed for a dry rice [2] from Champa in Indochina. This dry rice spread quickly from the coast of Fukien, where it was first cultivated, into other areas of China. Land which could not be levelled and irrigated, could now also be cultivated with rice, and although dry rice does not have the large harvest that wet rice does, rice always got a higher price than other grains. And hitherto unusable land could now be used for grain, i.e. rice, production.

Already in 500 A.D. the Chinese in some areas had two rice harvests a year; this was, as far as we know now, mainly possible by cutting the rice at harvest time (in June) above soil level; the roots made new sprouts and there was a second harvest in October. Naturally, this second harvest was much smaller than the first one. Incidentally, *we* are now experimenting with perennial rice and even wheat varieties—in order to save more labor [3].

From the twelfth century on, the Chinese began to experiment with new varieties of rice. Soon, they developed some varieties which were ripe so early that a second crop could be planted in warm enough areas. They also experimented with inter-seeding, i.e. mixing different varieties of rice in one field, or mixing rice with beans, and so forth. In such cases, one variety is always early, and after it is harvested, the other crop develops quickly and a second harvest is possible. Thus, in a few centuries, we find that the average Chinese farmer had at least 5 varieties of rice at his disposal: glutinous rice for ordinary meals; sweet rice, an inferior type; hard rice for noodles; soft rice, also an inferior type; and reddish rice for rice cakes and rice wine. Actually, by now, in Central and South China, the fields produced on the average more than one harvest. Cultivation rose from some 50 per cent acreage/year before 1000 to about 150 per cent acreage/year after 1300 or 1400.

---

[1] On early cotton in China see specifically M. Amano in *Tōyō gakuhō* 37, 1954, no. 1, pp. 1-45 and no. 2, pp. 61-94 (the later article in no. 3 does not deal with early developments).

[2] *Bulletin Academia Sinica*, vol. 10, p. 406 and vol. 11, p. 339.

[3] Sh. Kato, *Studies in Chinese Economic History*, vol. 2, pp. 647-651 discusses these and the following problems.

With the wider spread of rice cultivation, new techniques of irrigation were introduced, which saved water and produced even higher harvests. The water was periodically drained from the fields. Whether the Chinese farmers knew this or not, the fact is that this type of periodical irrigation destroyed the malaria mosquitoes. And this meant that large areas which before 1000 were famous as places in which almost everybody soon died (famous as places of exile), now became healthy places which could absorb a large population. In other areas, where periodic draining of water was not possible or not indicated, malaria was cut down by keeping fish in the shallow water in which the rice was growing. This technique, which seems to have been developed after 1100, has several advantages: the fish eat up the mosquito larvae; they produce fertilizer for the rice; they are a valuable source of protein as food. Incidentally, this process of eliminating malaria by rice cultivation functions only after the population has reached a certain density, so that the first settlers always were in great danger. In the Yünnan-Burma border area, which I visited recently, this problem of the first settlers was solved by seasonal migrations of farmers: they moved into the malaria areas in the time of the year when the danger was not acute, and moved out of it during the malaria season.

From the 15th century on, we hear of even more complex schemes: an entrepreneur in the field of pisciculture kept pigs in cages on piles in the middle of ponds. The pigs did not need any control, as they could not run away. Their refuse fell into the pond, so that there was no cleaning of the pigsties. In the pond he kept fish which fed on the refuse of the pigs. The pigs were much healthier than normal pigs; and the fish fatter than normal fish [1]. Although such schemes seem to have been comparatively rare, it became fairly common to make ponds for pisciculture where formerly fields had been [2]. By proper drainage, the ponds could from time to time be converted into deep-lying fields which gave very high returns [3]. Especially in the hinterland of Shanghai, which from this time on developed into one of the main centers of the textile industry, many such specially designed fields came into existence, in part because the owners could circumvent taxation, but in part in order to achieve high income in an area of high prices near the big city.

---

[1] *Li-shih yen-chiu*, Peking, 1955, no. 3, p. 99.
[2] In the present time cf. Graf zu Castell, *China-Flug*, Berlin, 1938, p. 53.
[3] See Yoshiyuki Suto in *Memoirs Inst. Orient. Culture*, vol. 10, 1956, pp. 229-300.

In addition to the agricultural changes in connection with rice, new plants were introduced, the importance of cotton in Chinese agriculture has already been mentioned. In the 13th or 14th century, sorghum came to China [1]. Sorghum gives high yields, much higher than wheat; it also gives valuable straw which can be used to feed the cow which does the plowing, to cover roofs, and to serve as fuel. With the discovery of America and the first contacts with Spanish traders, around 1500, tobacco and corn [2] came to China. The Chinese, apparently, took quickly to smoking, mainly pipe smoking. At first, farmers who grew tobacco did not have to pay taxes on the tobacco, so that its cultivation was quite profitable. More important, however, was corn, especially for the mountainous areas of Western China. Here, corn replaced buckwheat almost completely as a staple food, and corn even made inroads into the wheat areas. It can be cultivated on very small terraces; I have seen terraces which were so small that only 4-5 plants could grow there. Formerly, the cultivation of hillsides had been limited to hills which allowed the construction of fairly large terraces.

Let me summarize all this: from circa 1000 A.D. on, a great number of changes in Chinese agriculture began, one after the other, and altogether revolutionized Chinese agriculture. Productivity per acre was now more than twice what it had been, and much hitherto uncultivable land could now be taken under cultivation, so that also the total agricultural surface increased. Chinese food habits changed correspondingly: wheat in the north had to compete with rice (for the upper classes) and sorghum (for the lower classes); the increased need for rice stimulated not only higher intensity of cultivation, but also immigration into thus far underdeveloped areas, especially of South China, which were opened for rice cultivation. From 1500 on, corn became a main staple in the southwest and west and allowed a higher population there. We think that in addition to all this, improvements in the techniques of irrigation were made; I think especially of the spread of the so-called "Persian Wheel" which is a much more effective irrigation machine than the older methods.

Higher intensity of agriculture means that more labor is needed. We do not know how many 8-hour days an average Chinese farmer in, let us say, the year 1100 worked. Before 1949, he worked some

---

[1] Hagerty in *Harvard Journal of Asiatic Studies*, vol. 5, 1941, pp. 234-260.
[2] *T'ien-kung k'ai-wu-chih yen-chiu*, p. 72, states that corn was known in China at the latest in the middle of the 16th century.

200 or 220 days, while, to give a comparable figure [1], his Pakistani brother works only some 120 days per year, as do the farmers in many South American countries. I think, however, that there was less of an increase in the labor of the individual farmer, than an increase in the number of children whom the farmer raised: with as much land as before, he could now use the labor of more persons, and his own children were certainly the cheapest laborers. The higher productivity of his land allowed him to feed these children perhaps even better than before. Here are, I believe, the reasons for the sudden increase of China's population. This increase did not start at the moment when the new techniques appeared; it always takes time before the technological changes have spread so widely that a noticeable impact upon production is made. As far as we can see now, the last great changes happened around 1500, and by that time the combined impact of all earlier changes had become fully effective; the population curve began to rise greatly. I see, then, a definite correlation between the level of production (especially of agriculture, if food imports from other countries do not play a role) and the labor needs, and population density and growth. The new level of agriculture which was achieved by the innovations from 1000 A.D. on, made a much larger population and a much denser population possible and even desirable. But at the same time, the labor-intensity of agriculture prevented in the first period, before 1800, the growth of an underemployed or unemployed group which might have acted as a stimulant for industrialization. In addition, the possibilities of intensive agriculture may have turned the interest of Chinese inventors toward agriculture and away from industry, especially as there are few places in China where the two basic raw materials for modern industry, coal and iron, occurred together, and as the development of an all-weather communication system of high quality was difficult, due to the nature of the geography before the invention of railroads. When China's population increased from 100 to 400 millions between 1550 and 1800, the population of China reached the limits that could be supported by the new methods of production. At first, there was a need for more agricultural labor, and surplus food was available; therefore, the farmers could afford to have more children and could supply work for them. The farmer adjusted to the new situation of a larger family and kept this pattern beyond the point where it was

---

[1] The labor input has been calculated as 4.4 man/days per 100 m² or as 137 man/days per hectare (H. T. Fei, *Earthbound China*, New York, 1945, p. 33 note).

profitable. He then, theoretically, could select one of three ways:

a) he could decrease the number of children, so that a fair ratio between available land and people remained;

b) he could further decrease the number of children, so that the ratio became once again more favorable, i.e. a higher standard of living became possible; or

c) he could continue to produce as many children as before and lower his standard of living.

Apparently, he first lowered his standard of living by cutting down on meat consumption, by specializing more and more upon rice to the detriment of vegetables and other food which would supply necessary vitamins and minerals. We know that the ratio of men to acreage became smaller and smaller and is by now as low as it ever has been; on the other hand, no new techniques had been developed in the 19th century. There was even some loss in agricultural surface by erosion: continued corn production exhausts the soil; continued cultivation of hillsides leads to erosion which then affects even the valleys [1]. The firewood needs of a dense population led to the disappearance of practically all forests in China, especially on the hills; this, in turn, led to a decrease of moisture and to further erosion and loss of agricultural land. Decreased animal breeding and increased use of all vegetable refuse such as straw, and so forth, for the kitchen stove, reduced the amount of natural fertilizer and reduced fertility, although increased use of human refuse in the fields around the settlements kept fertility high in these choice areas.

Still other factors which we have not yet studied may have been active; I think, for instance, that possibly the change to white rice, i.e. highly polished rice, may have increased vitamin-deficiencies. The import of opium (opium had been known since at least 1000) and more general use of it as well as the impact of venereal diseases after contact with the Spaniards, may have been important additional factors which reduced life expectancy and decreased the rate of increase of population in the 19th century. We can say that by circa 1800, China was "filled up", but that the farmer still kept his pattern of fertility. He lowered his living standards and ran into a higher mortality rate.

At this very moment, the time was ripe for a transition to a new mode of production: industrialization should have started around

---

[1] See note 1, page 270 on the nitrogen level.

1800. But the impact of the West prevented this for a while; just long enough to produce a critical situation. Instead of starting to produce industries, China was induced and/or forced to buy foreign industrial products which prevented it from building its own industry in time. This, then, created the unfortunate picture of 19th- and early 20th-century China.

4) Migrations

An agricultural population which increases in numbers has to migrate; there is a marginal size for an agricultural settlement at which the distance from the farmer's house to his fields becomes so great that he decides to move out of the village. This, then, leads to the formation of a hamlet at first. Out of the hamlet grows a new village. The moment when this marginal size is reached depends largely on local, geographical factors. In Shantung, 188 families or slightly less than 1000 persons seems to be the "ideal" size [1], in Hopei it seems to be 169 families or roughly 850 persons [2]; in Chekiang it is only 54 families with less than 250 persons [3].

Once the marginal size is reached, a new village has to be created. This may be a settlement very close to the old village. Indeed, the pattern of settlement of our Wu clan in Kuangtung shows this type of movement before 1800. Slowly but steadily all possible places, valleys, canyons, hill slopes, are filled with fields and settlements. Then finally, the time comes when no more settlement is possible near by. And if the community still continues to grow, the surplus has to emigrate to a place far away. We have seen the possible patterns of these migrations.

We also tried to show that until the 19th century "emigration" was always to some degree possible in China. In Yen-yüan hsiang, near Ning-po in Chekiang, 3258 out of a total of 9252 families have clear records of having moved into this community between the 8th and the 19th centuries [4]; yet this community is a relatively old one. There are indications that it was well settled as early as the 13th century at the latest.

Settlers are the active elements in society: the persons who are willing to change, are willing to experiment. Chinese settlers normally

---

[1] H. D. Scholz, *Formen der ländlichen Siedlung in China*, 1949, p. 57.
[2] Makino, *loc. cit.*, p. 288.
[3] Makino, *loc. cit.*, p. 210.
[4] Makino, *loc. cit.*, p. 284.

did not come into areas which were completely empty. They usually came as a superior group into a place inhabited by more primitive groups. We find our immigrants in all kinds of "colonial exploitation": they introduce the culture of indigo and then sell blue cloth to the natives who love it and are willing to pay high prices for it; they set up little shops and sell Chinese textiles or metal or porcelain to the natives, and buy their raw materials: the gold they picked up in the rivers, firewood, mushrooms and medicinal herbs for sale back home. They make Chinese wine and liquor, which is more potent and better than the native brew, and the natives love to drink. They make the natives indebted to them, and finally take over their land, with the natives as tenants. And they even take the daughters of the natives as wives or sell them as prostitutes or concubines. They marry into native ruling families and become managers of their properties. They buy up cheap, uncultivated land, put in irrigation and reap big harvests. Finally they come as officials and rulers and take over the area—and a new district is born. All these processes are well documented, well known, common all through Chinese history. They are still going on before our eyes in Taiwan and in Southeast Asia, Central Asia or Tibet. It is in this zone, which is so hard to define, but may be said to be some 50 to 100 miles outside the official borders of China proper and 50 to 100 miles just inside the borders, in which we find the quickest changes, the greatest possibilities, the most frequent upward social mobility. It is also here that we find the greatest intellectual stimulation, because the processes are not one-sided as we may have described them just now. The Chinese settlers also learn from the local population: they take over new plants cultivate them, and introduce them into China proper; they import new implements, new materials, new ideas. It would be worthwhile to look into the biographies of some of China's greatest thinkers: Chu Hsi (1130-1200) may very well have conceived of some of his ideas on the family while he was an official in a half-barbarian coastal district. At least he is locally credited with cultural innovations which spread over large parts of the Far East [1]. Han Yü (768-825) may have been inspired to look more into Buddhism while he was an exile in a coastal district, for having attacked the Buddhist cult. Wang Yang-ming (1473-1529) is not only one of the first to copy

---

[1] *K'ang-yu chi-hsing* 14, 3a and *Sun Yat-sen University, Yü-yen li-shih*, no. 4, pp. 1-7. Makino, in *Minzoku-gaku kenkyu*, vol. 16, 1951, no. 2, p. 116, has discussed the influence of Chu Hsi over Korea and Annam.

Portuguese firearms and to use them in his campaigns against South Chinese native tribes, but it is conceivable that some of his idealistic ideas and the new spirit expressed in his philosophy actually were inspired by his contacts with the businessmen along the "frontier". And if we go back into early China, there can be, I think, no doubt that Meng-tzu formulated some of his ideas on civilization and the state after he had had contacts with "neo-primitives" who propagandized a bucolic anarchy, while his Taoist opponents seem to have modeled their ideal society after a Rousseau-type picture of "the noble savage".

The concept of the "frontier", perhaps, has been much overplayed. Yet I think that O. Lattimore was correct to point out that a "frontier" society could also be found in China. What he indicated mainly for the North and for the recent periods may be true also for earlier periods and for the South. It seems to be the marginal area which proves to be the place of the greatest challenge.

Perhaps one of the reasons why China followed a different development than the West is that there was always an "open" border around China: for at least the last 3,000 years, the country has been always surrounded by societies which were technologically inferior to the Chinese, which looked up to the Chinese, and which had a lower rate of population growth (as a consequence of their technological level) than the Chinese. The "underdeveloped" societies around China (and this includes—at least for the Chinese and the time before the late 19th century—also the Japanese and Koreans) never really could resist the Chinese colonists. Thus the individual settler profited from the challenge. In the West, many small societies of more or less the same level of technology existed, at least during the last 300 years.

An ordinary migrant in the West could not simply exploit the difference in cultural and/or technological level between his home country and his new environment; his government could not help him by "pacifying" the natives. Any such processes as we discussed for China, in the West invariably involved, after a short time several states—each one jealous of the other—and developed into wars. Wars between states of equal level are a challenge of a different type from "pacification" of natives. Much of Western progress in technology and science was a "by-product" of a development for war. China needed no higher and higher technology to subdue the primitive and "under-developed" societies around it.

APPENDIX

THE NAMES OF THE MEMBERS OF THE WU CLAN

Every Chinese has a personal name (*ming*); Chinese from educated families, when they reach a certain age, are given a special name in addition (*tzu*; often called "style"). Men with scholarly interests may adopt in their later life a third name (*hao*; often called "pen-name"). We can, therefore, say that the higher the percentage of *tzu* the higher their educational level, and the higher the percentage of *hao*, the greater is the scholarly activity of a family.

In our genealogy, the ratio of *tzu* to *hao* is

Generation 50-59	3 : 1
Generation 60-69	2 : 1
Generation 70 85	1.3 : 1

The general ratio of *ming* to *tzu* and *hao* in all families over the whole period is 4: 1. The percentage of *tzu* and *hao* is higher in the early generations (see Table 69). These changes, however, do not mean much, because the results are strongly influenced by the fact that for one house (the An-hai house) in most cases both the *tzu* and the *hao* are given which influences the totals. It seems to me that the percentages of *tzu* and *hao* for the individual families, although they might in part reflect the social status and the changes of the social status of these families, largely reflect the attention of the writers of the genealogies, and therefore do not have much importance as indicators.

Hao only occasionally show a consistent pattern. They are always two-character combinations.

Tzu also always consist of 2 characters. They often do show a consistent

TABLE 69. PERSONS WITH A *tzu* AND/OR *hao*

	gen. 50-59	gen. 60-69	gen. 70-85	total average
Lü-wei	36.8%	15.0%	19.1%	22.5%
Ch'iu-kuan	15.8%	49.4%	36.1%	26.7%
Han-yüan	50.6%	46.5%	16.8%	40.7%
Sha-pei	10.7%	0	0	1.1%
T'ien-hsiung	8.0%	3.5%	38.3%	7.8%
Lung-yen	33.3%	5.6%	10.7%	8.2%
An-hai	7.7%	138.0%	148.0%	134.0%
Jung-kui	2.8%	3.3%	8.8%	6.6%
Total	33.8%	14.0%	28.0%	24.6%

pattern: all sons of one generation may have one character (and mostly the second one) in common. Or the *tzu* may contain an element which is a typical character in the *ming* of other members of the same family. For an analysis of names, *tzu* and *ming* can often be used together.

The personal name (*ming*) of a Chinese in the last centuries consists usually of 2 characters; names with only one character were more common in early medieval times. Yet, down to the present, some *ming* still have only one character. In our families, the names consisting of only one character constitute 10 per cent of all names. (see Table 70), but individual families

TABLE 70. ONLY ONE CHARACTER IN THE NAME (MING), BY HOUSE

House:	%
Lü-wei	6%
Han-yüan	22%
Ch'iu-kuan	7%
Sha-pei	41%
Jung-kui	8%
An-hai	10%
Lung-yen	1.5%
T'ien-hsiung	7%

differ greatly: the Lung-yen house dislikes such names strongly; the Sha-pei house, on the other hand, shows over 40 per cent of one-character names. In this field the 2 competing houses (Lü-wei and Han-yüan houses) who are quite similar in other respects and who lived closely together for centuries, differ: the Lü-wei house dislikes one-character names, while the Han-yüan house, especially in some generations, likes this type of names.

A tabulation according to generations (Table 71) does not show a con-

TABLE 71. ONLY ONE CHARACTER IN THE NAME (MING), BY GENERATION

Generation	Generation	Generation
50: 36.3%	60: 34.5% (Ch'k;LW)	70: 5.4
51: *40%* (HY)	61: 10.8%	71: 3.3%
52: 5.3%	62: 6.2%	72: 4.2%
53: 7.7%	63: *38.4%* (Sha)	73: 3.0%
54: 1.4%	64: 22.3% (Sha)	74: 1.9%
55: 0.9%	65: 10.0% (Sha)	75: 0.5%
56: 17.3%	66: 1.0%	76: 0.0%
57: 8.7%	67: 2.4%	
58: 15.7%	68: 1.8%	
59: *45.2%* (HY)	69: 3.5%	

sistent pattern; it rather seems that one-character names were preferred strongly by one or the other house in one specific generation for reasons which we do not know, and then often abolished again in the following generation.

Since early medieval times, it has been a custom to use a definite pattern in naming sons: in names with two characters either the first or the second character was the same for all sons. It is more common to keep the first character constant, but in our sample, one house (the Lung-yen house) prefers to keep the second character constant and usually not the first. In *ming* with only one character several procedures can be used. Most commonly, the ming of all sons have the same 'radical'; but in other cases, the names belong to a set of concepts, such as the basic virtues, the auspicious trees, etc [1].

Our families follow this pattern in general, but there are exceptions. Table 72 shows that roughly 75 per cent of the sons have *ming* which follow the rule, but 25 per cent deviate. There is no significant change

TABLE 72. BROTHERS WITH SAME OR WITH DIFFERENT NAMES (MING), ACCORDING TO GENERATIONS

Generation	Number of cases (%) same	Different	Number of individuals (%) same	Different
50-59	214 (73%)	80 (27%)	603 (71%)	251 (29%)
60-69	160 (79%)	43 (21%)	458 (74%)	162 (26%)
70-76	97 (73%)	36 (27%)	309 (66%)	158 (34%)
Totals	471 (75%)	159 (25%)	1370 (70%)	571 (30%)

over the generations, and as Table 73 shows, there is no significant deviation between different houses. We cannot, therefore, explain the inconsistency as a consequence of a gradual acceptance of a custom, because in such a case we would expect a gradual increase or decrease of the percentages. We also cannot explain the inconsistency by saying that some families accepted the custom and others did not.

If we study which of the sons has the highest chance to get a name

TABLE 73. BROTHERS WITH SAME OR DIFFERENT NAMES (MING) ACC. TO HOUSES

House	Cases		Individuals	
Lü-wei	77%	23% (244 cases)	74%	26%
Ch'iu-kuan	69%	31% (75 cases)	68%	32%
Han-yüan	62%	38% (87 cases)	57%	43%
Jung-kui	100%	(8 cases)	100%	
Sha-pei	69%	31% (61 cases)	53%	47%
T'ien-hsiung	77%	23% (84 cases)	69%	31%
Lung-yen	68%	32% (44 cases)	83%	17%

[1] All details on customs concerning names which are studied here can be read in W. Bauer, "Das P'ai-heng-System in der chinesischen Personennamengebung", in *Zeitschrift d. deutschen morgenl. Gesellschaft*, vol. 107, 1957, pp. 595-634.

which deviates from the pattern used for the other sons, we find the following picture (Table 74):

TABLE 74. DEVIATING NAMES (MING)

First Son: 50 per cent	Percentage of First Sons:	42
Second Son: 16		26
Third Son: 22		17
Fourth Son: 6		7
Fifth Son: 4		5
Later Sons: 2		3

We do not think that the chances for any son to get a name which deviates from the names of his brothers are higher than we should expect, considering the distribution of sons in general. We can offer only a hypothetical explanation, as our data do not suffice for proof: we believe that a son from a concubine, i.e. a wife of lower social status, was often (or perhaps usually in the Wu clan) given a deviating name in order to indicate this different status. The implications of this hypothesis for an understanding of the family structure of polygamous families in China would have to be explored.

From the late medieval period on, at least some families used the same pattern of name not only for the sons of a man, but also for all cousins, so that a name became an indicator of the generation to which a given person belongs. We found this custom in our material in the time before generation 60, but we did not investigate whether the circle of names of the same pattern included also second or third cousins. A complete study of names would also have to include the *tzu* name, because sometimes cousins use the pattern in the *ming* while others use it in the *tzu* only. In the same way, often the son who has a *ming* deviating from the pattern, has the expected word in his *tzu*. By this expedient, a man can be identified as belonging to a certain generation and at the same time as a son of a concubine. We are, however, not at all sure whether this practice was general in China or even general in South Chinese clans.

The custom of using a name pattern in still later times led to the introduction of a "name code": at a certain moment in the history of the family, the chief of the family made a code for the following generations; usually this code was in the form of a poem of, usually, 20 words. Each word was to be used by the members of a certain generation. It was easy to check whether a man who claimed to be a relative really was a relative: in his own name (*ming*, or *tzu*) he had to have the code word, and, in addition, his father's and grandfather's names also should show the appropriate code word. If the claimant did not know the whole code by heart, and if the names which he gave as names of his father and grand-father did not have the right code words, he was exposed as an imposter.

Our genealogy published the codes of the Lü-wei [1], Han-yüan [2] and

---
[1] 2b, 22a.
[2] 2b, 22b.

284   APPENDIX

T'ien-hsiung houses [1]. They also published a code used by the Jung-hsien sub-branch of the Lü-wei house [2] and a code to be used when the existing code is exhausted [3]. With the exception of the T'ien-hsiung house code, all codes have 20 code words. The T'ien-hsiung code had only 10 words; another ten words were added in the middle of the 17th century.

The T'ien-hsiung code starts with generation 58, but we found that it was not used before generation 61, i.e. from around 1470 on. Generation 61 is, according to the traditions of the house, its 14th generation in South China. The code continued to be used by the house until the end of the first part, i.e. generation 67 (ca. 1645). The following two generations which should have used the first two words of the extended code, did not use the code, but from generation 70 (ca. 1730) on the code is used, down to the present time.

The Lü-wei house code begins with generation 62, which, according to the traditions of the house, is its 14th generation in South China, and is still in use. The Lü-wei house, therefore, began to use a code from ca. 1530 on.

The Han-yüan house code starts with generation 62, but it was not used in generation 62; the application begins in generation 63 which is the 14th generation in South China, according to the traditions of the house. Generation 63 of the Han-yüan house lived around 1640. The code is still used.

The Jung-hsien code began to be used by generation 71, ca. 1850, and is still used by the present 75th generation. This branch house of the Lü-wei house was created in generation 64 [4], i.e. around 1590.

The names in the other houses, too, seem to follow a definite pattern, and seem to be based upon a code; but if the code is not given, it is always difficult and unsafe to try to reconstruct the code from the names.

The Jung-hsien sub-house is an example of a branch which split away from the main house and established its own pattern. We do not know what circumstances led to the Jung-hsien members to make such a break; it was certainly not the distance from the main house, because other families just as far away from the main house continued to use the code. It is also not in connection with the lapse of time since the creation of the new settlement. Families which in the present generation 74 and 75 of the Lü-wei house still use the code names, belong to settlements which were, in the majority, created in the generations 64 to 67, but some were established as early as in generation 56, i.e. such families continue the use of the code names even after 20 generations of separation from the mother house.

There is no interrelation between the individual houses in this custom of giving names. We found that as soon as a new house was created, it adopted its own pattern of giving names; in fact, this was one of the main reasons we argued that the so-called houses were independent families which were tied together only by the work of the genealogists. Otherwise

---

[1] 2b, 22b.
[2] 2b, 22b.
[3] 2b, 22b.
[4] 4a, 59b-60a.

we should expect that the branch house continues to keep the name pattern of the mother house for a while, until it establishes its own rules. We know that such an action can be taken in the 5th generation after the separation.

Some similarity in the names of persons who were believed to have lived around 1250 seemed to have been the main reason for the genealogist's tying together all the houses to one clan (generation 53).

The independence of the houses is further obvious from the fact that the same code word occurs in different house codes, although in all cases the code word is assigned to generations so much separated from one another in time that no mix-up could occur.

As a rule, no name should be used by more than one person. Yet we find in our material a number of names which occur more than once. One reason for this is an error in interpretation: as the genealogy in some cases gives the *ming*, in other cases *ming*, *tzu* and *hao*, but in other cases either only the *tzu* or only the *hao*. I failed to identify two apparently different names if the one was a *ming* and the other a *hao* or *tzu* and found this out only after a general indexing of all names according to the alphabet (63 cases out of a total of 4,331 names; most of these cases belong to the Lü-wei house (52) and of the generations from 72 on) [1].

But we found another group of 231 names which occurred more than once and which apparently refer to different individuals. Of these 231 names, 192 occurred twice, 31 three times, 6 four times and 2 five times. It is interesting to note that 75 of the 213 names (32.5 per cent) are names consisting of one character only, while the general percentage of one-character names is only 10 per cent.

This expresses in my opinion nothing more than the higher percentage of incidence of identical names if the name has only one and not two characters. While most persons who had the same name belong to different houses, and while the difference in generation between such persons is on the average 6 generations, there are cases in which the same name occurs within the same house and sometimes even within the same generation. There are 22 such cases in the Lü-wei house, 5 in the Han-yüan, 3 in the Sha-pei and one in the Lung-yen house. The average difference in generation between persons with the same name within the same house is 5 generations. After a lapse of 5 generations, theoretically a name once used could be used again. On the other hand, if we consider the great number of clan members, their wide distribution, and the relatively limited number of possibilities for forming a name in which one part of the 2-character combination is given, we can understand that sometimes members of the same generation living in different settlements have the same name, and that in other cases by pure chance the names of persons belonging to different generations are identical.

We would like to add one remark here: if names occur in lists, names with only one character break the pattern of a list in which the majority of names has two characters. In such cases, several devices have been found

---

[1] For all these persons nothing but the name is reported. These men, therefore, do not re-appear in any of our statistical tables.

in the course of centuries: a) the one-character name can be enlarged by adding an "A-" to the name [1]. If, however, an "A-" occurs in front of a family name (*hsing*), this indicates in earlier inscriptions a woman [2]; in later texts a low-class familial type of adress.

b) the one-character name can be padded by repeating the character [3]. In such cases, the added word has to be left out of consideration when the names are analyzed.

In conclusion we can state: There is no developmental change in the customs of giving either one-character or two-character names (*ming*) in the 800 years of family history. *Tzu* and *hao* indicate the social status of its bearer, but our genealogy is not complete enough to allow us to use the occurrence of *tzu* and *hao* to measure social status. Sons usually carry names which are interrelated. If their names (*ming*) are not interrelated, it seems in the Wu clan to indicate that the son in question was the son of a concubine. He then often indicates by his *tzu* that he is related to his brothers. Cousins also often carry interrelated names, indicating their generation. We have the impression that the sons of a son of a concubine do not usually have names of the same pattern as their cousins who descended from a main wife, but we did not study this problem in detail.

We find the use of a name code in one of the houses as early as 1470; other houses adopted a code system later. Branch settlements often continue to use the code names even after 20 generations of independent living. For unknown, but certainly individual reasons, some settlements begin to use a code of their own, but not before a fair number of generations of independent living. The code names are still in use by the generation living at the present time.

---

[1] This system was used in the inscriptions of donors in the temple in Rangoon from the years 1868 and 1871. It occurs also fairly often in Tun-huang texts.

[2] Often in Tun-huang. As an example see A. Stein, *Serindia*, vol. 4, illustr. 62: a Mrs. Liu.

[3] Often in Tun-huang. As an example, see Paris no. 2685, quoted in Niida Noboru, *Legal Documents*, p. 614. Incidentally, while Buddhistic and even Taoistic names are quite common in Tun-huang even among lay people, our genealogy contains practically no Taoist and very few Buddhist names. Also, names which contain numbers are very rare.

BIBLIOGRAPHY

a) List of Books

Amyot, J., *The Chinese Community of Manila, a Study of Adaptation of Chinese Familism to the Philippine Environment*, University of Chicago, Philippine Studies Program, Research Series, no. 2, 1960 (mimeogr.).

An-p'ing Kao-shih tsu-p'u chih-lüeh 安平高氏族譜畧, Taipei 1955; text of Taipei, Taiwan Provincial Library.

An-yang Fa-chüeh pao-kao 安陽發掘報告. (Reports on Excavations at Anyang), Peking and Shanghai, 1929 f.; 4 volumes.

Balazs, Etienne, "Le Traité économique du 'Souei-chou'", in *T'oung Pao*, vol. 42, no. 3/4, 1953, pp. 113-329.

Balazs, Etienne, *Les Foires en Chine*, Editions de la Librairie Encyclop., Bruxelles 1953, 15 pages.

Buriks, P., *Fan Chung-yen's Versuch einer Reform des chinesischen Beamtenstaats*, Unpublished Ph.D. thesis, Göttingen 1954.

Castell, Graf zu, *China-Flug*, Berlin 1938.

Chang Chung-li, *The Chinese Gentry. Studies in their Role in 19th Century Chinese Society*, Seattle, U. of Washington Press 1955.

Chang Tê-tsui, *Agricultural Economics in Taiwan*, Taipei 1960, mimeogr.

Ch'en Cheng-hsiang, *Place Names in Taiwan*, Research Report no. 104, Fumin Geogr. Institute of Economic Development, Taipei 1960.

Ch'en Cheng-hsiang and C. H. Tuan, *Population of Taiwan*, Inst. of Agric. Economics, Taipei, 1951.

Ch'en Fu, *Nung-shu* 陳尃, 農書, Shanghai, Chung-hua shu-chü 1956.

Chen Han-seng, *Landlord and Peasant in China*, New York 1936.

Ch'en Meng-chia, *Yin-hsü pu-tz'u tsung-shu* 陳夢家, 殷虛卜辭綜述, Peking 1956.

Ch'en Shih-ch'i, *Ming-tai kuan-shou-kung-yeh-ti yen-chiu* 明代官手工業的研究, Wuhan 1958.

Chen Ta, *Emigrant Communities in South China*, New York, Institute of Pacific Relations, 1940.

Ch'en Ta, *Population in Modern China*, Chicago 1946.

Chieh-hu-chi 堅瓠集. Author Ch'u Hsüeh-chia, Manchu period, Edition Pi-chi hsiao-shuo ta-kuan 筆記小說大觀, Shanghai, Chin-pu.

Chin-shu 晉書. Edition Erh-shih wu shih, Shanghai, K'ai-ming.

China International Famine Relief Commission, Geneva, League of Nations 1924.

Ch'ing-ho tsu-p'u 清河族譜 (Text in U. of California Library, Berkeley).

Chiu Wu-tai-shih 舊五代史. Edition Erh-shih wu shih, Shanghai, K'ai-ming.

Ch'ü T'ung-tsu, *Chung-kuo fa-lü yü Chung-kuo shê-hui* 瞿同祖，中国法律與中国社會, Shanghai, Commercial Press 1947.
Ch'ü T'ung-tsu, *Local Government in China under the Ch'ing*. Harvard East Asian Studies, vol. 9, Cambridge. Mass. 1962.
Ch'ü-yu chiu-wen 曲洧舊聞. Author Chu Pien. Sung period. Edition Pi-chi hsiao-shuo ta-kuan, Shanghai, Chin-pu.
Ch'üan-shan yao-yen 勸善要言. Manchu period.
Chung-hua ch'üan-kuo feng-su-chih 中華全國風俗誌. Author Hu P'u-an, Shanghai, Ta-ta 1935, 4 volumes.
Cuisinier, J., *Les Mu'ò'ng, Géographie Humaine et Sociologie*, Traveaux et mémoires de l'Institute d'Ethnologie, vol. 45, Paris 1948.
Eberhard, W., *Conquerors and Rulers*, Leiden, E. J. Brill 1952.
Eberhard, W., *A History of China*, Second edition, London, Routledge 1960.
Eberhard, W., *Kultur und Siedlung der Randvölker Chinas*, Leiden, E. J. Brill 1941.
Eberhard, W., "Zur Landwirtschaft der Han-Zeit", in *Mitt. d. Seminars f. Orient. Sprachen*, Abt. 1, vol. 35, 1932, pp. 74-105.
Eberhard, W., *Lokalkulturen im alten China*, vol. 1, Leiden, E. J. Brill 1942; vol. 2, Peking, Monumenta Serica 1942.
Eberhard, W., *Das Toba-Reich Nordchinas*, Leiden, E. J. Brill 1949.
Eberhard, W., *Typen chinesischer Volksmärchen*, Folklore Fellows Communications no. 120, Helsinki 1937.
Eberhard, W., *Volksmärchen aus Süd-Ost-China*, Folklore Fellows Communications no. 128, Helsinki 1941.
Ennin's Diary, The Record of a Pilgrimage to China. Transl. by E. O. Reischauer, New York 1955.
Fairbank, J. K. (ed.), *Chinese Thought and Institutions*, Chicago 1957.
Fei Hsiao-t'ung, *Earthbound China*, Chicago 1945.
Feng-su-t'ung 風俗通, as quoted by *I-lin* (see there).
Fischer, Johanna, *Fan Chung-yen*. Unpubl. Ph.D. thesis, Göttingen 1954.
Franke, Otto, *Geschichte des chinesischen Reiches*, Berlin, de Gruyter, 1930 f. 5 volumes.
Freedman, Maurice, *Lineage Organization in Southeastern China*, London, U. of London 1958.
Gamble, Sidney D., *Ting Hsien. A North China Rural Community*, New York 1954.
Granet, M., *Danses et Légendes de la Chine Ancienne*, Paris 1926.
Granet, M., "Catégories Matrimoniales et Relations de Proximité dans la Chine Ancienne" in *Annales Sociologiques*, Série B, Paris 1939.
Grimm, T., *Erziehung und Politik im konfuzianischen China der Ming-Zeit*, Mitt. d. Ges. f. Natur- & Völkerkunde Ostasiens, vol. 35B, Hamburg 1960.
Groot, J. J. M. de, *Religious System of China*, Leiden, E. J. Brill, 1892-1910.
Groot, J. J. M. de, *Les Fêtes Annuellement Célébrées à Émouy*, Paris 1886.
Han Fei-tse 韓非子. Author probably Han Fei, 3rd cent. B.C.
Han-shu 漢書. Author Pan Ku et al. Edition T'u-shu chi-ch'eng.
Han Yü, *Han Ch'ang-li ch'üan-chi* 韓昌黎全集, T'ang period.
Hou-ching-lu 侯鯖錄. Author Chao Ling-chih, Sung period. Edition Pi-chi hsiao-shuo ta-kuan, Shanghai, Chin-pu.

Hou Han-shu 後漢書. Edition Erh-shih wu shih, Shanghai, K'ai-ming.

Hou-tê-lu 厚德錄. Author Li Yüan-kang, Sung period. Edition Pi-chi hsiao-shuo ta-kuan, Shanghai, Chin-pu.

Hsiao Kung-chuan, *Rural China; Imperial Control in the 19th Century*. Seattle 1960.

Hsin-an Ch'eng-shih t'ung-tsung shih-p'u 新安程氏同宗世譜. Ming edition. Text in National Library, Taichung.

Hsin-hui hsien-chih 新會縣志. 1840 edition.

Hu Hsien-chin, *The Common Descent Group in China*, Viking Fund Publ. in Anthropology, no. 10, New York 1948.

Hua-man-chi 畫墁記. Author Chang Shun-min. Sung Period. Edition Pi-chi hsiao-shuo ta-kuan, Shanghai, Chin-pu.

Huai-nan-tzu 淮南子. Author probably Liu An. Han period.

Hulsewé, A. F. P., *Remnants of Han Law*, vol. 1, Leiden, E. J. Brill 1955.

I-chien-chih 夷堅志. Author Hung Mai. Sung period. Edition Pi-chi hsiao-shuo ta-kuan, Shanghai, Chin-pu.

I-lin 意林. Author Ma Tsung, T'ang period. Edition Pi-chi hsiao-shuo ta-kuan, Shanghai, Chin-pu.

Ju-Shu-chi 入蜀記. Author Lu Wu-kuan. Sung period. Edition Pi-chi hsiao-shuo ta-kuan, Shanghai, Chin-pu.

Jung-ch'uang hsiao-p'in 湧幢小品. Author Chu Kuo-chen. Ming period. Edition Pi-chi hsiao-shuo ta-kuan, Shanghai, Chin-pu.

Jung-shih p'u-tieh 容氏譜牒. Text of U. of California Library, Berkeley.

K'ang-yu chi-hsing 康輶紀行. Author Yao Jung. 19th century. Edition Pi-chi hsiao-shuo ta-kuan, Shanghai, Chin-pu.

Kato Shigeru, *Studies in Chinese Economic History* 支那經濟史考證, Tôyô Bunko Publications, Series A, no. 34A-B, Tokyo 1952/3, 2 vol.

Köymen, Mustafa, *Der Einfluss des Handels mit Zentral- und Vorderasien in der T'ang-Zeit auf die chinesischen Märchen*, Dil ve Tarih-Côgrafya Fakültesi, Sinoloji Enstitüsü neşriyatı 5, Istanbul 1941.

Kracke, E. A., *Civil Service in Early Sung China*, Cambridge, Mass. 1953.

Ku-liang-chuan 穀梁傳.

Kuan-tse 管子 (references to a translation are to L. Maverick (ed.), *Economic Dialogues in Ancient China*, Carbondale 1954).

Kuhn, Franz (transl.), Li Yü, *Jou Pu Tuan*, Zürich 1959.

Kung-yang chuan 公羊傳.

Kuo-yü 國語.

Lamson, Herbert D., *Social Pathology in China*, Shanghai 1935.
Lang, Olga, *Chinese Family and Society*, New York 1946.
Lattimore, Owen, *Mongols of Manchuria*, New York 1934.
Lattimore, Owen, *Inner Asian Frontiers of China*, New York 1940.

Lattimore, Owen, *Pivot of Asia*, New York 1950.
Li-chi 禮紀 (references to a translation are to E. Couvreur, *Li Ki* or to R. Wilhelm, *Li Gi, das Buch der Sitte*, Jena 1930).
Li Chi, *The Formation of the Chinese People*, Cambridge, Mass. 1928.
Li-chia tsu-hsien shih-tsu p'u 李家祖先世簿. Manuscript, 10 pages. Seen in Taiwan.
Li Yü 李漁 (see Fr. Kuhn).
Lieh-tse 烈子 (references to a translation are to R. Wilhelm, *Liä Dsi*, Jenal 1921).
Lin-shih tsung-ch'in lu 林氏宗親錄, Taipei 1937, 196 pages.
Lin-shih tsu-p'u 林氏族譜, Taichung 1935.
Ling-nan Wu-shih tsung-p'u 嶺南伍氏綜譜. Text in U. of California Library, Berkeley.
Liu-Kui ts'ung-k'an 六桂叢刊, Taichung 1957, 297 pages.
Lo Chen-yü, *Liu-sha tui-chien* 流沙墜簡, 1914.
Lo Hsiang-lin, *An Introduction to the Study of the Hakkas in its Ethnic, Historical and Cultural Aspects* 客家研究道論, Hsing-ning, Hsi-shan shu-yüan, 1933, 292 pages (quoted as "K'o-chia" or as "Introduction").
Lü-shih ch'un-ch'iu 呂氏春秋. Compiled by Lü Pu-wei, 3rd century B.C. (translation R. Wilhelm, *Frühling und Herbst des Lü WeiBu*, Jena 1928).
Lun-heng 論衡. Author Wang Ch'ung, First century A.D. (references to a translation are to A. Forke, *Lun-heng*, Leipzig & Berlin 1907-1911).
Lun-yü 論語. (References to a translation are to R. Wilhelm, *Kung Futse, Gespräche*, Jena 1923).
MacNair, H. (ed.), *China*, Berkeley, U. of California Press 1946.
MacSherry, Ch. W., *The Impairment of the Ming Triburaty System*, Unpubl. Ph.D. thesis, U. of California, Berkeley.
Makino, Tatsumi: 牧野巽，近世中國宗族研究, Tokyo Nikko Publishers, 1949, 329 pages.
Marsh, Robert M., *Mandarin and Executive*, Ph.D. thesis, U. of Michigan 1959 (in a revised form published later under the title *The Mandarins: Circulation of Elites in China*, Glencoe 1961, 300 pages).
Maspero, Henri, and J. Escarra, *Les Institutions de la Chine*, Paris, Presses Universit. 1952, 184 pages.
Maybon, P., *Essay sur des Associations en Chine*, Paris 1925.
Meng-tzu 孟子. Author Meng K'o, 4th cent. B.C. (references to a translation are to R. Wilhelm, *Mong Dsi*, Jena 1921).
Ming-chai hsiao-shih 明齋小識. Author Chu Mei-hsiang, Manchu period. Edition Pi-chi hsiao-shuo ta-kuan, Shanghai, Chin-pu.
Ming-shih 明史. Edition Erh-shih-wu-shih, Shanghai, K'ai-ming.

Nan-Ch'u hsin-wen 南楚新聞. Author Yü-ch'ih Shu, T'ang period (quoted in *T'ai-p'ing kuang-chi*).
Naumann, Hans, *Primitive Gemeinschaftskultur*, Jena, E. Diederichs 1921.
Neng-kai-chai-man-lu 能改齋漫錄. Author Wu Tseng, Sung period Edition Pi-chi hsiao-shuo ta-kuan, Shanghai, Chin-pu.
Niida Noboru, *Chinese Rural Families* 中國の農村家族, Tokyo, Tokyo University Press 1952, 419 pages.
Niida Noboru, *The Critical Study of Legal Documents of the T'ang and Sung Eras*, 唐宋法律文書の研究, Tokyo, Tôhô Bunkwa Gakuin 1937, 857 pages.
Niida Noboru, *T'ang Law* 唐令拾遺, Tokyo 1933.
Nivison, D. (ed.), *Confucianism in Action*, Stanford 1959.
Pa-tou-tse Yü-ts'un t'iao-ch'a pao-kao 八斗子漁村調查報告. Authors Sun Tê-hsiung et al., Fumin Geogr. Institute, Taipei, 1959, 43 pages.
P'an Kuang-tan, *Ming Ch'ing liang-tai Chia-hsing-ti wang-tsu* 潘光旦, 明清兩代嘉興的望族, Shanghai, Commercial Press 1947, 145 pages
Pelzer, K. J., *Die Arbeiterwanderungen in Südostasien*, Hamburg 1935.
Pelzer, K. J., *Pioneer Settlement in the Asiatic Tropics*, New York 1945.
Po-hu-t'ung 白虎通. Editor Pan Ku, First cent. A.D. (references to a translation are to Tjan Tjoe Som, *Po-hu t'ung, the Comprehensive Discussions in the White Tiger Hall*, Leiden, E. J. Brill 1949).
Preliminary Report: A Study on the Impact of Farmer's Association and Extension Program on the Development of Agriculture in Taiwan, a Project, jointly sponsored by ECAFE, National Taiwan University, and JCRR, Taipei, June 1959, mimeo.
Ruben, Walter, *Eisenschmiede und Dämonen*, Internat. Archiv für Ethnologie, Leiden 1939.
San-kuo-chih 三國志. Edition T'u-shu chi-ch'eng.
Scholz, H. D., *Die Formen der ländlichen Siedlung in China*, Ph.D. thesis Bonn 1949, 185 pp.
Schurmann, Franz, *Economic Structure of the Yüan Dynasty*, Harvard-Yenching Inst. Studies, no. 16, Cambridge, Mass. 1956.
Second Socio-Economic Report on Rural Taiwan, Taipei 1959 mimeo. (editor St. Kirby).
Serruys, H, *The Mongols in China*, 1959.
Shih-lin yen-yü 石林燕語. Author Yeh Meng-tê, Sung period. Edition Pi-chi hsiao-shuo ta-kuan, Shanghai, Chin-pu.
Shirokogoroff, S. M., *Social Organization of the Manchus*, Shanghai 1924.
Shuo-wen 說文. Author Hsü Shen, Han period.
Shuo-yüan 說苑. Author Liu Hsiang, First cent. B.C.
Skinner, G. W., *Chinese Society in Thailand*, Ithaca, Cornell University Press 1957.
Smith, Robert J., *Kurusu*, Univ. of Michigan, Occasional Papers, Center for Japan. Studies, no. 5, 1956.
Studia Serica, Bernard Karlgren Dedicata, Copenhagen 1960.
Studies in Chinese Econ. History (see Kato, Sh.).
Su, Sing Ging, *The Chinese Family System*, New York 1922.

Sung-chuang meng-yü 松窓夢語. Author Li Chi-k'o. Sung period. Edition Pi-chi hsiao-shuo ta-kuan, Shanghai, Chin-pu.

Swann, Nancy L., *Food and Money in Ancient China*, Princeton 1950.

Ta-Tai Li-chi 大戴禮紀. (References to a translation are to R. Wilhelm, *Li Gi, Das Buch der Sitte*, Jena 1930).

T'ai-pei-hsien Chung-ho-shê-ch'ü-chih yen-chiu 台北縣中和社區之研究. B.A. thesis, National Taiwan University Library, 1951.

T'ai-pei Lu-chou t'ien-yeh mei-pen chih-shih-hsi tsu-p'u 台北蘆州田野美本支世系族譜, ms.

T'ai-p'ing kuang-chi 太平廣記. Author Li Fang, 10th century. Edition Pi-chi hsiao-shuo ta-kuan, Shanghai, Chin-pu.

T'ai-p'ing yü-lan 太平御覽. Author Li Fang, 10th century. Edition Szu-pu ts'ung-k'an, Shanghai, Commercial Press.

T'ai-wan Ch'en Ta-tsung tz'u Tê-hsing-t'ang chung-hsiu chi-nien t'ê-k'an 台灣陳大宗祠德星堂重修紀年特刊, Taipei 1958.

Tamai Korehiro, *Shina shakai keizai-shih kenkyu* 玉井是博，支那社會經濟史研究, Tokyo 1937, 618 pages.

T'an-shih chih (Tam Family Record). Author Tam Yeu-wa 譚耀華，譚氏志, Hongkong 1957.

T'ang hui-yao 唐會要. Author Wang Fu, Sung period.

T'ang liu-tien 唐六典. Compiler Li Lin-fu, T'ang period.

T'ang-lü su-i 唐律疏義. Author Chang-sun Wu-chi, T'ang period.

Tawney, R. H., *Agrarian China*, New York 1932.

T'ien-kung k'ai-wu-chih yen-chiu 天工開物之研究. Transl. by Su Hsiang-yü et al., Hongkong, Chung-hua Publishers, 1956, 250 pages.

Togan, Zeki Validi, *Umumî Türk Tarihine Giriş*, Istanbul 1946.

Tso-chuan 左傳.

Tung-hsien pi-lu 東軒筆錄. Author Wei T'ai. Sung period. Edition Pi-chi hsiao-shuo ta-kuan, Shanghai, Chin-pu.

Van der Sprenkel, S., *Legal Institutions in Manchu China*, London, London School of Economics Monographs, 1962, 178 pages.

Vital Statistics, *Special Report* no. 44, publ. by the U.S. National Office of Vital Statistics.

Vreeland, H. H., *Mongol Community and Kinship Structure*, New Haven, Human Relations Area Files, 1952, 321 pages.

Wan-li yeh-huo pien 萬曆野獲編. Author Shen Tê-fu, 16th century. Shanghai, Chung-hua Publishers 1959

Wang Chen, *Nung-shu* 王禎，農書, Shanghai, Chung-hua Publishers 1956.

Wang-Liu Hui-chen, *The Traditional Chinese Clan Rules*, Monogr. of the Assoc. for Asian Studies, vol. 7, New York 1959, 264 pages.

Wei-shih tsu-p'u 韋氏族譜. Text in U. of California Library, Berkeley.
Wei-shu 魏書. Edition Erh-shih wu shih, Shanghai, K'ai-ming.
Wen-hsien t'ung-k'ao 文獻通考. Author Ma Tuan-lin, Sung period. Shanghai, Commercial Press.
Wiens, Harold J., *China's March Towards the Tropics*, Hamden 1954, 441 pages.
Wilbur, M., *Slavery in China during the Former Han Dynasty*, Publ. of the Field Museum, Anthropol. Series vol. 34, Chicago 1943, 490 pages.
Winfield, G. F., *China, the Land and the People*, New York 1947, 437 pages.
Wittfogel, K. A. and Feng Chia-sheng, *History of Chinese Society: Liao*. Philadelphia 1949, 752 pages.
Wu Hsiang-hsiang (ed.), *Chung-kuo chin-tai-shih lun ts'ung* 中國近代史論叢. Series 2: 社會經濟. vol. 2, Taipei 1958.
Yang-chou hua-fang-lu 楊州畫舫錄. Author Li Tou. 18th century. Shanghai, Chung-hua Publishers 1960.
Yang Lien-sheng, *Money and Credit in China*, Harvard-Yenching Inst. Monograph Series, vol. 12, Cambridge, Mass. 1952, 143 pages.
Yeh-k'o ts'ung-shu 野客叢書. Author Wang Mou. Sung period. Edition Pi-chi hsiao-shuo ta-kuan, Shanghai, Chin-pu.
Ying-shih 桯史. Author Yüeh K'o. Sung period. Edition Pi-chi hsiao-shuo ta-kuan, Shanghai, Chin pu.
Yü chih t'ang t'an-wei 玉芝堂談薈. Author Hsü Ying-ch'iu. Ming period. Edition Pi-chi hsiao-shuo ta kuan, Shanghai, Chin-pu.
Yü Ch'ü-yüan pi-chi 俞曲園筆記. Author Yü Yüeh, 19th century. Shanghai, Ta-ta publishers 1934, 2 vol.
Yüan Mei, *Hsiao-ts'ang-shan-fang wen-chi* 小倉山房文集, Yüan Mei, 18th century. Edition Shanghai, Hsin-wen-hua 1935.
Yin-chien chü-mu ch'ao 雲間據目抄. Author Fan Lien, Ming period. Edition Pi-chi hsiao-shuo ta-kuan, Shanghai, Chin pu.

b) List of Periodicals

Annales Sociologiques, Paris.
Anthropos, Vienna & Fribourg.
BOSS, see: *Bulletin School* ...
Bulletin Academia Sinica, see: *Bull. Phil. Hist.* ...
Bulletin of Chinese Studies 中國文化研究彙刊.
Bulletin of the Institute of Philology and History, Academia Sinica, Nanking and Tai-pei. 歷史言語研究所集刊.
Bulletin of the Museum of Far Eastern Antiquities, Stockholm.
Bulletin of the School of Oriental and African Studies, London University, London.
China Post, English language newspaper in Taipei.
Ch'ing-hua Journal 清華學報, Peiping and Taipei.

Comparative Studies in Society and History, Chicago.
Deutsche Akademie der Wissenschaften, Berlin, Institut für Orientforschung, East Berlin.
Economic Development and Cultural Change, Chicago.
Economic Geography.
Folklore Studies, Catholic University, Peiping and Tokyo.
Frontier Affairs 邊政公論.
Frontier Studies 邊疆研究論叢.
Geography and Industries, Taipei.
Harvard Journal of Asiatic Studies.
Historical Annual 史學年報, Yenching University, Peiping.
Hsin shê hui 新社會, Taipei.
Japanese Journal of Ethnology 民族學研究, Tokyo.
Journal for the Economic and Social History of the Orient.
Journal of Asian Studies.
Journal of Oriental Studies, Univ. of Hong Kong, Hong Kong.
Li shih yen chiu 歷史研究, Peking.
Memoirs of the Institute for Oriental Culture 東洋文化研究所紀要, Tokyo.
Memoirs of the Research Department of the Toyo Bunko, Tokyo.
Minzoku-gaku kenkyu (see *Japanese Journal of Ethnology*).
Nankai Weekly Statistical Service, Nankai University, Tientsin.
Oriens, Leiden.
Oriens Extremus, Hamburg.
Orientalistische Literaturzeitung, Leipzig.
Ostasiatische Zeitschrift, Berlin.
Population Studies.
Shien 史淵, Fukuoka.
Shih-huo 食貨.
Sinica, Frankfurt.
Sinologica, Basel.
Sociologus, Berlin.
Sun Yat-sen University, Yü-yen li-shih 中山大學語言歷史研究所週刊.
Ta-lu tsa-chih, Taipei 大陸雜誌.
T'ai-nan wen-hua 台南文化, T'ai-nan.
T'ai-wan shih-shih yen-chiu, 台灣史事研究, Taipei.
T'ai-wan ta-hsüeh, Wen-shih chê-hsüeh pao 台灣大學文史哲學報, Taipei.
T'ai-wan wen-chien 台灣聞見, Taipei.
Tôhô gakuhô 東方學報, Tokyo.

T'oung Pao 通報, Leiden.
Tôyô gakuhô 東洋學報, Tokyo.
Tôyô shigaku 東洋史學.
Tôyôshi kenkyu 東洋史研究.
Transactions of the Asiatic Society of Japan, Tokyo.
Tsing Hua Journal (see *Ch'ing-hua Journal*).
Wen-shih hui-k'an 文史薈刊, Taipei.
Yenching Journal of Social Studies, Peiping.
Yü-kung 禹貢, Shanghai.
Zeitschrift d. deutschen morgenländischen Gesellschaft.

INDEX

Aborgines, assimilation of 198f, 221, 278; trade with A 241 (s. Tribes)
Abortion 171n (s. Infanticide)
Academies (shu-yüan) 246, 261
Adoptions 159f, 234; ceremonial A 161; rules for A 199-200
Age difference husband/wife 132f, 143; A and social class 193
Agriculture, improvements 40, 271f (s. Irrigation)
Amano, M., scholar 272n
Amoy, city 218, 222n
An, clan 199n
An-hai, district in Fukien 67, 75; A house 82f
Anhui, province 58, 59 (s. Hsin-an)
Annam (Vietnam) 91, 167, 168, 278n
Apprentices 230
Army 268 (s. Soldiers, Military)
Artisans 177, 236f
Australia 78

Bandits 71, 89; Salt B 91 (s. Liu-min)
Bangkok, city 94, 104, 105n
Banks 255-6
Bauer, W., sinologist 282
Beggars 228
Besleme 160n
Bielenstein, H., sinologist 33n, 115n, 201
Birth rate 164f (s. Population)
Blacksmith 244
Blockprint 261
Bodde D. sinologist 8n
Borneo 256
Bourgeoisie 259f
Broker(ya) 244
Bronzesmith 244
Buckwheat 274
Buddhists 47; B names 286n; B and Social Work 254 (s. Monks, Monasteries)
Burghers 23, 10-11 (s. Patricians, Middle class)
Burma 91, 104, 273 (s. Rangoon)
Business families 116; B organisation 256f

Businessmen 118, individual B 71, 75, 78, 82-3, 87, 89, 90, 91, 94, 109, 65 (s. Merchants, Hong, Shopkeepers, Entrepreneurs)

California 167, 214 (s. Colima, San Francisco, Marysville, Weaverville)
Canton, city 55, 60, 65, 70, 72, 73, 74, 75, 76, 77, 78, 83, 89, 91, 93, 175, 181, 202, 258n, 266n, C clans 61
Capital formation 254f
Castes 18, 244
Castle 266 (s. Fort)
Cemeteries, Chinese 119
Census, reliability 166
Champa, state in SE-Asia 272
Chan, Wingtsit, philosopher 7n
Chang, clan 65-66
Chang Ch'ien, industrialist 246
Chang Chiu-ling, scholar 61
Chang-chou, district in Fukien 215
Ch'ang-sha, district in Hunan 110
Chao-ch'ing, district in Kuangtung 85
Chaste widows 135f, 233
Ch'en, clan 178-9, 64, 125f
Ch'en Hsien-chang, scholar 77n, 179, 180
Ch'en Kang, author 52
Ch'en Pai-sha (Ch'en Po-sha) see Ch'en Hsien-chang
Ch'en K'ai, author 52
Ch'en Yüan-kuang, general 215
Cheng, clan 178, 194, 123f
Chi-an, trade-city in Kiangsi 107, 115n, 110
Chia-hsing, district in Chekiang 121n, 147n, 155, 166, 185n, 245n
Chiang Chia-chin, scholar 256, 257
Chiang-shan, district in Chekiang 52
Chien-ch'ang, district in Kiangsi 59
Children, age of parents at time of birth of C 141f; illegitimate C 131n; number of C and social status 188; number of C 153f
Chin, dynasty 70
Chin-shen (degree holders) 204
Ch'ing-chiang, district in Kiangsi 110-1

INDEX

Ching-tê-chen, town in Kiangsi 268n
Ch'ing-yüan, district in Kuanghsi 102, 107
Ch'iu-kuan house 70f
Ch'iu Ying, painter 261
Ch'u, ancient state 58, 199n, 200
Chu-chi hsiang (see Pearl street)
Chu Hsi, philosopher 8, 278
Chu, Samuel, scholar 247n
Ch'ü T'ung-tsu, sociologist 204n
Ch'üan-chou, place in Kuanghsi 107, 109, 110
Ch'üan-chou, district in Fukien 79, 111, 215, 258n
Ch'üan Han-sheng, historian 255n, 258n
Chün-tzu („gentleman") 10
Chung-ho, district in Taiwan 214
Chung-shan, district in Kuangtung 88, 119, 150-1 (s. Hsiang-shan)
City, the free C 258n; C life 227-8; trade C 267; C as place of refuge 211; C in wartime 267n; C God 176
Clans 33; federations of C 212-3; C fights 211n; C names of aborigines 199; relations between main C and banches 206f; C rules 40f; C splits 206; C villages 48-9 (s. Lineages)
Class, definition of ruling C 30
Colima, suburb of SanFrancisco 50, 119
Colonial development 116; C society 202
Colonies, military 225
Colonization, of South China 198f; patterns of C 221f
Colonizers 2
Commoners 10, 16-18
Concubines 129, 130f, 219, 229, 245; imperial C 62, 64; age difference C/husband 134; social status and C 188-9
Confucian value system 162, 170, 171, 247, 252
Confucius (K'ung-tzu), philosopher 5, 7
Contraceptives 171n
Convicts 20, 23 (s. Criminals, Exiles)
Coolies 227
Corn(maize) 274
Corruption 24
Cotton, cultivation 271; C mills 246; C trade 260
Courtesans 261 (s. Geisha)
Craftsmen 12-14, 236f

Creel, H. G., sinologist 23n
Cripples 218
Crime 48; Criminals 225 (s. Convicts)
Cross-cousin marriages 177, 213

Death, age at time of D 149f; D-marriage 172n
Divorce 135
Doctors 41, 43, 218, 230, 232-3
Donors, portraits of D 216n

Earth God 215
Eckstein, A., pol. scientist 243n
Edo (Tokyo) 259
Education of children 209-210 (s. schools)
Eichhorn, W., sinologist 11n
Elite, lists of families of E 38 (see Gentry, Upper Class)
Emigration, general 221f; E Overseas 167f, 172; E to United States 119-120
Employees 250
En-p'ing, district in Kuangtung 66, 78, 90, 92, 97, 99, 100 (s. Nan-en)
Entrepreneurs 71-2, 91, 93
Erosion 276
Erotic paintings 261
Estate 41-2 (s. Manor)
Europe, social mobility 32
Examination, system 22-24, 68
Exile 51, 56, 226 (see Criminals)
Exogamy 47
Expulsion from clan 228

Factories 109; organisation of F 256f
Fairbank, J. K., historian 243n, 258n
Fairs 241; temple F 243-4
Family, development of F 33-35; size of F 34, 117n; size of farm F 219-220 (s. Household)
Fan-hu (social class) 17-18
Fashions, change of F 262n
Fecundity 153f
Feng-ch'eng, district in Kiangsi 76
Feng-ch'uan, district in Kuangtung 87, 88, 91, 96
Fertility 153f (s. Children)
Feudalism 200; F period 37; marginal F 222
Fish (s. Pisciculture)
Food habits, change of F 269f
Foreign merchants as promoters 245
Formosa (s. Taiwan)
Forts (pao) 212n, 266n

INDEX

Foundations, charitable 39, 208 (see schools)
France 95
Frick, J., anthropologist 170n
Friese, H., sinologist 238
Frontier concept 244, 279
Fujii, H., historian 260n
Fukien 33, 198, 199, 201, 202, 203, 212, 213, 217; cults of F 214

Gambling 248, 250
Geisha houses 262 (s. Prostitution)
Genealogies, general 2, 37-50; G and marriage 37; rules for composition of G 46-8
Generation, length of G 146-7
Gentleman-merchants 245f
Gentry 15-16; G class 6, 204f; G families 31; schools for G 25-6; G society 31 (s. Upper class, Elite)
Geomancers 41, 230
Germany 95, 104
Go-between 245
Gold digging 167
Gotha, almanac of European aristocracy 38
Granet, M., sinologist 177, 213, 252
Great Britain 92
Guilds 228, 230
Gypsies 244

Hainan, island 98-9
Hakka 2, 55, 67, 103, 105n, 115, 120
Han-k'ou, city 59, 67, 72
Han-lin, academy 65
Han Yü, scholar 7, 278
Hao, part of name 280f
Harriman, E.H., U.S. industrialist 93
Hawaii 167
Heng-chou, district in Hunan 110
Ho-fei, district in Anhui 59
Ho-nan, place in Kuangtung 67, 75
Ho Ping-ti, sociologist 29, 184, 186
Ho-p'u, district in Kuangtung 97
Ho-yüan, district in Kuangtung 106
Holland 93
Hong merchants 83, 246
Hong Kong 84, 91, 78, 93, 104, 94, 167
Houses, origin of clan H 38-39; H of the Wu clan 52f and Tables 1-2
Household, size of H 34
Hsiang-shan, district in Kuangtung 121 175, 177, 194 (s. Chung-shan)
Hsiao-jen, social term 10

Hsin-an, trade city in Anhui 115n, 260-1
Hsin-feng, district in Kuangtung 109
Hsin-hsing, district in Kuantung 78, 79, 88, 89, 90, 92
Hsin-hui, district in Kuantung 51, 64, 79, 88, 89, 91, 93, 96, 94, 107, 175, 177, 179
Hsin-ning, place near Canton 51, 67, 85
Hsing-ning, district in Kuangtung 105
Hsing-hua, district in Fukien 65
Hsiu-ning, district in Anhui 121
Hsiung-nu, tribal federation 21n
Hsün-tzu, philosopher 8
Hsün Yüeh, philosopher 7
Hu Shih, philosopher and politician 5n
Hua-hsien, district in Kuangtung 114
Huai-chi, district in Kuanghsi 73
Huang, Mr., 115n, 158n
Huang Tien-ch'üan, historian, 45n, 132n, 149n, 216n, 217n, 233n
Hui-ch'eng, district in Kuangtung 99
Hui-chou, trade city in Anhui 260 (s. Hsin-an)
Hummel, A., historian 27, 185n
Hunan 202, 203

I-ho yang-hang, business firm 83
I-ning, district in Kuanghsi 111
Illegitimacy, 47, 48 (s. Children)
Indigo, plant 75, 278
Industries, modern 239-240 (s. Factories)
Industrialists 71-72 (s. Jung Hung, Chang Ch'ien)
Industrialization, problems of 275
Infant mortality 131, 154
Infanticide 131 (s. Abortion)
Infertility 132n
Inheritance 35-36 (s. Primogeniture)
Inn 232
Intercourse 171n
Irrigation, investment in I 91, 97, 110; techniques of I 270n, 271

Japan 94, 160n, 167, 168, 218, 222, 227, 230, 259, 261, 262, 263, 268, 279; clan rules in J 45; J craftsmen 12; J pirates 260n (s. Edo)
Joint ownership of land 207, 220
Ju-hu, sociological term 15, 68, 204
Jun-chou (old name for Chen-chiang), Kiangsu 218
Jung, clan 121

INDEX

Jung-hsien, district in Kuanghsi 88, 91, 92
Jung Hung, industrialist 246
Jung-kui house 102f
Juvenile delinquents (s. Beggars, Criminals) 254

K'ai-Chang temples 215
K'ai-feng, former capital, in Honan 60
K'ai-p'ing, district in Kuangtung 119
Kan river 115
Kanda, N, historian 200n
Kang-chou (s. Ku-Kang-chou)
Kao-chou, district in Kuangtung 75, 76, 85
Kao-yao, district in Kuangtung 85, 88
Keelung, city in Taiwan 234
Kiangsi 86, 88, 89, 97, 114, 115, 202, 203
KMT (Kuo-min-tang), Party 46, 78, 118, 195
Korea 202, 278n
Kroker, E., anthropologist 35n
Ku-Kang-chou, former district in Kuangtung 61, 63, 65, 76, 78, 79
Kuan-ti, God 216n
Kuan-yang, district in Kuanghsai 107, 110, 111
Kuang-ning, district in Kuangtung 79, 86, 97
Kuhn, Franz, translator 262n
Kui-hsien, district in Kuanghsi 97
Kui-lin, district in Kuanghsi 111
Kui-p'ing, district in Kuanghsi 105
Kui-shan, district in Kuanghsi 96
Kung-szu, form of organization 256-8

Laborers 21, 42; origin of L 223; migrations of L 226; recruiters of L 226-7
Lan-fang, form of organization 256
Lantern-makers 244
Lattimore, O, pol. scientist 279
Leisure class 7
Levirate 140n
Levy-Strauss, C., anthropologist 177
Li Chen, author 51-2
Li-p'u, district in Kuanghsi 111
Li Yü, writer 262-3
Liao, aboriginal tribe 200
Liao-tung, peninsula 51-2
Library, of a clan 43, 45
Life expectancy 147f; L and social status 191f; L of women 192

Lin, Fukienese clan 212n; L and the deity T'ien-hou 214
Lineages 33, 34
Lin-ch'uan, district in Kiangsi 109
Ling-ch'uan, district in Kuanghi 108, 111
Ling-shan, district in Kuangtung 71, 72, 73, 75
Liu-min (vagabonds) 12, 223, 240
Live-in daughter-in-law 132n
Live-in son-in-law(chi) 226n, 233-4
Lo Hsiang-lin, historian 256n
Lolo, tribal group 37
London 93
Lou Tzu-k'uang, folklorist 214n
Lu-ch'uan, district in Kuanghsi 114
Lung-yen, house 111f, 114

Maladjusted persons 216-7
Malaria 175, 176, 273
Managers of business firms 246; M of estates 41-2
Manchu invasion 71, 88
Manchuria 84, 203, 223
Manila 94
Manor (chuang) 42, 206-7 (s. Estate)
Mao-ming, district in Kuangtung 107, 113, 114
Markets in city 242; farmer's M 241; village M 176
Marriage age 140f, 145; endogamous M 213n; eugenic M 213n; M pattern 121f; preferential M 121, 123f, 177, 193-4, 267; M system 36; M time 145-6, 173n (s. Exogamy, Polygamy, Wedding, Death marriage, Cross-cousin marriage)
Marysville, city in California 119
Maspero, H., sinologist 20n
Medicine 93 (s. Doctor)
Mei-hsien, district in Kuangtung 103, 104, 105
Meng-tzu, philosopher 7-8, 279
Merchants 14-15; M class in Sung time 197; types of M 231f, 239f (s. Businessmen, Peddlers)
Mexico 91, 93
Miao, tribal group 73
Middle class (s. Burgher, Merchant, Craftsmen)
Migration, attitude towards M 19-20; M into Chekiang 49; M of 97 families 63; M of Wu clan 115-6

Military career 235; M service 20-21, 235-6; M settlements 19-21
Millet 269
Ming, part of name 280
Minorate 34n
Mobility, attempts to calculate M 27-30; downward M 117-8; upward M 118
Modernization 169f
Mohammedans 243-4
Monasteries 235 (s. Monks)
Mongol businessmen 255; M dynasty 21; end of M dynasty 73; M invasion 64, 65, 70, 76, 77, 79, 85-6, 96, 178, 181; M settlement policy 225n
Mongolia 223
Monks 23, 41, 47, 234-5
Moskow 93
Moso, tribal group 199n
Mortality 132 (s. Death)
Mou Jun-sun, scholar 38n
Mu, clan 199n

Nakamura, J., scholar 26n, 245n
Name code 206, 283-4
Nan-ch'ang, city in Kiangsi 87, 109
Nan-en-chou, ancient district in Kuangtung 66
Nan-hai, district in Kuangtung 75
Nan-hsiung, district and trade center in Kuangtung 61, 62, 63, 64, 65, 66, 70, 71, 73, 75, 76, 107, 115, 123, 174, 175, 177, 225
Nanking, capital 262
Natives 66 (s. Aborigines)
Ning-hua, district in Fukien 52, 66, 105
Ning-po, district in Chekiang 277
Nishijima, Sadao, scholar 21n, 225n
Niu-t'ien (Oxfield), ward of a district 61, 62, 63
Nobility 24, 10 (s. Gotha, Elite)
Novels 262

Office, sale of O 188
On Kidea, scholar 38
Opium 250, 276; O War 133
Ortaq, form of organization 255
Osaka, city 259
Ou-yang Hsiu, historian 39n
Oversea's emigration 119; O trade expeditions 83, 255

Pa, local culture 200n
P'ai, social group 176

Pai-pai, Taiwanese religious festival 214-5
P'an Kuang-tan, sociologist 166, 185n
P'an-yü, district in Kuangtung 72, 73, 96
Pang-liao, town in Taiwan 214
Pao-an, district in Kuangtung 82, 92
Patrician families 259
Pearl Ward (Chu-chi-li), 61, 64, 211, 225
Peddler 231
Pei-liu, district in Kuanghsi 113, 114
Peking 178, 181, 212, 225n, 236; settlement around P 21
Penang, city 94
Pharmacist (s. Doctor)
Philippines 94, 95, 167, 168, 213 (s. Manila)
Pien (old name for K'ai-feng) 67
Pig, culture of P 273
Pin-yang, district in Kuanghsi 71, 72, 75
P'ing-lo, district in Kuanghsi 102, 111
Pisciculture 273
Plough, iron P 269
Polygamy 35, 47, 129f (s. Concubines)
Population, periods of growth 165, 269f (s. Fertility)
Porcelain industry 268n
Portraits 216n
Potters 244
Pregnancies in relation to the month of the year 145
Primogeniture 34, 163
Prostitutes 160n, 248, 250 (s. Courtesans, Geisha)
Pu-ch'ü, social group 17n
P'u-ning, district in Kuangtung 105
P'u-t'ien, district in Fukien and trade center 51, 65, 66, 67, 75-6, 82, 213; P house 75f
Pulleyblank, E. G., sinologist 11n

Rangoon, temple inscriptions in R 50, 56, 119, 286n
Ranks 10; list of R 68-70
Registration of citizens 21
Re-marriage 47, 135f
Rice, new varieties 272-3

Salt administration 69, 84; S makers 175f; S trade 246
San Francisco 50, 78, 93, 119, 120, 167, 211n
San-shan, place in Kuangtung 55

San-shui, district in Kuangtung 106
Scholz, H., geographer 22n
Schools of clans 43, 208, 209, 224; S as financing agency 245; S system 25-6 (s. Academy, Library)
Sculptors 238
Seepage migration 222
Serfs 222, 223 (s. Commoners, Slaves, Fan-hu)
Servant 229-230; S girls 42 (s. Concubines)
Settlements (s. Colonies, t'un-t'ien) 225
Sex ratio 131
Sha-pei, place in Kuangtung 73, 75, 96; S house 82f
Shaman 43, 230
Shantung 203, 277
Shanghai 94, 219, 257-8, 273
Shang Yang, politician 34
Shê, city in Anhui 262
Shih (gentry) 6, 10
Shih-lin, town in Taiwan 214
Shih-pi-hsiang (s. Stone Wall county)
Ship-building 13
Shops in city 241-2; Shop-keeper 14
Shu-jen, sociological term 26
Shu-yüan (s. Academy)
Shun-tê, district in Kuangtung 73, 91, 96, 97
Simony 118
Singapore 91, 93
Skinner, G. W., sociologist 34n, 131n, 154n
Slaves 11, 16-17, 160n, 245
Smallpox 94
Smuggling 260n
Social change 169f
Social classes 5-10 (s. Class)
Social security 39
Social Welfare 91, 109, 209 S activities of merchants 252-4; S institutions of clans 206; S for the poor 228n (s. Foundations, Schools)
Soldiers 19-20, 181, 217 (s. Military)
Sons, of concubines 283; fate of second S 163, 168
Son-in-law selection 127f (s. Live-in son-in-law)
Sorghum 274
South Africa 104
Spencer, J. E., geographer 241n
Squeeze (extra-legal ways to get income) 229

Standard of living 276
Stange, H. O. H., sinologist 23n
State factories 236f; S industries 13; S slaves 17
Statistics, question of reliability 166
Steam engine 258-9
Stone Wall County 66-67
Students 183-4
Suburban settlements 232
Sugar factories, rules 256f
Suicide 250
Sun Tê-hsiung, geographer 160n
Sun Yat-sen, president 93, 96, 121
Sung, end of S dynasty 60, 66
Sung P'ei, author 51
Suto, Yoshiyuki, scholar 273n
Swatow 92
Szuch'uan 93, 202; S sugar 257
Szu-min (Four classes) 5-6

Taeuber, I., demographer 166n
Taipei, capital of Taiwan 239-240
T'ai-p'ing rebellion 72, 90, 92, 109, 110, 113, 114, 126, 162, 164
T'ai-shan, district in Kuangtung 78, 82, 88, 89, 90, 91, 92, 119
Taiwan 2, 217, 218, 220, 222, 231, 232, 256, 257, 258; T aborigines 201n; T colonization 201, 213, 253
T'an clan, 211, 212, 235; origin 62f
T'ang Yin, painter 261, 263
T'ao-yüan, district in Taiwan 133f
Taoists 43, 47, 279, 252
Teacher 230
Tea houses 248
Temple 176, 209; T and business 254; T fairs 243; T festivals 214f; T for Wu Tzu-hsü 59; function of T 215-6; T inscriptions 49; T land 207-8; T as meeting place 256; T as shop-owners 242-3
Tenancy 223, 224
Thai languages 199n
Theatre 262
T'ien-hou, female deity 214, 215
T'ien-hsiung house 105f
Tin-smith 244
Title bearers as upper class 182f; list of T 68-70
To-min, a caste 18, 244
Tobacco smoking 251, 274
Tokyo (s. Edo) 84
Toshikazu, Oshima, scholar 20n, 225n
Tou-tung, place in Kuangtung 51, 66, 85

Tribes 200; customs of T 233n (s. Aborigines, Natives, Liao, Lolo, Miao, etc)
Triplets 146
Tsa-hu, social group 18
Ts'en-ch'i, district in Kuanghsi 73
Tseng-ch'eng, district in Kuangtung 67, 82, 75.
Tseng Ti, author 51
Tso Tsung-t'ang, general 247
T'u-szu, administrative term 200
Tuan Chi-hsien, demographer 132n, 141n, 145n, 151n, 153n
Tun-huang, district in Kansu; data from T 134, 142, 149n, 174, 286n
T'un-t'ien system (settlement) 20-21, 225n
Tung-wan, district in Kuangtung 82
Turkey 160n, 217n, 254n
Twins 146
Tzu, part of name 280f

United States 84, 92, 93, 94, 95, 104, 195, 226; Chinese in U 120; U universities 78 (s. California, Hawaii)
Upper Class (see Gentry, Nobility)

Vagabonds 12 (s. Liu-min)
Vagrants 223 (s. Vagabonds)
Venereal diseases 276
Versailles 95
Vietnam (s. Annam)
Village, size 266; V size and clans 48-49; in-V marriages 126, 129; V-city relations 266f
Vitamine deficiency 276

Wada, H., historian 22n
Wan-hua, ward of Taipei city 215, 232
Wang An-shih, politician 109
Wang Chen, author 8-9
Wang (-Liu) Hui-chen, sociologist 40n, 44n, 139n, 170n
Wang Mang, emperor 37n
Wang Nai-chi, demographer 166n
Wang Yang-ming, philosopher and general 278
Ward, Barbara E., anthropologist 256n
Wang-tsu, sociological term 204n

Wang Yi-t'ung, sociologist 18n, 21n
Weaver 110, 236, 238n
Weaverville, town in California 119
Weber, Max, sociologist 247
Wedding, cost 171n
Wen, clan 199n
Western influences 169; W trade 218
Wheat culture 269, 271
White Lotus, sect 109
Wholesaler 231
Widows 46-7, 189; remarriage of W 135f (s. Chaste Widows)
Widower 137f
Wine 44
Wife: main and secondary 129f; obligations of W 43-44 (s. Concubine)
Wu, ancient state 58
Wu-chou, district in Kuanghsi 89, 90, 92, 94, 100
Wu Kuo-jung, merchant 83
Wu-ling, district in Hunan 59
Wu Sheng, author 52
Wu Tzu-hsü, politician 58-9
Wu Yao-kuang, author 52
Wu Yen-shou, author 52

Ya, middleman 244-5
Yang, clan 123f, 177, 178, 181-2, 194
Yang Ch'ing-yü (Mrs.), sociologist 35n, 159n, 160n, 215n
Yang-chou, city in Kiangsu 261-2
Yang-ch'un, district in Kuangtung 87, 88, 98
Yang Lien-sheng, sinologist 23n, 24n, 25n, 243n
Yao, tribes 98
Yeh, clan 132n, 149n, 152n, 153n, 158n, 217f
Yen-yüan-hsiang, rural area in Chê-kiang (s. Ning-po) 48
Yin privilege 25, 86
Ying, type of settlement 225
Ying-hu, social group 21
Ying-tê, district in Kuangtung 114
Yü-nan, district in Kuangtung 73
Yüan Mei, essayist 9
Yünnan 91, 154, 199n, 202, 273
Yung-an, district in Fukien 107
Yung-chou, district in Kuanghsi 110
Yung-p'ing, district in Yünnan 109